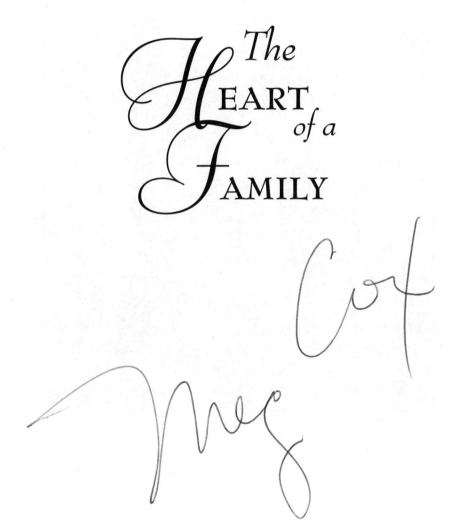

The
HEART
of a
FAMILY

RANDOM HOUSE · NEW YORK

The
HEART
of a
FAMILY

★ · ★ · ★ · ★ · ★ · ★ · ★

Searching America for
New Traditions That Fulfill Us

Meg Cox

Illustrations by Janet Payne

Library of Congress Cataloging-in-Publication Data

Cox, Meg.

    The heart of a family: searching America for new traditions that fulfill us / Meg Cox.

      p.   cm.

    Includes bibliographical references.

    ISBN 0-679-44863-2

    1. Family—United States.   2. Family festivals—United States.

  3. Rites and ceremonies—United States.   4. Holidays—United States.

  5. United States—Social life and customs.   I. Title.

  HQ536.C765   1998

  306.85′0973—dc21   98-9585

Random House website address: www.randomhouse.com

Manufactured in the United States of America on acid-free paper

98765432

First Edition

Design by Mercedes Everett

To the memory of my mother,
JOANN HOHENSTINE COX

Contents

INTRODUCTION

I wrote this book because I needed it.

When I finally decided in my mid-thirties that I wanted children, I was terrified that I wouldn't know how to be a good parent. I had fallen in love with my husband partly because I was touched by the way he treated his teenage daughter, so I felt sure that he would be excellent at this. But I felt so unprepared. We both were intensely independent, career-minded city people, and I panicked at how to shape a different kind of life. What did I know about making a family feel like a family, and not just a random collection of busy people living together?

One morning I woke up with the vivid realization that what I needed was ritual; if I could understand family rituals and knew how to create satisfying ones of my own, we would be fine. I was sure I could find plenty of information about how to feed and care for a baby, but I knew I wanted to be able to provide more than simple nourishment. Rituals seemed like protection, insurance, talismans. And the thought came to me, virtually simultaneously, that there was a book to be written about family rituals, what good ones feel like and how to start them. I was sure I wasn't the only person desperate for this knowledge.

I read what books I could find on the subject, but they didn't contain the wisdom I sought. Either they featured a laundry list of traditions without explaining how they fit into families' lives, or they were all practiced by a single family, one that had nothing in common with mine. Too often they were only sentimental suggestions, not actual rituals that had been road-tested in the muddle and stress of contemporary family life.

Early in 1994, when we discovered I was pregnant, I started my quest in earnest. Using my skills as a journalist, I set out to try to learn first-hand the secrets of families across the country who were really good at ritual. I also wanted to get the answers to such basic questions as: What is a ritual? Why does ritual work? When it doesn't, why doesn't it? I wanted to know why I felt this need so strongly, to find out how rituals really affect families. I read books on anthropology and sociology and ritual studies. I interviewed prominent psychologists and religious educators.

I quit my job and devoted my time to my family and my search. My son, Max, was growing out of infancy and my need for family ritual was becoming more urgent. My husband and I started trying ritual ideas out on him, and watching his reactions. Everything I was learning began to make sense.

I spent more than three years researching, writing, and interviewing more than 200 families around the country, and, in the end, found the answers to most of my questions.

I have learned that ritual and the craving for it are ageless and every-where. There are rituals not just for celebrating holidays but also for wag-ing war, falling in love, playing sports, and running governments. Rituals commemorate events and connect people, either to others in their family, or to history. In the Mescalero Apache tribe in Mescalero, N.Mex., girls still celebrate the beginning of womanhood by dancing for four nights in a row, while ceremonial singers perform up to sixty-four different sacred songs each night. And there are *Titanic* fanatics who get together once a year and eat an eleven-course feast just like the meal served on the liner the night it sank.

But the most important thing I learned is that people *need* ritual, and they need it for many reasons.

In a recent study of 90,000 teenagers, researchers tried to figure out why certain kids were less likely than others to engage in "risky behav-iors," everything from drugs to sex. Only one factor stood out: it wasn't that all these teenagers had mothers who stayed home, it was simply that they felt emotionally close to their families. And what is it that makes families feel truly connected? Good family rituals.

Rituals not only help thriving families; they help heal the pain of life's greatest tragedies. Think of the ceremony conducted in Oklahoma

City on the day that Timothy McVeigh was found guilty. Families of the dead and survivors gathered by a tree that had endured the blast and, in a ritual of cleansing and rebirth, together poured water onto its roots.

One recent United Nations study of Bosnian children whose villages were bombed and their parents killed found that standard forms of "talking therapies" were absolutely no use in helping these children rebuild their psyches. The only effort that helped was an attempt to re-create some of the festivals and other rituals that had filled their childhoods; having that continuity to hang onto made it possible for them to go forward.

If ritual can do that, imagine the difference it makes in the everyday lives of children. The power of ritual to comfort and heal and teach is enormous, and all parents have this power: they just need to know how it works. The basic principles are the same, whether a ritual is designed to help ease children to sleep at bedtime, celebrate a major holiday, or navigate the profound transition from childhood to adulthood. But in our technologically hypercharged world, we seem to have lost touch with our roots as ritual makers and ritual needers.

As I interviewed families, I discovered that many of the people who have vital, inventive rituals didn't have them when they were growing up: their passion came from a determination to give their kids something they didn't have, and they figured ritual out for themselves. I wasn't deprived of ritual, but I wanted more and different rituals from those I had known as a child. I grew up in a patchwork family of adopted and biological children (including me), and though I felt my parents' love and approval profoundly, we weren't big on family outings and events.

To be fair, I treasured many of our family rituals, including our holiday traditions and Saturday morning outings with my dad. The four kids took turns doing Saturday errands with him; I can still smell the gas at Howie's filling station and still taste the hot chocolate with fake whipped cream I ordered monthly at the coffee shop.

My bond with my mother was ferocious and I miss her desperately since her death, but she prepared me to nurture a career rather than a family. The great lessons she passed on to me were about pursuing only work I love. Her personality combined with her circumstances made copious ritualizing unlikely: raising four kids is challenging enough, but she also had to cope with a chronic illness. She was a loner rather than a joiner all her life. And though she spent her career as a professional artist doing everything from puppeteering to calligraphy, she never felt that she achieved her artistic ambitions. At home, she knitted matching sweaters for the whole family, and stitched Raggedy Anns with our names painted on their hearts, but family celebrations weren't her forte. I inherited much of her temperament, but I became desperate to learn how such things are done.

These days, like many in my generation, my family is scattered across the country and I'm lucky to see even my father twice a year. My husband's mother died long before I met him, and his father, too, lives far away. There's nothing nuclear about my own household, either. My family holidays include myself, my husband and son, my grown stepdaughter, and my husband's ex-wife. I confess that the ex-wife and I did not become friends on first meeting, but by now I can't imagine holidays without Anita, and not just because she's a fabulous cook. She adores my son and I adore her daughter and we share the same basic values. We may not seem like a conventional family, but the reality is that there is no such thing anymore.

Which brings us to another reason why family rituals are more important now than ever before. As Americans loosen their ties to organized religion, ethnic heritage, and even the commitments of marriage, what will bind families together?

We all know that the people who surround us by accident of birth and marriage, siblings and parents and the whole extended menagerie, often aren't the same people we'd choose as bosom buddies. So what will make them matter to us? What will provide the kind of emotional connection to them that lasts a lifetime? How can this group of people embrace and sustain us against all the hurt and grabbiness and pain of an intrusive culture? Rituals will, at least rituals that have meaning and depth. And the rituals of our childhood can teach us how to live all our lives in a focused and caring way.

It's no accident that interest in ritual is growing. It isn't just New Agers waving incense or men banging drums or teenagers dabbling in Native American spirituality. Educators across the country are creating rituals within school programs in an effort to provide meaning and teach basic values. Some juvenile justice authorities, having found nothing else works, are using the structure and sanity of good rituals to show young lawbreakers another path. Religious leaders from many different denominations are trying to renew and strengthen the formal religious rituals performed in their churches and synagogues, while encouraging families to personalize religious rituals at home. And more and more therapists are prescribing rituals to dysfunctional families, finding that the action and symbolism of rituals carry enormous power to heal rifts and forge a healthy family identity.

The rituals I collected on my search are of a staggering variety: some are religious, quite a few have ethnic roots, and many are just the sheer invention of thoughtful and attentive parents. I talked to families of four different ethnic backgrounds who all have an Easter tradition of cracking eggs together. A Yupik Indian in an Alaskan village described to me her tribe's "first catch" ritual, in which the families feast when a firstborn son captures his first fish or game. I have included an ancient Greek Orthodox naming ceremony, and, for the celebration of an open adoption, a wildly unorthodox ritual that includes the biological mother.

The sheer quantity and variety of rituals routinely practiced in this country-of-many-cultures is beyond the scope of any single book. It's impossible to include traditions from every American religious community, but equally impossible to write a meaningful book about family ritual and ignore religion.

I have tried to include the widest possible range of rituals and to reflect the best of what I've discovered, emphasizing rituals that struck me as original and unusually thoughtful. I found myself drawn most powerfully to rituals that don't require a lot of money and props but do meet the deepest needs of children.

I have included rituals from families that are white and black, Christian and Jewish, intact and divorced. Not surprisingly, I discovered that many families who teach their children at home are also big believers in family ritual, so there may be a greater percentage of home-schoolers in my book than in the general population. I also can't help being affected by my own roots. I am a white, Protestant baby boomer from the Midwest, of long-faded, mixed-European ancestry. So while I did track down some wonderful Kwanzaa rituals, I've got many more about Christmas, my favorite holiday, than any other occasion. I'm a fanatic about bedtime, so I may have gone overboard on bedtime rituals.

Readers may well quarrel over omissions, but I didn't set out to write a book that was exhaustive, or exhausting. I didn't want to just share great rituals, but to show readers how they can create glorious ones of their own, and to prove to them why they should.

For that reason, the book is divided into three sections, Why, What, and How. The first section is about the psychology, history, and sociology of rituals, and attempts to show how rituals really affect children. The second section, What, serves as an extensive catalog of family rituals, covering everything from holidays to one family's ritual for breaking bad news. I have tried to describe these rituals within the context of the families that observe them, and, in many cases, to show how children feel about their rituals. The final section demonstrates how to create rituals from scratch, and change them when they stop working.

I offer these rituals for inspiration. I wouldn't want them to be slavishly followed like a gourmet recipe, but used as a jumping-off place, the outline of a good idea. For example, my friend Ellen Levine, the editor-in-chief of *Good Housekeeping*, once told me that whoever in her family has a birthday finds masses of cards tucked in unexpected places. I took her idea, but used it for my husband on Valentine's Day. He got up that morning to go to work and found valentines everywhere: in the refrigerator, taped to the inside of the front door, in his briefcase.

Remember, rituals are like jokes: it isn't the words themselves, but the timing and the telling that matters. That's where the creativity enters, the stamp of someone's personality that makes all the difference between something done mechanically and something done joyfully. Creating new rituals isn't easy and it doesn't always work, but it's worth it.

I've learned a lot about family ritual in the last three years that has given me countless new ideas and the confidence to try them. Writing this book has changed my life and I hope made me a better parent. I share the fruits of my search, in the hopes they enrich your family life, too.

—Meg Cox, Princeton, 1998

Part 1

WHY

One

★ ★ ★ ★

DEFINING RITUAL

Upon reflection, is it not odd that human beings, everywhere and in all ages, have engaged in the making and performing of rituals? Why have they done this, when life is full of dangers and challenges that would seem to require more practical kinds of activity? Contrary to common-sense expectation, rituals are not, in most cases, the product of affluence and leisure.

—Tom F. Driver, *The Magic of Ritual*

The Siegal family of Alexandria, Va., had started to eat dinner one night when two-year-old Rebecca, sitting in her high chair, suddenly got very quiet. Tears rolled down her cheeks, while her confused parents and older sister tried frantically to figure out what was wrong. She didn't seem sick or in pain. The food on her plate was something she liked. What could be missing? What had they done differently? Suddenly, it came to them: they had forgotten to sing grace.

So they held hands and sang. "For thy gracious blessings, for thy wondrous works, for thy loving-kindness, we give thanks, O Lord." It was a simple blessing, a grace Rebecca's older sister, Judith, had picked up at her Episcopal private school. As they sang it, Rebecca's crying escalated into loud sobs, then subsided quickly. She calmed down and ate her dinner. And the family never forgot grace again.

Ask any parent: kids love routine. And ritual is routine with sprinkles and extra sauce. Special words are usually included, and sometimes special costumes, food, and songs. It's a chance to act really loud, or really goofy, or deeply quiet. Behavior that is often forbidden—like eating sweets— may be required, especially during holiday rituals. For young children in particular, ritual times are the rare occasions when they are full equals in the family drama, or even the stars. Family comes first, attention is guaranteed, and they don't have to wonder what comes next or what is expected of them.

But children don't merely love family ritual, with its wondrous combination of predictability and specialness; they *need* it. The story of Rebecca Siegal's blubbering over a forgotten grace barely hints at that need, and it begs the question, Why did she cry? Why is ritual important? Why is it worth enduring what can sometimes be a great deal of bother?

Think about what it means to be a small child like Rebecca. You never know when you wake up each day where you'll be taken, what you'll wear, which foods will be put before you. You haven't totally mastered the language yet, so you're not entirely sure if somebody, even somebody who loves you, will understand what you're hungry for or where you hurt. The world is vast, unpredictable, and beyond your control or comprehension.

It isn't unlike the experience of being an adult in a foreign country, where you don't know your way around or speak the language fluently. Everything feels a little chaotic, tentative, even scary. Remember that triumphant feeling when a concierge or waiter actually understood what you said and replied in the way you expected him to? Maybe he even brought the dish you thought you ordered. Or how you begin to relax after finding your way to the same café three mornings in a row? You think, "I can do this," and you begin to feel at home. Because you have a secure base to start from and return to, you feel more confident about setting out to explore the strange city around you.

With small children, ritual is an anchor, a home base. And there is a triumphant gleam in their eyes when they say or do their part in rituals both routine and spectacular, and when an adult response is just what they expected. They feel thrilled with their competence, secure that their world is in order. They expected you to say "Good morning, merry sunshine" when you lifted them out of the crib, and you did.

Rituals provide far more than mere comfort of habit, and are vital not just to babies and toddlers. Children of all ages are grappling with their own constantly changing bodies in the context of an ever-enlarging world. As they get older, they'll grab onto anything that seems to help them make sense of all that, and how much better for them if their parents, in the reassuring setting of ritual, serve as their guides.

We all have our rituals for getting dressed, reading the newspaper, doing our chores. In his book *From Beginning to End: The Rituals of Our Lives,* Robert Fulghum describes in loving detail one woman's regular morning routine, which includes wearing a different bathrobe for each season and sitting quietly with her dog, Elvis. He concludes that an anthropologist analyzing this woman "would see ritual behavior of the most classic kind—the kind that gives structure and meaning to daily life. Behavior that is regularly repeated because it serves a profound purpose."

Personal rituals make our lives smoother and more predictable, at least in the areas we can control. But family rituals are another beast, more complicated, less predictable, apt to be more vocal and dramatic, and, I would argue, possessing the potential to be far more powerful because of the interactions between people. After reading many authorities in anthropology, sociology, and psychology, I would narrow the basic elements needed to make family ritual down to three or four, including action (people have to act, not just speak); repetition; order (a prescribed sequence of events); and what one psychologist calls "an attentive state of mind," a focused, heightened mood.

But these things are not set in stone. The "mood" may be the end result of the ritual rather than a starting point, produced because of its special drama, music, repetition, or other elements. And events don't have to be repeated to qualify as ritual, as weddings, funerals, and rite-of-passage ceremonies show. Even action isn't compulsory, or can be astoundingly minimal.

Take the good-bye ritual of Elinor Craig and her son, Mose. Each day as they drive to preschool the boy thinks up a special code word based on something he sees. Later, when he turns to his mother and says "snowman" or "truck," or whatever it is, he's saying it's okay for her to leave him there. Think of it: a ritual of one word. But it gives this child an ultimate power and security, and reinforces his intimate bond with his mother, all the more delicious for being conspiratorial. The other kids never have to know he has a qualm. I can't imagine many rituals that would make a child feel more loved.

The bottom line: I would argue that ritual is almost anything, big or small, that families perform together deliberately, providing there is repetition or some dramatic flourish that elevates the activity above the ordinary grind. Eating meals together is automatically a ritual and can be organized to provide far more than the basic need for nourishment. Taking time to blow bubbles with a child wouldn't be a ritual by itself, but if, over time, blowing bubbles together on Saturday morning developed into a regular thing, usually after breakfast, say, then it would become a bubble-blowing ritual.

Some might argue that such a modest activity as bubble-blowing belongs in the category of mere habit, but I think many families have much too grandiose an idea of what ritual means and thereby sell themselves short. Perhaps because ritual is a word associated with religious practices, people assume that a ritual means something that takes props, crowds, and special training to perform. It doesn't. One of Webster's main definitions for ritual is simply "any practice or pattern of behavior regularly performed in a set manner." Thus, I believe that even very simple activities can be transformed into satisfying and memorable rituals, such as singing a certain song whenever you give your child medicine, or always declaring an  evening study break for hot cocoa on winter weeknights. Call those habits, if you insist, but your children will remember them as something more.

Even chores can be ritualized, with just a little extra attention or a conscious ordering of events, as with Sandi Nolan, who comes close to making a game of doing laundry with her daughters during "Friday video nights." At "intermission," the girls wheel their own dirty clothes into the laundry room in doll carriages.

The evolution of an event into a ritual often goes like this: something happens, certain foods are eaten, words are said or read, an occasion normally ignored is celebrated, and someone says, "This is fun. Let's do it again." That's why Mary Bonner sang "Silent Night" to her sons as a lullaby every night for three years. And why Patrick McIvor's family eats shrimp cocktail and carryout Chinese food every Christmas Eve. To paraphrase a popular expression, ritual happens.

Later in the book, you'll meet families with rituals for everything under the sun. Rituals to celebrate full moons, April Fools' Day, the last day of school, adopting a newborn baby, and even one for breaking bad news. Some are huge affairs, like reunions that run four or five days. But many are amazingly simple: Kathy Schuessler of Loveland, Colo., always drops her kids off at night in their rooms by linking them all together in a trainlike file and "choo-chooing" down the hall.

A Primal Urge

Scientists tell us that many animals have rituals and anthropologists report they haven't found any human societies without them, which alone is compelling evidence that rituals must be a human necessity.

Tom Driver, in his book *The Magic of Ritual,* says there is much reason to believe that even prehuman animals were "ritualizing," repeating behaviors in part to pass on to young ones survival skills in a hostile world, like monkeys teaching their offspring how to wash fruit. Later, rituals were the vehicle for teaching language, culture, religion. (Like other experts on ritual, Driver distinguishes ritualizing, which he describes as less conscious and more automatic, a kind of compulsive, patterned doing, from more formal ritual, which takes some of its special meaning from memory and association.)

In any case, the experts agree that somewhere in our basic genetic makeup is a need, a compulsion to perform actions in repetitive, ritualized ways. In one attempt to understand the underpinnings of this drive, psychiatrist Eugene d'Aquili and anthropologist Charles Laughlin tried to figure out the neurobiology of ritual, its physical effect on the brain. In an essay first published in 1979 by Columbia University Press, they concede their work is more of a suggested model than "scientific dogma."

But they say they believe that the "repetitive rhythmic behavior" found in some rituals produces a kind of "discharge" within the nervous system, which results in a pleasurable sensation akin to a state of ecstasy.

They also say that studies of brain activity have convinced them there is something about ritual that stimulates both hemispheres of the brain simultaneously, briefly creating a state of mental intensity similar to that achieved in meditation. They predict that "although ritual behavior does not always 'work,' it has such a powerful effect when it does work that it is unlikely ever to pass out of existence within a social context, no matter what the degree of sophistication of society." (This may help explain why "drumming therapy" has been so successful in recent years with the elderly and the mentally ill: therapists have found that even Alzheimer's patients can focus their minds in limited bursts while rhythmically beating a drum.)

Whatever the biology of ritual may be, it isn't hard to imagine how vital its practice was and is to primitive tribes, partly as a way to organize society, regulate behavior, and pass on culture. In such tribes there are no books, movies, or Bible-study groups to teach children about their world. Rituals must be taught for eating, communicating, becoming responsible adults, and making war.

Take a puberty ritual for girls described by the late Mircea Eliade, a scholar of religion, in his *Rites and Symbols of Initiation*, first published in 1958. Among a tribe called the Dyaks in Borneo, pubescent girls are isolated from the rest of the tribe for an entire year, living in a white cabin, dressed in white, and eating white foods. When a girl emerges, she "sucks the blood from a young man's opened vein, through a bamboo tube," Eliade writes.

Primitive puberty rites for girls vary in the length of time the girls are segregated after their first menstrual period, ranging from several days to several years. But in virtually every case, the tribal elders use that time of isolation to pass on substantially the same kinds of information: the "secrets of sexuality and fertility" and the customs of the tribe, including religious traditions.

Young girls today need to be taught pretty much the same stuff, and most will learn the sex part and be "sexually initiated" whether or not parents choose to actively participate in the teaching. The point here isn't so much that old ways are best, but that the basic need for education about life and culture never changes, and that meaningful ritual may still be the most powerful way to package and pass it along.

In fact, today's kids may actually need ritual *more* than their counterparts in primitive tribes. They aren't surrounded by the secure, familiar world of tribal life, that until recently didn't have to compete with other notions of identity, values, and lifestyle. Good family rituals can be a steadying compass in today's fragmented culture. At a time when families are so isolated from even their own clans, they can help make a family function more like a tribe.

We've all heard the disturbing statistics that mothers who work outside the home spend an average of eleven minutes a day communicating with their kids, while stay-at-home mothers spend about thirty minutes (it's only slightly more for both on the weekends). For fathers, it's less than ten minutes of daily interaction. Psychologist Mike Lewis, who has devoted years to researching American family dinners, found that the average at-home dinner lasts fifteen to twenty minutes, and most families eat together less than half the time. On the other hand, kids spend an average of twenty-five hours a week watching television, a ritual of sorts, but often not a healthy one. No wonder that Mary Pipher, a family therapist in Nebraska and the author of *Reviving Ophelia: Saving the Souls of Teenage Girls*, lectures about a generation raised by "appliances" instead of parents.

"Contemporary American families are entropic, meaning they drift toward falling apart," says William Doherty, head of the Marriage and Family Therapy program at the University of Minnesota. "Rituals combat that entropy and help hold families together. Whenever you do a ritual, you are saying 'No' to other activities or people, and becoming what I call an intentional family. Most of us just drift into habits, doing what is most convenient. But ritualizing means to take a hold of activities and ask: does this meet the needs of our family? If it's something like sitting in front of a TV night after night for dinner, then the answer is 'No.' "

As Susan Abel Lieberman writes in her book *New Traditions: Redefining Celebrations for Today's Family*, "Tradition is family insurance against outside pressures that threaten to overwhelm our days and weaken our ties to each other. . . . With the weight of permanence and the force of habit, tradition demands our attention."

Increasingly, therapists are creating rituals to help heal dysfunctional families. Evan Imber-Black, a pioneer in this area, says in *Rituals in Families and Family Therapy* that rituals are also a kind of diagnostic tool: just asking about dinner routines can provide important clues about what issues are troubling a family.

When Dr. Mary Pipher "prescribes" rituals to troubled families, she starts by suggesting they keep their televisions and computers turned off as much as possible during nights and weekends, and that they set aside time for a special family night or afternoon every week. "One of the things parents must teach kids is how to protect time and the essence of ritual to me is that ritual sanctifies time," she says. "Ritual makes a statement that the moment we're in is important and that the family itself has a greater value than other things. I don't think you can have too many rituals."

The effectiveness of rituals in contemporary society isn't just a sentimental fairy tale. Various sociological studies back up the anecdotal claims of success. Steven J. Wolin, a psychiatrist and professor at the George Washington University Medical School, has long been fascinated by cases where children from extremely troubled families still manage to grow up healthy and well-adjusted. In a series of groundbreaking studies in the '70s and '80s, Wolin and his colleagues researched rituals in families with a history of alcoholism. They learned that the more serious a family was about its rituals, the less likely the alcoholism would be passed on to the next generation.

Over time, the studies of alcoholics focused on different variables, including how adaptable a family's rituals were and whether they had been passed down or newly created. But they found the best predictor of alcoholism in future generations to be what they called "deliberateness," the degree of importance rituals held within each family. Thus of twelve couples in one study who were extremely "deliberate" about family rituals, only 25 percent passed on alcoholism to their children. But among thirty-one couples whose rituals were haphazard, 77 percent were "transmitters" of alcoholism.

In another study, psychologist Dr. Barbara Fiese examined the family rituals of a group of college students and discovered that those with solid, meaningful family rituals adjusted much more easily to college life.

The study focused on seven categories of family ritual, including those used during dinnertime, weekends, vacations, annual celebrations, special celebrations, and religious and ethnic traditions. After questioning the students about their specific rituals, the researchers tried to evaluate their level of adjustment and maturity, looking at characteristics such as self-esteem. The survey, reported in a 1992 issue of the journal *Family Process* as "Dimensions of Family Rituals Across Two Generations: Relation of Adolescent Identity," convinced Dr. Fiese that "adolescents who came from homes with special traditions adjusted better to college. It gave them a firm grounding, a sense of identity and these things made them feel more worthy of being liked."

But Fiese also discovered that some rituals could be harmful. "Where we found that many of the rituals were fairly hollow and rigidly strict, such as, 'You have to be home at such-and-such an hour no matter what, and never speak at the table before your father does,' then the kids seemed to have a harder-than-average time making the transition to college." This doesn't, of course, mean that having rules is bad. But if most family rituals are in the form of relentless rigid and joyless rules, children may grow up with more negative than positive feelings about their families.

My friend Jill Ciment, a novelist, says she grew up completely without rituals: her family virtually never ate together, didn't celebrate much of anything, wasn't religious. But evidence to the contrary appears in her brilliant memoir, *Half a Life*, about her bad-girl childhood in California.

She writes about Saturday car rides with her mother and brothers, touring model homes they couldn't afford in new housing developments. "Just as some women try on expensive dresses to see themselves anew, my mother and I tried on model houses...." It was something they did repeatedly, and something she says they found compelling, if not exactly satisfying. Clearly, for a time, this was one of the family's defining rituals. (Jill turned out very well, as did her three brothers, a fact that can be traced in part to a much healthier Ciment family ritual: frequently reading books aloud.)

The message here is that ritual is pretty much inevitable, but the form and quality of it are the responsibility of parents. If they don't push for events and activities that draw the family together in a healthy way, the rituals that evolve on their own will likely fall prey to the entropy Bill

Doherty talks about, with every person sitting in front of his or her own screen—television or computer—for the night. Or the ritual of the kids banging the front door as they leave to play with their more exciting friends, or the arguments and squabbles that exist in every family, but sadly dominate some. Or even more negative rituals may result.

Janine Roberts, a professor of family therapy at the University of Massachusetts at Amherst, notes in the book *Rituals in Families and Family Therapy*, which she co-edited, that a lot of the compulsive behavior patterns in dysfunctional families, such as "... bingeing, handwashing, alcoholic drinking, drug abuse ... can have intricate rituals attached to them." She adds ominously that "such rigidly ritualized symptoms often appear in families lacking more meaningful rituals."

Roberts is understandably reluctant to conclude that the lack of good rituals automatically leads to such serious problems. Maybe it would be more accurate to say that meaningful rituals seem to serve as a kind of preventive medicine. If you never brushed your teeth, you might not necessarily get cavities. But what careful person would risk such a thing, knowing that even a minor ritual has the potential to provide major benefits?

Two

★ ★ ★ ★

Ten Good Things Rituals Do for Children

"Rituals simplify life. On Christmas, we do this, and it's Saturday, so we're eating pizza. Thursday nights are family nights, and Sunday, we eat waffles."

—L'Tishia Suk, mother of four in Evanston, Ill.

"The importance of rituals is that they give my children tangible tokens of my love."

—Kate Smith, mother of two, Santa Barbara, Calif.

"I'm hoping that the rituals I create . . . will eventually lead my kids to [religious] faith."

—Mary Bonner, mother of three, Baltimore, Md.

fter several years of research and interviews with several hundred families that do this well, I have compiled my own list of Ten Good Things Rituals Do for Children. I think it covers all the important basics. Not every ritual accomplishes all ten goals, but most rituals are a means to multiple ends. In reviewing existing rituals and designing new ones, families should consider which goals are most important to them, and adapt their traditions accordingly.

A thorough understanding of the diverse and powerful benefits of ritual in the ten areas mentioned below will make it abundantly clear why kids need ritual, why it is worth the work.

Ten Good Things Rituals Do for Children

1. Impart a sense of identity
2. Provide comfort and security
3. Help to navigate change
4. Teach values
5. Cultivate knowledge of cultural or religious heritage
6. Teach practical skills
7. Solve problems
8. Keep alive a sense of departed family members
9. Create wonderful memories
10. Generate joy

Identity

Researchers are amazed at how tightly people cling to their family rituals as the virtual definition of their family. When most people are asked to explain their family to a therapist (or indeed to almost any stranger), rituals are often the first thing mentioned.

In *Rituals in Families and Family Therapy*, Stephen Wolin and his team of alcoholism researchers write in an essay that "family rituals contain, better than any other aspect of family life, the myths, history, and identity of the family. . . . There is no better route into the themes of particular families than to interview its members about their cherished (or despised) rituals. 'The way we do Thanksgiving,' one man reported, 'with all our repeated stories, our recurrent fights, our great traditions and our petty disputes, the day is really us. It's really our family!' "

This supremacy of family ritual above and beyond all other family activity was first detailed in *Ritual in Family Living*, a groundbreaking 1950 study of modern family rituals by sociologists James Bossard and Eleanor Boll. It took eight years to complete, included a survey of 400 families, and concluded that rituals comprise "much of the behavior of which a family is proud and of which its members definitely approve."

Some of their analysis now seems dated or just plain silly. They had wild ideas about how rituals differ by social class, declaring that middle-class dads get boring gifts from their families while upper-class dads don't, because they have time and money for interesting hobbies. But they were wise and insightful about the big picture: they understood what ritual means to families. They assert that if rituals are practiced with "frequency and intensity," they will create "a feeling of belonging to a family and of not just living in it. . . ."

Doesn't everybody remember a family they were jealous of as a child, a family they fantasized about being adopted into because it looked like so much fun to "belong" to that household? Chances are it was a family whose celebrations were frequent and festive, and whose other habits included a kind of playful, spontaneous acting out: things like special family jokes, expressions, songs, treat foods, or maybe a gag gift that was recycled year after year. In other words, a family rich in rituals.

Of course, such families still exist, and it's easy to see why the people born into them feel good about "belonging" there. In Cindy Grubb's family, the Trieschmans, the extended family includes her parents, her four siblings, and their children, a total of twenty-one.

Every Memorial Day and Labor Day weekend, the whole clan troops out to Cindy's parents' beach house. There's the Easter-egg hunt every year, and the annual Christmas caroling expedition in a hay-filled wagon. On the day before Christmas, they go to a greenmarket in downtown Baltimore to buy holiday food, get their shoes shined (they try to go to the same guy every year), eat raw oysters, buy last-minute presents, and get their pictures taken with Santa Claus. They've been doing it for twenty years.

And whenever a baby is born into the family, a seven-foot-tall wooden stork arrives on the proud parents' front lawn and stays for a week. "They know by now at the hospital that if it's a Trieschman baby, the entire hall will be full of people. We all just drop everything and go," says Cindy. It's no wonder that, as she tells it, when her only unmarried brother breaks up with a companion, "the girl says she can't bear to leave the family."

Or take the Love family from Columbia, S.C. Their semiannual family reunion lasts four days, attracting about 300 people from four generations to the cookout, talent night, golf tournament, and other events.

The family is so organized that they have a formal mentoring program that pairs up every child between seven and fifteen with an adult other than his or her parents: every six months, the child must update a contract with his mentor, stating what he wants to be when he grows up and a list of five actions he'll take soon to reach that goal.

Leon Love, one of the reunion's principal organizers, says the family has traced itself back to "three boys sold as slaves in Mississippi in the early 1800s." The reunions started twenty years ago, and have gotten bigger and more sophisticated ever since. "Our theme is that it's a huge social event, but it's also about creating legacy," he says. "Most of us didn't inherit much money, but if we work hard, we can create something wonderful for Loves yet unborn."

Indeed, the reunion has even become a draw for friends who have heard the reunion stories for years and want to "belong." "We joke and call them wannabes," says Leon, but there is actually a ritual during the reunion in which the friends in attendance can be adopted as "honorary members" of the Love family "from this day forward, unless you break our strong family ties."

There's no question that any children born into the Trieschman or the Love family will have a strong sense of what that means, and will sooner or later realize how lucky they are.

In the case of the Trieschmans, Cindy's mother was the ritual engineer, "determined that, because her own family wasn't close growing up, her kids would have the biggest celebrations for everything," says Cindy. "And we do."

Leon Love says that he and two cousins who had been researching the family tree got the idea of having a reunion in 1976, and started with fairly simple dinner or weekend get-togethers. A decade later, it had expanded to four days and required quarterly planning meetings to work on such projects as the family's tax-exempt scholarship fund. The committee that organizes the reunions also acts as a permanent family news hotline, helping the scattered relatives to stay connected between the big fetes: when a Love gets sick, dies, or gives birth, designated family members spread the word quickly.

Of course many of us don't live near our siblings or parents, or don't always have a lot to say to them when we do get together. Lots of us are dreadfully busy and couldn't possibly fit the Trieschmans' schedule into our already crowded calendars.

But family rituals that are a whole lot simpler than these can still help create a genuine sense of family esprit de corps. The Freebern family of Lakeland, Fla., declares occasional "Freebern holidays" where the whole family calls in sick. In Merchantville, N.J., Susan Lynch and her husband and two daughters lift their spirits on down days with a Lynch Family Happiness Party, for which elaborate ice-cream sundaes are mandatory. The Laughtons of Reno greet each child with his or her special family hand signals and the Densons in Winnetka, Ill., do a special "jumping hug" when someone celebrates a birthday.

Charlie Brown was never more poignantly miserable than in a 1990 Sunday cartoon, where he bemoans his family's lack of traditions to his friend Linus. He talks about how other families have great vacations, always "go to the opera on opening night," or "have a big dinner on Sunday," but sadly declares that his family's only tradition consists of his parents saying "Home again, Finnigin" as they drive in the driveway. He says they do it because "Gramma used to say it, too."

Obviously, creating rituals so your kids will know what it means to be part of your family is a valuable expression of who you are together. Teaching them their phone number and address when they reach the right age will help them get home if they get lost, but family rituals will teach them where home truly is, beyond mere geography.

Comfort and Security

As the Fiese study of college students showed, children raised with rituals that make them feel they belong to something and are special will automatically have a greater sense of security and sense of place in the larger world. Let's go back to Rebecca Siegal, crying because the family forgot to sing grace. Experts in early childhood development say that young children can't comprehend the abstract notion of time; the present has a kind of hyperreality to them and they need to have some things repeated regularly so they don't feel adrift, without a structure.

Indeed, rituals are one of the ways "kids first start making sense of time," says Amy Dombro, an authority on how children under three learn, and coauthor of the book *The Ordinary Is Extraordinary.* "When you think about it, it takes them a lot of experience to learn that it works best to put your sock on before your shoe. Ritual helps them learn through its sense of order: first we do this, and then this."

Ms. Dombro goes on to explain that ritual "has both a cognitive and an emotional element," and that Rebecca probably felt a pull in both areas. In other words, the heightened atmosphere and emotion of ritual go beyond just being a habit or routine, and missing that emotional buzz, if you will, could have been very powerful to the toddler. "There is something about actually enacting rituals that accesses touch, smell, a sense of being in our body, and a sense of being close to other people that isn't like just having a conversation," says Janine Roberts, a professor of family therapy at the University of Massachusetts who has written about the use of rituals in therapy. Thus, skipping a ritual like grace would leave a bigger hole than, say, forgetting to tie a shoe.

Every parent has experienced the way children, from a very early age, gravitate toward repetition. They want the same books, stories, songs, games, and videos over and over again, often in the same order. Even if you do some basic chore or activity twice in the same way, they're apt to notice and demand further repetitions. Professor Bill Doherty talks about driving his wife and kids to visit his family in Iowa, and how they happened to stop at the same ice-cream stand on several trips in a row. "After the third time, my kids declared it a tradition," he says, "and now the car just sort of drives itself off the road at that spot."

These repeated activities, however prosaic, are immensely satisfying and comforting. And the security aspect of ritual and repetition is more significant in the current age than ever before. For families who move constantly or who endure divorce and remarriage, job insecurity, and all the other constant unknowns, rituals are comforting simply because they are one of the few things over which families still have control. You may not be able to prevent your children from being hit by a terrorist bomb or eating a tainted hamburger, but you can make them *feel* safe in the security of your loving rituals. And you can have the satisfaction of knowing you have done your part.

Indeed, a whole category of family rituals has been shaped specifically to be reassuring, to send a message to a child that he or she will be protected. Many bedtime rituals fall into this category, including such classic good-night pronouncements as "Don't let the bed bugs bite." Allison Dafferner of Huntington Beach, Calif., continues a bedtime ritual that her mother shared with her: she and her thirteen-month-old daughter open the front door and "touch the darkness" before the child goes to bed.

In her book *Safe & Sound: Protecting Your Child in an Unpredictable World*, Vanessa Ochs includes a whole section on "protective rituals" and writes about how they help to comfort parents as well as children. She talks about a grandfather of hers who had a special ritual when his children or grandchildren left for an overseas trip. She says he would give the departing child a dollar and instruct him or her to give the bill to a beggar or anyone seeking charity as soon as possible after arrival. "My grandfather believed that a person who was in the process of carrying out a divine commandment would be protected by God from the time the deed was begun until the time it was completed," and thus he was able to deal with his own fears for the safety of the child.

Much of her book is of a very practical nature, including what safety precautions are important for children to learn at different ages, and how parents can avoid becoming so overprotective that they stifle a child. But Ochs, a teacher of religion and writing, is most poignant when detailing protective rituals that she acknowledges are useful only in a psychological sense. She talks about prayers, talismens people carry, and the ritual warnings most mothers dispense on parting—"Don't forget to look both ways," and so on.

"Disregarding the outcome of the protective ritual, we perform it, giving concrete expression to our fears," she writes. "In performing a ritual, we face the reality of our fear and own it; we are reconciled with the fact that there are issues over which we have little control. Through the ritual, we let our children know how profoundly we care."

Indeed, part of the special power of ritual comes from the naming of emotions and events in front of witnesses, as in weddings and baptisms. Saying something out loud helps to make it real, and yes, whistling a happy tune really does make you less afraid. Especially if you're a young child.

In an article in *Parents* magazine about preschoolers and nightmares, Dr. Lawrence Kutner, who teaches at Harvard Medical School, suggests an appropriate ritual to help a child get over a nasty nightmare: have him or her draw a picture of whatever was terrifying in the dream, then tear it up and throw it away.

In a wonderful essay called "Imitative and Contagious Magic in the Therapeutic Use of Rituals with Children," psychologists John J. O'Connor and Aaron Noah Hoorwitz write about some remarkable case studies in which ritual was used to help alleviate the suffering of terminally ill children, including a five-year-old boy dying of cancer of the spine and brain. A therapist told him that a stuffed animal he had just been given, a rabbit named Fluffers, was "very, very strong and could take some of the pain David had now in his head and neck." The therapist suggested the boy could hold the rabbit to his head and count to ten, and the pain "would lessen and lessen." The boy died several months later, but he kept Fluffers by his side to the end.

The two also tell of an eight-year-old boy who would wake up screaming five or six times nightly from terrible night fears. A therapist told the boy that his stuffed toy raccoon, Ralph, was strong, and if the boy squeezed or held Ralph, the animal would absorb his fears. Over a period of months, the boy's mother reported that he would squeeze or punch the raccoon when he got scared, and eventually sleep through the night with no problems.

The coauthors explain in their essay in *Rituals in Families and Family Therapy* that such "magic" makes perfect sense to a child. Children are predisposed to ritual because of the way they think; they constantly make up rituals of protection themselves, such as saying, "If I hold my breath long enough between thunderclaps, my parents will be safe. . . ." (And we all remember that childhood sidewalk game of trying not to step on the cracks, to protect our mothers' backs.) "Like gods, children give life to inanimate objects and are themselves the center of the universe. Magical thinking is also characteristic of this stage. In children's minds, a thought is equivalent to a deed. That is, if they wish in anger that a parent were dead, then they feel as if they have performed the act. . . . Compulsion and repetition, combined with a bit of magic thinking, is all that it takes for the creation of a ritual which will undo whatever it is the child fears."

That principle is proven in a modest way every night in millions of households, as kids clutch their "blankies" and lopsided stuffed animals to their chests and fall asleep. Psychologists call such things "transitional objects." Children transform these treasured belongings in their imaginations into an extension of their parents. They cling to such objects and drift off, confident they won't be sucked into the dark vacuum left by their parents' absence.

Thoughtful parents know from experience that fears must be addressed or they'll only grow. There are all kinds of small daily rituals that tame such fears by naming them.

Mail-carrier Mary Routh, who lives in Ankeny, Iowa, knows her youngest child worries about her parents while she is at school and they are at work. So she started a little ritual when the girl was in day care: in the car, on the way, the two sing a morning song and say a prayer. The prayer is usually along the lines of hoping that "Daddy is working hard and Mom won't get wet in the rain, and to help us remember to pick up milk on the way home."

Like Elinor Craig's day-care ritual of a single magic word by which her son can tell her it's okay to leave, the Rouths' ritual is meant to provide security in a moment of transition.

Navigating Change

A vast percentage of rituals from time immemorial have to do with change, including tribal rites of passage. Many rituals simultaneously celebrate a change and enact it: it is the ritual of saying "I do" publicly, along with the attendant hoopla, that changes two people from being single to married. Carl Jung has written eloquently about how each human life consists of a series of passages and transformations, deaths, rebirths, and ordeals of initiation. He warns that "stagnation and desiccation of the soul" are inevitable unless a person learns to handle these transitions.

Changes of all sorts can go more smoothly and be felt more powerfully if appropriate rituals surround them. And childhood is the best time to start learning this. Anybody who has raised a child knows that contradictory stage where toddlers cling one minute and push you away the next. Children need to be both celebrated and soothed when going through transitions, applauded for their new achievements, but also reminded of their family's unchanging love. And this applies to all kinds of significant changes, from giving up bottles to starting school, learning to ride a two-wheeled bicycle, reaching the age of ten (the first year of double digits) to, later, getting a driver's license.

Eliane Proctor of Westmont, Ill., was struggling to nurse both her newborn and her daughter Cassandra, nearly three, whom she felt was ready for weaning. She kept telling Cassandra that some day she would be old enough to stop nursing, and "We'll have a wonderful party." She eased the girl down to four breast-feedings a day, then two, and then announced that the next day would be her last. The weaning party was set for the day after that, and her mother baked a chocolate cake with candles, wrapped some modest gifts, ordered Cassandra's favorite kind of pizza, and invited some friends over to celebrate.

Afterward, Cassandra would occasionally see her baby sister nursing and decide she wanted to, too, but her mother would gently remind her that she'd been weaned. "She would say, 'Oh yes, I had my weaning party,' and she was so proud of that," recalls Eliane. The party, with its special foods, gifts, and words of praise, registered the transition very boldly in the child's mind, giving her a sense of accomplishment powerful enough to carry her through subsequent moments of regret or wistfulness for her past state of babyhood.

Just as significant are rituals for the daily transitions children weather again and again, like bedtimes and saying "good-bye" before work or school. Because they are woven so tightly into our lives, these are among the most satisfying rituals of all.

At the Bonner household in Baltimore, Md., a complex bedtime ritual for John and Kevin includes the reading of many books, specific songs, and a family prayer. Just before prayers, the boys, aged four and five, are entitled to a series of special hugs they request by name: squirrel hugs, kitten hugs, rocket-ship hugs, and so forth. Some hugs have been established over time, others their mother must improvise on the spot. New hugs will soon be added for their baby brother.

As with all good bedtime rituals, this one lets children wind down with direct reminders of parental love; it allows children to let go of the day by demonstrating that their parents, emotionally at least, won't let go of them.

Says Janine Roberts: "Everybody has transitions and changes—as simple as going from waking hours to sleeping hours, or as overwhelming and total as a death in the family. How do we bring forth some kind of sacred and protected space to make meaning out of those transitions? Ritual is where we have that space. That is what ritual can do."

I think this last point didn't really become clear to me until the death of my mother. She died on April Fools' Day, 1995, five days before she would have seen my five-month-old son for the first time. She had long been sick with emphysema and was bedridden, but her doctor had recently told me she might hang on for years. Suddenly, the trip I'd planned with Max to North Carolina took on a new and grim purpose: to attend her memorial service. I was overcome by the brutal reality that in one moment I had gone from being a person with a mother to a person without one.

It wasn't until much later that I knew how greatly the memorial rituals had helped me through that transition. A parade of family members entered the church wearing brightly colored vests my mother had quilted. My sister's daughter read a poem she'd written about her grandma, and as she did, she placed on the podium some worn rag dolls my mother had made for my sister and me that had also been special to Jenny. I got to talk about how I wanted my mother to be remembered, and to hear people speak who had become her friends long after I left home, including the woman who was with her when she died.

As powerful as the memorial service was for me, it was nothing compared to the simple ritual of scattering my mother's ashes at sea, as she had requested. The only nonfamily member was the minister from the church. He read a short prayer, and then we all stood at the edge of the dock and released the ashes slowly into the water.

Having never seen her dead body or had a chance to say good-bye, at least I had some sense that my mother's essence was freed to move on, away from pain. And it was important to me that, at least in this most final thing, she got what she wanted. I almost didn't go down to the dock that day because it was windy and my son had his first cold. But I thank God that I took the trouble, because those few minutes helped carry me from my mother's death into the rest of my life. What that modest ritual provided was exactly what Janine Roberts talked to me about later: a protected place to "make meaning" out of this saddest of life changes.

Anthropologists talk a lot about the "liminal" period in rituals of change, or the in-between phase that occurs, for example, after an initiate has been separated from his family and ordinary life, but before the transformation to manhood has been completed. Taken from the Latin word for threshold, the liminal phase is a kind of no-man's-land: a person is no longer what he has been in the past, but is not yet what he will be when the ritual concludes, like a bride in the middle of a marriage ceremony. While passing through this highly charged, magical state of transition, major change can occur, knowledge can be absorbed, and a great deal of the performance aspect of ritual is enacted.

But it's also a scary time, because the outcome, the extent and nature of the change, can't always be predicted. There have always been young people who don't survive their rites of passage, including the unfortunate victims of some contemporary fraternity initiation rituals.

Parents who are thoughtful about ritual can help create and enact ceremonies and celebrations that help their children through such liminal moments, so that the changes that happen will be as positive and complete as they need them to be. And so the children can get on with their lives, embracing change as exciting rather than dreading it, as many do.

Janine Roberts has written that ritual combines doing with believing. When a person is under stress, both action and belief are a tremendous help, and together their force can be transforming. The belief may be of a religious nature, or a simple but profound faith that the ritual will be effective.

The single biggest source of the rituals that help most people through major life transitions is religion; baptisms, confirmations, bar mitzvahs, weddings, funerals. The best are ancient and deeply meaningful ceremonies where the doing and the believing that Janine Roberts talks about work powerfully together.

Patricia Gianakopoulos of Bexley, Ohio, remembers the complex and beautiful Greek Orthodox christening ceremonies for both of her young children. During the ceremony, the priest blesses each part of the baby's body, making the sign of the cross with oil on the eyes, nose, mouth, arms, legs. "He blesses the arms so they can be strong, the feet so they will carry him and never tire," says Mrs. Gianakopoulos.

Then the child's godparents are given oil to rub all over the child's body. The priest cuts three locks of hair, a gift to God that shows gratitude and obedience. Later, the baby is dressed all in white and wears a necklace with a cross. Prayers are said, and the priest and the godparents, carrying the baby, walk to the altar, light candles, and walk around the baptismal font three times. Finally, the priest hands the baby back to the parents and says, "We present to you your son [or daughter], baptized and confirmed."

"Spiritually this is very important because the child is anointed and welcomed into the Orthodox faith," says Patricia, who converted from Catholicism when she was married. "Having friends and family witness this adds to the feeling that he or she is being welcomed into both a spiritual and an ethnic community. It is such an aesthetically beautiful and emotional ceremony."

Religious rituals can't and shouldn't be ignored or underestimated, because they have the potential to be among the most compelling experiences in the life of a believer. In the next section, covering specific rituals for various occasions, some religious rituals will be discussed in detail. But, as with rituals of any kind, religious rituals will turn hollow unless the participants exhibit real conviction and concentration in enacting them.

Some change rituals will automatically be part of a person's religious life, like bar mitzvahs, but people must demand more than a generic version of such milestones and build in elements that reflect their families and personalities. This may involve adding special touches to a ritual in a synagogue or church, or designing a party afterward that reflects the unique importance of the event to this person.

Marilyn Labendz of Montville, N.J., created a special ceremony around the weaving of a prayer shawl for her oldest son's bar mitzvah. An elderly woman was commissioned to weave the shawl, but before she finished, Marilyn assembled seventeen family members at the weaver's house. Each aunt, uncle, and sibling pushed the shuttle once to the left and once to the right, then said a personal blessing to the boy, and gave him a hug and kiss. Each of these blessings was thus woven into the prayer shawl, which the boy is meant to wear for daily morning prayers once he is declared an adult.

These days most religions and houses of worship are a little more flexible and user-friendly than they were in the past, recognizing the complexity of the times and the extra meaning that comes when people add their individual stamp to a ritual. Thus, even when planning a ritual that doesn't appear on anybody's liturgical calendar, families that consider themselves religious shouldn't rule out the participation of their church or minister.

At Gail Simpson's Unitarian church in Oakland, Calif., a simple naming ceremony for babies is performed during regular services, and Gail and her husband took part in one when they adopted their first child. But when the family adopted a second time, Gail wanted something more. In open adoptions such as this, adoptive parents get to know the biological mother and often plan to keep in touch over the years. In Gail's case, the mother had also lived with the adopting family for the last stages of pregnancy and the bond was closer than usual.

So Gail wrote a ceremony that included lines, vows in a way, for the minister, the congregation, the adopting family, and the birth mother. Her minister was willing to include it as part of a regular Sunday morning service, and members of the congregation participated. One woman, who had given up a child for adoption years before, agreed to stand up with the young mother so she wouldn't have to speak her lines alone. Others who had been adopted as children rose to read lines on behalf of the adopted child. The mother placed her three-week-old baby in the arms of Gail, the woman who will raise her. The ceremony ended with a poem by William Blake about how joy and sorrow are tightly entwined throughout life. Gail says the event was overwhelming and more than a little scary, and she wondered "whether I was out of my mind to put us all through it."

But the poignant ceremony (reprinted on pages 341–342) left many in the congregation weeping, and has accumulated power for Gail, an economist and entrepreneur. Looking back, she feels thrilled that the handing over of the baby was "witnessed by the community in which that child will be raised" and that the event was "attended by all the appropriate emotion which such awesome acts should engender."

Equally nontraditional was the ritual Paula Penn-Nabrit and her husband, Charles Nabrit, created at their Pentecostal church to cap a scholarly rite-of-passage program for each of their teenage sons. During the Saturday morning ceremonies, each boy, then thirteen years old, read a series of scriptures as well as essays he had written about the past, present, and future of African-American men. After a speech about what the

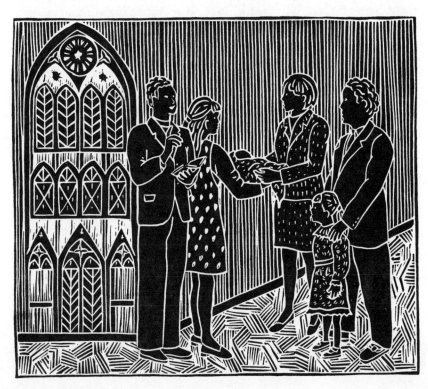

process had meant to him, each boy was acknowledged and celebrated as one after another of his relatives stood up to honor him. The pastor concluded each program by saying, "We welcome you to the honored realm, challenges, and responsibilities of black manhood."

Though some members of the congregation complained to the pastor that the church was being used for a ritual that wasn't part of its tradition, most fellow members were extremely supportive. The choir volunteered to sing, and the pastor met regularly with the boys as they composed their essays. Paula, a lawyer who owns a consulting business with her husband, is the fourth generation in her family to be raised in the Pentecostal-Apostolic faith, and she wanted religion to be a major component of her sons' preparation for manhood.

Both Gail and Paula seized occasions often ignored and transformed them into memorable milestones that are now an indelible part of their family histories. When you ask the Nabrits' sons about their rites of passage, they will grumble about how hard they had to work to prepare for them and how the ritual didn't really turn them into men. "I can't vote or drive yet: where are the privileges that come with the responsibilities?" asks Charles Nabrit, Jr., now fifteen. And yet, there is a kind of bragging in the detailing of their ordeals, and a composure and directness about these boys that is very rare for their age. You get the feeling that the real impact of these rituals will be compounding for years to come. Someday they will feel like men, and these experiences will have helped determine what kind of men they have become. Similarly, Gail Simpson's baby will grow up in the atmosphere her adoption ceremony helped inaugurate, one of honesty and outspoken love.

Obviously, not everybody is as ambitious and creative as these two women. However, good, meaningful rituals can be and have been invented for both these occasions that aren't nearly as much work. And they certainly don't require a religious context.

Teaching Values

"Family values" has become such a trite, overworked phrase that it has practically lost all value itself. But the preachers and politicians are right when they say that teaching values is one of the most important duties of parenting. And it's something kids won't absorb just by hearing and reading moralistic fairy tales. Some kind of action is required, and that's where family rituals come in. Rituals combine doing and believing, words and action. Rituals don't just talk about values, they enact them.

There is no arguing that the Nabrit rite-of-passage ritual, or the average bar mitzvah for that matter, is in large part about passing on values to kids. But what isn't so obvious is that family rituals of all kinds do this automatically and on many levels. All the more reason that parents should be thoughtful not only about what values they want to share via new rituals, but about what they are already transmitting through existing rituals. Family rituals are family priorities: the message children get very powerfully is "we do these things and not others because we value these things more."

If a family's members grab dinners on the run, or regularly eat in silence with the television blaring, they are participating in a ritual and sharing a value, but it is a negative one of mutual disrespect. Similarly, being spanked or beaten with a particular belt for misbehavior is a familiar ritual for many children. But child psychologists are in almost total agreement that the lesson being imparted by that ritual is a harmful one: that the biggest guy has the right to prevail by using violence. If, instead, the ritual for correcting misbehavior is heavily weighted on the side of praising and rewarding good behavior, a very different set of values is being imparted, including the message that people of all ages deserve respect.

It may be equally obvious, but including children in a regular extended-family holiday that always degenerates into a shouting match is also an example of a family ritual that doesn't teach meritorious values. Just getting the family together in one place isn't enough, though such gatherings are a good starting point.

Most religions offer distinct guidelines for families on how to transmit their religious values, including holiday traditions, weekly worship sessions, grace at meals, and daily prayers. These are important and useful occasions, but families who don't practice a standard religion shouldn't feel closed out of such activities.

Grace, for example, is a wonderful daily ritual that can be focused on values without being specifically religious or limited to a single religious viewpoint. Robert Fulghum, the author and Unitarian minister, writes, in his book *From Beginning to End: The Rituals of Our Lives*, about the very basic evening grace used by his family, especially when they have company for dinner. They hold hands, observe a moment of silence, and then say, "In this house we believe the finest blessing is fine companionship during a meal. With such company as we have now, we are blessed, indeed. May God bless us all. Amen." The simple act of appreciating friends or other blessings we take for granted is a value worth sharing with children every day.

In the same way, a bedtime prayer that includes blessings for family, friends, and even strangers is a practical daily exercise in thinking about other people, something that doesn't come easy to children whose egos are new and overwhelming.

Linda and Richard Eyre, parents of nine children and coauthors of the bestseller *Teaching Your Children Values*, have also written about the importance of family traditions. They write about their own family rituals in the book *3 Steps to a Strong Family*, and make clear how they have passed on values to their own children, especially the importance of service and attending to the needs of others. Yes, the Eyres are regular churchgoers (they are Mormons) and talk a lot about the values expressed in scripture. But they also live those values as a family, and have specific rituals that reward family members for actions based on them.

For example, the entire family gets involved in service work: one summer, the parents and the seven youngest Eyres went to help out at a Romanian orphanage for handicapped kids. Every September, the entire family sits down and picks two topics to study together for the whole year, a "major" and a "minor." One year the major was Spanish and the minor was Mexico, but in 1993, the major was current events and the minor was volunteerism. And there are Sunday "awards" during dinner for "value-based behavior." Regular categories include neatness, honesty, and being a self-starter (doing chores without reminders). Family members nominate one another, and the winner gets the award pinned to his door for a week.

Weekly family nights are another good forum for focusing on values. Jim and Susan Vogt, parents of four kids in Covington, Ky., are Roman Catholics who add a religious element to pretty much every family ritual.

They started family nights when their oldest child was four years old, and continued them for a decade. They do it sporadically with only one child still at home.

"Our kids weren't going to Catholic school, and we thought of it as our time to impart a religious education, but through activities rather than preaching," says Susan. Vogt family nights, which are conducted at the dining-room table and last between ten minutes and an hour, always start with the lighting of a candle and end with a special dessert.

Indeed, Susan Vogt got so experienced and creative about family nights that she was approached by the Parenting for Peace and Justice Network, a nonprofit group, to prepare a book of ideas for other families. In *Just Family Nights: 60 Activities to Keep Your Family Together in a World Falling Apart* she suggests activities to teach kids "stewardship, nonviolence, tolerance, action and spirituality." Her examples often start with a suggested Bible verse, and her themed activities teach about everything from homelessness and the environment to how to watch television critically. One exercise about racism has every family member but one wear a blue paper armband. The family members take turns ostracizing the only person wearing an orange armband, leading to a discussion of how racism feels to its victims.

This might seem like a lot of work, and not every family has the time or inclination for weekly research and preparation, let alone the effort and commitment of the actual meetings. But there are other ways. For many families, holidays seem to provide the ideal background for rituals that center around values, particularly the importance of sharing with less fortunate people.

The Vogts sometimes work with their kids in a soup kitchen at midday on Christmas. But families should think about how every aspect of their holiday celebration reflects their values, for good or bad. Families whose Christmas or Hanukkah focuses exclusively on giving lavish gifts to one another are teaching their children to place a high value on *things*, especially costly ones, whether or not they mean to.

The Michael family of Minneapolis reduced their children's Christmas gifts down to one each to avoid the holiday's materialistic focus. For three days each holiday season, the family retreats to an isolated rented cabin without phone or television. There they read together, especially M. Scott Peck's *The Friendly Snowflake*, about a little girl who has a snowflake land on her nose. "She thinks it happened on purpose and names it," says Martha Michael. "This usually leads us into a discussion about whether there is a God or not. We don't specifically talk about what happened in Bethlehem, more about the idea of love and what it means and how you know it exists."

The idea was first brought up at a family meeting, and the three kids, now between eight and fourteen, weren't thrilled. They usually get one package, a bunch of small things like T-shirts or toiletries.

Which brings up the issue of how kids react in general to new rituals, particularly those blatantly designed to upgrade their values. Research for this book showed again and again that thoughtful, well-respected parents can command a pretty amazing degree of effort, commitment, and flexibility from their kids in this area. As with the Michaels' children, there may be some grumbling, but in most age groups the desire to please parents is still a strong motivator, along with a real desire to do something together.

Also, though they cling to well-worn routines, kids are born experimenters and have a pretty high tolerance for novelty. In her book *Family Prayer for Family Times: Traditions, Celebrations, and Rituals*, Kathleen O'Connell Chesto writes that, despite this childhood trait, parents shouldn't be reticent about introducing rituals such as bedtime prayers. "Remember, even if you feel uncomfortable with this, a young child will view a simple prayer ritual in the same natural way that he or she accepts any new game or activity. The sign of the cross is not far from 'Itsy, Bitsy Spider' in the mind of the two-year-old."

Asked how she felt about giving up most presents at Christmas, the Michaels' daughter, Chelsea, a sixth-grader, replies philosophically, "In a way it's better, and in a way it's not so great. It's great that my parents don't have to spend a lot of money and that Christmas is more about family time than presents. The bad part is that after vacation my friends will brag about what their parents got them. One of them got a horse. I'll just act like being with the family more is the best present in the world."

And while there is no study that proves such values-oriented family rituals automatically produce compassionate, values-centered children, the anecdotal evidence is everywhere you look. Once they left home for college, two of the Vogt children, Brian and Heidi, got involved with the organization Habitat for Humanity, and helped build houses for low-income families during school vacations. Wendy Wright, the oldest of nine kids in a family from Idaho, grew up playing a game her father called "Sneak." About once a month, the family would spend a day in the mountains chopping a truckload of wood, which they would "sneak" onto the front porch of a local family in need. When Wendy and her sister went away to college and got their own apartment, they immediately started thinking of ways to help others. For starters, they became "secret Easter bunnies" to some little girls who lived in their apartment building.

Cultivating Knowledge of Cultural or Religious Heritage

Anybody who grew up in an even moderately religious family doesn't need convincing of the validity of rituals for this purpose. My family was pretty lackadaisical about religion, even though my father's father was a Methodist minister. I spent a lot of hours at Sunday school and church teen programs and was confirmed, but I was bored much of the time. Nonetheless, as an adult, I am glad I did these things.

What little I know about religion and the Bible I learned because of my family's commitment, however wavering, to churchgoing. And there were periods of time and isolated moments of spirituality that were uniquely fulfilling. As a preteen, I remember a New Year's Eve when each youth-group member took a lighted candle and scattered throughout the sanctuary to greet the new year privately, with quiet reflection. It may have been the single most solemn moment of my young life. I was a bit of a loner as a child, and given to contemplative moods, but something about assuming this attitude in a hushed, dark church, assembled with but not close to others of my age, and holding a burning candle turned a familiar solitude into sacred ritual.

Childhood experts and the average parent can tell you from experience that children have an incredible, innate capacity for wonder. And wonder is the root of spirituality.

Barbara DeGrote, a mother of three from Long Prairie, Minn., who has cowritten two books with her pastor husband about simplifying lifestyles, says, "I have found that kids really respond to holy moments, like lighting a candle in silence. I think kids have a sense of holiness that adults lose. I was a teacher and I know some people think they've succeeded with a group of kids when they get them to scream. I think they respond better when it's quiet: they feel as if they'll be heard."

During the four weeks of Advent, Barbara and her husband and three kids keep their Advent wreath on the kitchen table. Every night, an Advent candle is lit, a short passage is read from a church pamphlet, and one carol is sung. "Sometimes we all hold hands, and everybody gets to say one thing or one word." With the candle lit, the day's Christmas cards are opened and shared, and one new figure is added to the manger under the Christmas tree.

Some parents argue that they don't want to inflict a single system of religious beliefs upon their children: they want them to be free to choose for themselves. But I believe that excuse ignores the primal instincts of children. Any religion I've ever heard of will give kids a sense that there are forces greater than man, teach about right and wrong, and offer the vivid parables and stories of scripture. The children might decide later they'd rather be Jewish, Buddhist, or Episcopalian, but they will have a basis upon which to judge. And in the meantime, a childhood religious education will provide them with a grounding experience, helping them explore the big "whys" that inevitably pop up.

In his book *The Spiritual Life of Children*, Robert Coles describes how children have a natural and fervent hunger to know why they're here, what life means, and what lies ahead.

> Biblical stories, or lessons in the Koran, have a way of being used by children to look inward as well as upward. It should come as no surprise that the stories of Adam and Eve, Abraham and Isaac, Noah and the Ark ... get linked in the minds of millions of children to their own personal stories as they explore the nature of sexuality and regard with awe, envy or anger the power of their parents, as they wonder how solid and lasting their world is, as they struggle with brothers and sisters. ... The stories are not mere symbolism, giving expression

to what people go through emotionally. Rather, I hear children embracing religious stories because they are quite literally inspiring—exciting their minds to further thought and fantasy and helping them become more grown, more contemplative and sure of themselves.

Coles found again and again that when issues of God and heaven, good and evil, were raised with schoolchildren all over the world, they stopped fidgeting and prolonged, intense discussions ensued.

"To children, the invisible seems to be even more real than the visible," says Sofia Cavalletti, head of a religious education center in Rome that is based on Montessori principles. "Children do not have the least difficulty in looking through the liturgical signs," she writes in an essay from the journal *Montessori Talks to Parents.* "The light in Baptism is for them goodness, as if they really saw goodness and not the light of the candles."

When religion is infused into family life, it can work for kids like a map in the hands of an intrepid explorer. It will probably be years before they understand what it *really* means to be Baptist or Muslim, but they are desperately trying to figure out what it means to be alive.

As discussed previously, religions come with built-in family rituals for everything from daily meals to major life changes. But individual families make a big difference in whether these rituals pack real power. Family rituals can make religion come alive to kids far more vibrantly than coloring in drawings of Noah's ark in Sunday school.

Mary Bonner, a Catholic mother of three sons, has thought about this issue a lot. She says she wants her children to grow up with lots of family religious rituals, as she did, but feels she can be more creative and attentive to three than her mother was with eight kids. "To me, faith is a personal thing and ritual is shared, but I believe ritual can lead a person to deeper faith. I am hoping that the rituals I help create will be a foundation that will lead my kids to faith eventually. But for now, I just want it to be fun for them."

The Bonners gave all their sons first and middle names of Catholic saints, and on the "name days" or feast days for those saints, the child with that name is given a special dinner. "We don't give gifts, we simply read stories, give them their favorite foods, and talk about the life of that particular saint. It's a fun way for them to learn more about the culture of our church and to identify with qualities of honor, courage, bravery, and even the possibilities of miracles."

During the forty days of Lent, Mary cuts out magazine and newspaper photographs of children "who don't have a nice house to live in or enough food to eat. Nothing too alarming, but they have led to very interesting questions." The Bonners look at the pictures and discuss them during dinner. "To me, Lent doesn't have to be a season of sackcloth and ashes literally, but forty days of enhanced awareness about poverty in the world," she says.

All across the country, thoughtful parents are putting their personal stamp on traditional religious rituals to deepen their meanings within the family. Passover, an eight-day Jewish holiday that celebrates the freedom of the early Israelites from slavery, begins with a special ritual dinner called a seder. There are many traditional elements to a Passover seder, including the eating of bitter herbs (usually horseradish) to commemorate slavery. But one family I know puts a special plate on the Passover table to which each person contributes something that represents liberation in his or her own life. Friends and family have contributed everything from termination papers from a job they hated, to a timer that reminded them when to take the medication that keeps them alive. Part of the evening's ceremony consists of letting each person at the table tell the story of their liberation symbol.

Ilene Cohen of Pittsburgh is a firm believer in Jewish family ritual, but she wants her rituals to have an element of creativity and fun. She and her husband and two young children have a Shabbat dinner every Friday night, lighting the traditional two candles and saying the kiddush, the blessing over the wine. Special foods are often served, but at the Cohen household, continuing a big family tradition from Ilene's childhood, one of them is liable to be "Shabbat Jell-O," a kind of rainbow or confetti gelatin, in which red, green, and orange Jell-O is folded together and spread with whipped cream.

"I only serve this on Friday, though not every Friday," says Ilene. "We might make brownies together instead. But there is always something special, different, or unique. I want my kids to have a memory for every holiday."

Family rituals are doubly important when it comes to emphasizing cultural and ethnic heritage, because often there isn't as much celebration and activity built into the calendar as there is with religion. Families who want to keep their ethnic traditions alive consciously work at doing so, and make it fun for their children.

Deborah Pecoraro of Livermore, Calif., felt her husband's Italian roots were crowding out her Irish heritage, so she decided to make a big deal out of St. Patrick's Day for her two children. She would fix corned beef and cabbage and a green cake for dinner, and dye the eggs and the milk green for breakfast. But mere food wasn't enough, so she got her son, now ten, into the habit of building a "leprechaun trap" every year with his grandfather.

The trap, a white box with pennies and shamrocks all over it, is chained to the boy's bed. There is a hole big enough for a hand to go through, and a few pennies are left inside to entice the leprechauns. Bells and other noisemakers are positioned to go off if someone tries to take the money. The trap is set the night before St. Patrick's Day, and when the leprechauns finally come, either during the night or the next day, they make a mess in the room, but leave behind a cache of gold-covered choco- late coins for both the boy and his sister.

Brandi Kuhlmann of Placerville, Calif., is one-eighth Cherokee, but grew up learning nothing about her Native American roots. About five years ago, she began to get very involved in Native American rituals and traditions, and has taken her daughter, now ten, to a weekly activity at the local intertribal Indian center called a "drum." The sessions include drumming, singing, and praying, and start with a ritual act called "smudging," in which a stick wrapped with smoldering herbs (usually sage) is waved over each participant in turn so the smoke can purify them.

Now Brandi's daughter has become intensely involved too, and recently completed a ceremony called "coming out." After she performed a series of good deeds for her community and made beautiful gifts for some of the elders, the girl appeared in a special dance wearing an elabo- rate costume.

Some families introduce rituals about ethnic heritage that have little or no connection with their own backgrounds, because they wish to teach their children respect for different cultures.

The Lewis family of Wisconsin shares the dilemma of many modern American families. Jeanne Mollinger-Lewis grew up in a strict Catholic family, while her husband had no religious affiliation whatever. Both their children are adopted: the older child, a boy, was born in Korea, and his sister is part Filipino.

Jeanne's response to all this has been to let her children sample a wide variety of traditions. For example, the family's Christmas rituals vary from year to year and have included elements from the African-American harvest celebration called Kwanzaa, and the Jewish winter holiday, Hanukkah. They call their Christmas tree a solstice tree, and have a big celebration at the winter solstice, but they also set up a traditional Christian manger under the tree. The family has even celebrated Santa Lucia Day, the Swedish holiday that opens the Christmas season, by making a Santa Lucia crown for their daughter and baking traditional Swedish sweet buns together.

Jeanne also wants her children to learn about their natal cultures. Korean flags hang in the dining room and in her son's bedroom. Her son takes lessons in tae kwondo, a Korean self-defense discipline, and he decided at age seven, with his parents' blessing, that he would like to try following Buddhism.

Clearly, Jeanne's moves have come partly because she felt her religious upbringing was too conservative and, in response, has herself moved to the highly undoctrinaire Universalist Unitarian church. But her wish for her children goes beyond a question of religious affiliation. "We want them to grow up in a global community," she says.

Teaching Practical Skills

Ordinary rituals teach all kinds of practical skills, such as how to set the table, even though this is not what most parents think about when they contemplate family rituals. One family has a tradition that during summer vacations and on snow days, when the kids are stranded at home, they will be taught the nuts and bolts of what makes the house work, things like how to restart the hot-water heater and replace a fuse.

Kids who bake with their mothers at holiday time, for one obvious example, will grow up knowing how to make cookies and cakes. Children used to sitting down to holiday meals with extended families and friends will gain valuable practice in carrying on social conversations. If you have a tradition of family camping trips, your kids will learn to pitch a tent and build a fire, while vacation rituals that include water sports may teach kids sailing, waterskiing, or fishing.

A special bonus gained from all this is that as children learn practical skills in festive settings under their parents' watchful eyes, they are also learning responsibility. The Dreys of Des Moines, Iowa, go to a tree farm every year to cut down their own Christmas tree. Their son, Paul, has gone from eagerly watching the proceedings to holding the tree while his father chopped, to cutting it down himself.

But let's use some imagination here. Deborah Pecoraro, the lady with the leprechaun traps, did. The Pecoraros have a tradition of "full-moon sundaes": every month when the moon is full, her two kids get to make themselves lavish, gut-splitting sundaes. But there's a catch. The sundaes only happen if the children, aged ten and thirteen, take responsibility and keep track in the newspaper of when the full moon is coming. And there's a little lesson in finance involved: if the kids buy ice cream or other items using a cents-off coupon, they get to keep the money saved.

Clearly, blending any kind of lesson into a special occasion will make it seem less like school and more like fun. And the possibilities are endless. One idea: give your children special occasions to practice and show off the skills they've learned. Table manners, for instance. Sociologists say that some families' dinners become dreaded battlegrounds instead of cherished rituals because the whole meal is spent criticizing and correcting kids on their behavior.

In her book *New Traditions: Redefining Celebrations for Today's Family*, Susan Abel Lieberman writes about the unusual "no-reason" dinner parties given by Sally and Richard Singleton for their three children. The table is set with the best china and decorated with flowers. The kids get all dressed up, go out the back door, then walk around to the front, where their parents usher them in as honored guests.

"[The kids] love it," says Sally Singleton. "We do, too, because it is reassuring to see your children as guests. Has your child ever been out and the host family glowingly reported on his or her nice manners, leaving you delighted and mystified? Well, these dinners seem to bring out that best self."

Solving Problems

Many well-loved family rituals were initially created to solve problems. Bedtime rituals, for example. One mother, concerned about her kids getting sick from too much Halloween candy, started a savvy annual dinner ritual: nobody can go out trick-or-treating on an empty stomach. They must first eat at least one bowl of her special homemade Halloween soup, containing noodles, potatoes, and rice. I myself have fond memories of waking up early on Christmas morning to grab the bulging stocking propped outside my door. But what seemed like a treat to me was really my exhausted mother's technique of keeping four hyperexcited kids in their beds until dawn.

Sally Pennington, a mother of five grown children, laughs to think that many of the "rituals" her kids fondly recall were actually rules or other ways to resolve problems. Even the cherished ritual of having annual calendars printed up that included family activities and family photos was an effort at what she calls "managing the family."

"Living with five kids is chaotic. We found that if you had a ritual or a rule for things, you didn't have to revisit an issue every time it came up. We even had a rule about seats in the family room for TV-watching: if a person wanted the same seat back, they had to say 'Coming right back,' and there was a time limit of five to ten minutes."

Of course, not every rule qualifies as a ritual, but the Pennington children have so many memories of their childhood rituals/rules, that they once created a Family Trivia game as a gift for their parents. Says Sally, "Quite a few of the trivia questions start out, 'What was the rule for . . .'"

But an inventive parent might want to begin thinking whenever he or she faces a recurring problem: what's a recurring ritual that would counteract this?

One of my favorite examples is the brainchild of Polly Mead, whose oldest son, Walter, is one of my dearest friends. Walter is one of four children, and just as you might expect, every time the family went on an extended trip by car, at least one child whined, fussed, or started a fight. Deciding that it was inevitable, but that collective fussing was preferable to consecutive fussing, Polly instituted "fuss towns," selected because they were halfway to the destination. In between fuss towns, the children had to behave. It was only while driving through the fuss towns that the kids could yell and whine and carry on, and they did so with a vengeance, letting off lots of steam but over a short, endurable period of time.

The Meads also grew up with a glass jar on their kitchen table that the kids called the "talking against jar." Anytime they said something nasty about a sibling during meals, a child had to put a certain amount of money in the jar. After money had accumulated, it was given to charity. Walter jokes now that the chief lesson he learned from this is that "my sister's reputation was worth a dime," but his mother swears the jar cut down on sibling slander. "After a while, it was more symbolic than anything. Just sitting there, it was a reminder."

Brandi Kuhlmann was concerned when her six-year-old daughter was being teased by other kids and felt weird about being home-schooled. Before bed, she would recite a litany of woes and insecurities, so Brandi started a bedtime ritual she calls "good things." After her daughter is tucked in bed with the lights out, she can express discontent about the day, but then she has to list three things: What she liked best about herself that day. What she liked best about the day itself. The thing she liked best about whichever parent is putting her to bed. (Then that parent has to recite his or her "good things.")

"At first she had trouble saying anything good about herself," says Brandi. "She might say, 'What I liked about myself today was that I got through the day.' It took practice, but it definitely helped lift her self-esteem and keep it lifted."

Obviously, rituals alone aren't going to be able to solve every problem facing a family, but their power to help heal troubled relationships is immense, and more and more family therapists are using them as one of their trustiest tools in solving the problems of dysfunctional families.

The 1988 book *Rituals in Families and Family Therapy*, edited by Evan Imber-Black, Janine Roberts, and Richard Whiting, gathered essays by a number of therapists using rituals with adolescents, the mentally ill, terminally ill children, remarried families, and families with a history of alcoholism. In an opening essay, Janine Roberts explains that one reason ritual is so powerful within the context of family therapy is that "ritual allows strong emotions to be safely experienced, at the same time that interpersonal connections are made. Families in treatment have often put a rigid boundary around difficult events in their lives. . . . The use of ritual in treatment can provide a safe place to explore intense emotions" related to such past traumas.

If paralyzed and tormented families find themselves unable to get past a tragic loss, therapists may help them invent a healing ritual. Roberts writes about her younger brother, Mark, who disappeared from an alcoholism treatment center and was missing for five years. Blame flew between family members and the situation was made worse by the fact that Janine's mother and father were divorced and the family members lived far apart.

Finally, a therapist suggested to Janine's mother that she "create some memorial that would both honor him and acknowledge her pain." Her mother decided to create a memorial in the garden outside her window, and later family members went to a mountain path where Mark loved to hike and selected a rock. During a small ceremony, it was placed in the garden and the family took turns sharing memories of Mark. His mother brought out a scrapbook with photos of her lost son and written recollections, which were supplemented at the gathering. "There were many tears and some laughter as people talked and moved closer together," Janine writes.

Clearly, the ritual helped them live with this tragedy, which had a happy ending when Mark turned up again, having pulled himself together, and, Janine says, the scrapbook and memorial gave him powerful, concrete proof of how deeply he was missed.

Keeping Alive a Sense
of Departed Family Members

Not everybody is so lucky. Inevitably, as we have children and grow older, we will all lose family members. Grandparents, parents, aunts and uncles, brothers and sisters will die and so, saddest of all, will children.

The ritual of grief contains many rituals, and lasts for years after the funeral or memorial service. Every time you bake Great Aunt Maud's apple pie, you are performing a ritual of mourning, remembrance, and appreciation. Even better if you have some of her flowered china to serve it on. The smell, the taste, the look of that pie brings her back into the room, and you remember her favorite sayings, the kind of dress she wore, the way she hugged.

Finding the means to express these things as a family makes it easier for everybody to survive the grief of loss. Through ritual, a family member who is gone physically can still be present emotionally and spiritually. And children who never knew, or barely remember, the person who is gone, can be given the gift of "knowing" that person.

I understand this from my own experience. My son will never meet my mother, and I can't do anything to change that. But on the first anniversary of her death, I lit candles in front of her picture and promised her that I would pass on to Max the lessons she taught me. I also sat down and started writing him a long letter about her life, and began collecting materials for a scrapbook about her. When he gets older, I plan to observe her birthdays with him by looking at the scrapbook and engaging in an activity related to her passions, probably puppetry. We could see or perform a puppet show every year in her memory, and I can show him the only puppet of hers that I still have: the devil from *Punch and Judy*.

For the tenth anniversary of her dad's death, Julie Hoddinott of Columbia, Conn., revived what had been a beloved summertime family ritual: a summer clambake. Her extended family had come together for the baptism of one of the Hoddinotts' two adopted sons. After the church ceremony, the eighteen people trooped back to Julie's house for the festivities, which included looking at an album of pictures of the absent grandfather. "When the anniversary rolls around, I miss my dad a lot," says Julie, "but I also remember that party."

Linda, a New Hampshire woman who asked to keep her last name private, lost her oldest son in a car crash when he was twenty-two. She says the rituals she has created were for comfort, remembrance, sanity, and to keep Michael's memory fresh for his four siblings. "You loved this person and you can't just give him up and forget about him," she says. "There is a need to remember. Like every other parent I've met who has lost a child, you are afraid this person is going to be forgotten by the rest of the world."

Clearly, he won't be forgotten by his family. Michael loved planting things and outdoor work, and dreamed of being a farmer, so it seemed natural to make a special garden for him in the backyard, with fruit trees, flowers, a birdbath, and a bench with an angel sitting on it. The first Christmas after his death, Linda's family gave her and her husband a bird feeder, as well as filling Michael's stocking with special notes about things they'll never forget. "Though I cried many tears, it was so good to have them remember him outwardly," says Linda.

The family has a special year-round Christmas tree in the living room. The six-foot-tall artificial tree is covered with silk flowers, baby's breath, lights, and special ornaments representing Michael's passions. The family has dubbed it "the giving tree," and it has become a gathering place in the house. When a special gift is given to a family member or friend, Linda will say, "I have something under the tree for you." When her daughter graduated from high school, everybody gathered near the tree to honor her and present her with gifts.

"It was like including Michael in everything," says Linda. "For a month I cried when I thought about her graduation, mostly because Michael wouldn't be there. But I found a picture of the two of them together and bought her roses, which he would have done."

The Moreheads of Springfield, Ill., lost their daughter Lucie at thirteen months, after heart surgery, and they, too, have developed rituals to celebrate and commemorate her, including her love of balloons. "On special occasions, including her birthday and the Fourth of July, we buy helium balloons and just release them into the air," says Tina Morehead. "People used to tell children when they lost a balloon, 'It's going up to heaven, and it will meet you when you get there.' "

On Lucie's birthday, the family also sends balloons to kids in the intensive-care unit of the hospital where she died, and every Christmas they buy an ornament for her, either an angel or a star. Since they can't buy her a present, they buy and donate one to a needy child the age she would have been. Through these and other rituals, the Moreheads' infant son and Lucie's cousins will continue to celebrate and remember Lucie.

Wonderful Memories

When you ask parents why they are creating and perpetuating rituals, usually the first thing they say is that they want their kids to have great memories. But children don't always remember rituals in the way parents expect. Those that took a lot of preparation and went off without a hitch may be long forgotten, but the ones with a few kinks here and there are imprinted forever.

Ask the McNurlan kids of Indiana about their weekly family-fun nights, which almost always include watching a movie, eating pizza, and following rhymed clues to find a special dessert. The fun nights have continued for a decade, but the night the kids *really* remember and tell friends about is the time their mother, Deena McNurlan, hid cupcakes in the clothes dryer and forgot about them. Until she did the next load of white clothes. . . .

Every year on the last day before school starts, Margaret Simon and her four sons pile into the car and enjoy a last-blast-of-summer outing at the beach or park. Their most memorable excursion? The time Margaret drove them to Pioneer Waterland only to find it closed for the season. So they went to a state park instead and rented two motor boats, one of which died and had to be towed. By day's end, the boys were already calling it their "Griswold vacation" after the family in the Chevy Chase movies about horrendous holidays.

To hear even grown-ups talk about their memories of ritual is to learn all over again that simple and heartfelt always beats fancy and forced. A ritual that singles out a child and makes him or her feel special is likely to be remembered long after the noisy, boisterous birthday parties that destroyed the family's budget—and the furniture.

Tarrant Figlio, a mother of two in Eugene, Ore., is a real believer in rituals and has added plenty of her own to the ones she cherished as she was growing up. But though she loved her mother's elaborate Easter-egg hunts enough to pass them on to her children, the childhood ritual that left her with the fondest memories was a far simpler one. "The biggest ritual to me growing up was going to get doughnuts with my dad on Saturday mornings. Just me and my dad. That was the coolest thing. My father and I would always make up songs on the way, like one about our kitty."

Tarrant says she can't name more than two or three Christmas presents she received in her entire childhood. But what she'll never forget is that "I always got an orange in my stocking and there was always something really special in the toe. And we always ate eggs Benedict for Christmas breakfast."

Repetition adds to rituals: silly family rituals that keep getting embellished get more and more memorable the longer the gag runs.

Barb Brock now lives in Oregon, but whenever possible she takes her family back to Iowa, where she was born, to participate in her family's annual Christmas Eve bingo game. The game has been going on for more than forty years, and each year fifty some adults and kids gather to play again, with each family contributing presents for the winners. Some of the gifts are nice: homemade fudge, attractive picture frames. But a few have been recycled for decades, including an enormous pair of red silk panties: "My husband and I once hid them in a test tube inserted into a freshly baked loaf of bread," says Barb. Everybody roars hysterically when the panties reappear each year. They also anticipate the beat-up horse figurine that comes with its own photo album (whoever wins the horse each year takes it to the most exotic locale they visit, to take a snapshot—it's been all the way to Israel).

Pamela Pinegar has learned for herself that when it comes to memorable rituals, it's not the economy, stupid—it's the caring and creativity. The first year she was divorced, Pam's daughters were nine and five, and she was worried about Christmas because her budget was tight. Those are very acquisitive ages, and the girls were deep into their Barbie phase ("In those years, I could swear Barbie was a third dependent," says Pam.) The older girl was desperate for a Barbie Dream House, but what she *needed* was underwear and socks.

"At the least I wanted there to be lots of boxes under the tree, because kids are into volume," says Pam. So she bought six pairs of panties and put them in six different boxes. Plus, she got inexpensive fun gifts like bubble-blowing liquid, jigsaw puzzles, and paperback books. Each present was wrapped in a box that was decorated with a catalog picture of something expensive, and a note. "Pretend this is a Barbie Dream House," read one.

"At the time, I didn't know if it would fly with them," recalls Pam. "The first gift they opened, the reaction was like, 'What *is* this?' But then it grew on them and they started treating it like a game." The game became so popular that the ritual is an indelible part of the family's

Christmas celebrations. "Every year now, they give me at least one BIG box, with a picture of a diamond ring or a new car," says Pam with a laugh. "Inside is a can of Pledge, or a pair of panty hose. They think it's so funny, they've even started to do it to their friends."

Often, memories are a side effect of rituals. As with Pam Pinegar, the creators of new rituals can't always tell which traditions will stick and which will fade, both on the calendar and in memory. But some rituals are designed around memories; they are created to capture and save them, and when they work, they can be treasures for a lifetime.

One mother I know has begun a ritual of asking each of her children's teachers to write a letter at the end of the school year. Her oldest daughter is in sixth grade, and the mother has been collecting letters secretly since the girl was in kindergarten. The letters recollect the highlights of the year, not just academically but anecdotally, escaped frogs and all. When each daughter graduates from eighth grade, she will receive the entire collection of letters, enclosed in an album of photos that correspond to the years.

Much of family ritual, even the celebration of modest occasions, includes specific foods and other festive elements, such as music or decorations. In effective rituals, the emotions and memories associated with a particular ritual and time of life can be instantly triggered when those senses are stimulated again in the same way.

One of the most famous works of literature in this century, Marcel Proust's *Remembrance of Things Past*, pays homage to the powerful hold of childhood ritual on memory and helps explain why this is so. Proust writes about tasting a *petite madeleine*—a little yellow cake baked in the shape of a scallop shell—and being thrown viscerally back to childhood. He recollects a ritual of sitting in an aunt's bedroom on Sunday mornings, when the aunt would dip a madeleine in her tea and offer it to her nephew. Once he recognized the familiar taste, an image of the aunt's room, the house, the street, and the entire town rose up like a stage set in his mind.

Who doesn't have madeleines? Mine are plain doughnuts, served at the annual elementary school Halloween party. I can feel the crisp fall air, see the playground and my childhood house up the hill, and taste the doughnut and cold apple cider in a plastic cup. We can't select or control what will be the equivalent for our children, but we must create rituals thoughtfully, knowing just how vivid the memories will be.

Generate Joy

Ultimately, the memories will take care of themselves, but joy comes with the moment. Experts in rituals say that while they should include a scripted, repeated element, they should also include a spontaneous, creative segment, and joy is a child of spontaneity.

It is also a product of whimsy and foolishness, two other qualities that belong in ritual. This is well understood by parents who do things like leave baking-soda footprints from Santa in the living room at Christmas; eat sundaes on Sunday; and celebrate the first day of spring as Big Bird's birthday. Although ritual is a powerful tool for teaching everything from table manners to morals, it can also create a special climate for fun. That's because ritual time isn't ordinary time; it doesn't follow everyday rules, it gives permission to be extreme.

Ken Scott, a divorced father in Suttons Bay, Mich., instituted an occasional ritual of "opera meals" with his two young children. No talking is allowed, just singing—even requests for butter and salt must be sung, and that goes for him, too.

Receiving not just permission but encouragement to act silly is guaranteed to generate joy in a kid. If, in addition, a ritual adds the spectacle of grown-ups acting silly, the bliss will be virtually boundless.

Some of the most joyful rituals are those that inherently acknowledge the disadvantages of being a child—like the need to follow lots of rules—and turn propriety on its head.

Dawn Hale of Clinton, N.J., loves to surprise her three children with an April Fools' Day ritual. "When they get up in the morning, the house is all mixed up," she says. "The table will be set with candles and their orange juice is in wineglasses. Instead of serving them regular breakfast food, I'll give them dessert, like cake or a plate of cookies. They think it's a riot, that Mom has just gone crazy. Then it finally hits them what day it is."

And then there's "King Henry VIII Night," a ritual from Ellie Just's childhood that is probably the dream of every child. Ellie's mother started the ritual because she grew up in a household where table manners were strictly enforced, and she knew Ellie had to endure special scrutiny when she dined at her grandmother's once a week. So every so often, at home, Ellie's mother would declare a "King Henry VIII Night," at which table manners *weren't allowed*. "We would eat outside and throw our chicken bones and corncobs on the ground," Ellie recalls. "There was smacking of lips, burping, and plenty of elbows on the table. I always invited friends, and it was so much fun."

One final bonus benefit: how many of you want your kids to visit often when they grow up? Rituals can help here, too.

Mike Lewis, the research psychologist who has studied family dinners, talks about his family's "International Reptilian Hunt." This tradition started during a family vacation in the Caribbean, when someone came up with the idea of "seeing how many different kinds of lizards we could catch, and let go." The four Lewises had so much fun on the trip that they now take a vacation together every summer to look for reptiles. Every year, special T-shirts are made for the trip, which each family member takes a turn designing. One child is in college and the other has graduated, but they still come together every year for the reptile hunt. "I could never just say to them now that they're on their own: 'Hey, I miss you, let's spend a week together,' " says Mike. "They'd say, 'No, Pop, I'm busy.' But they can't stand to miss this ritual. It is somehow bigger than the family; it has a life of its own."

Worthwhile though it is, ritual isn't always easy. It takes time, which everybody seems short of, and thoughtfulness, which is a form of work. Even with the best of intentions, the world intrudes: Dr. Stephen Wolin, the psychiatrist who has studied resiliency in children, once conducted what he called "the family dinner experiment" on *Oprah*. Five families selected from around the country made a pact to have dinner together at least four times a week for at least half an hour each time. Not one family lived up to its promise.

Obviously, we can't wish ourselves back to some primitive, tribal society or even a supposedly simpler time in this century; indeed, research shows that earlier periods weren't so family-focused as we like to think. The vital question facing us now: What rituals can we fashion in the late twentieth century, using the tools of our own culture, that will make the most positive difference in the lives of our children?

"The saying is that you give your children two things: roots and wings," says Marilyn Labendz, the woman who created the special ceremony for weaving her son's prayer shawl. "I think the rituals are the roots. You can fly off anywhere if you know where you come from."

Part 2

WHAT

Three

★ · ★ · ★ · ★

CELEBRATING HOLIDAYS AND THE SEASONS FROM NEW YEAR'S THROUGH HALLOWEEN

For everything, there is a season,
and a time for every matter under heaven:
a time to be born, and a time to die;
a time to plant, and a time to pluck up what is planted;
a time to kill, and a time to heal;
a time to break down, and a time to build up;
a time to weep, and a time to laugh;
a time to mourn, and a time to dance....
                                                    —Ecclesiastes 3:1–4

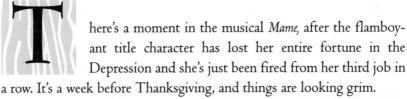here's a moment in the musical *Mame*, after the flamboyant title character has lost her entire fortune in the Depression and she's just been fired from her third job in a row. It's a week before Thanksgiving, and things are looking grim.

But the ever-resourceful Mame plunges into her closets and pulls out tinsel and wreaths and the few presents she has stashed away, and, with her nephew Patrick and what's left of her household staff, she celebrates Christmas early. The four of them sing and dance, act silly, exchange gifts, and declare their love for one another. They sing a number called "We Need a Little Christmas." "We need a little music, need a little laughter, need a little singing, ringing through the rafters. . . ." And wouldn't you know it? Just then a rich, available man rings the doorbell looking for Mame.

Well, Santa Claus doesn't always work that quickly, but holiday rituals can indeed perform a kind of restorative magic, unleashing a balm of remembered good times the way potpourri distills and intensifies the scents of dried flowers. The power of holiday traditions comes from all the memories packed away in them, but also the knowledge that even in tough times those ritual activities can still make us laugh and sing when nothing else can. There are times when we *all* need Christmas, or its emotional equivalent. Life has a way of getting tough, and even when it isn't, it needs spice, anticipation, and pageantry. In truth, we crave occasions that require living up to.

According to the eminent child psychiatrist Bruno Bettelheim, such events are especially vital to children. In his book *A Good Enough Parent,* Bettelheim argued that holidays are critical to psychological development, because they provide a reliable, regular occasion when children find themselves "in the center of affectionate attention and are made to feel important. If such occasions are celebrated in the right spirit, the glow from these days can spread out over the rest of life."

Holiday celebration hasn't always been such a big deal in this country. The Pilgrims didn't believe in celebrating much of anything and forbade most holidays. Thanksgiving wasn't a national holiday until President Lincoln declared it one in 1863, and Father's Day wasn't official until 1966. Some people might argue that the pendulum has swung too far the other way from Pilgrim minimalism, and we've become a tad excessive in our fervor to party and commemorate. Are you aware that February is Humpback Whale Awareness Month and September 7 is Grandparents' Day?

But Americans are, if nothing else, a people who love having choices, and our holiday smorgasbord truly offers something for every appetite. The important thing is to fill in the family calendar with events that mean something to the people involved, and that requires both passion and practice. Don't be afraid to celebrate new things and don't neglect the most ancient holidays of all, the changing of the seasons. This year, welcome spring the way the Reichman family does, by raising butterflies from caterpillars and setting them free. Or celebrate autumn like Shirley McDonald and her daughter by catching falling leaves. "If you catch twelve in one outing," says Shirley, "it means twelve months of good luck."

All the ideas in this and the following chapter have one thing in common: they've stood the test of time, and real kids. So be of good cheer, and party on.

New Year's

New Year's is a good place to start, and not just because it comes first in the calendar year. Unlike a lot of annual holidays, it doesn't carry much baggage in the expectations department. For most people, it isn't one of those holidays marked by complicated logistics, umpteen relatives, and de rigueur decorating: it is hardly ever celebrated with the kind of command family performance one friend of mine calls "an Occasion of State." Indeed, many families are perfectly happy ignoring it altogether, and brag about not being awake when the new year starts.

But the lack of ingrained tradition associated with this holiday is an advantage, because it grants families freedom and flexibility to shape it in whatever way suits them. Parents with small children don't have to wait until midnight to celebrate. Families can have a spectacular family brunch on New Year's Day, or host an annual afternoon open house and reconnect with old friends. Age-old traditions like opening the door at midnight to welcome in the new year can be combined with a family's invented rituals, such as attaching resolutions to helium balloons and releasing them to the heavens.

The day automatically holds plenty of portent about fresh beginnings, symbolism that families can tap into to make their festivities more meaningful. It's a perfect occasion for families to plan the year ahead together, or to reminisce about the year just past. Often, people are so worn out from the Thanksgiving-through-Christmas marathon that they can't seem to handle much more than drunken collapse on New Year's. Perhaps if families could be a little more imaginative and whimsical about their rituals on this occasion, it would inject creative energy into the household and set a more hopeful tone for the year ahead.

Parties and Celebrations

At the Butman house in Walkersville, Md., New Year's Eve dinner is a family-only "cocktail party" in the family room, with the five Butmans eating a meal consisting of just appetizers. As at any cocktail party, they balance paper plates on their laps, or eat standing up while talking. Each person prepares his or her favorite appetizer, whether it's shrimp or piles of crunchy vegetables with creamy dip. Everyone wears a funny hat and blows a noisemaker, and after people finish eating, the family plays oldies rock-'n'-roll songs from the '60s and '70s and dances up a storm.

One of the evening's highlights is the ritual viewing of family videos from the past year. Because this has become such an expected part of the family's New Year's Eve tradition, family members now make a joke of shouting "Happy New Year!" all year long whenever the video camera rolls. The twin boys and their sister may be standing by a pool under a hot July sun, or blowing out the candles on a birthday cake, but they rarely forget to bellow out that greeting, knowing that, come New Year's Eve, they'll all be sitting in the family room watching their year on television.

"I guess it got started because one New Year's Eve someone said, 'We never had a chance to see our Christmas video; let's do that,' " says Karen Butman. "We watched the Christmas footage, but there was also some stuff from summer and we kept watching and one of the kids said, 'That was fun. We'll have to do it again.' " Now that her kids are entering their teens and complaining about their family more, Karen finds that the simple act of watching the year's events replayed consecutively reminds them how much they've shared. "They'll say things like, 'Gee, we did do a lot of stuff together this year, didn't we?' " she says.

Now that the Butman boys are thirteen and their sister is eleven, the kids are allowed to stay up until midnight. When the new year hits, they all cheer and yell and throw glittery confetti all over the family room and drink ginger ale out of champagne glasses. "The funny thing is that as much as the kids love making this big, super mess in the family room, they also have fun vacuuming all the confetti up," says Karen. "They never leave it till the next day."

Many cultures over countless generations have placed special significance on the first person to step over a household's threshold on New Year's, and that's another element people can play with in designing rituals. The superstition is taken especially seriously in Scotland, with a tradition known as "First Footing." Because it was considered a bad omen for a fair-haired man to be the first person over the threshold (except in a few districts where brunettes were bad luck), in some places dark-haired men were actually hired to be the first to enter a house in the new year. It's a tradition that has been adopted and lovingly embroidered by Jim San-ford of Warren, Vt., whose grandmother is Scottish though she never practiced this custom or even told him about it.

"I read about it in *Gourmet* magazine," explains Jim, an architect and father of three sons. "In Scotland, they say the first person to cross your threshold at the new year should be a dark, handsome young man in a kilt or black tie, and he brings four gifts: coal, to symbolize warmth; a black bun for healthy food; a bottle of Scotch whiskey for prosperity; and then some salt, to remind you that all the good things of life don't come with-out sadness." In Jim's variation on the ritual, logs are substituted for coal, and he has added a fifth item, cashews, "to promote a sense of humor" (nuts, get it?). At first, the family would just grab a muffin or even Won-der bread to serve as the food offering, but lately, Jim's wife has taken to baking the traditional Scottish black buns that are much like fruitcakes.

The handsome young man who crosses local Vermonters' thresholds is the Sanfords' middle son, Owen, who was about seven when the prac-tice began, chosen for the honor because "he owns a dinner jacket," says his father, and because "he loves doing it." Also, the oldest Sanford boy is blond, and the Sanfords go by the tradition requiring a dark man for luck. Jim Sanford is a man who believes in having special rituals for each one of his children; First Footing is Owen's.

Unlike the Scots, who carry out the ritual shortly after midnight, Jim and his son leave their house about 8:30 AM on New Year's Day, visiting eight or nine friends, who aren't warned in advance. Some households are repeats from the previous year, while others have no idea that they're about to experience a very unusual intrusion. (Jim swears they haven't been mistaken yet for burglars.)

Owen and Jim walk in a family's front door without a word and put the logs on the hearth or wood stove and a bun on the kitchen table. They then sprinkle salt and the nuts on the table. Jim reads a small printed text explaining the ritual and as he reads it, he pours two shots of whiskey. He raises the Scotch in a toast to the head of the household, wishing him or her "Happy New Year!" Without another word, Jim and Owen leave by the back door, and head to their next stop.

"People are surprised and delighted," says Jim. "If they've never seen it before, they're baffled, but they call up later and say how fabulous it was." The ritual has evolved so much over six or seven years that the Sanfords actually have a computer rating system, designed by Owen, to track people's reactions to the ritual. "If they are wildly enthusiastic while we're there, and call later to thank us, they get a ten, and we keep them on the list for next year," explains Jim. "If they're grumpy we subtract points, and if they don't drink the Scotch, we don't go back; they're off the list.

"For us it says to our friends, 'We feel good enough about you guys to come over and wish your family well,' " says Jim. "I just love the fact that you have to drink with somebody early in the morning; it makes a man out of both of you. Also, I love that this is unique to us. Lots of folks send Christmas cards, but who goes around drinking Scotch with their friends at 8:30 AM on New Year's?" (Keep in mind this is a man who wears a tie each year on the first day of deer-hunting season, to show respect for the deer.)

In Merchantville, N.J., Susan Lynch isn't quite ready to have her girls, aged ten and twelve, stay up till midnight. At the Lynch house, the "ball" drops at 8:00 PM, which simply means that the family does its own countdown after dinner, shouting out the seconds before the hour as though it were midnight. The new year is toasted with sparkling apple cider, served in crystal wineglasses. And the stone bulldog that stands guard outside the front door wears a silly party hat just like everybody else in the family.

"My husband and I hate going out on New Year's, but the kids thought they were missing something, so we started having our own early party at home," says Susan. "We eat in the dining room, off the good china, though it's a dinner of all appetizers and maybe some soup for nutrition. After we eat, we go around the table and each of us makes a resolution about something we'll do in the new year to make us a better person. Plus, we say what we were most proud of in the year just ending." After dinner, it's time for a board game chosen by the girls, and then the countdown begins.

A few traditional superstitions are observed: the girls always put pennies on the windowsill, because their grandmother told them it would mean money for them in the new year. And on New Year's Day, the big meal at noon must include lentils (usually in soup) and greens, both said to assure prosperity. "Kids love that superstitious stuff," says Susan. "It seems so mysterious and old."

★   ★   ★

In Tucson, Ariz., Karen Swift's mother started a New Year's ritual some twenty years ago when she noticed how let down Karen's kids started to feel every year after Christmas. "They would complain that the holiday season is over and it was so much fun, and now they have to go back to school and all that stuff," says Karen, who has one biological child, six adopted children (so far), and numerous foster children who stay for varying lengths of time. "So my mother started the tradition of 'The Last Gift of the Old Year, The First Gift of the New Year.' We call it 'Last-Gift Night' for short."

To prepare for the last gift of the old year, the names of everybody in the household are dumped into a hat and everyone picks a name, their "secret pal." Immediately after Christmas, Karen bundles the kids into the car and heads for the mall, so New Year's gifts can be purchased on sale, usually with money the kids got for Christmas. Price limit: ten dollars. "People often buy a small thing that was on a kid's Santa list but Santa didn't bring, or something that's an accessory for something Santa brought," says Karen.

The gifts are bestowed on New Year's Eve during a celebration that includes rented movies, popcorn, and sparkling apple cider at midnight.

The "First Gifts" come the next morning, at breakfast, and are given by Karen and her husband, Stan, to each of the kids. These are fairly modest gifts and are chosen to match the children's interests: Grace, for example, who is now sixteen, loves music and was given a compact disc for New Year's.

"This just helps combat the feeling that everything is over," says Karen, "and now that my mother is dead, it's another way to help keep her memory alive."

Resolutions

The Hilton family of Henderson, Nev., has an unusual way of recording and reviewing its New Year's resolutions. On New Year's Eve, each member of the family writes his or her resolutions down on a small strip of paper and folds it inside an empty walnut shell. The walnuts are glued shut and ribbons attached to the ends, and the nuts are then hung on the family's still-standing Christmas tree.

When the tree is taken down and the ornaments packed away, the walnuts are stored with them (the family learned the hard way to also write the resolutions on the family calendar, otherwise they'd all be forgotten long before the year was out). The next Christmas, the walnuts go back on the tree with the other ornaments. And when New Year's rolls around, it's time to open the walnuts to review last year's resolutions, and write new ones for the year just beginning. The littlest children state their resolutions aloud, and an adult takes dictation and makes a few suggestions.

"I'm not sure where I heard about it, but it's worked great for my family," says Nanette Hilton, an illustrator and mother of three small girls. "It's great because you take turns and have each person review their resolutions for the past year and say how well they did. It makes the children realize they can accomplish things and life is fluid, a continuous process. They also see Mommy and Daddy working on goals, struggling, succeeding, and sometimes failing."

Nanette adds that the key to the exercise for small children is "being realistic. Suggest goals that are appropriate for their age, not something where there is little chance of success. You can just see it on their faces when they've accomplished something. One of their goals might be 'To fight less with my sisters,' which will be an on-and-off kind of thing, but when the almost-three-year-old said one year, 'I hope to be potty-trained for nighttimes,' and she was by the time the walnut was reopened, she was thrilled. They can see real progress."

The walnut-opening ritual is part of a New Year's Eve celebration at the Hiltons that includes a dinner of homemade pizza (everybody helps); a lengthy board game, usually Monopoly; and often, the breaking of a colorful piñata. After the walnuts are opened and just before bed, the kids get to run out on the front porch and bang pots and pans together.

Looking Back, Planning Ahead

Kate Smith, who lives with her husband and two children in a California mountain house without electricity or telephone, is a ritual virtuoso. Ever

since her time as a peace marcher at Berkeley in the '60s, Kate has been a big believer in—and producer of—ceremonies and rituals. With her family, she celebrates not just the usual holidays but also the solstices and equinoxes. She has even adopted a traditional good-luck ritual for the first day of every month, which consists of saying the phrase "rabbit, rabbit" before another word is uttered.

"Some people say you have to jump off the edge of the bed when you say it, but I don't subscribe to that," says Kate. "When I go to my kids' rooms first thing on those days, I whisper 'rabbit, rabbit' in their ears and they know to say it back. It means they'll have a great month."

Just as you'd suspect, New Year's is an important holiday in Kate Smith's book, and she thinks it's vital for her kids to ceremonially put the last year behind them. There is a long-standing tradition of putting an object over a child's cradle, sometimes a gargoyle, that is meant to protect the baby from harm. Kate's children have a "cradle guard," a four-foot-long bronze sculpture hanging in their room, featuring hundreds of tiny bronze squares welded together. The family's tradition is to hang one item of memorabilia per child on the cradle guard for each special occasion during the year: one valentine, one Christmas ornament, a paper four-leaf clover for St. Patrick's Day, a paper crown from a birthday party.

On New Year's Eve, the family of four takes down all the souvenirs from the cradle guard and either burns everything that was hanging from the sculpture in an outside bonfire, or, if they can't bear to destroy the assorted trinkets, packs them away in a box. "They have to let go of the old year and get ready for a new one," says Kate. "Then we can start all over decorating the sculpture."

The Reichman family of New Rochelle, N.Y., makes a special New Year's collage on a big piece of poster board. The first time, Francine Reichman, the mother of two, glued red yarn to the top to spell out "Farewell 1996" and then the family started adding photos and mementos chronologically.

To remind themselves of the previous winter's big snows, they cut out magazine photos of snow scenes and made a large paper snowflake. Then there were photos from family trips, a flyer for the house they bought that year, pictures of birthday parties and other big events, and ticket stubs, including some from the *Nutcracker* ballet the Reichmans had just attended.

"To me, the new year is such an important passage and a great time to look back on the old year, but there aren't enough traditions to celebrate it," says Francine. "Creating the collage together helped us savor memories of some really wonderful things we'd almost forgotten."

Like the Hiltons, Cheryl Humphrey's family, the Frickes of Yorktown, Va., used walnuts in their New Year's celebration. But instead of using them to hold resolutions for the future, the Frickes used them as a way to look back through several generations of family history. Each year since 1900 was represented by a tiny "boat" made of half a walnut, with a birthday candle stuck in each one like a mast. As each candle burned down, family members would sink the shell boat and call out a year, chronologically. (The first boat to sink would be 1901, then 1902, and so on.) Everybody would shout out an event or events that happened that year: "Grandma got married," "the war ended," "Cheryl was born . . ." The last boat floating was dubbed "The New Year," and was saved for the next year's ceremony.

Ahead of time, Cheryl's parents prepared the shells, splitting them open, hollowing them out, using a little hot wax to fix a birthday candle into each half. Right before the annual ritual, every family member would pick one shell and write his or her name on the bottom: if that "boat" was the very last to go down, and thus the one that represented the new year, the person was supposed to be outrageously lucky for the whole year.

"My parents have no idea how it started; it came from my father's mother," says Cheryl. "At first, they used to do it in the kitchen sink, but by the time I was a little girl in the '50s, there were over fifty candles and we did it in the bathtub, with Dad lighting all the candles at once with a small propane torch. I had friends who couldn't believe my family celebrated New Year's in the bathroom!"

By the 1990s, the Fricke family had abandoned the practice, "because nobody wanted to mess with floating ninety boats," says Cheryl. But with a new century about to dawn, this seems like a fun idea for young families to adopt.

Of course, there are many ways to vary the practice without waiting for the millennium, and it doesn't have to be done in the bathroom. Each person could take a certain number of walnuts and write on the bottom of each an event or personality trait of the past year they want to put behind them. There could be a special toast or cheer when all the nuts had sunk. Then perhaps a new white votive candle in a floating holder could be launched on the water, representing all the hopes for the new year.

L'Tishia Suk of Evanston, Ill., is a supremely well-organized mother of four and a Lamaze teacher who occasionally lectures on family ritual. For her family, the focus is on New Year's Day, "when we do what we call the year in review," she says.

At brunch, somebody pulls down the kitchen calendar and the whole family relives the year. "What do you remember about last January? What was the best month? The worst day?" says L'Tishia. "We keep going for a while, but it has to be done in time to watch all the New Year's Day football games."

There are lots of other ways to review the year and the family's experiences together. Some families save their photographs from the entire year for New Year's Day, then spread them all over the dining-room table and fill a special album together. The Malfaro family of Pottstown, Pa., gets together, eats a whole lot of snacks, and sits down for a long viewing of the family's entire slide collection. In addition, the family always reads aloud from a journal called "the funny book," in which everyone's humorous and embarrassing sayings have been duly recorded.

The Hodges of Saratoga Springs, N.Y., start the year with a New Year's survey, in which the five family members record their answers to such questions as: what's your favorite color? favorite place? and what do you want to be when you grow up? As in other such traditions, half the fun each year is rereading the results from earlier years. Asked to finish the question "I wish I had . . ." the three kids answered, youngest to oldest: a chocolate bunny, fifty dollars, and a twin sister. At age six James knew exactly what he would do with a million dollars: "Buy Legos and give to charity."

There are many possibilities for planning the new year, such as getting together to fill out a calendar for the year ahead: little ones can add minidrawings for holidays and special events like their own birthdays. If there is more than one child, make more than one calendar, and let each kid have one for his/her room.

Some families like to use this time to plan their big vacation for the year ahead, debating the pros and cons of favorite past trips like theme parks or the tropics in winter. The children can do research on different possibilities, then report back later. If you know you'll be visiting a foreign country or a national park or historic site, the kids can start a journal full of research from encyclopedias and other sources, or the family can plan some simple at-home language lessons to memorize useful phrases.

OTHER IDEAS

★ The Minich family of Garland, Tex., blows up over 500 balloons (with an inexpensive, handheld balloon pump), which are stuffed into a small room emptied of furniture. Most of them contain a piece of candy or money and some have dollar bills. At midnight, the family's kids and their friends get the signal that it's time to dive in when their mother tosses a roll's worth each of quarters and nickels among the balloons. The ensuing free-for-all makes for compelling family video.

★ In Cleveland, Ohio, the Webb family camps out in the living room every New Year's Eve. The parents and their two daughters eat popcorn and other snacks, watch a video, and read together, usually whatever children's classic their dad is reading to them at the time. They sleep in sleeping bags or on the sofa, and the Christmas tree lights stay on all night.

★ The Rivkins of New York City found a use for the purple glass cornucopia they got for a wedding gift years ago. It has become the centerpiece of their annual New Year's Eve party, and all their friends know to bring a small symbol of something they wish for in the new year to stick inside it. Over the years, people have brought such things as tiny toy cars and little flags representing countries they hope to visit on vacation. After dinner, the assembled company goes through the pile of objects one by one and, when necessary, people explain what their item means. One couple used the cornucopia to announce they were going to have a baby: they put in a small plastic doll.

★ The musically adept might want to follow the practice of David Tarpley, a Nashville, Tenn., lawyer, who stands on his front porch at midnight and plays "Auld Lang Syne" on either his French horn or cornet. His wife, Sara, took years to convince him that he wouldn't get arrested for this, and now he always gets scattered applause from the neighbors. His six kids find the tradition amusing too and stand on the porch with him for the neighborhood serenade. Up until midnight, they watch a rented movie or play games.

★ The Leventry family of Summerhill, Pa., favors quiet New Year's celebrations, but they always leave the front door open and the house lights on until midnight "to let the good luck in," says Karen Leventry. And they observe German traditions of "lucky" foods for New Year's Day, including sauerkraut. Karen actually hates sauerkraut and refused to eat it one year, to her regret. "We came back from Granny's and found our refrigerator broken, and that year, almost every appliance in the house broke," she says. "I kept hearing, 'If you had only eaten your sauerkraut,' so now I eat it."

VALENTINE'S DAY

One of our more ancient holidays, Valentine's Day is named after a number of Christian martyrs—nobody seems quite sure how many—whose feast day happened to be February 14. In medieval times, some people believed that this was the day birds chose their mates. Printed valentines weren't available until the late eighteenth century, but for centuries there has been a tradition on this day of wooing one's lover with conspicuous proofs of affection.

Despite the historical emphasis on romantic love, Valentine's Day has the potential for good family ritual. Family love runs deep, but people need to be formally reminded of it. Besides, this holiday comes in the midst of the winter doldrums, after Christmas and New Year's, and before Easter and spring. By now, most people *need* something to celebrate.

One of the charms of Valentine's Day is that, as with New Year's, there really aren't any rules. Valentine's Day cards, while fun, aren't the only way to go. Why not bake heart-shaped cookies with your kids, buy and decorate a small rosebush that the whole family can plant outside in the spring, or send heart-shaped balloons and a silly rhyme to a grandparent far away?

Another good thing about Valentine's Day is that while most major holidays seem to be the province, even duty, of mothers, Valentine's Day generally puts pressure on guys: husbands and fathers. I like that in a holiday. They may not all be comfortable doing it, but most men feel a certain compulsion to express their feelings at this time, and more and more of them are finding that their families love hearing the specifics. I know how much I look forward to the little treats my father continues to send on Valentine's Day even now: one year, a gorgeous amaryllis plant waiting to bloom, the next year a teddy bear holding a box of chocolates. And it is one of the rare times he still uses the pet name I gave him when I was a toddler, signing his cards with it.

In one family I know, the father buys each of his three daughters an enormous box of chocolates. The boxes are left on the kitchen table the night before Valentine's Day, with a note telling each girl how much she is loved. The girls know that when they wake up on that day they'll get a love note from Dad, plus the recurrence of one of their favorite rituals of all time, the annual "chocolate breakfast."

Here are some other Valentine family rituals from around the country:

Kathleen Chesto, who has written numerous books about Catholic religious family ritual, used Valentine's Day in her family not just to show her kids how much they were loved, but to celebrate the qualities that made each child unique.

When the kids were small, Kathy would bake a heart-shaped cake and frost it pink or red, then write something on it for each child. One year it was just their names, while another year she wrote one word characterizing each child and made them guess who she meant. "One year, I quoted qualities from the Beatitudes (Matthew 5:1) for each of them," recalls Kathy. "Mercy was for my son Jon, while Becky was justice, because she's the child who was always upset about injustice. Pure in heart was for Liz."

Some years the Chesto family would make what Kathy calls "an affirmation tree," made by sticking a bare branch into a pot filled with sand, stones, or marbles. The day before Valentine's Day, the kids would cut out red paper hearts for each of the people they loved, write the names of the loved ones on them, then hang the hearts on the tree. At dinner, Kathy would put a heart on each child's plate, paying tribute to some special quality that made that child especially lovable.

At the Straw household in Plano, Tex., Valentine's Day dinner is known as Red Food Night. The meal consists of red food only, which requires some imaginative cooking. Sue Straw serves red vegetables such as beets or red cabbage (or mashed potatoes with food coloring) and red fruits like apples and red grapes. The main dish might be pasta with red sauce, or such red meats as rare beef, or pink ham. It's all washed down with red fruit punch, or maybe pink lemonade. For dessert, of course, there's a heart-shaped cake or heart-shaped cookies. Earlier in the day, the Straw kids open their lunch boxes to find valentines from Mom, along with a sweet treat like a heart-shaped lollipop.

Sally and Robb Dine Fitch of Columbus, Ohio, have a "validation book" for Valentine's Day, a simple little notebook embellished with hearts. The couple started it when their oldest son, Corey, now seventeen, was eight or nine years old.

"The opening page of the book says, 'Happy Valentine's Day. We love you so much. This notebook is to help us keep track of all the ways we do love you.' " Then at the bottom of that page are the words, "We love you because . . ."

Sally says that every year, she and her husband sit down with the book and answer that question, often illustrating their points with an anecdote about Corey. "It's funny because the book chronicles his stages and phases," says his mother. "Not just what he was like over the years; even his reaction to the book over time is very revealing. For years, it was hidden except for Valentine's Day because he was too embarrassed that his friends would see it. Now it's on the shelf, and he'll grab it himself and say to his friends, 'There's a cute story my parents tell about me here.' "

Sally says that one year she wrote, "We love you because you're so persistent about accomplishing a task." She told a story about her son, then about three, and a time she was busy and asked him to "go jiggle the toilet" because the water was running. The young Corey didn't reappear any time soon, so Sally went into the bathroom, where she found him kneeling down, hugging and squeezing the toilet bowl with all his might. "Mom, this is hard," he said.

Now, the Fitches are starting the process all over again with their four-year-old twins. "They've gotten to the age where they love hearing stories about themselves, so it seems like a good time," says Sally. "I've got two books ready and have saved up some stories about them I want to share."

Nancy Rey of Lakeside, Calif., is one of those people who recognizes and celebrates every month of the year. When a new month comes around, she changes the banner flying outside her house, putting up an angel for December, a snowflake for January, and so on. Every month she also replaces the runner that decorates the center of her dining-room table, and changes the recorded message on her answering machine.

This is her February message: "Roses are red, violets are blue, the Reys aren't able to talk to you. So leave your name, number, and time for starts, and we'll get back to you, cross our hearts."

OTHER IDEAS

★ Starting many years ago, the first time Nancy Dodge got a live Christmas tree for her family, she got the idea of decorating it again on Valentine's Day. The Dodges used to get a sapling small enough to sit on a table, and plant it in their yard when spring came. To give it a Valentine treatment, Nancy put up a string of tiny white lights and made heart- and teddy-bear ornaments from red oak tag (thin cardboard used for craft purposes). As her family grew to five children, the tradition of live trees at Christmas got replaced by the cheaper, easier one of cut trees, and the Valentine's tree ritual died with it. Until last year. "My eleven-year-old daughter hates change and got upset last Christmas when it was time to take the tree down," Nancy explains. "So I promised to get a small, live tree in time for Valentine's Day and decorate it as before."

★ One large family has a Valentine ritual of giving each other "warm fuzzies." They buy little pom-poms at a craft store, to which they glue eyes, plus heart-shaped mouths, ears, and noses. The fuzzies are given out like awards. The mother of the family gave her nine-year-old son a warm fuzzy for helping a younger sibling learn to read. The nine-year-old, in turn, gave his father one for helping him in Boy Scouts.

★ In Cleveland, DeeAnn Pochedly celebrates the holiday with her three kids after school, setting the dining room up for a Valentine's "tea." It's actually milk dyed pink and served in champagne glasses. The kids are also offered red, heart-shaped Jell-O jigglers, heart-shaped pieces of bread with pink butter, and Valentine cookies or cupcakes. The room is decorated with candles and red and white balloons, and each child gets a card and a few token gifts.

First Day of Spring/Vernal Equinox

It is probably safe to say that most people in this country don't have a ritual for the first day of spring, which is truly a shame. You don't have to be a pagan, witch, or New Ager to appreciate the primal importance of the earth's seasonal rhythms, and the natural urge to revel in the rebirth of trees and plants and the return of the sun. For children, this occasion can be used for pure, memorable celebration, or a lesson in biology, astronomy, or miracles.

The official beginning of spring, March 20 or 21, is marked by the vernal equinox, at which time the sun crosses the equator from south to north. This results in an astronomical oddity that happens only twice a year: day and night will be equal in duration. (The other day this occurs is the autumnal equinox, September 22 or 23.)

This is one of those occasions that is fertile for new ritual because it comes without a script or rules, leaving individuals and families complete freedom of invention. My son and I always plant flower seeds together in an indoor pot on the actual day. The season deserves to be warmly and appropriately welcomed, as it is every year by the Reichmans, the family that makes a New Year's collage. Every year in late winter, Francine and her two kids order a butterfly kit, feed the tiny caterpillars inside, and watch them make cocoons. Eventually, lovely painted lady butterflies emerge, and as soon as it's warm enough outside (a specified temperature that is rarely reached by mid-March), the family sets them free.

Susan Lynch of Merchantville, N.J., celebrates Big Bird's birthday on the first day of spring, because her daughters saw that happen once on *Sesame Street.* The two girls invite some friends, make a cake themselves in the microwave (it always has the fudge icing they love, and sprinkles on it, to represent birdseed), and hand out party favors like kites, flowers, or pinwheels. Her daughters have been celebrating this birthday since they were toddlers, and even though they are now a mature ten and twelve years old, they wouldn't think of celebrating spring any other way. Big Bird, by the way, turns six every year.

"Now that they're bigger, our Big Bird stuffed animal lives in my closet, but we always bring him down for his birthday," says Susan. "You used to be able to pull his string and make him talk, but now he just speaks gibberish." Also, as the girls have gotten older, they are less likely to invite children their own age. "We usually invite younger kids," says Susan. "We also ask anybody we know who's in a crappy mood; people who need to come to a party. This always cheers them up."

In places where winter is brutal, the first day of spring is a special occasion for joy, as with the Suk family near Chicago. L'Tishia Suk prepares picnic food such as deviled eggs to celebrate the first spring day, and the family heads to the nearest park, along with a Frisbee or baseball and bat. If it's still bone-achingly cold, the Suks will eat their feast in the heated van, but no matter how brutal the weather, they won't skip their ritual spring kickoff. Even with gloves on, they can throw the Frisbee around a few times before diving back into the heated car.

Do Mi Stauber and Trisha Whitney, a lesbian couple in Eugene, Ore., celebrate the spring equinox every year with their adopted daughter, Alex. They have sometimes wakened at dawn to welcome the spring, but these days the three wake up naturally, then wrap up in blankets and drink hot tea or cocoa on the porch. They each recite a poem, either something one of them has written for the occasion or something they've found in a book.

After welcoming in the new season, the three decorate eggs, which Do Mi and Trisha hide. Alex, now nine, doesn't just hunt for the eggs, but also for more than a dozen baskets that are hidden around the house and the yard. The baskets contain more eggs and also candy and presents, usually outdoor toys for the spring.

Do Mi grew up Quaker and Trisha was raised in another Christian denomination, but the two have been spiritually restless for much of their lives. Do Mi especially experimented with everything from Buddhism to paganism. Their rituals as a family tend to be very personal, borrowing elements from many traditions and fashioned to their own needs. They don't celebrate Easter, for example, but many of the rituals they use to celebrate the equinox, such as an egg hunt, are familiar from their childhood Easter celebrations. Indeed, they have persuaded Trisha's mother to send chocolate bunnies and other treats to her granddaughter before Easter, so those items can be included in her equinox baskets.

Passover

The oldest holiday in Judaism, Passover celebrates the liberation of the Jewish people from slavery in Egypt some four thousand years ago. The festivities last eight days, but the highlight is the seder, or formal family dinner, that begins the holiday. Many American Jewish families have two seders every Passover, one the first night of the holiday and one on the second night. The fifteen-part seder conducted by the family is guided by a special book called a Haggadah, and it can take well over an hour of readings, prayers, and songs before any food is served. But this is meant to be a fun holiday even for children and most branches of Judaism provide enormous leeway in how the ceremony is conducted in order to engage them in the festivities.

Children play an active role in the seder, which starts with the youngest child asking a series of four questions. The first of them is "Why is this night different from all others?" To begin the last section of the seder, the children leap up from the table and go searching for a special hidden piece of matzoh, an unleavened bread. Matzoh is eaten because of its symbolism: the Israelites had no time to wait for their dough to rise, and fled to the desert with unleavened bread. Both the text and related ceremonies practiced at Passover seders vary enormously between families, with some updating the liberation theme to include Holocaust references. Others have a tradition of acting out the biblical story in very theatrical ways.

Along with Hanukkah, Passover is one of the most widely celebrated Jewish holidays. And because it exists to celebrate and retell the history of Judaism (the word *Haggadah* is Hebrew for "the telling"), this is a holiday many Jewish families like to share with non-Jewish friends. There are even some non-Jewish families and Christian churches that hold Passover seders, in appreciation of another religion and because Jesus was a Jew.

When she was growing up on Long Island, Allison Dafferner's favorite part of the Passover seder was the description of the ten plagues. These were disasters that God called down on Egypt when Pharaoh broke his repeated promises to free the Israelites. The recounting of these biblical plagues—everything from frogs and lice to turning the Nile water to blood—is part of the Haggadah that has been read at Passover seders for centuries. In Allison's family, the three kids sat down in the afternoon while her mother was cooking, picked a plague, and creatively illustrated it or its effects. "We used crayons, yarn, anything that was around," says Allison. "We always had company, so there were plenty of people to cover all the plagues."

The finished artwork was taped to the wall of the dining room, creating an ad hoc mural. Later, when the plagues were referred to in the Haggadah, the person responsible for a given plague would proudly point to his or her depiction. "Sometimes, if we were feeling silly, we would also act out our plagues," recalls Allison. "If it was the plague of frogs, you might just hop around."

As in many Jewish families, the Passover text and rituals evolved over the years. When Allison's sister was in college, she wrote a feminist Haggadah that the family used for a while, and the section on the plagues included the naming and drawing of ten modern plagues, including AIDS, along with the ancient ones.

Now Allison is married and starting a family of her own. Though her graphic-designer husband is Catholic, the two plan to teach their daughter, now under two, traditions from both their religions. And she, too, will soon be drawing the plagues at Passover. "It's just nice to know that some things will always be the same," says Allison. "I've moved to California and my sister lives in Israel, but at Passover I can close my eyes and envision her doing the same thing I am, cutting out and drawing the plagues. It makes me feel close to my family no matter how far away they are physically."

To appreciate Julie Stockler's Passover seder, which has been known to include troll dolls playing God, it helps to know that her two daughters are adopted and that Passover is Julie's favorite Jewish holiday.

"I worried that since they weren't born into Judaism, they might reject the religion if they didn't see the joyful parts of it," says Julie, a divorced medical writer who lives in Upper Makefield, Pa. "I worry that they'll resent things like going to Sunday school, and say later, 'If you hadn't adopted me, I wouldn't have to do this or that. . . .' "

Julie says she knows the purpose of Passover is to tell the story of the exodus of the Jews from Egypt, and she set out to make that story as vivid as possible to her children.

"In the first place, we always watch *The Ten Commandments* with Charlton Heston," explains Julie. "I wanted them to be able to visualize things like the ten plagues, including the Nile turning to blood. Well, DeMille did that: let them see it." The movie night usually occurs the week before Passover, while Julie is in a frenzy of cleaning and cooking.

Then there is the family's seder. "There are long-drawn-out prayers in Hebrew, the parts when I was growing up where we would fidget and misbehave," says Julie. "The way we do those parts is to literally tell the story, and I help the kids do that. When they were younger [the girls are now seven and ten], they would use puppets. The older one, Elana, would tell the story and her little sister, Rebecca, would act it out with her troll dolls. The troll with a star in his hand was God." Julie also recalls the time Elana wanted to demonstrate the story of baby Moses, and dragged her little sister across the room in the laundry basket.

But for the first Passover after her divorce, Julie was stumped. Without in-laws and others coming over, she didn't want to spend days cooking foods her kids wouldn't eat anyway. And now that her older daughter was in fifth grade, "she was less interested in performing," Julie explains. In the end, the three of them decided to take a different but historically based approach to the holiday.

"Tradition says that seders were conducted in a reclining position (since reclining while eating was a sign of freedom in ancient times), so we sort of did that," she explains. "The girls dressed up like ancient Hebrews, or what they think ancient Hebrews looked like, in sheets draped around them and over their heads. I cooked them what was basically chicken nuggets, not the traditional foods at all. But we had our seder and we had a great time."

One thing Julie hopes never changes at her seders is the making of her haroset, a mixture of chopped apples, nuts, wine, and spices that is one of the foods on a traditional seder plate. It is meant to symbolize the mortar that the Jewish slaves made for bricks in Egypt. Julie has a wooden bowl and a special knife for the purpose her grandmother brought from Russia years ago and passed down to her. "I only take that bowl out at Passover and use it to chop the apples and nuts," she says. "The kids help now, and I tell them that when I was little, I heard that same sound every year, the knife against the wooden bowl."

A family tragedy provoked revisions in Sally Weber's Passover ritual.

Sally grew up in a Jewish family but she describes it as "nonreligious to even antireligious." She later married Jerry Weber, a leader in the Los Angeles Jewish community, and she became much more observant of religious family rituals. Sally particularly looked forward to her young family's Passover seders, led with passion by her extremely knowledgeable husband.

But Jerry Weber died tragically in 1989, killed during an ATM holdup. Sally, whose daughters were then thirteen and fifteen, not only mourned him, but the rich body of tradition he created for his family. Just before Passover later that year, Sally's mother also died suddenly, and Sally panicked about how she could possibly conduct a seder.

Sure, she had cooked the holiday foods before, but Sally didn't have any experience leading a seder, and was intimidated by the reputation of the Weber family seder: it was among those featured in Ron Wolfson's excellent book on Passover seders (see Bibliography). Jerry not only read most of the service, much of it in Hebrew, but also led prayers and songs. With virtually no formal Jewish education, Sally didn't speak Hebrew fluently, and was too self-conscious about her poor singing voice to be comfortable leading the songs (she says Jerry couldn't carry a tune either, but it didn't bother him in the least).

Sensing her panic, Sally's friends volunteered to help her through that first Passover: they would assist in the cooking and lead the seder in her husband's place. They made her promise to use only paper plates and napkins, for convenience's sake, leaving the hard-to-iron embroidered tablecloths from her maternal grandmother in the closet. Sally gratefully accepted their help and thought the evening went reasonably well. But her daughters disagreed.

"They said it was a nice seder, but it didn't feel like ours," recalls Sally. And the next year, when Sally suggested they repeat the previous year's arrangement, the girls refused. "I said, 'Paper goods are great,' but they said, 'No, you can't ever use paper again, and we don't want strangers running our seder,'" says Sally.

The girls' refusal "was enormously moving," Sally says. "I realized that if I wanted to keep this tradition, I would have to take responsibility for learning how to do it. I realized if I didn't own this ritual, we would lose it as a family." Newly determined, Sally took some workshops, including one offered at her synagogue, read a great deal of religious literature, and now is the primary leader of the seder her family conducts every Passover for about thirty-five people.

"I figured out what things I could do myself, such as prepare a theme and orchestrate the evening, but I also realized it would be okay to use other people to do the things I couldn't," says Sally. "I read only English, but there are some parts of the seder I really want in Hebrew and I ask people who are proficient in Hebrew to read those parts. For the songs, I lean on people who can carry a tune." Other parts of the ritual changed too: Jerry's mother is no longer up to making a complicated appetizer she'd had during her childhood in Palestine, so Sally learned how. "It's made with rhubarb stuffed with ground meat and a sweet-and-sour tomato sauce. It's a lot of work, but if I threaten not to make it, people threaten not to come," says Sally, "and it wouldn't seem like Passover without it to me, either."

This experience has proved valuable in her work. Sally is regional director of Jewish Family Services of Los Angeles, adult and children's counseling services, and she sometimes conducts workshops about Jewish holidays. "I see families in the shoes I was in, uncomfortable about rituals because they think they don't know enough," she says. "The most important message I can give them is that the point isn't knowing everything, but having the desire to do the ritual and then helping other people to help you fill in the blanks."

The basic format of the Weber seder was developed by Jerry nearly twenty years ago and is more demanding than most: this seder is famous for requiring guests to do research beforehand.

"I send out the questions about three weeks ahead," says Sally. "When the seder was smaller, everybody got a question, but now that isn't always the case. I've got about thirty-five or forty questions in a computer database; some questions I use over and over, but there are fresh ones each time. In the past, Jerry and I developed questions together; it's been a real thrill to me that every year I develop new ones on my own."

A few years ago, Sally asked two guests to write and perform their own Passover song. One Weber tactic is to ask someone to argue an issue of religion like a lawyer arguing a case in the courtroom. For example: there is no mention of Moses in the Haggadah despite his importance to the story, because tradition has it that this would elevate a man to the status of a god. So Sally has twice asked guests to "prepare an argument to include Moses in the Haggadah."

"This is the most profoundly Jewish thing I have ever done and it's exhausting," concludes Sally, "but I love it." It also satisfies a promise Sally made to herself: she was at Jerry's side when he was shot, and ever since, she has thought about his killer and vowed "not to let him take anything else away from my family."

Marilyn Heiss, a video and film editor, has no children of her own, but her annual Passover seders in San Francisco include fifty people, some of whom have attended for a decade. Marilyn started hosting the seders when she moved to California from the East Coast in the '80s. Over the years, her seder has become so popular that people beg to attend, and she's even got a waiting list.

Although the basics of her seder come directly from her mother, Marilyn's has been designed for maximum participation by guests and the welcome inclusion of non-Jews. "My rules are that everybody has to bring a dish, and that everybody has to read" something from the Haggadah, explains Marilyn. "I'm so organized, I have a database of recipes and I'm faxing them right and left beforehand. The recipe reserved for non-Jewish rookies is cucumber salad. I cook the main dish—my mother's brisket—along with some peripherals that I just have to do." She adds, "My mother invades my body at this time of year: if there's an open burner, I find something to put on it."

Marilyn has added various poems and readings to the Haggadah over the years, and lately has been adding family history to the ceremony. This year, slides of the Ukrainian village where her immigrant grandfather was raised will be projected on the wall during the seder. "I'm going to weave some stories from the family into the Haggadah and also ask if some of the other people at the seder have family immigrant stories to add," says Marilyn.

Another unusual Passover tradition, also in San Francisco, is that of Laurie Salen, a medical social worker. Laurie, a lesbian who celebrates the holiday every year with a circle of about fifteen close friends, instructs them beforehand to bring a symbol of their own liberation to put on the table. The significance of Passover isn't just to relive ancient history, but to remind Jews of the importance of freedom in every sense and in every time, and like many who fashion their own seders, Laurie wants to help give the occasion the relevance it deserves.

"The traditional seder plate is very standard," says Laurie, and includes things like horseradish, symbolizing the bitterness of slavery, and a vegetable, often parsley, that represents spring and rebirth. "But the Haggadah teaches us to bring the message of the seder to our own lives. You are supposed to live the story, as though it had happened to you," she says. Over the years, her guests have put a wide range of objects on the seder plate to symbolize their own struggle for liberation, including termination papers from a hated job and a timer used by an AIDS patient as a reminder to take the medicine that kept him alive.

"I had one friend who was a total workaholic, but had always wanted to dance," says Laurie. "She finally took up ballroom dancing and absolutely loved it: she put her dancing shoes on the table."

Two families that have acted out the fleeing from Egypt in especially vivid ways are the Elkins and the Brosbes.

One year, Judy Elkin and her husband, who live with their three children in Boston, decided to start their seder in a tent, to make it more realistic. They had warned their guests in advance, and the guests got together and decided "to come as slaves," recalls Judy. "We looked out the window, and there were about twenty people walking down our street dressed in sheets and singing a parody song one of them had written based on a tune from *Aladdin* [the Disney animated film]. The leader of the group even carried a staff."

As for the Brosbes of Santa Rosa, Calif., they've tried various dramatic ways to create the sensation of urgency prior to flight. For several years, at the appropriate moment in the seder, they had someone ring the front doorbell then run away, leaving a note on the steps with the letters cut from magazines: GET OUT OF EGYPT NOW! Then all the family members and their guests were instructed to put on backpacks, as though quickly collecting their possessions, before running out the door and marching around in the backyard singing a traditional Passover song.

Ellen Brosbe, the mother of four children between eleven and seventeen, has also been creative in such areas as depicting the ten plagues: "We have these little wind-up frogs zipping around the table," she explains. She also often supplies her family and guests with modeling clay at the start of a seder; they use it to form various objects and symbols mentioned in different parts of the service.

"What amazes me is that the adults love this as much as the children," she says. "When they're done, I put the finished things on little plates for everybody to admire."

Then there's the Butman family of Maryland, whose New Year's ritual was detailed earlier. Karen Butman was raised Catholic, her husband grew up Methodist, and the two now attend a Baptist church, yet the family has held a Passover seder annually for more than a decade.

Some Jews would undoubtedly be uncomfortable at the idea of Christians trying to celebrate this Jewish holiday, and indeed, when Karen first called around to area synagogues to ask for advice, the reaction of the rabbis she talked to ranged from puzzlement to horror. But to Karen, her reasons are perfectly logical and religiously sound, and there are other Christians who share her thinking.

"We started doing it even before the children were born," says Karen. "Easter is such a holy time for us, and we were looking for a way to make that time of year even more spiritual. We've been reading the Bible more and more over the years, and Passover to us is about the roots of our religion. Jesus was a Jew who celebrated Passover and the last supper was a seder."

The Butmans don't follow Jewish traditions for a thorough cleaning, which includes disposing of all the leavened bread in the house and replacing all the pots and dishes with cooking and eating implements reserved just for the eight days of Passover.

"We have the basics of Passover, from what I understand," explains Karen. "We have the bitter herbs and the parsley, and other things on a plate, though not a special plate reserved for that purpose, as a Jewish family would."

Similarly, the Haggadah used by the Butmans isn't one any Jewish family would use: it's a version put out by a Christian publisher, and explains the steps in the ritual from a Christian perspective. For example, the Butmans put a glass of salt water on the table, just as a Jewish family would. But while the understanding in Judaism is that the salt water represents the bitter tears of slavery, the version used by the Butmans explains the symbolism in a different way. "We say, 'It's the tears we no longer have to cry, because now we have a savior,'" says Karen.

Karen and her husband find their Passover very meaningful. What has surprised her is the reaction of her three children. "It just amazes me how much they look forward to it. It's simply a familiar part of their year, something they've done all their lives."

Easter

We read in the Bible that Christ's empty tomb was discovered at dawn and many Christians observe the tradition of starting their Easter at that time. Some attend sunrise church services, while other families and groups create ceremonies of their own. Like Tammy Patchin of Monroe, Wis.

The family of six is deeply involved with a Christian community of about twenty-five people. Though the individual families don't share the same church or even the same religion, the group owns a building together and uses it for weekly community dinners and special occasions, like Easter. These families, part of a national trend toward what some have called "intentional communities," also pool a percentage of their joint salaries for charitable causes they all choose together.

Tammy's husband plays in a band connected with their church, and many of their friends are musically inclined. On Easter morning, the families in their ecumenical community climb to the top of a hill in a meadow on the Patchins' property for a special sunrise service that always includes a trumpet fanfare.

"We have five trumpets and a French horn usually," says Tammy. "They do the fanfare right as the sun is coming up. Then we have singing and reading, which includes a bunch of Christian Easter songs and somebody reads the Easter story from the Bible."

As part of the tradition, the families have dragged their Christmas trees to the top of the hill months before, and as a prelude to the sunrise service, one of the fathers is dispatched to set fire to the pile of old trees. "The bonfire helps keep us warm," explains Tammy. "I guess it doesn't really have significance that we use the old Christmas trees, but somebody suggested it one year and it seemed like a nice idea." (Or perhaps it actually means a lot, since Christmas celebrates the birth of Jesus, and Easter his death and resurrection.)

After the brief service, the group, which swells to a total of about thirty-five people including guests, walks down the hill to the community hall. The Easter morning feast includes such traditional fare as hot cross buns and someone always brings quiche. "People bring their specialties," says Tammy. "Sometimes, after we eat, the kids will put on a play for us, or do a reading of something."

For some Catholics, especially those with Eastern European backgrounds, a big part of the holiday is the day before Easter, Holy Saturday, when baskets of food are taken to church to be blessed by the priest.

Kim Blaney, a single mother in Chicago, grew up in a Polish Catholic community and loved Holy Saturday as a child. "I would put homemade bread, homemade horseradish, homemade wine, and homemade butter in the basket, plus my dad's homemade sausage. You also put some colored eggs and candy. After it's blessed by the priest, we come home and light a candle at the kitchen table and have a little sausage with horseradish and rye bread with butter and egg and salt, which also was blessed. The idea is everything is blessed for you throughout the year."

Kim isn't very close to her family, and she wanted to find her own church, because she couldn't imagine not celebrating Holy Saturday.

"I called around to Catholic churches and a number of them said they didn't do it any longer because they consider it a pagan ritual," says Kim. "I finally found a church that still does it. I don't know why it means so much to me—to me this one is bigger than Christmas. But it makes me feel pure and like a child again. It just makes me feel as if I'm starting spring right. I feel this is a gift I'm handing down to my three-year-old daughter."

Holidays are hectic enough with six kids, but Julie Young was really in a bind one recent Easter because the family was in the middle of moving to a new house in Gilbert, Ariz.

"I was afraid that the Easter season would get lost in the shuffle, but I needed to come up with a no-frills ritual, and fast," says Julie. "So I took some pretty candles we had left over from Advent, and placed them on the entertainment center in the living room. Every night of Holy Week, the week leading up to Easter, the kids took turns lighting the candles. Then they sat in the dark while I read, with a flashlight, the events of Jesus' last week on earth."

Julie says she read from a book called *The Book of God for Children* by Walter Wangerin, Jr., which had small sections for each day. After she read, the kids would each blow out a candle, one at a time, then go up to bed.

The most amazing thing to Julie was how much her children loved her ad hoc ritual. "I'm sure they'll ask for it again next year, and that taught me a valuable lesson," she says. "That I don't need to go all out to provide meaningful, memorable experiences for the kids. Sometimes the simplest rituals are the most effective."

Rain Mako, who lives in the Ozark Mountains in Arkansas with her husband and three sons, has abandoned many of the religious traditions she grew up with in Minnesota. She still celebrates Easter, but views it more as a seasonal celebration heralding the rebirth of the earth.

"On Easter we go out to our garden and put a stake with a flag at each of the compass points and do a kind of Easter blessing," says Rain (who changed her name from Jean Marie in her twenties). "Each flag is a different color representing the sun, water, the earth, and the air. We talk about how the garden needs these four things and we are celebrating the fact that these four elements are also provided for us by the earth. As we drive in each stake, we talk about what it represents and how that particular element helped grow the garden and helped grow our spirits."

She adds, "We dress up in our party clothes to do this, and this past year, my husband and I stayed up all night beforehand just to have that time together. I had gotten a drum for Christmas, so we walked into the garden beating the drum, which my sons loved. After we pounded in the stakes, we sang a couple of songs that we picked up at their school or on tapes they have." The story of Jesus' resurrection isn't entirely ignored: "We talk about this as a time of rebirth for the earth, and also talk about Jesus being reborn."

Then it's time for the family's annual egg hunt, which involves the three boys finding about a dozen colored plastic eggs, usually filled with yogurt-covered raisins. "What's so funny is that every time they find them and open them, they want us to hide them again," says Rain. "So even after they get the goodies out, we may hide the eggs eight times."

★   ★   ★

Unlike most kids, the Meisenheimer boys get something of a vacation from bunnies at Easter.

The boys, now ten and twelve, live in Suisun City, Calif., and have been raising rabbits for some years now, having started to do so as a 4-H project. Around Easter, there are loads of baby bunnies and so the family started a tradition about five years ago of "loaning" the bunnies out to children in the neighborhood for a week.

"Parents like this because the bunnies aren't permanent guests, and the boys like it because they have the week off from bunny duties," says their mother, Kim. But her sons do keep track of how their charges are being handled, checking in to see that their "foster parents" are giving them proper food and care. Last year about ten children signed up for Easter-bunny duty, and each carried one home in a small cage.

The older bunnies in the Meisenheimer brood do, however, play an important role in the family's Easter celebrations. Every year, usually on the day before Easter, the kids put on a "bunny parade" in the family's yard. The two boys make little costumes, then parade the bunnies around, either in their arms or on leashes. "We call our bunny enterprise Mt. Olympus Rabbits, so one year the bunnies were all mythological gods," explains Kim. "They got the idea because they had to do a parade when they first started showing the bunnies for 4-H. The only rule is that the outfit can't hurt the bunny."

The boys are also busy with other Easter crafts, including making books and sugared eggs.

"We always have them make Easter books that tell the story of Easter starting with Palm Sunday," says their mother. "When they were little, the books were all handwritten, but now they usually do them on the computer." Copies go to selected family members, of which there are tons in the area, including four sets of great-grandparents.

The sugared eggs, Kim insists, are easy to make using molds made by a holiday novelty company, or by slathering wet sugar on tinted plastic eggs and allowing it to dry. To decorate the insides of the eggs, the Meisenheimers buy little wooden figures at a craft store (last year it was bunnies with carrots), and glue them into the eggs along with a verse from the Bible on a small strip of paper.

One final Easter ritual for the Meisenheimers: starting to plant their garden. "We plant vegetables and also herbs and part of the fun for the kids is to keep picking new varieties of things to grow every year. We plan carefully, in order to start the garden work the week before Easter, which helps make it one of our favorite times of year. Planting the garden and waiting for new life creates such a feeling of joy."

I was surprised to find how many cultures have Easter traditions that involve knocking eggs together, in some cases hard-boiled and in one instance hollowed-out eggshells. Families from Greek, French, Lithuanian, and Mexican backgrounds told me about such traditions.

Andrea Majewski is both Polish and Lithuanian, and, like Kim Blaney, she takes a basket of food to be blessed at the Polish Catholic church on Holy Saturday. On Easter Sunday, after early Mass, her family has a long-standing tradition that they refer to as "bucking eggs." Everybody in the Wilmington, Del., family selects a dyed, hard-boiled egg, and they smash it against another person's egg. Andrea's mother boils her Easter eggs with leftover onion skins, which tints them and, she believes, makes the shells stronger.

"Each time two people buck eggs, you wind up with one champion egg and one getting broken—and eaten," explains Andrea. "This results in a lot of eggs being consumed, since we have a rule that you have to eat 'em if you lose."

Vicky Adkins's Easter-egg tradition comes from her Mexican-American heritage. Hollowed-out eggshells are filled with confetti, decorated, and hidden for an egg hunt. Once they've all been found, family members smash the eggshells on each other's heads.

"We call them *cáscarones,* which means *shells* in Spanish," says Vicky. "We end up saving eggshells all through Lent. We make a good-sized hole in the egg and empty out the inside, usually for scrambled eggs. We rinse and dry the shells, then paint them with watercolors or markers. Then we fill the egg with confetti and seal the hole with tissue paper, which is glued around the edges of the hole."

Vicky says she didn't meet anybody until she was nineteen years old who *didn't* do *cáscarones,* and it was a big shock. Now she lives on Bainbridge Island, Wash., with her three kids, and they love the tradition. "Just the other day, my thirteen-year-old told me how proud she was to be able to cite this as a special family cultural tradition in her social-studies class," says Vicky.

Egg Hunts

For many families, regardless of how religious they are, Easter wouldn't be Easter without an egg hunt. In my own family, the Easter baskets were set out before we woke up so we could take a peek at them before toddling off to church in our new Easter outfits. But many parents make their children work a little to get the goodies.

Tarrant Figlio in Eugene, Ore., says her mother was "the family tradition queen," and one of her specialties was the annual Easter-egg hunt. Tarrant was one of three kids, but even the children's father got an Easter basket, and just like the kids, he had to hunt for it by following clues.

"The Easter bunny would leave a list, saying, 'Tarrant has five purple eggs and three pink eggs,' and so on through the family. The eggs were plastic and each one contained candy, plus three of them included a clue. You had to find all your eggs and follow those clues to find your Easter basket. If finances were good that year, your Easter basket would be on the dinner table, and the clues in the eggs would lead to an extra prize, like a new spring outfit."

Tarrant decided her son was ready to learn the family tradition even though he was only eighteen months old. "We read all the clues to him and they were very direct like 'look under your bed,' she says. "He had a great time, and the eggs had stuff in them like goldfish crackers, which he likes to eat. We'll make it harder when he gets older." And his baby sister can join in, too.

Of course, there are a thousand and one versions of Easter-egg hunts. Here are some approaches taken by other families.

The Scicchitano family of Lititz, Pa., takes part every year in a giant neighborhood egg hunt, which families take turns hosting. Most years two families' yards are needed to accommodate the crowd. A few days before, each child who wants to participate brings a dozen colored eggs, either hard-boiled or plastic, to the host house, along with a few little prizes.

Often one of the fathers rents an Easter-bunny costume and the kids can have their pictures taken with him. The kids are divided into age groups, with the littlest ones usually hunting in the front yard and the older kids in back. The older the age group, the more tricky the hiding spots.

The children get to keep all the eggs they find, and for each egg marked with an X or a sticker, they are also given one of the prizes. (A few extra prizes are reserved for children who don't find any specially marked eggs, or fewer than the others.)

There's a special twist to the egg-hunting tradition in Betsy Muir's family.

Betsy grew up in California, the youngest of five Jagger children, and as with all the major family holidays in the household, the kids had to line up, youngest first, and do a countdown before starting the egg hunt. The countdown went "ten Easter bunnies, nine Easter bunnies, eight Easter bunnies," and so on.

As Betsy grew up, her older siblings started the tradition of a second, expanded hunt, that included the real eggs plus a bunch of plastic eggs filled with candy or money (mostly coins, but one always contained a five-dollar bill). This time the eggs were also outside in the yard.

Over the years, the Jagger family egg hunt has gotten even more elaborate, now including Betsy's two children, aged one and five, and her twenty-one nieces and nephews. After church, about thirty-five family members gather at Betsy's mother's house, at around 11:00 AM, and the children do the Easter bunny countdown. After the first, inside hunt, the kids wait upstairs for the grown-ups to prepare for the second, expanded hunt, with this added flourish: both real and plastic eggs are hidden both indoors and in the yard, but now many of the plastic eggs are stashed somewhere on the assembled grown-ups.

"There might be one under Grandpa's trademark golf cap, in Uncle Randy's cowboy boot, Grandma's apron pocket, and so on," explains Betsy. "It's a riot because all the grown-ups really get into it, trying to act natural with these things bulging out. If you only hide one egg on a person, they'll get jealous that somebody else has two. The funniest time was when I hid a purple plastic egg behind my cousin Debb's eyeglasses, and she sat there for half an hour with this thing protruding from her face while the kids ran back and forth right in front of her!"

This Easter-egg hunt "is probably my family's favorite all-around ritual," says Betsy.

OTHER IDEAS

★ One Michigan family with four kids hides the Easter baskets, then ties a different colored ribbon to each one. The ribbons are twisted around furniture and through various rooms, with the other ends tied to the foot of the childrens' beds. After the kids are all awake, each follows the appropriate ribbon, getting all tangled up in the process. It's part of the family's tradition to videotape this antic scene.

★ When Andrea Majewski was growing up, her mother always snipped a lock of hair from each of her children on Good Friday "to protect against future baldness." So Andrea does the same for her two children. Unfortunately, she says, "I was too late to help my husband, Vince."

★ The Mettier children in Patterson, Calif., make a special "nest" each year for the Easter bunny, so he knows where in the living room to put the baskets. The nests are made from shredded newspapers and when the Easter bunny comes, he leaves not only a colorful basket of goodies, but scatters eggs and candy throughout the nest. Heidi Mettier is passing on a tradition that her mother started when she was a child, and it gives her almost as much pleasure as it does her son and daughter.

May Day

This is an old-fashioned holiday that has pretty much faded into oblivion. But there's a simple sweetness to it, which I believe deserves a revival and should preferably be celebrated with lots of flowers. The first day of spring is a great occasion, eagerly awaited, but in most parts of the country, there still aren't any flowers blooming. To me, the spring equinox is about anticipation, and May Day should celebrate a promise fulfilled.

Laura Hench, a mother of three in Maine, just started celebrating May Day.

"Here in Maine, spring really takes its time," she says, "but I decided to take a special walk with my kids on May 1 and look for early signs of spring. We found a bird's nest, some daffodils and crocuses peeking through the ground, tiny green leaves on shrubs and yellow forsythia." The four of them also listened to birds singing and talked about how "they sing while they build their nests and look for food." Her son and two daughters, who range in age from three to six, had a glorious time, and Laura expects this simple search to become an annual ritual.

In Casper, Wyo., Mary Sutton's family May Day tradition is a very old one. "It may go back to the pagans, who knows?" says Mary. "We did it as children, and my children still love it, even though the oldest is fifteen now."

Mary and her three children make May baskets filled with goodies, candies, and cookies. (Flowers would also work well.) These are very simple baskets you don't need Martha Stewart to diagram: the Suttons fold paper plates into cones and glue a pretty ribbon to the top as a handle.

"There are a lot of elderly people in our neighborhood," says Mary, who works in the education division at Catholic Family Ministries of Wyoming. "The kids hang the baskets on doorknobs, then ring the bell and run away."

Of course, an even older tradition for celebrating this holiday is the maypole. And there are people and communities across the country intent upon keeping this ritual alive.

One of them is Nancy Goddard, who lives in Sebastopol, Calif., with her teenage son and his girlfriend. They own their house but live on a property they share with three other families in what Nancy calls "a co-housing intentional community." The group, which calls itself La

Tierra, shares such things as a garden, tools, washers, and dryers, and the group eats together four nights a week, with the adults taking turns cooking.

"I love it because I find I can be as involved or as withdrawn as I want to be," says Nancy, who makes her living leading wilderness rites of passage for various groups, especially women and teenagers. The trips usually include some intense time alone in an isolated natural spot for each of the participants, an experience modeled to a degree on the Native American concept of vision quest, a period of soul-searching conducted in solitude.

But Nancy and her son also take part in their community's annual May Day festival, which involves up to 300 celebrants including invited guests. The centerpiece of the festivities is a tall, thin pine pole nearly forty feet high.

"Every year, we lower the pole and staple new ribbons to the top. We'll probably put on about sixty ribbons each year. It takes a long time to wind the ribbon all the way down, so it's a progressive kind of thing: whoever wants to start doing the dance jumps in. People are positioned so that every other person around the pole faces the opposite direction. They dance over and under each other while holding the ribbon. When one person gets tired, somebody else picks up their ribbon and keeps going. Everybody sings. Then, when the ribbons are all woven down to the end, and the people are all clumped together close to the pole, everybody hoots and hollers and we tie the ends down so it doesn't pull apart.

"This ceremony is about the renewal of life," Nancy says. "It's a celebration of the season of fertility and growth and the weaving together of our lives and our community. And it's great fun."

A maypole doesn't require 300 people or a forty-foot pole. Your local lumberyard will be happy to cut you a ten-foot-long wooden pole in a standard diameter of one-and-five-eighths inches for less than fifteen dollars. There are various ways to lodge it firmly in the ground, including planting a metal cylinder (from the hardware store) in your yard and then slipping the pole into the cylinder. Half a dozen or so eager children would be sufficient to weave the ribbons in their dance. If you need music and don't know any May Day songs (nor do I), you can always bring along a boom box and play a tape of Beethoven's Sixth Symphony (the *Pastoral*) or the "Spring" section of Vivaldi's *Four Seasons*.

★ ★ ★

Kate Smith, whose New Year's ritual was discussed earlier, is a big proponent of May Day celebrations. On May Day she usually leads a whole program with her children's classes at school, working with kids between five and seven. Her ideas could easily be adapted to a family gathering or neighborhood party.

First, she has the parents send their kids to school with fresh flowers, and she helps the children make a crown by taking a long strand of ivy and stripping off the leaves (Kate brings ivy growing wild near her house, but also recommends honeysuckle vine or other flower vines). The naked vine is shaped around a child's head in the form of a circle, and sealed with green florist's tape. Additional vine is wound around the first circle and sealed with more tape. She takes three flowers in a tiny bunch (she recommends statis and roses) and binds them to the circle with more tape. She adds more bunches of flowers until the front half of the garland is decorated. Long ribbons are then attached to hang down from the back of the crown.

The dancing takes place in the school gym. Kate and another parent make a ten-foot maypole with three-inch-wide ribbons, about thirty in all. Kate nails the bottom of the pole to a plywood board as a platform and then uses sandbags or rocks to hold it securely. "I create the singing and dancing part of the day, and before we start I teach the kids the song ''Tis a Gift to Be Simple,'" says Kate. "They weave in and out and I play Beethoven's *Pastoral* symphony (the sixth) on a tape recorder."

To top off the festivities, Kate crowns the Queen of the May, "who is always the teacher, but I pretend it's a big surprise," she says. "We make a crown for the teacher too, and put a cape made of a floral fabric on her and sing a song. The idea is to get the children to learn how to honor other people."

Other May Day activities Kate Smith advocates: have children press flowers between pieces of cardboard, weighted down with a few telephone books. When they dry, glue them to picture frames or to paper that then becomes pretty stationery. The dried flowers can also be glued to new candles.

Who knows what other lessons this minor but worthy holiday could teach if given half a chance?

MOTHER'S DAY

Here's a little quiz to start: who invented Mother's Day? If you answer "Hallmark Cards," *bzzzzzzt*, you lose.

Generations ago there was an annual custom in England known as "mothering Sunday," during which it was traditional to visit one's mother, take her a cake, and cook the midday meal so she could attend church. In this country, the "mother" of Mother's Day was a woman from West Virginia named Anna M. Jarvis. Miss Jarvis, a genteel spinster who spent her life caring for a blind sister, lobbied for a day to honor mothers because she so revered her own, a minister's daughter and Sunday school teacher. Mrs. Jarvis died in May of 1905, and starting on a Sunday in May several years later, her daughter began a full-fledged campaign that included sending letters to congressmen.

There is some argument about who should get the credit for the practice of Mother's Day in this country: there were others lobbying for some such special tribute. But it seems Miss Jarvis was the most persistent champion of the idea, helped in her crusade by one of the leading evangelists of the day.

Now founders of all sorts are often dismayed by how their causes and philosophies evolve over time, and this was certainly true for Anna Jarvis. She wanted Mother's Day to be observed strictly in the context of church services and personal visits, and she was appalled as her holiday became increasingly commercial, ballyhooed by the peddlers of cards and flowers.

I'm sorry if Anna was bitter at the end, because I must say that I think she started a good thing. As a late-blooming mother, I simply adore having an extra day where everyone is supposed to be nice to me and I don't even have to get another year older. I remember the very first Mother's Day card I got, from my stepdaughter when I was pregnant, and I was amazed at the wonderful electric thrill it gave me. I hadn't yet started to buy baby things and this was the first time it all seemed real; I would soon be a member of the sisterhood of mothers.

There are a few time-honored ways of celebrating Mother's Day, including the obligatory card, possibly flowers, and sometimes breakfast in bed. But even those elements can be rethought and rearranged in interesting ways.

★ ★ ★

Judy Elkin, whose Passover seder in a tent was described earlier in this chapter, didn't tell her three children for years that she detested breakfast in bed, but now she's glad she did.

"I just dislike the whole thing: crumbs in the bed, and then me eating upstairs alone, or everybody having to watch me eat," says Judy. "I finally said: 'Please let me stay in bed reading, which is a treat, then when you have breakfast cooked, another treat, call me to come down.' " (She also had to make it clear that "part of the gift is you guys working together without fighting.")

Anyway, her kids added on to the ritual by asking, "How about a menu?" So what they do is come upstairs, speak in a pinched British accent while handing her a menu, and then carefully take her order. When it's time to eat, they get the dining-room chair with arms on it, place a pillow on the seat, bring it to the kitchen table, and ceremoniously seat her. They let her start breakfast alone, then quickly join in, taking care of all the cleanup once the meal is over. (P.S. They also make lots of homemade cards and give her flowers.)

Nancy Rey, on the other hand, loves breakfast in bed and bought a special tray for serving it. Every year, her husband and son bring her an elaborate breakfast and her son always crawls into bed to help her eat it.

Some mothers celebrate the day by reversing tradition and giving gifts to their kids. Californian Mindy Robinson, a mother of four, loved that her own late mother celebrated in this way. "Every year, my mom would buy a small present, maybe a book or some candy, for both my brother and me," she recalls. "There were times when we really annoyed her and she'd be yelling at us a lot, but every year when this happened we got the message that we were a blessing in her life."

FATHER'S DAY

In many families, fathers don't do quite as much of the hands-on grunt work of parenting as moms, and may feel they get slighted when it comes time for recognition. So let's not forget Father's Day here.

I like the ritual followed in the McCandless family, outside Philadelphia, which honors all the men (and even boys) in the family at once.

"About ten years ago we got sick of just buying another shirt for Father's Day," says Sue McCandless. "So we started planning a special 'guy day' for all the dads. Every year it's a new adventure, and it includes my father, my father-in-law, my husband, and our teenage son. The first year it was a local air show, another year a naval shipyard tour, and another year a visit to a train museum."

The womenfolk, "who would be bored by these things," says Sue, pay for the whole excursion and appear only at the picnic dinner that ends the day.

INDEPENDENCE DAY

Maybe it's because they've stopped teaching civics courses in school or because we've all grown so cynical and unforgiving about government, but this seems to be another one of those traditional holidays undergoing a quiet decline. Sure, a lot of fireworks still get sold, and many Americans still stick a flag in the front yard. But when was the last time most of us really celebrated the great ideals our country stands for? I mean, who does anything for President's Day other than shop? Many Americans actually seem embarrassed to appear patriotic, as though it were synonymous with simplemindedness or might encourage scumbag politicians to raise taxes.

I've been accused of being sentimental *and* an optimist, but I think grabbing ahold of July Fourth with a little ritualistic gusto, both individually and as communities, would be a real good thing. Heck, maybe a majority of the population would even start voting in elections. If there is one national holiday that could really use some dusting off and reimagining, it's this one. So here are a few modest proposals now practiced by some thoughtful families.

If anybody would celebrate July Fourth, it would be L'Tishia Suk, the Evanston, Ill., woman who even has a ritual for the first day of spring. On the Fourth, all six of the Suks wear red, white, or blue, or any combination of the three flag colors. In the morning, the family gathers on the patio for breakfast of red raspberries, blueberries, and whipped cream on waffles.

During breakfast, there is a quiz, including such questions as who wrote the Declaration of Independence and why? And who was the king of England at the time? Then the Suks pass around the family encyclopedia and take turns reading the Declaration out loud. After that, they head into town for the local parade.

Kim Meisenheimer's Fourth of July celebration centers more on family than patriotism, packed with a mix of private activities and town spectacles.

This is the time for her annual "big family get-together." Like the Suks, she and her husband and their two sons dress up in red, white, and blue and head downtown for the morning parade. They listen to the bands, look at the floats, and laugh at the Shriners in their tiny cars.

After they return home, Kim's family and that of her husband head to the annual carnival in their town, Suisun City, Calif. It's on the waterfront, so there are ships to tour, paddleboats, and dunking tanks. Local businesses provide a reptile-petting zoo, and there are pony rides, booths, and kiddie games.

After a few hours, they all head back home and fire up the barbecue, usually for shish kebab or grilled chicken. Everyone brings a special dish and looks forward to Grandma's potato salad. Long tables set up in the yard are covered with white paper and one of the traditions is that everyone there writes his or her name on the "tablecloth" or leaves a self-portrait. After dinner, it's time to set up the portable basketball hoop close to the street and play a free-form game where everyone can jump in and out at will.

At dark, everybody heads back to the waterfront for fireworks. The day always ends with the kids playing on their own street, setting off rockets and running around with sparklers. Says Kim, "This is one of the only nights of the year when our two kids don't get to bed until after midnight. I love this holiday."

Halloween

This is one of those holidays whose rituals are enticing for the very reason that they *require* children to do things that are normally forbidden.

They are expected to dress up in outrageous costumes; play tricks (though not dangerous ones); yell, scream, and act melodramatic; and eat their fill of candy. Even grown-ups aren't immune to the thrill of make-believe, of getting the rare chance to act out and act up, becoming characters of fantasy for one magical night a year.

For those parents who abhor violence and fear that Halloween could glorify it, there are alternatives to celebrating with ghouls and gore. A family Halloween party can be just as tame as the grown-ups wish and, as with any family celebration, there are ways to communicate values without becoming preachy and boring.

The Gines family treats Halloween mostly as a harvest festival. "We basically celebrate the whole month of October as the beginning of yet another great fall season and harvest," explains Sydney Gines, mother of four. "We watch the moon as it changes all month long until it gets golden and full and we talk about the olden days when farmers would have barn dances and celebrate a great harvest."

Over the years, the Gineses have developed a series of four basic Halloween-related rituals, one for each week of October. Being Mormons, the activities and celebrations normally occur on Monday nights, which are dedicated to "family home evenings" through the dictates of the Church of Jesus Christ of Latter-day Saints. For starters, the family goes to a fabric store and the kids pick out "happy" Halloween fabric (no ghostly or creepy images), which their mother sews into pants, using existing pants as a pattern. They wear these pants several times a week for the rest of the month.

The second week, the family puts together a scarecrow and surrounds him with cornstalks from their garden. On the third week, they collect fall leaves, grasses, and flowers and make "suncatchers," by laying them on waxed paper, then shredding wax crayons on top of the paper, then covering it with another layer of wax paper and ironing the layers. The Gineses hang their finished suncatchers in the windows.

During the fourth week, near dusk, the family goes to a cider mill not far from their home in Canton, Mich. There they watch apples being pressed into cider, buy a jug of cider and fresh, hot doughnuts, and take a hayride into the orchards. After picking apples and pumpkins, they head home to carve pumpkins and make caramel apples. The kids also make costumes for a Halloween parade at school, which also doesn't allow attire with a gross or violent theme.

For the past several years, the family has been living in a small farming village in France, where Sam Gines works as a manufacturing engineer for Ford Motor Co. They have managed to observe many of their usual October rituals there, though an attempt to grow pumpkins failed. Since they didn't have a porch, their straw man lounged in the foyer of their house, and when they couldn't find any Halloween fabrics in local stores, they took out leftover fabric from the previous year's pants and made pillowcases instead. There was no cider mill nearby, so they settled for finding some local fresh apple juice and making homemade scones to go with it.

"My mother had a deep love for the change of seasons and set an example for me," says Sydney, whose four children are between three and eleven years old. "I never liked the dark side of Halloween, and there always seemed so much more to celebrate in October. Now I'm finding that the older my kids get, the more they anticipate this season. Shifting the focus away from Halloween has helped in that: this extended celebration really ties our family together."

Here are some other ideas worth adapting:

Neighborhood Parties

In Des Moines, Iowa, Janet Drey's family started a Halloween tradition that spread to their entire block and evolved into a block party no one wants to miss.

Janet knows a farmer who grows giant pumpkins, each weighing upward of a hundred pounds, with walls four inches thick. About ten years ago, the Drey family started buying one of these pumpkins every year (Janet's husband carves them with power tools) and Janet's sister embraced the idea too. It's hard to hide a jack-o'-lantern that big, and neighbors started asking where they could find such colossal specimens.

Now the festivities include a pumpkin-judging contest. Two or three nights before Halloween, families walk from house to house to examine the "contestants," and it is understood that every pumpkin will win a ribbon for something, whether funniest, scariest, or best eyes. That same night, the ribbons are awarded and the families meet at one neighbor's garage for cookies and hot cider. Each family brings a plate of cookies. Once it became a blockwide event, Janet got the idea to call a local television station, and for three years in a row, the station featured the giant pumpkins on the news at 6:00 PM and again at 11:00 PM.

In Columbus, Ohio, the Fitch family also has a Halloween block party, one that started when they first moved into the area and wanted to make friends.

When Sally Fitch, a social worker, went trick-or-treating with her two younger kids, "we asked people to stop by our house afterward. We just had a kind of open house, with apple cider and pumpkin doughnuts. It's especially nice because there are some elderly people in our neighborhood, as well as young families." The Fitches have a seventeen-year-old son and twins who are four.

"One year, I wasn't going to do it, but the neighbor kids saw me beforehand and said, 'We'll be there for the doughnuts.' It dawned on me that the children in the neighborhood look forward to this. I guess to them it feels like the last chance to celebrate before winter hibernation hits." So the tradition continues.

Some might say that Nancy Rey and her family are playing up the whole ghoulish tone of Halloween, but their tradition transmits a moral message. For years, they have decorated their front yard for the holiday, turning it into a graveyard full of cautionary tales. The Reys have half a dozen gravestones made of wood painted white that are arranged across the lawn. Written in black letters on each one is a poem that describes how bad behavior of some sort curtailed a life.

A few samples:

> Here lies Frank.
> Alcohol he drank.
> Made him feel brave.
> Now he's in the grave.

> Here lies Tom, Harold's son,
> Tried to play with Harold's gun.

Found it in a dresser drawer,
Now Harold has a son no more.

Here lies Matt.
Junk food made him fat.
Too big for a box,
So just covered with rocks.

In front of each gravestone is a candle to shed an eerie light, and some object or objects associated with the bad behavior, such as empty potato-chip bags or beer bottles. Scary music is piped out into the yard to accompany the scene.

"We all just love Halloween, but we wanted to decorate in a way to help kids learn something," says Nancy Rey, who wrote all the gravestone poems when her thirteen-year-old son Trevor was six or seven. "We all dress up, including my husband and me, even if it's only to hand out candy. I'm usually a ghoul and he's Frankenstein's monster, but this year he wore a gorilla suit and ran around the lawn in it. We only recently moved to California and did the gravestones here for the first time. When we used to live on a very quiet road in Virginia, we'd see people bring other people out of their way just to show them our yard."

Kyna Tabor in Salem, Ill., takes her kids to the nearby Civil War–era graveyard every Halloween Eve's day, and the three make tombstone rubbings. Kyna says her son Michael, now ten, suggested the idea himself when he was about three. "We get butcher's paper from my aunt, who works in the meat department at the supermarket," says Kyna. "I usually use charcoal and my kids use sidewalk chalk. We pick headstones with intricate carving on them, and each of us does one rubbing."

At Karen Leventry's home in Pennsylvania, the chief decorating feature consists of a straw man holding court on the front porch, a ritual started and continued by her four children.

"My second oldest son, Wade, came to me when he was ten or eleven and asked, 'Hey, Mom, can we take some of these old clothes and stuff 'em and make a man?' " she recalls. Wade is now seventeen and his straw man has gotten more elaborate over the years. "I pretty much let them run the whole show, except for the year I caught them dashing out the door with my husband's best suit and a dress shirt," says Karen.

The four Leventry kids draw a face on the corner of an old pillow-case, then tuck it inside a flannel shirt stuffed with old newspapers. Straw sticks out in a few places so he'll look like a straw man. He wears a beat-up, Indiana Jones–style fedora and a pair of Dad's crummiest old work boots. Ratty pants are held up with rope. The man might or might not have a quilted vest to keep him warm, but he always wears work gloves. Every year, the straw man sits on a swing or on a porch chair.

The Leventry kids also hang ghosts from the big Norway maple in the front yard. The ghosts are made by bunching up newspaper or rags into a ball, putting a white sheet over the ball, and tying it tightly with white yarn. The bottom of the sheet is usually cut into one-inch-wide strips to flutter in the breeze, and the ghosts are strung from the tree on fishing line. "Because you can't see the fishing line, the ghosts really look like they're floating in air," says Karen.

A Healing Ritual for Halloween

Lucinda Herring is a writer and educator who teaches a course about rit-ual called "Living a Spiritual Year." She lives with her daughter, Eliza, on Whidbey Island off the coast of Washington State. The end of the island on which they live is heavily populated with self-described healers, therapists, and what Lucinda calls "people interested in changing the world." In this setting, she has created community-wide rituals for all sorts of seasonal holidays including the solstices and equinoxes, May Day, and Twelfth Night.

Many pagans, witches, and others have believed that the barrier sepa-rating the living from the dead, what some call "the veil between worlds," is lifted on Halloween. Disguising oneself as a spirit would allow a living person to mingle with the unleashed otherworldly beings without notice or harm. Hundreds of years ago, the Celts chose this day to celebrate the dead and the Celtic new year, and they performed rituals designed to cast out anything evil from the past year, as well as ones to contact their ances-tors. Similar impulses are found in the Mexican holiday Day of the Dead, which falls in early November although celebrations start the last week of October. Mexicans and Mexican-Americans eat sweet treats in the shapes of skeletons, coffins, and skulls, and visit the departed in graveyards.

Lucinda, too, believes in remembering the dead on Halloween, and in dealing directly with dark issues, personal demons of all kinds. On this day, Lucinda and her daughter take out photographs of Eliza's grandmothers and great-grandmothers.

"We put them in a special place, and honor them. We make a sort of altar with the pictures and I often put beautiful fall leaves and candles on the altar. Then I recall their lives, telling stories about who they were, what they did, the hard times they had. I might even write down questions I want to ask them and then have my grandmothers speak through me. Maybe they don't literally do that, but I believe the ancestral voice is in us, in our genes, and it can be a powerful experience even if you're creating it yourself."

Lucinda also teaches a regular course for children in the area, and, together with those children, she likes to perform a Halloween ritual exorcising what she calls "the glooms," the things and feelings kids hate about their lives.

"First I get them to write down their glooms: these range from 'I wish my parents weren't divorcing' to 'I'm sad I didn't make the soccer team.' Then we make a little doll that looks like a ghost. First, they take the paper with their glooms written on it, and crumple it up in a ball. That's the doll's head. We take a square piece of white cloth, often an old sheet, then fold it in half to make a triangle. The paper is stuck in the middle of that and you tie under the 'head' with string or yarn. The two sides of the triangle hang down, and you can tie off the corners to make them look more like hands. Then we make a big fire and burn the gloom dolls. It's as if you're burning the past year and all its struggles."

Four

CELEBRATING HOLIDAYS AND THE SEASONS FROM THANKSGIVING THROUGH KWANZAA

Christmas is come, hang on the pot,
Let spits turn round, and ovens be hot;
Beef, pork, and poultry now provide,
To feast thy neighbors at this tide;
Then wash it all down with good wine and beer,
And so with mirth conclude the YEAR.
—*The Virginia Almanack for the Year of Our Lord 1765*
(Williamsburg: Joseph Royle, December 1765 issue)

In a poem called "April Yule, Daddy!" Ogden Nash wrote, "Roses are things which Christmas is not a bed of..." Not surprisingly, a Nashian Christmas features children tearing down the curtains to play dress-up rather than amusing themselves with "the dictator's ransom" of fancy toys and bicycles beckoning under the tree. These people are not having a jolly time, which is too often the case on major holidays that demand a great deal of logistics, cooking, whining, and protracted anticipation.

The last six weeks of the year can be either holiday nirvana or hell. Even non-Christians can't avoid the hugeness of Christmas in the American culture, developing "Christmas rituals" by default. Many Jews, for example, traditionally go to the movies or eat Chinese food on Christmas because those are among the few venues open. Every year, articles appear about how depressed people get at this time because their lives and celebrations don't seem to match up to some lavish ideal. Because this is the season of the highest expectations, it is potentially the time of greatest disappointment.

But simple rituals that focus more tightly on the meaning and purpose of these days can make the great occasions as satisfying as they ought to be. This season marks the highest peak in the holiday terrain, so think of it like climbing a mountain. If you plan ahead and bring the right equipment, you'll still have to exert yourself mightily, but you will get to the top with less strain, and the view will be breathtaking. The family photo you take as you plant your flag will be worth treasuring, and the process will be worth repeating.

Alternatively, many families across the country are finding greater satisfaction by spreading their celebrating more evenly across this holiday period, smoothing out this treacherous terrain to make it a more gradual climb, with multiple sights and rewards along the way. Some, for example, mark the whole period of Advent. Others are focusing new energy on the ancient holiday that crowns this season, the winter solstice.

THANKSGIVING

Like a lot of contemporary American holidays, this one has come under some attack in recent years because of increased sensitivity to Native Americans. There's no denying that the Pilgrims of Plymouth invited the local natives to a celebration in 1621, partly to give thanks for a bountiful harvest that owed much to good advice from the Indians. We don't even know for sure what they ate during that three-day celebration, other than some deer the Indians contributed: the "fowl" mentioned in records of the time may not have been turkey at all. (Indeed, turkey didn't become the entrée of choice for this holiday until after a post–World War II marketing campaign by the poultry industry.)

In any case, the years following British colonization brought a sustained extermination campaign to the Native American population. Some find it impossible to celebrate this day, but many families have found ways to honor the whole history in their rituals.

In the end, many feel, and I agree, that regardless of the crimes of our forefathers, a holiday the chief purpose of which is to give thanks deserves to have a place on our calendars. This land is still bountiful and thanks should be given. And our families should be appreciated, along with all the good things we take for granted in our lives. Our nation's history hasn't always been as noble as our ideals, but this is one of the few holidays that belongs exclusively to us; we can celebrate as Americans together despite our enormous differences.

Besides, now that families are so scattered geographically and even workaday family dinners have become so far from routine, it is wonderful to have at least one night a year when family feasting is expected and all of Grandma's good china comes out of the closet.

Finally, Thanksgiving is probably so popular because it is one of those ritual occasions when behavior that is normally shunned—i.e., gluttony—is exuberantly encouraged. I firmly believe that the primal instinct for celebrating thus runs much deeper than the history of America; if primitive man hadn't been gluttonous when the opportunity arose, we wouldn't be walking this planet today. So, looked at from this perspective, Thanksgiving celebrates not just an episode in our national history, but also our deepest roots and earliest instincts as human beings, for good and for bad.

Giving Thanks and Sharing the Bounty

Every year on Thanksgiving morning, the Butman family of Walkersville, Md., unrolls a huge scroll of white paper on the kitchen table. The scroll, which consists of two rolls of art paper glued together, is about three feet wide and about forty feet long.

To get things started, Bryan Butman or one of his three kids picks out a Bible verse that has to do with giving thanks, and writes it across the top. The paper is then taped down and divided into five sections, and each family member draws and colors things or events from the past year for which he or she is thankful. (If family members from out of town are present, they're invited to add their own panel to the scroll.)

"The kids might be thankful for a vacation, good grades, or a pet," explains Karen Butman, the mother of twin teenage boys and a preteen daughter. "They've been known to draw pictures of the beach, their friends, or Nintendo games, but we also try to focus on something spiritual, like giving thanks for the pastor. It might also be something sad: something we didn't realize we should be thankful for until it was gone."

The Butmans have now been illustrating their thankfulness for half a dozen Thanksgivings and have filled up an entire roll of paper. After they've finished their artwork for the current year on a new scroll, the old finished scroll is spread out from the breakfast nook through the kitchen and on into the family room, basically the width of the house. "It usually stays open for a couple of hours," says Karen. "The kids' friends come in and out of the house constantly and everybody stops to admire it."

At dinner, the family gets a chance to translate its thanks into words: five kernels of corn are placed by each person's plate, and everyone takes turns counting off five blessings. "I can't say for certain these exercises have made the kids more aware of their good fortune," says Karen, "but I believe they have. I know they feel our tradition with the scroll is something special that others do not have. At this age, the fact that they spend a considerable time concentrating on the activity and don't complain is telling in itself."

Elsewhere in Maryland, Nancy Mendez and her family have a tradition of sharing their Thanksgiving with "the birds and beasts." Before the family's big feast, Nancy's two children and their assembled cousins take a walk in the woods accompanied by at least one grown-up and a bucket of seeds and food scraps.

"On the way, they talk about being thankful and being generous," says Nancy. The walk is also a quiet lesson in recycling, because the goodies being delivered to the woodland creatures include "pumpkin seeds saved from our Halloween jack-o'-lanterns, bread crumbs that didn't make it into the stuffing, and mushed cranberries that didn't pass inspection for my cranberry relish. On the way back, the kids fill up the empty bucket with twigs and kindling for the fireplace."

Like many rituals designed with children in mind, this one sprang out of very practical concerns: "The kids were always bouncing off the walls before Thanksgiving dinner, asking 'When is everybody coming?'" But what started essentially as a problem-solving ritual immediately became an annual practice treasured for the pleasures it provided.

Kim Meisenheimer, whose sons are now ten and twelve, has thought a great deal about giving thanks, and her family's Thanksgiving rituals have evolved over the years.

"When the kids were little, we started making Thanksgiving trees in the hallway and the leaves were cutouts of their handprints," Kim explains. "Either the kids or my husband and I (when they were really small) would write a short note about what they were thankful for on the handprint 'leaves.' "

But Kim and her husband thought that the process left something out. "We realized that many of the people we were so thankful for were not receiving the message," says Kim. Now, on the weekend before Thanksgiving, the boys make personalized thank-you cards, by hand or on their computers.

"The notes are all very personal and very specific," says Kim. "To a martial arts instructor, one once wrote, 'Thank you very much for helping me so many times with the new forms I am learning. I get really impatient when I can't do it right the first time, but you always show me how patience pays off. Thanks for all the time you share with me. I appreciate it.' "

Sometimes a note alone is sent, but other times, an entire Thanksgiving tree is given to a family or a grandmother. In recent years, the boys have also given some recipients heart-shaped cookies to express their thanks, or included with the note a photograph of a special time they shared together. All of the thank-yous are delivered in person before Thanksgiving.

When it comes to the actual holiday, the Meisenheimers give thanks once again, especially to God. The two boys find Bible verses "containing praise and promises from Jesus," says their mother. These verses are written on small slips of paper that are rolled into tiny scrolls and inserted into the family's special oatmeal rolls before they are baked.

When the family sits down to its Thanksgiving feast, everybody tears into the rolls and reads their "thankfulness fortune" aloud; this is followed by a traditional family prayer.

After the feast, everybody pitches in to clean up before the football games begin. The day concludes with a fancy dessert and a viewing of *It's a Wonderful Life*. By then, the Meisenheimers have been fully and creatively reminded of all they have to be thankful for.

Do Mi Stauber refused to observe Thanksgiving as a teenager. "I used to fast out of protest, not wanting to celebrate the oppression of Native Americans. By fasting, I wanted to make myself more aware of that suffering."

Now, raising a child with her partner, Trisha Whitney, Do Mi has refashioned the holiday for herself. "We don't make it a celebration of the first Thanksgiving," she says. "What we do is spend the day with close family and it's about appreciating that."

Do Mi and Trisha have added a Thanksgiving ritual that was inspired by something Garrison Keillor did on his radio show on National Public Radio, *A Prairie Home Companion*. He had been known to ask members of his live audience to turn in slips of paper listing something for which they were particularly thankful. By the end of the show, Mr. Keillor would take a selection of those blessings, juxtaposed in an amusing manner, and turn them into a whimsical song. On hearing the result, Do Mi decided it would be fun to translate that process, minus the song, into a family ritual.

"We have this cardboard box that we call the Thankful Box, and during the day, we write down things we're thankful for on little slips of paper and stuff them in," she explains. "Then, after dinner, we open the box and read them out loud to one another. Part of what makes it so much fun is the order; that you'll have something really major followed by some mundane household thing. Like someone will write, 'I'm thankful for Trisha's family recipe for Jell-O salad,' and that'll be followed by, 'I'm thankful that they are allowing lesbian marriages now.' "

Giving thanks starts around the breakfast table for L'Tishia Suk's family.

"Since we invite lots of friends and strays for Thanksgiving dinner, morning is our family time," explains the Lamaze instructor and mother of four. "We set up a round card table in the living room and this breakfast is the only meal we eat in that room all year. I always dig out my Handel's *Messiah* and it's like the kickoff of Christmas music season."

Every year the Suks eat the same thing, a baked egg dish called an "egg strata," made with eggs and cheddar cheese, that is mixed the night before and stuck in the oven that morning. It's a Suk tradition to drink the season's first eggnog along with it.

While eating breakfast, each family member gets his or her turn listing "what we've been thankful for in the past year." Being stunningly well-organized, L'Tishia writes all these things down in a fabric-covered journal. (She didn't get this organized until a few years ago, after years of saving the thankful list on scraps of paper and three-by-five index cards. And one year, the family tape-recorded the things they were thankful for, and promptly lost the tape.)

"We've been doing this Thanksgiving list for fifteen years. And the really fun part now is to look back and see what we were thankful for in the past. The seventeen-year-old gets the biggest kick out of hearing that fifteen years earlier he was thankful that his tricycle didn't get stolen!"

Macy's Parade

I grew up watching the Macy's Thanksgiving Day parade on television, and I can't imagine starting the holiday without it.

In Merchantville, N.J., the Lynch family has a tradition of watching the parade on TV while wearing their pajamas and eating bacon sandwiches. In another family I know, blueberry muffins are the preferred dish.

In many households, including my own, the parade helps keeps kids occupied while mothers rush around trying to make the stuffing, finish the desserts, and set the table. But in many families living in or near New York City, attending the parade or watching the balloons being inflated the night before is de rigueur.

Take the Rivkin family, which lives in an apartment overlooking New York's Central Park.

"When we moved here in 1959, we discovered that the parade starts right in front of our apartment on Seventy-seventh Street and they blow up the balloons the night before on our street," says Lois Rivkin, mother of three children. "So we started the tradition of a big house party on Thanksgiving Eve. Only people who live on the block are allowed to watch them set up, so the kids would all invite friends and we'd go watch. I always order pizzas, six-foot hero sandwiches, sodas, and if it's real cold, we make hot chocolate, loads of it."

As the children got older, the ritual evolved into an all-night party. "Staying up most of the night is part of the fun," says Lois. "The kids and their friends would all sleep in the living room and dining room, even under the dining-room table, which would already be set with all our best china and crystal. There were often twenty kids or more sleeping in our apartment that night."

On Thanksgiving morning, everybody gets up early, puts away their bedding, and goes down to the street to get a good view of the parade as it passes.

If she ever needed evidence that this Thanksgiving ritual was important to her kids, Lois has gotten plenty of it in recent years. Not only did her two sons and daughter consistently return from college to attend this celebration, usually bringing friends, but as adults they still can't bear to miss it. David Rivkin comes all the way from Brussels, where he works for Reuters television, for the parade party.

The Feast and Decorations

I love to cook turkey. The first time I discovered as a novice and very hesitant cook that turkey was almost impossible to ruin, I was hooked for life. Not only do I love the taste of it, but turkey looks great coming out of the oven, all golden brown and massive.

Unlike many people in my situation, I have a great relationship with my husband's ex-wife, and my Thanksgiving feasts are made easier and more festive by the fact that she usually brings fabulous appetizers and desserts. Our Thanksgiving feast *has* to include a huge turkey, stuffing with sausage and nuts, gravy, homemade cranberry sauce, and sweet potatoes. Beyond that, the side dishes vary a lot and we don't always stick to pumpkin pie.

But some people have very distinctive food rituals, like one family I know whose main dish at Thanksgiving is turnips. It seems that the great-grandfather skipped town after harvest one year, leaving his wife with a house full of hungry kids and nothing to eat but a field of turnips. The turnips kept those kids alive until the next season of crops, but when they grew up, they vowed never to eat another one. Well, when one of those turnip-hating sons died, his grandchildren made a vow of their own: to focus Thanksgiving around that modest root vegetable, "to remind ourselves to be thankful for whatever we have, no matter how little."

Now, four generations, up to thirty people, sit around the table and though they also serve turkey and ham, "some of us just eat turnips," says one family member. The turnips are just boiled and mashed with a little butter and salt.

It impresses me that this family created a tradition to help them remember a painful history of desertion and deprivation. It has made me realize that while my ancestors never suffered quite so horribly (as far as I know), I should find a way during my plentiful Thanksgiving feasts to honor those who lived through wars, depressions, and other hard times. Perhaps we can at least talk about the onion sandwiches my father, as the son of a preacher struggling to make ends meet, remembers eating during the Depression, and be thankful for our bounty.

As much as I love to cook turkey, I must admit to being completely charmed by the wonderful tradition of the Hughes clan of Galeta, Calif.: the men do all the cooking for Thanksgiving.

Indeed, the Hughes men don't confine themselves just to the Thanksgiving feast itself, but prepare all the meals for their extended family during the long holiday weekend, usually stretching from Wednesday night through Saturday night. And all the cleaning up is done by kids, along with adults who have no children (and thus don't need a break as badly as the mothers do).

Paul Hughes, a technical writer living in Albuquerque, N.Mex., says his father's family has been holding their patriarchal Thanksgivings for nearly twenty-five years. Between fifteen and fifty people gather for the weekend, usually in a rented mountain lodge with an extra-large kitchen. Before that, explains Paul, his father's mother cooked a Thanksgiving feast every year.

When the old matriarch died in the early '70s, her children realized "they would have to make time to get together, otherwise it just wouldn't happen," says Paul. Combined with that urge was the notion that "the women should get a break from cooking, maybe partly because Grandma was strong on making sure her three sons and two daughters could do lots of things; she didn't make gender distinctions when it came to chores, including cooking."

Various female family members do contribute pies and other treats. "My dad makes great cinnamon rolls. His two older brothers always make the turkey. The women are supposed to enjoy themselves, and they usually play cards, especially pinochle and cribbage."

Allison Dafferner loved her family's tradition of dressing up for Thanksgiving: everybody had to make the proper headgear to portray either a Pilgrim or an Indian.

"It started because my two older siblings and I would drive my mom crazy while she was cooking, and she wanted to give us something to do. She'd give us construction paper and glue and we'd make feather headdresses or Pilgrim hats with a buckle in front. Everybody ended up with a slightly different style, and we always made new ones every year. It was fun, partly because we would invite neighbors and friends, and they had to make hats, too."

Allison's daughter Mackenzie is only two, but she has already participated in the ritual twice: both years she was an Indian. In one recent year, Allison and her husband were invited to a friend's house for Thanksgiving, and took the tradition with them, initiating the dozen or so other guests.

"It's funny what you get used to," says Allison. "I had never had Thanksgiving anywhere but home until I went to my husband's family's house at the age of twenty-one, and I asked them, 'Where's the construction paper?' I thought everybody did this."

You might be wondering what happens if all the family members and guests want to be Indians, or all want to be Pilgrims? Well, family tradition has it that the kids pick first, and then the adults balance things out. Lately, that's meant the adults are mostly Pilgrims; ever since Disney's *Pocahontas*, little girls insist on portraying the Indian princess.

★　★　★

Betsy Muir's family always attends a four-day gathering at a church camp near her home in La Mesa, Calif.

"It's very corny in a way, but everybody plans on it and everybody loves it," says Betsy. The program is run by the Congregational church Betsy attended as a child. "We do crafts, sing Christmas carols, have a square dance. The turkey has always been good, but the other food has greatly improved over the years, and it's wonderful not to have a mess to clean up." (Even though the food has improved, says Betsy, part of the family tradition remains—skipping the turkey soup served the Saturday after Thanksgiving, and sending someone into town for fast food.)

Around 150 people usually attend the church camp weekend, including about twenty-five members of Betsy's family, who are grouped together in two cabins. Her family has been going to the camp at Thanksgiving for thirty-eight years now, and although Betsy remembers dropping out of the camp ritual during her late teen years "when it just wasn't cool," so far her two kids love this way of celebrating Thanksgiving. "My son conveyed his enthusiasm the first time he went at only a year old," she says, "and my daughter, at six, has a case of cousin-worship, so she talks about it all year long. She loves the crafts and the hanging out and the big slumber-party feel."

Actually, Betsy says, the outing may be an even bigger treat for the slightly older kids in the family. "They love it because they get such freedom—they can roam between cabins and the crafts lodge and the mess hall and the woods and the creek. They can play sports, do crafts, drink as much hot chocolate as they like, and check in with the authority figures once in a blue moon." Now that's something to be thankful for.

Monica Hall is thankful she revised her Thanksgiving rituals to make them more kid-friendly.

"In the past, we all wound up with indigestion because I tried to make the kids eat a little of everything, while all they wanted to do was play with the friends and relatives we see so rarely," explains the mother of four children between the ages of one and eight. "This year I finally said, 'Enough!' Holidays are supposed to be about spending time with family and friends and remembering Our Lord. How can my kids have good memories of Thanksgiving if it's always a struggle over food?"

So this year, Monica relaxed her rules: the kids not only sat at their own table, but had their own version of the feast. Instead of being forced to try things they considered "yucky," they were served cranberry Jell-O jigglers, and all the mashed potatoes and rolls they could eat. And Monica made enough extra turkey drumsticks so there was one for every kid.

"They were allowed to get up and go play in the basement as soon as they were full, while the adults sat and talked and ate and ate and ate. So the kids had a blast and the adults stayed calm. My eight-year-old told me this was the best Thanksgiving ever, and even told the Lord so during his prayers." Monica will repeat the new ritual next year.

The unusual thing about Mindy Robinson's family's celebration is the tablecloth.

"My mother was a kindergarten teacher and a great seamstress and she had good ideas for almost every occasion," says Mindy, who has four children of her own. "Twenty years ago, when I was about nine, she decided it would be fun for everybody at our Thanksgiving dinner to pick up their plate and write their name under it, right on the tablecloth. She said she would embroider all the names afterward, and we could do it again next year."

So began a tradition that Mindy keeps alive and cherishes to this day, doing all the embroidery in the five years since her mother's death. Considering the size of the clan today, this is not a trivial sewing task: Mindy's father had six brothers and sisters and counting all the generations, between thirty and forty people attend these Thanksgiving feasts in San Diego, Calif. In fact, there are two tablecloths.

"Every year we embroider all the names in one color," explains Mindy, and as a color guide, all the years are embroidered on the edge of the cloths in the color used that year. "The problem is we eventually ran out of colors, so recently we started a new round: we do the first letter of the name in black and the rest of the letters in a color.

"It's so much fun to see the signatures change as children grow up, people are added in marriage, you see names of old friends. It also means a lot to me seeing my mother's name on there."

Mindy's in-laws were so captivated by the stories of her family tablecloth, they asked her to start one for them too. There was a family discussion about what holiday to choose, but they really liked the idea of a Thanksgiving cloth. In the end, Mindy decided, "Why not?"

OTHER IDEAS

★ The Gines family has a great pre-Thanksgiving tradition that unites members of the clan scattered all over the world. On the day before Thanksgiving, at a time designated by the family matriarch (and adjusted for time zones), all of Grandma Betty's six children and their families make Thanksgiving pies. The recipe for the crust is a basic "no-fail" one handed out beforehand by Betty Gines, and each family chooses a filling. Any visiting grandchildren help Grandma Betty make pies. But during the pie-making time, she calls each of her other kids and briefly talks to every grandchild.

★ For the McCarthys of Caspar, Wyo., Thanksgiving ushers in the holiday game-playing season. When the four kids were smaller, they would play board games with their parents constantly, but now they are older, between fifteen and twenty-five, other activities keep them occupied. So every Thanksgiving, the family buys a new game and gets all the old favorites out of the closet. The family of six play their way through the bunch till the Christmas holidays end.

★ In a ritual that has no historical significance (except for family history), the three kids of Judy and Josh Elkin always dunk their dad in the bathtub sometime after the Macy's parade. Judy says the tradition got started when the kids were very small: one year, their dad was bathing them on Thanksgiving and one of the boys dumped water on Josh's head. Josh Elkin, a rabbi, stunned and delighted his kids by jumping into the tub with them fully dressed. Now that the children are older, between seven and eleven, they get into their bathing suits first, and so does their father. First, they "water" their dad with cups, then work their way up to buckets. By the time it's over, all are howling with laughter and soaking wet.

Hanukkah

Hanukkah, also known as the Feast of Dedication, celebrates a miracle, and because that miracle had to do with lighting a lamp in a temple, the chief symbol of the holiday is a lamp, the light of which symbolizes religious freedom.

Ironically, Hanukkah is the only major Jewish holiday that has no basis in the Bible, but it is the most historically documented, says Michael Strassfeld, who has written extensively about Jewish religious rituals. Syrian-controlled forces took over Israel in the second century B.C. and banned the practice of all Jewish religious rituals, killing and torturing Jews who refused to worship their Greek gods. In Jerusalem, the Syrians

desecrated the Jewish temple by using it for pagan sacrifices and setting up figures of Greek gods.

Religious persecution set off a guerrilla war, led by a village priest and his sons, including Judas Maccabaeus. The Maccabees eventually liberated the temple in Jerusalem and they wanted to relight the "eternal lamp" within. Unfortunately they found that the Syrians had desecrated all the oil, except for one small container holding only enough to keep the lamp burning for a day. They lit the lamp nonetheless, and miraculously it continued burning for eight days.

The ritual focus for most Jewish families today is on lighting the candles (or oil) in the menorah on each of the eight nights of Hanukkah. It is a festive occasion: the candle-lighting is accompanied with prayer and songs. Whether candles or oil are used, they are supposed to stay lit each night until they burn out, and while the menorah is lit, no work can be done in the house. So families play.

The most popular game is a very old form of gambling played with a square top called a dreidel. Depending on which of four Hebrew symbols on the dreidel lands facing up, the spinner does nothing, takes all the pot, takes half the pot, or adds to it. Families generally play for pennies or candy.

Oil is so vital to the miracle celebrated that foods fried in oil take center stage, especially potato pancakes called latkes. It was traditional even in ancient times that children were given *gelt*, or money, during the holiday. But in recent years, gift-giving has become more elaborate, partly because many Jewish families felt they had to compete with Christmas, which falls within a week or two after Hanukkah.

Just as many Christian families have been rethinking the commercialism of Christmas, many Jews have worked to make their Hanukkah rituals less about getting and more about doing and giving.

Like Ellen Brosbe's Hanukkah in Santa Rosa, Calif.

Ellen says, "I think the only ritual my father had was to buy a tie every time a friend died." When she and her husband started raising their four kids, they basically had to start from scratch, and as they found themselves becoming more deeply religious, they crafted rituals to reflect their beliefs.

"The kids *really* want gifts and there is always tension about Christmas. But we try to downplay the presents. There are absolutely no big-ticket gifts. When they were little, I gave them only books, but they eventually protested. In recent years, they have gotten money, but it's a modest amount." Last year, for example, the Brosbe children were given money each night in an amount dictated by the number of candles lit in the menorah, one dollar for each candle. By the last day of Hanukkah, they had each collected $44.

The major focus of the Brosbes' Hanukkah celebration is food. "Every night has a different theme, and as long as it's fried, everybody gets a turn to pick whatever they want," Ellen explains. "One night it's tempura and another night fish and chips, and so on. Also, whoever picked the night's menu gets to pick which food we'll use for playing dreidel, usually a candy like M&M's."

Hanukkah has also evolved a lot for the Elkins of Boston.

"When our kids were little, we used to give them a present every night of Hanukkah because that's the way we were brought up," says Judy Elkin. "But then we started asking ourselves, 'Why?' With three kids it costs a fortune and it's crazy."

Over the years, Judy, who runs a Jewish family camp, and her rabbi husband worked out various ways to make every night special for their children, even though they only receive gifts from their parents every other night.

"We start a week or two before Hanukkah and we take all the kids out shopping so they can buy for each other," explains Judy. "The price limit is ten dollars per gift, and my husband and I bring his mother so that each kid has an adult along. The first night of Hanukkah is always kid-giving night, and we find they can't wait to give their gifts to each other."

Another night is reserved for charity, called *tzedaka* night. Judy explains that the Hebrew word comes from the word for justice. (The root for the English word *charity* is the Latin *caritas*, and the concepts are not the same.) "In the Jewish religion, you don't do this out of love, but because you ought to. If you wait till you're in a loving mood, someone could die of starvation." The Elkins set some money aside every Friday, before their Shabbat dinner. The money isn't counted until Hanukkah, at which time the family decides together how it should be donated.

Last year, the money saved amounted to $95 and the Elkin kids voted to give it to a homeless shelter that especially helps children. Another year, the family bought toys and delivered them to a battered women's shelter.

Another of the giftless nights is a family fun night, usually including dinner out and a movie or bowling outing.

Of course, the Elkin children receive gifts from each other on kid-giving night, and on another night their grandparents give them each a gift. But the end result is that their parents give them half as many gifts as they used to and yet they don't feel deprived: the holiday is full of activity and more diverse in its pleasures.

Growing up Jewish in South Africa, clinical geneticist Adele Cohen never paid much attention to Hanukkah.

"Hanukkah came in the middle of summer vacation in South Africa, and it just wasn't a big holiday. But when I moved to the States and started my family, I saw all the hubbub around Christmas and I wanted to make Hanukkah more special for my three kids."

One thing Adele did was to start making a special South African pastry every year at the holiday. Because it is fried in oil it fits the theme foodwise. These doughnutlike braided pastries called *koeksister* were widely popular in South Africa and available in stores year-round. Adele didn't eat them as a child, but she came across a recipe for them one day in *The Philadelphia Inquirer,* and saw a way to share her South African roots with her kids, and at the same time create a new ritual.

"We just have the best time making them. The kids roll the dough flat and cut it into three-inch-long strips, and braid them. After I deep-fry the pastries, the kids dip them into a syrup made from water and sugar and honey, and then we let them dry."

The Cohens light their menorahs, of course, with each child responsible for his or her own, and a few simple gifts are given. But the making and eating of the South African pastries, which are included in a festive meal with latkes and other Jewish specialties, is the highlight of the holiday.

★   ★   ★

Marilyn Heiss has an annual Hanukkah football party. Since Hanukkah lasts for eight days, there is always a Sunday during the holiday, and that's when the party is scheduled.

One year when San Francisco was playing, Marilyn's invitations read: "Come celebrate the miracle of the lights and the magic of the Rice" (Jerry Rice, the San Francisco wide receiver, that is).

"I invite my Jewish friends, but always include a few rookies who don't know Hanukkah. Some of them bring their kids and I give them dreidels. It's like an open house, and I make latkes all day."

At halftime, Marilyn pops a videotape into the VCR that tells the story of Hanukkah with animated characters. Marilyn, who is a video and film editor, made the video herself. "I make everybody watch it, even the grown-ups, and I ask for questions when it's over. Then, after the football game ends, we gather around and light the candles in the menorah. People love it."

Everybody gets involved in the lighting. "I have two big menorahs and a bunch of little ones, and there are plenty of candles, so that everybody can light some."

Lisa Gibbs, a Brooklyn elementary-school teacher, started a Hanukkah ritual with her nieces and nephews that she hopes they will now pick up for her recently adopted daughter.

"I'm tired of Hanukkah being a mini-Christmas. When I grew up, I lived on a farm but I attended a yeshiva, a Jewish school, and I didn't feel inundated by Christmas the way kids do today. My father didn't believe in giving Hanukkah gifts at all, and my mother thought we should because it's the American way. But my brother and I only got a book or record every year and the last gift we ever got, when we were ten, was a prayer book."

Once her brother started a family, Lisa wanted to play the doting aunt and do something special for Hanukkah, but she didn't want to encourage extravagant gift-giving either.

"The only gift that is really traditional for Hanukkah is *gelt*, or money," explains Lisa, "and you can buy these chocolates wrapped in gold foil like coins. I decided to put boxes together for each of my brother's kids, with each one getting the chocolate coins plus special chocolates just for them. My littlest niece plays violin, so one year she got a chocolate violin, and another child got a soccer ball. When I find things like chocolate in Hanukkah-related shapes like Maccabee warriors, I throw in some of those."

Each box also includes a dreidel, in a new style or color every year. And each package is beautifully wrapped. "One child gets all the pinks and reds (including the wrapping on the chocolates inside), another all shades of blue, another all yellow and gold."

Even in college the children look forward to the boxes from Aunt Lisa, and when her infant daughter is old enough to eat chocolate, she hopes they'll start sending her Hanukkah *gelt*.

Finally, there are countless families of mixed religions where both Christmas and Hanukkah are observed, a sometimes difficult balance.

Sally Dine Fitch, a social worker in Columbus, Ohio, is Baptist, and her husband, Robb, is Jewish. Sally was raised in a household where ritual was important; she grew up with four siblings and a changing cast of foster brothers and sisters, twenty-eight in all. She really loves Christmas, especially Advent, but she has embraced the rituals in her husband's faith as well, and believes in celebrating the major holidays of both religions with their three children.

"Hanukkah became the toughest holiday to do, because Christmas is simply so overwhelming," says Sally. "We love it when Hanukkah comes early in December, but we try very hard to do justice to both. We have rules for this, like not decorating the Christmas tree until after Hanukkah is over: when the twins were three and heard their grandma singing a Christmas carol, they said to her, 'Not yet! It's still Hanukkah.' "

At Hanukkah, the Fitches light the menorah candles every night, and sing a prayer. They often share the holiday with families who aren't familiar with the holiday, and enjoy telling them about its historical background. To make the story as vivid as possible, they have done things like help the kids act it out with puppets made from construction paper and tongue depressors.

"We do the whole thing: play dreidel and gamble with nuts or pennies. We teach our guests that the four Hebrew letters on the dreidel stand for the phrase, 'A Great Miracle Happened There,' " says Sally. "Like a lot of the Jewish holidays, Hanukkah has to do with freedom of conscience and we talk about how people are still persecuted for their religious beliefs: we challenge the kids to come up with current examples."

Winter Solstice

Imagine how it must have felt before the invention of electricity—to have darkness close upon you earlier and earlier every day of the summer and fall. How fearfully you would sit in your house, or a cave, guarding your fire, craving light. But your family or your tribe would offer reassurances, because the shortest day of the year would finally arrive, and that day would signal the cycle's reversal, the return of the light. It's no wonder the winter solstice has been the cause of great jubilation and celebration for centuries, and for some families, it still is.

Rain Mako, for one, didn't think much about the seasonal variations until she moved with her husband to a cabin in the Ozarks and lived without electricity. "I found the darkness really affected me," says Rain, "and when the winter solstice came, it meant that the days would start to get longer. The promise of that change just really struck home. I found myself thinking, 'Yeah, this is really something to celebrate.' "

Even before her kids were born, Rain had become disillusioned about all the commercial hoopla surrounding Christmas, and decided to begin putting most of her winter energy into celebrating the solstice. But she wasn't immediately sure how to do this.

Later she found herself moving to a new house with her husband and two children and a third on the way. The family had to make many trips to their old house over rough country roads. One night, attempting to turn their truck around, the bumper got hooked fast to a tough, thick old grapevine, some sixty feet long. Rain and her husband used every tool in the truck; it took strength, patience, and ingenuity, but they finally freed themselves.

"At the time, we were broke and my husband had cancer. Our lives were chaos, and I was about to have another child," says Rain. "For some reason, when I got home and looked at my bare walls, I got the idea to turn that vine into a solstice wreath. It was so fitting. The vine seemed to represent all the intractable problems in our lives, and turning it into a symbol of hope became a very powerful action for me."

Rain had already been making solstice wreaths for the kids, each about two feet in diameter, and had invented myths about the "Solstice Spirit" to explain the holiday. "I told them the Solstice Spirit is a woman, with a face that is half white and half black and she wears a long skirt covered with amazing pictures of the seasons," says Rain. "She is always turning and turning, reaching out to people. If we reach out and take her hand, she will turn our hearts around to love, trust, happiness, and gratitude."

Her new winter solstice wreath, made from the old vine, is a full six feet in diameter. To decorate it, the family cuts lots of cedar and yellow-pine boughs and inserts the greens easily into the woven vine. Ornaments and Christmas lights are added. "The wreath is our chief symbol of the holiday," says Rain. "The circle shape reminds us of the ever-turning circle of the seasons and the lights remind us that solstice is when the light returns. We always leave one small section of the wreath bare of greens, to represent the barrenness of winter."

To create a mythology relevant to her family's situation, both emotionally and geographically, Rain came up with a story about "the people who first came to the Ozarks, where we live. They lived under these big rock overhangs in the caves and they listened to their dreams, which told them what to eat and how to solve problems. I tell the kids that as the winter came, the people got crabby and struggled and fought. Then one of them had a dream and saw they needed to give each other small presents and tell stories by the fire to cheer each other up, and to sing all night long."

And that celebration was winter solstice. Rain says she told this story because "I was trying to heal the emotional turmoil in my own family, trying to make the point that when bad times come, people have difficulty rising above them, as we had, but there are things they can do to make it easier." When the family puts up the wreath, Rain retells the story, and everyone talks about the things for which they are grateful.

Rain always felt that when the kids got all their presents at once on Christmas Day, they didn't feel very grateful for each thing, so during the week leading to and including the winter solstice, the boys each get one present a day. When they wake in the morning, they find it on the floor near where the wreath hangs. (Later, for Christmas, the family will visit Rain's parents, where the kids will experience a traditional Christmas.)

"I think the most important test of whether my kids took the solstice ritual to heart is that I hear them tell other people about it without embarrassment," says Rain. "They tell them that we celebrate the solstice and get presents from the Solstice Spirit, though they often add, 'They're really from our parents.' "

She can't prove that the Solstice Spirit had anything to do with it, but the family's fortunes have turned around: her husband is healthy, as is their third child, and their new home is as cozy as they hoped.

This time of year, Jeanne Mollinger-Lewis celebrates just about everything including Hanukkah, when the family lights a menorah even though they aren't Jewish. But the biggest emphasis is on the winter solstice, which falls on December 20 or 21, and almost overshadows Christmas in the Lewis household.

"We started celebrating winter solstice about five years ago, simply lighting a candle on that day and saying, 'Goody, tomorrow we start getting more daylight on the clock,' " says Jeanne. "Now, we have a special dinner on solstice eve that includes food the sun helps grow, things like nuts and fruits and sweet potatoes. And my children get their biggest gifts on solstice, like a dollhouse for my daughter and a tape recorder for my son."

For the Lewises, even Advent has become a countdown to solstice rather than to Christmas, and they call the tree they cut at the local tree farm a "solstice tree," decorating it not only with traditional Christmas ornaments but also with a growing collection of sun symbols. "We buy a new sun ornament every year and we put that on first," says Jeanne.

On the last day before the winter solstice, events include the lighting of candles. Then there's a special meal with an extra-special dessert and the opening of the solstice presents. The Lewises read aloud from several books about the winter solstice and recite some poems about winter. The family also puts out luminarias, candles in paper bags weighted down with sand, along the walk to their front door.

After the kids put on their pjs, they watch from the window as their father sets off some modest fireworks and sparklers saved from the

Fourth of July for this occasion. "The colors look so beautiful against the snow," says Jeanne.

"I see Christmas as more materialistic and the earth-related emphasis of solstice seems more meaningful and universal. I want my children to have an appreciation of the cycles in our lives, and our connectedness to the earth."

The Ridimans of Fort Thomas, Ky., love both Christmas and winter solstice. The heart of their solstice celebration is a "feast for wildlife."

"We invite one or two other families," explains Kathy Ridiman. "The kids help with things like spreading peanut butter on pine cones and tying ribbons on them so you can attach them to a tree. We buy a few sacks of corn ears at the feed store and we do things like take a plastic Coke bottle and cut a hole in the middle, like the door in a birdhouse, and pour in liquid suet."

Stale bread is cut into fun shapes with cookie cutters, and these are also attached to trees.

When everything is ready, the Ridimans and their friends prepare their feast in the woods behind the house. They also sing songs, mostly circle songs and rounds, including some Native American songs (Kathy is part Cherokee), and they often light sparklers. "There's an old Celtic tradition that you're supposed to turn on every light in your house and throw open the doors, to convince the sun to come back the next day." The Ridimans do that, too.

Nancy Goddard also has special rituals for winter solstice, but they are community celebrations just like the May Day one described previously.

The four families in Nancy's community invite other friends as well. The evening starts with an all-dessert potluck, supplemented with either eggnog or mulled wine. Then, the lights in the room are turned out.

The group has been holding its winter solstice gathering for some years, so they reuse simple wooden candleholders—long, narrow pieces of two-by-fours with holes drilled through them to hold candles. Washers on the top of the holes prevent the candles from burning through the wood. These wood strips are laid out on a table like the spokes of a wheel, with a basket in the middle containing small candles and one large winter solstice candle.

A prayer is said about the returning of the light and the middle candle is lit. Someone announces the group's "intention to call in the light," says Nancy. "We acknowledge the dark as well as the light in our families, and we acknowledge the passing of time and the seasons. Then individuals or families take a candle, light it from the center candle, and say a prayer or declare an intention." Nancy says her prayer is usually "to bring more consciousness into my life, or I pray for the leaders of our country, or for the people suffering from AIDS."

The ceremony continues until each person present has lighted a candle. "If there are candles left over, people keep doing it," says Nancy. "It winds up being this wonderful unifying thing, because you have all these adults and children walking up lighting candles one by one and it feels as if we've filled the room with prayers covering every aspect of life."

Then the group sings some solstice songs together, and watches as the candles burn down.

CHRISTMAS

We've come a long way since the Puritans fined citizens for feasting or even taking off from work on Christmas Day. The Puritans wanted to set up a purely religious community and hoped to forestall forever the bacchanalian drinking, feasting, and commercialism of Christmas celebrations back in England. Indeed, the tug-of-war between piety and paganism at Christmas goes back centuries, and in this country the tension between religion and commerce has never ended.

In his book *Consumer Rites: The Buying and Selling of American Holidays,* Leigh Eric Schmidt quotes various religious tracts going back to 1712 that bemoan what Cotton Mather called the "mad mirth" of the season, and details the formation of the "Put Christ Back in Christmas" movement in 1949. Along the way, Schmidt shows how the country's merchandisers groomed and elevated the folk character of Santa Claus, perfecting the message that gift-giving is the truest expression of the Christmas spirit. He notes that the beloved Rudolf the Red-Nosed Reindeer was created by an advertising copywriter at Montgomery Ward in 1939, so that the retailer's Santas could hand out free booklets to kids.

The battle continues to this day. An organization called Alternatives was formed in 1973 by a clergyman to protest the commercialization of Christmas, and provides pamphlets and videos about how to celebrate "more responsibly and joyfully." And a 1982 book called *Unplug the Christmas Machine* by Jo Robinson and Jean Coppock Staehli (see Bibliography) continues to find new readers every year among families sick of feeling more exhausted than exalted from the holiday grind. On the other hand, statistics suggest that gift-giving, especially to children, is still escalating out of control: in 1995, according to the Toy Manufacturers of America, parents spent an average of about $350 per child for Christmas toys!

Still, it seems to me that at least a little more balance and reason have begun to take hold in thoughtful families. The Victorians may have invented the lavish family Christmas we all fantasize about—and Martha Stewart hasn't helped by suggesting we should all be gilding our own wreaths—but I believe there are sensible, even inspired, ways to embrace both the religious and secular traditions. I have found families all across the country whose celebration of Christmas honors the holiday in all its depth; they don't forget the religious significance, but also use rituals that allow them to revel in the family spirit inherent in this occasion, and yes, buying special presents can be an important expression of that. As a child, I valued beyond measure the rag dolls my mother made, but I'll never forget the joy I felt the year Santa Claus brought the pink Barbie convertible.

And let's not overlook the seasonal custom of charity, important to most Americans regardless of whether or not they consider themselves religious. In my search for families with creative rituals, I've found all kinds of people who haven't forgotten what Christmas really means, and have created celebrations to reflect it.

Counting Down: Not Just Advent Calendars

The word *advent* means *coming* or *commencement;* Advent with a capital *A,* the four-week period that culminates in Christmas, celebrates and anticipates the coming of Christ. Practicing Christians of all stripes observe the entire Advent season with daily or weekly prayers and candle-lighting. A typical Advent wreath is a simple circle of evergreens decorated with four candles, traditionally three of purple and one pink. The first week, one candle is lit, the next week two candles, and so on until the last week, when all four candles are lit. The pink candle is for the third Sunday, a signal that the waiting is nearly over. Often a fifth candle, white for Jesus, sits in the center of the wreath and is lit on Christmas Eve.

Many of the families who observe Advent are given booklets by their churches with suggested prayers and scriptural readings to use when candles are lighted. Others fashion their own scripts.

Within the simple activity of lighting candles lies a world of ritual and much history. The flame of the lighted candles represents the light and hope of Jesus, but also carries ancient solstice meaning about a season that heralds the return of light and warmth to the earth. Indeed, Christian leaders in the fourth century declared that Christ's birth be celebrated on December 25 not because that was when historians believed he was born, but in order to supplant various pagan celebrations related to the solstice. The greens, too, represent both the hope and renewal brought by Christ, and the earth's cycle on its way back toward spring. Families all across the country have taken these symbols and added other traditions and activities, making Advent more meaningful and memorable.

The Suks of Evanston, Ill., for example, light Advent candles every night of Advent, and read scriptures L'Tishia Suk has chosen for her family of six. A simple ceremony is observed each evening: "We light a candle, sing a Christmas carol, and read the scripture," explains L'Tishia. "I also save the Christmas cards every day until we celebrate Advent. Then each night we pass them around and say a prayer for whoever sent the card."

Barbara Brock of Cheney, Wash., loves celebrating Advent so much that for half a dozen years she has created a thirty-page Advent pamphlet for her church. The booklet provides her fellow church members with suggested scriptures, stories, and other material to help them conduct four weekly Advent ceremonies at home. She even includes a short multiple-choice quiz on Christmas trivia for each week (Who established the tradition of decorating the Christmas tree with candles? The answer: Martin Luther).

Barb's kids love lighting candles so much they demand an Advent ritual every night. "Sydney just turned four and for her, candles are like magic," says Barb. "My son, Adam, at eight, has recently started reading, so he wants to read something every night." Barb has had to hunt down additional stories and scriptures, and the family used up one set of candles and had to buy more.

Depending on how a family uses them, Advent wreaths and other Advent-related rituals can help children focus on the spiritual and historical roots of the holiday, a noble end indeed. But they can also be used as classic problem-solving rituals, helping calm antsy children and offering concrete counting tools. Also, by spreading the excitement and fun throughout the month, parents are helping to refocus the celebration from a single day of orgiastic gift-giving to a season with multiple pleasures and deeper meanings.

There are all sorts of Advent calendars in paper or fabric, allowing kids to open a little window every day or stick a felt ornament on a wall hanging, or reach into a small pocket for a tiny sweet. But some innovative ways of counting out Advent don't use calendars at all.

Being a bookaholic, I was thrilled to copy Nancy Giehl's practice, a kind of literary Advent countdown. Nancy, who lives in Boulder, Colo., wraps twenty-five books in Christmas paper, and she and the kids open one together every day, starting December 1.

"It's one of the best things that happens every year," she says. "We don't have quite that many Christmas books of our own yet, so I mix in a few library books and some stories torn out of magazines." Christmas videos are also a good addition. On Christmas Eve, there are always two selections, including *The Night Before Christmas,* and a book that retells the Christmas story from the Bible.

Nancy has a seven-year-old daughter and six-year-old twins, and what surprises her most about this ritual is that "the books they get most excited about are the ones they remember from when they were just two, like *Spot's First Christmas.*" (Nancy says she got the idea from *Family Fun* magazine's letters column.)

★   ★   ★

Kyna Tabor, a mother of two in Salem, Ill., was being driven to distraction by her son, then four, as he nagged her daily about how long he had to wait until Christmas. So she started a tradition of filling his stocking on the eve of December I with a series of tiny wrapped gifts on a related theme that he could open one at a time. "I always buy a cheap set of Army men or cars or farm animals. By Christmas Eve, Mikey has a whole troop of soldiers or a whole car lot to play with, and in the meantime, he doesn't bug me anymore." Kyna has started the practice with Mikey's sister, Kerstina, now three.

It wasn't quite as successful, but Sara Tarpley of Nashville, Tenn., tried what might be called a Good Deed Paper Chain. She hung a multicolored paper chain by tape across the bay window in the dining room, with a family member's name written inside each link of the chain. The idea was that each day one person would break a link off the end and do a good deed for the person whose name was written there (if they got their own name, they passed it on). "I always wanted to avoid those commercial Advent calendars where the kids get something for themselves every day, like a piece of candy," she explains.

But Sara, the mother of six, says that her teenagers in particular weren't too conscientious about completing their good deeds. "We were supposed to open a link every night around dinner, and that's a crazy time in this house, so some nights we didn't get it done and doubled up the next night. Also, I'm not sure what happened with a lot of the supposed good deeds, but I know one of my kids responded by giving his sibling a five-dollar bill. I don't know what value was taught there, but it's not what I had in mind." The two oldest Tarpleys were away at college, and Sara at least hopes that when their names were drawn their siblings "sent them their prayers."

Barbara Gardiner's clever idea is to put a daily surprise in Christmas tins, one for each of her three daughters. Every morning starting December I, the girls run to the windowsill in the family's living room to see what's in their tins. Some days it's a Christmas poem, or a puzzle or riddle made up by their father, a pithy proverb about generosity, or a coupon. Once their parents surprised them with tickets to a local production of

The Nutcracker a few days hence. "If I've really run out of ideas, I give them each a piece of candy," says Barbara. "We do it all the way up to January 1, and they hate for it to end."

Polly Schroeder of Edwardsville, Ill., uses all sixteen of the characters in her nativity set in her Advent ritual. Nightly, after dinner, her four kids take turns unwrapping a person or animal and placing it in the stable. Whoever has the honor that night also gets to pick which carol the family sings. Before the ritual starts, all the lights in the dining room are turned off and at least a dozen candles are lit. After the figure is set in the stable, a carol is sung, and a Christmas story recited, it's time to snuff out all the candles, a privilege that is divided up among the kids.

The baby Jesus doesn't get placed in the Schroeders' manger until Christmas morning, when the kids sing "Happy Birthday, Jesus" and blow out the candles on a birthday cake (usually angel food) before they open presents. One final touch of genius on Polly's part: the kids wrap up the nativity set pieces after Christmas, while all the wrapping paper is still out. By the next year, they've long forgotten which is wrapped in what.

The two Lang boys of San Jose, Calif., look forward to seeing what the Christmas angel left each morning in the small stockings that hang on their bedroom doorknobs. Most days, the angel leaves either a piece of candy or a small toy in each stocking. But on Christmas, the boys wake to find an ornament there, always something connected with teddy bears. Theresa Lang, who loved the ritual when she was growing up in Oregon, starts it as her mother did, on December 12, but the practice could run all the way through the Advent season.

In Clinton, N.J., the Hale family's Advent calendar has a big felt Christmas tree against a red background, and every day one of the three kids takes a felt ornament from the little pockets along the bottom and puts it on the tree. And every day, the family moves the wise men and animals one step closer to the nativity scene under the Christmas tree: on Christmas Eve, the youngest child gets to put baby Jesus in the manger.

★ ★ ★

Another way of celebrating Advent is the Jesse tree, a bare tree branch that is decorated with symbols of characters from the Old Testament. These biblical people, among them Adam and Eve, Noah, Moses, and Jacob, waited and prepared for the Messiah. The bareness of the branch represents the world devoid of Jesus. Focusing on their stories provides a good Bible lesson. Many families make homemade ornaments for each character, such as a paper apple for Adam and Eve, and hang one on the tree each day.

Mary Routh started the ritual of a Jesse tree with her four kids more than a decade ago. "We were trying to decommercialize Christmas and I didn't want Santa to rule our house," explains Mary. "I stumbled on the Jesse tree idea in a book. In November, we cut a dead branch from an old tree and 'plant' it in a pot in the living room. Years ago we made all these little symbols—a tiny basket for Moses and an ark for Noah—and we reuse them every year. During Advent, we light a candle each night, read some scripture, and have a family prayer while hanging one symbol on the Jesse tree."

Another Routh tradition that seems to be gaining in popularity is celebrating St. Nicholas Day, December 6. St. Nicholas was a bishop in Asia Minor (now Turkey) who was elevated into sainthood because of supposed miracles related to the rescue of children. Legend has it that St. Nicholas was a very wealthy man who freely gave away his gold, at times dropping it off anonymously with sleeping recipients. The celebration of St. Nicholas Day has been common throughout Europe for centuries, and in Holland gifts are placed in children's shoes that have been left outside their doors overnight. Part of the legend is that St. Nicholas traveled with an assistant named Peter, who carried a switch with which to punish children who hadn't been good and didn't deserve treats.

Like many parents, Mary Routh embraced the St. Nicholas tradition partly to stretch out the holiday season. In her household, the children get their stockings filled on St. Nicholas Day and the stockings always contain sweets and books about the Christmas story.

Teresa Schultz-Jones celebrated St. Nicholas Day during her teenage years in Belgium, but she has freely adapted the ritual for her family. Her ritual brings together St. Nicholas and the mythical Santa Claus. And she doesn't stick to the real date, celebrating it on a day that is best for the family of five.

"In our family's version, St. Nicholas comes by around 9:00 PM and knocks on the door. If the kids aren't asleep, then we don't answer the door and St. Nicholas goes on his way, knowing this is a house where children don't heed their bedtime," says Teresa. "If all is quiet, we let him in and discuss how old everybody is, what their interests are, how they behaved, and whether there are any new children. We say that St. Nicholas reports all of this back to Santa Claus, solving the problem of how Santa knows so much." Then St. Nicholas leaves a gift for each child and even a note.

The tradition evolved over time: as the oldest child, now eleven, got to school age and wanted to be able to give gifts herself, St. Nicholas started leaving craft kits that could be used to make presents for others. "This is just so much better than having *all* the excitement revolve around Christmas Day," says Teresa. "Now they get very excited about what they'll get for St. Nicholas Day and the prospect of what gifts they can make afterward."

Jennifer Olson of Spokane, Wash., celebrates St. Nicholas Day with her family first thing in the morning so her husband can be included if it falls on a workday. Candles are lit, sweet treats are served with sparkling cider, and the boys each get the gift of a new Christmas book. "I tell my sons that St. Nicholas was a real person who did good things for people. This way we emphasize the spirit of St. Nicholas and then get back to the birth of Jesus on Christmas."

The Tree

As I interviewed people for this book, I soon noticed that those who were most fervent about their family's rituals either wanted to pass on something they loved dearly as a child, or were determined to compensate for a deprivation they felt keenly. I think most people, when they grow up and fashion their own holiday celebrations, relish the chance to re-create their favorite traditions in all their remembered glory, while eagerly junking and replacing the rituals that grated and chafed. In my case, that meant literally tracing my mother's homemade stockings to use as a pattern, while gleefully bidding farewell to her hideous aluminum Christmas tree.

What I wanted, what I needed, what I craved, was a *real* tree. The dense and regal look of it, the sweet sensual smell of it, the unpredictability, the bother, the chance of finding an even grander one next year—I consider this a major part of the Christmas traditions my husband and I built together even before our son was born. Dick is a Christmasholic who won't take down the last Christmas decoration until precisely the first day of spring, and, every year, the two of us can't wait to start opening those attic boxes full of half-forgotten treasures.

For us, it isn't Christmas without a tree that reaches almost to the ceiling, covered with white lights (no colors) and a jumble of ornaments. I abhor the idea of those women's magazine theme trees: all red decorations, all homemade, all anything. I think Christmas trees should be as sloppy and all-encompassing as life: crumpled waxed-paper stars you made as a kid next to delicate handblown glass bulbs and little handcrafted things you picked up on your travels.

Obviously, I'm not the only person with fierce notions about what makes a proper Christmas tree.

It would fill volumes just listing the traditions behind different families' Christmas ornament collections, which are one of the real joys of the season. This assemblage of small, mostly delicate objects collectively tells the whole, complex history of a family, its tastes, adventures, and ethnic background.

I will share the most unusual and moving tree-decorating ritual I've found, that of Karen and Stan Swift. The Tucson, Ariz., couple have one son of their own and a big brood of adopted kids they initially took in as foster children. Many foster kids are in their home only briefly, but for every one a gold Christmas ornament is purchased. On it is engraved the name of the child and the year he or she entered the Swifts' home. Over the years, the family has collected 150 such ornaments and they are the *only* ornaments that grace their tree each Christmas. "These are our babies," says Karen, "and putting up the tree every year helps us remember them all."

Families use their trees as a backdrop for many Christmas-related activities. In Cincinnati, Ohio, the Ober family always has a "slumber party" under the tree. "It's usually the weekend before Christmas," says Darla Ober, the mother of three kids under ten. "We drag out the sleeping bags and snuggle together. If there's a Christmas show on television that night, we watch it, or else we rent a videotape. We also usually read a Christmas book. We keep all the tree lights on until the kids fall asleep."

The Hiltons in Nevada conduct a wonderful ritual that ends at the foot of their Christmas tree but reminds everyone of the holiday's history and purpose. "We call it our 'Journey to Bethlehem Night,'" says Nanette Hilton. "One evening during December, we walk all through the house and the backyard, as though on a journey. Because there wasn't any electricity when Jesus was born, we turn the lights off and use candles, though we do switch on the tree lights. We wind up at the tree and spread out a blanket and eat a meal that is what we think Mary and Joseph might have eaten, things like sandwiches in pita bread, fruit and dates and nuts."

Barb Brock has a special outdoor tree ritual she borrowed from a children's book by Eve Bunting called *Night Tree.* The family in the book visits the same tree in the woods every Christmas Eve and decorates it with lots of treats for birds and other outdoor creatures. After the tree is decorated, the family drinks hot cocoa and sings carols.

The Brocks' ritual takes place on their own property in Cheney, Wash. They pick a new tree each year. "We gather in our pasture on Christmas Eve, between eight and fifteen of us including members of my husband's family," says Barb. "Before we go out, we read the story again and the kids take flashlights to help pick out the tree. We bring ornaments we've made earlier, things like pine cones covered with peanut butter and dipped in birdseed. We also string cranberries and breakfast cereal to make garlands. When we find the tree, we sing some songs, put on the ornaments, and have some hot chocolate."

Barb says her Christmas Eve tree ritual usually starts at about 5:00 PM and doesn't last too long. Even with the hot drink, the kids get pretty cold and the singing doesn't usually go on longer than two or three songs. "It's always fun to check up on the tree occasionally afterward," she adds. "We've never actually seen 'wild animals' eating our treats, but often there are deer tracks and it's great to imagine animals like the bears and raccoons they show in the book." (Eve Bunting says she got the ritual from

a Minnesota schoolteacher whose family did it every year, and that she has received "dozens of letters and photographs" from families who have adopted the tradition.)

Celebrations

For Mary Lou Scicchitano's daughters and their cousins, the Christmas season really gets under way once their great-grandmother puts on the annual church Christmas pagent.

Grammy Mayhew has directed the production and played the organ at her church in Strasburg, Pa., for years. Family ritual intersects church ritual, because as soon as the congregation leaves on the night of the pagent, the four cousins rush to the front of the church to reenact the first Christmas.

Many families start seriously celebrating on Christmas Eve by attending evening church services or opening gifts. Other traditions on this night are designed to build anticipation and set the mood for the next morning.

The Straw family of Plano, Tex., celebrates Christmas Eve as "Candle Night." Traditionally, the family of four starts the evening with a special dinner and an early church service. When they get home, every candle in the house is gathered up and placed around the family room.

After the candles are all lit, the lights are turned off and the family reads the Christmas story from the Bible. "When they were little, especially, the kids loved the candlelight and being snuggled under quilts with their parents and grandparents," says Sue Straw. The ritual has long been that after the Bible story is read, the kids can pick whatever other books they want to be read, which used to include *Good Night Moon* and *One Fish, Two Fish, Red Fish, Blue Fish.* After all the stories, the family has Christmas cookies and milk.

The ritual has been adjusted as the children have grown. Sue's son and daughter are now twelve and fifteen, and they light the candles themselves and read the Bible to their parents.

Another ritual involving candles takes place in the Taylor family of New Bedford, Mass. After dinner on Christmas Eve, an unlit candle is given to each person as they sit around the tree. A lighted candle is on a nearby table. The first person starts by telling about one prayer that God has answered during the past year, then prays aloud for something in the coming year. That person then lights his or her candle from the one on the table. The next person gets a light from the first person, and so on.

"One of my kids thanked God for getting his driver's license," says Joyce Taylor, "and I remember when my husband said, 'Thank God for my wife: she's been my strength all year.' The most moving time was the year my brother stopped drinking and gave God the glory for his healing." Joyce says the ritual was her idea and that it started off a bit awkwardly the first year. "They looked at me like, 'We're doing what?' But once the first person spoke, it was easy for everybody else."

When all the candles are lit, the family sings Christmas carols. Then, the youngest child present is given the honor of putting baby Jesus in the manger, and the family sings "Happy Birthday" to him.

★ ★ ★

In East Stroudsburg, Pa., the Mastroberte family conducts a very old tradition called Holy Night supper (*Svjatyj Večer*) widely observed by Christians in the Eastern Orthodox church in Poland and parts of Russia. The ritual meal is quite complex, including twelve courses that represent the twelve apostles. The visual symbolism includes a rope that is tied around the legs of the dining-room table to symbolize "the unending bond of the family," says thirteen-year-old David Mastroberte. Hay is spread on the table to remind the family of the manger.

"The meal starts after the first star appears in the sky," explains David. "Then we wash our hands at the table in a basin. The food is blessed with holy water from the church, and if there are any animals, they are blessed with holy water too. Since we don't have any sheep or goats, we bless our cats. Then you sit down and eat."

The Mastrobertes serve a variety of meatless dishes, including beans, cabbage, rice, and potatoes, and the ritual demands that nobody skip any dish: at least one bite must be taken. Also, says David, "We eat a clove of garlic dipped in honey. That represents the bitterness of the world mixed with the sweet." After eating, the family says a prayer and sings traditional Christmas *kol'ady* or carols, and then gets ready for church. Their immediate family doesn't live nearby, so in addition to David, his little sister, and his parents, the evening usually includes some family friends who have the same ethnic background but may not be familiar with the traditions.

It was David himself who pushed for making the Holy Night supper more ethnically complete after studying up on the holiday, adding touches like the rope around the table. His father, Raymond, grew up in Passaic, N.J., in a household that observed the holiday, but it had gotten "watered down" over the years, admits Raymond, who makes his living painting Orthodox religious icons. "My father is half-Italian and half-Slovak," he says, "and I married a woman whose background is Carpatho-Russian. Our son was brought up in those traditions and has always been a prober and did a lot of research on his heritage."

David's father says he believes he is the only member of his family who still observes the tradition of Holy Night supper, but clearly the ritual has caught fire in his son. David has already begun helping his father paint icons, and he says, "I think I might like to be an Orthodox priest. I'm studying Greek now."

Polish tradition reigns on Christmas Eve for the Kuligs of Rutland, Vt. Theresa Kulig and her husband, Jack, take their three daughters to his mother's house after an early-evening church service. First, the family "breaks bread," using a special wafer much like a communion wafer, which Jack's mother has received from the local Polish church. It is broken into small pieces that are passed around to each family member. Then everybody goes around the room and wishes the others "good things for the new year."

Next comes a traditional Polish meal, including pirogis and mushroom soup. Then it's time for the annual Santa sighting. Either Jack Kulig or his brother dresses up as Santa and is seen fleetingly out the window, walking away from the house. That's a signal for the kids to rush to the door, where there is a bag of gifts for each of the grandchildren on the doorstep. These bags were made by Grandma and are reused every year; each is stenciled with Christmas symbols and the name of one of the four children. Inside the bag are gifts from the grandparents and from aunts and uncles. (The kids will get presents from Santa the next morning.)

Suzy Kellett, a single mother of quadruplets living in Seattle, has many long-standing traditions for Christmas Eve, including a dinner of beef tenderloin, baked potatoes, and little pearl onions, as well as the reading of Christmas books by the light of a single lamp in the living room. The quads end the evening by hanging up their stockings and each lighting a candle, which they carry up to bed. Even now, at twenty-one, the four kids wouldn't hear of skipping a single step.

Christmas Eve is also when Deborah Pecoraro's son and daughter start using the special, handmade Christmas pillowcases she has painted and stenciled for them. Her son's, for example, has a Christmas tree, his name in red piping, and stenciled pictures of gifts under the tree. The kids sleep on these for the twelve days of Christmas.

Before going to sleep, the Pecoraros go to Mass at their local church. When they get home, they sing "Happy Birthday" to Jesus, and eat a special birthday cake. Deborah's husband is first-generation Italian, so this is always a cannoli cake, frosted with whipped cream and decorated with glittery sprinkles. Then, it's time to put the baby Jesus in the empty manger of the family's nativity scene.

Indeed, the practice of baking a "Jesus birthday cake" appears to be spreading, as mothers across the country eagerly embrace a way of focusing on the holiday's real meaning in an undogmatic way designed to enchant children. Debbie Morgan in Tulsa, Okla., also bakes a Jesus cake, usually chocolate, for her five kids. The family blows the candles out together and Debbie's husband reads the Christmas story from the Bible.

But many Christmas food rituals are much more idiosyncratic and less thematic than Jesus cakes.

The traditional Christmas Eve meal in Patrick McIvor's New Jersey boyhood home is shrimp cocktail and carryout Chinese food. That's because one year Patrick's mother found herself on Christmas Eve with three children in various stages of chicken pox. The family had been planning to travel to a relative's house and hadn't stocked up on holiday food. About all that was in the fridge was the McIvors' contribution to the family party, a large quantity of shrimp cocktail. Suddenly, with the travel plans canceled, the shrimp wasn't enough for a meal. Patrick's father was dispatched for food and found only a Chinese takeout restaurant open. The story became part of family lore and the menu has been repeated on Christmas Eve for twenty-five years.

Pharmacist David Ridiman cooks two Christmas Eve feasts every year, one for his two daughters and a second one for his wife after the girls are in bed. "He plans the menus for weeks," says his wife, Kathy. "For me he cooks all these delicate dishes, like orange soufflé, and serves champagne. The girls get whatever they want, within reason, and they get candlelight too. My nine-year-old loves caviar and this is the only time all year when she gets it. They also get Cracker Jacks."

For Catherine Duke, a divorced mother living outside Seattle, the traditional Christmas dinner was something to be dreaded. When she was growing up, her parents, even after they were divorced, insisted on going to a big Christmas Eve feast at her grandmother's house. The atmosphere was one of forced goodwill through clenched teeth, and when the kids grew up they fled into separate lives. But once Catherine had a house and a child and her brother was established in a happy marriage, they thought about getting together for the holidays once again. Several years ago, Catherine was asked to host a Christmas Eve family gathering and, immediately, "a big knot of Christmas fear began churning in my stomach."

Before the stress got out of hand, Catherine decided to abandon all the old traditions of turkey and forced gaiety and prepare a totally unorthodox and relaxed celebration. "We all grew up around the water and love seafood, so I served buckets of clams and mussels, fresh bread and salads," says Catherine. "We spread a big tablecloth on the floor of the living room and ate picnic-style. We drank too much wine and laughed till our faces ached. No one got cranky and goodwill abounded."

Preparing for Santa is another beloved Christmas Eve tradition that takes many forms. Countless children leave a plate of cookies for the rotund gentleman and carrots for his reindeer, and are delighted to find only crumbs and sometimes a thank-you note next morning. But some families go further. One couple partially grinds the carrots in their kitchen-sink disposal and tosses the "half-chewed" bits out into the snow near the front door. Elisabeth and Robert McCarthy of Algonquin, Ill., sprinkle a special "reindeer mix" of oatmeal and glitter across the lawn, promising it will lead Santa's sleigh team right up to their front door.

Many families help keep the magic alive by making baby-powder or baking-soda Santa footprints every year, dusting the powder around a paper outline of a big boot sole. One woman I talked to remembers fondly how her father would climb up on the roof once the kids were settled in bed, shaking jingle bells as he stomped around loudly. (This was in the balmy South: fathers who live in snowy climes probably shouldn't try this on an icy roof.)

Children who don't have chimneys must, of course, take extra precautions to ensure Santa's arrival. Like the children of Colby Beutel in Chicago, who put out a skeleton key on a special Christmas plate so that "the fairies can unlock the front door and let Santa in," Colby explains. The two kids, eight-year-old Zoë and her brother, Max, two, also help

Santa by letting him know when they're going to bed. They grab little enameled bells off the Christmas tree and run through their apartment ringing them, a practice dreamed up by Colby's sister Robin for her four kids.

Christmas morning, too, has its own rituals of anticipation, unveiling, and worship.

The Penningtons of Maine have a sheet blocking off the door to the present-filled living room, and nobody can peek or enter until after breakfast. The stockings are left on the stairwell, and the kids can delve into those beforehand. Breakfast itself includes a treat for the kids, in that they are allowed to eat sugar-covered cereals forbidden for the rest of the year: a small box of such cereal is always one of the stocking presents. But then there's the two-cups-of-coffee rule: the kids have to wait for all the grown-ups to finish their second cup before presents can be opened.

"Now that I'm an adult, I so look forward to that second cup of coffee!" says Nellie Pennington. "When I was a kid growing up, I was chomping at the bit." When it's finally time to enter the living room, the kids line up by age, youngest first, but it's Grandpa, with the video camera, who lifts the sheet and enters first. To prevent total chaos, gifts are opened in rounds: kids first, one present each, and then it's the grown-ups' turn.

The Penningtons aren't alone in creating a barrier to hold eager children at bay until the proper moment. Debbie Midcalf of Palm Desert, Calif., tapes a four-foot-high wall of wrapping paper across the hallway that leads to the living room. Her three children aren't allowed to go into the living room until everybody in the family is awake; then they collectively burst through the paper.

The Leventry family, which lives near Summerhill, Pa., used to have a tradition of stretching a piece of yarn across the living-room doorway, with a little bell on it that would ring if one of the four kids tried to get to the presents before the appointed hour of 7:00 AM. Once everybody was assembled, "they would break through the string as if they were winning a race," says Karen Leventry, who stopped the practice when her kids reached their teens and weren't so eager to wake at dawn.

★ ★ ★

When Betsy Muir was growing up as the youngest of five kids, one of her fondest Christmas-morning memories was the "countdown" the children had to perform before bursting into the living room for presents. "We had to count down from ten, only it was 'ten candy canes, nine candy canes, eight candy canes,' " she recalls. Now that Betsy's second child is old enough to participate, she plans to start the tradition in the next generation. The Reichmans of New Rochelle, N.Y., have a rule that nobody in the family can see the tree with all the lights on until Christmas morning: Rob Reichman runs downstairs first thing and flips the switch before his wife and two children enter to open presents.

Of course, not everybody celebrates Christmas in the ways we've come to think of as traditional. For some families, in some situations, that model doesn't suit their needs, means, or wishes.

Take the case of Mary Kay Havens of Dallas. A few years back, she found her family buffeted by death, divorce, illness, and unemployment and she needed to create an inexpensive Christmas celebration that focused "more on being together than giving presents." The family had changed so much (Mary Kay's ex-husband had died, her eighty-year-old mother was newly remarried, various relatives had sold their homes) that to repeat old Christmas traditions would bring up too many memories of what was lost. But Mary Kay, having been laid off for six weeks, certainly couldn't pull off a lavish celebration.

"We had to face the fact that we weren't the Cleavers anymore," she says. "Things had turned out differently from what we expected, and we had to sit back and look at ourselves and say, 'This is our family now.' " Which meant creating a fun, new way of experiencing the Christmas holiday, one that could also include Mary Kay's new stepfather and the fiancé of her older daughter, plus the fiancé's mother and sister.

The idea came from Mary Kay's younger daughter, Meredith, then thirteen, who had long been clamoring to have Christmas at home instead of traveling to out-of-state relatives. "Meredith had been to church camp and she came up with the idea that we invite everybody to our house and schedule a lot of activities and call it 'Camp Christmas,' " says Mary Kay. "Her thought was that with a name like that, it could be very informal so people wouldn't mind things like having to sleep on sofas and in sleeping bags and we wouldn't have to spend a lot of money."

Invitations were sent out to relatives and friends, complete with a checklist to send back so that invitees could pick and choose which events or days they planned to visit:

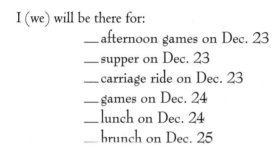

I (we) will be there for:
        ___afternoon games on Dec. 23
        ___supper on Dec. 23
        ___carriage ride on Dec. 23
        ___games on Dec. 24
        ___lunch on Dec. 24
        ___brunch on Dec. 25

For the sixteen people who attended there were activities such as a tetherball tournament and a scavenger hunt. When the whole crowd was indoors, there were a series of "centers" guests could choose from such as making cookies, singing Christmas carols, decorating Santa hats, or playing games. Presents (modest ones) were opened on Christmas Eve before an optional candlelight service at the Methodist church. Mary Kay's kitchen wasn't big enough to feed everyone, so she hosted buffet-style meals, and the whole crew traveled to her sister's house for the traditional Christmas feast the afternoon of Christmas Eve.

The highlight of Camp Christmas was a carriage ride that Mary Kay arranged in an area of Dallas called Highland Park, the night before Christmas Eve. It took two carriages to hold everyone, wearing Santa hats and bundled up in blankets, and they rode around town looking at Christmas lights. The cost of the carriage ride: just eight dollars a person. "Everybody just loved Camp Christmas," says Mary Kay. "The message was that we are together, and it was such fun to do things a little differently."

Presents: What and How

The Michael family, whose Christmas in an isolated cabin was discussed earlier, are not alone in trying to downsize Christmas gift-giving.

Barbara DeGrote and David Sorensen of Long Prairie, Minn., are part of the "simple living" movement that's been sweeping the country. About a decade ago, these parents of three children exchanged their big house for one half its size and downshifted their entire lifestyle. Barbara quit working and David, a Lutheran pastor, cut back his hours to emphasize family time. They also cowrote several books including *'Tis a Gift to Be Simple.*

One of their biggest targets for change was Christmas. "You can't change it overnight, but every year we get a little better at detaching from the commercialism," says Barbara. "You have to redefine what is a successful Christmas, and we have changed from defining it as getting so many presents you can't get through them to believing that a happy Christmas is a slow one."

Barbara says that what helped convince her of the need to change was observing her own son at Christmas. "We were at Grandma's and he opened his first present, a harmonica. He stopped to play with it and I had to remind him to open all the other presents. He was so content with this one present, but once he had opened his other gifts, he said, like all kids, 'Is that all?' "

So, over the years, the family has cut way down on the number of gifts the children get. On one recent Christmas, the family bought cross-country skis for all the kids and added a few minor items, like some sheet music for Kate, who plays the flute. "We opened the skis on Christmas Eve and then we all went out skiing on our town's golf course," says Barbara.

Barbara also believes that the kids should learn how much fun it is to give creatively to others, so she and her husband give the kids a small amount of money before Christmas to buy things for each other. "I believe kids need to hear a 'Thank you' and say a 'Thank you' at Christmas," she says. "Those two words are almost more important than 'Merry Christmas.' "

Indeed, many people's happiest memories are of Christmases when their family didn't have much of a budget for fancy gifts and had to improvise.

"The Christmas I remember most fondly was the year when I was seven and my dad's employer had shut down and he hadn't found a new job," recalls Kim Meisenheimer. "My mother had four children between six months and seven years old, and basically no money. They went to a lot of trouble to make games for each of us, with us two biggest kids helping to make the presents for the little ones."

Kim's mother took her two daughters on what she called "garage-sale hunts," looking for used adult clothing, costing nickels and dimes, that could be used to fill a special dress-up trunk. An actual trunk would have been too costly, so she fixed up an old wooden box and covered it with a floral sheet. For the two littlest ones, Kim's dad made a set of wooden blocks from an old pine table, plus two games, one a beanbag toss and the other a ring toss, using wooden clothespins and rubber canning rings.

"My sister and I helped with the sanding and painting. Some of the designs on those blocks are memories we won't forget," says Kim. "I don't know why, but that Christmas is still fresh in my memory. Maybe it was all the work and planning, but it was so much fun. And each of us kids has saved something from that year: we each have a couple of the blocks, my brother kept the ring toss, and my sister the costume trunk. My mom has the beanbag-toss board and the grandkids still play with it when they visit."

So precious are those memories that Kim and her siblings have continued a tradition of giving homemade gifts to their own kids. "My brother makes the kids wooden guns that fire rubber bands or carves a motorcycle rocking toy. I keep buying 'finds' at the Salvation Army to add to my kids' costume trunk, and my sister buys her kids a Rubbermaid tub and fills it with craft materials like old greeting cards, pipe cleaners, and empty paper-towel rolls they can use to make things."

Some families have taken to setting a specific limit on the number of Christmas gifts each child receives, scaling back to three or even one. Those who espouse the three-gift limit generally say they chose the number not merely because it is modest, but also because the Christ child was given three gifts by the wise men.

The Suks of Evanston, Ill., are one of the families that limit the number of gifts to three for religious reasons, but the wonderful thing about their gift-giving tradition is that they've found ways of making a few gifts seem very special.

"We decided many years ago that if three was good enough for Jesus, it was good enough for our children," says L'Tishia Suk, the mother of four. "We always give each child one book, one toy, and one game. Over the years, the toys have gotten to be pretty big, like a bicycle or an electric guitar. The ritual is that the book and the game are wrapped and under the tree, but the big gift is hidden. We hand out the first clue and then that clue leads to other clues, until they find the present."

Tradition has it that the youngest child gets to hunt first, but in each case, the entire family troops around following each child as he or she hunts for the big gift. Sometimes the hunt involves leaving the family's home. "One year, a kid's bicycle was in a neighbor's garage," explains L'Tishia. "One clue led our daughter to a garage-door opener, and eventually to the bike.

"This routine makes gift-opening much more leisurely than in many households, and a lot more fun for everybody," says L'Tishia.

Julie Young, the mother of six (pregnant with child number seven), decided to shift to the three-gift rule with her family several years ago.

"It took a couple years to see that it was workable. Before we started, I brought it up by saying that someone in my Bible study group told me an interesting tradition about how her family celebrated Christmas, and then shared the idea. That way the kids could talk about it objectively in reference to another family instead of immediately focusing on themselves and their own wish lists. It seemed better than just announcing a new 'law,' and when we did decide to try it, it seemed like a shared decision. Actually the rationale made perfect sense to them, given that baby Jesus got three gifts."

Having done the three-gift routine now for several years, Julie has found that it has multiple benefits, in addition to saving money and helping pass on her values to her kids. "Knowing that they won't get gobs and gobs of presents, the kids (who range in age from one to ten) have become very choosy in what they ask for," says Julie. "They don't want to 'waste' their requests." Julie adds that this system has another advantage: "Now I *know* when I'm finished shopping for each person."

Julie says she and her husband sometimes feel a little twinge when the family is spending Christmas at a relative's house and the cousins still have heaps to open when her children are done. But, she adds, "We are trying to teach them that 'stuff' won't make them happy, so we persevere. And after all, they do get stockings and a few additional gifts from relatives and friends."

In Chicago, Colby Beutel's kids, who put out the skeleton key for Santa on Christmas Eve, only get a single big gift from the jolly man.

"I wanted to establish this tradition early on because sometimes money is tight and sometimes it isn't," says Colby. "When Zoë, now eight, started making Christmas lists it was always, 'I want this and this and this.' I would say, 'Why not just ask Santa for one thing you really, really want?' "

One year, for example, Zoë got a beautiful dollhouse. Her stocking, which was placed under the tree, was filled with related gifts, including a family of dolls.

Large, extended families often find that the only way to deal with the too-muchness of buying for everybody is to create a gift exchange. One of the silliest and most creative ones I've found is the Trieschman family's, which they call a Kris Kringle.

The Trieschmans' Kris Kringle gift exchange has been going on since 1980, and with the twelve adults involved spending up to $250 on each other, the gifts are none too shabby. Recipients often get major household appliances, generous gift certificates, or a serious article of clothing such as a leather jacket.

"It had gotten to the point where we were buying for all our siblings and spending way too much on each one," says Cindy. "Although $250 seems like a lot, since we only buy for one person in our extended family we actually spend less than we did before." And have more fun doing it.

Those involved in the Kris Kringle include Cindy Grubb and her parents and four brothers, and everybody's significant other. A "wish list" is kept on Cindy's mother's refrigerator so all the adults can communicate their needs and wants. Names are drawn on Thanksgiving and the big gifts are exchanged at Christmas, but joke gifts are delivered between Thanksgiving and Christmas. The extra challenge here is that the joke gift is supposed to arrive without revealing the identity of the giver.

"You have to deliver the joke gift to the person's house or workplace without them seeing you," explains Cindy. "That can be tough around here because we all live within ten minutes of each other and three live on dead-end streets. We always do things to disguise our handwriting, like cutting letters out of the newspaper." The joke gifts are often related to the "wish-list" gifts. For example, Cindy's dad always wanted a farm animal, so when Cindy drew his name, she "rented" a miniature donkey and delivered it to her father's shed. "It woke him up in the middle of the night," says Cindy, laughing. "It was great."

When it comes time for the actual gift exchange on Christmas Day, each person tries to guess who their secret Kris Kringle is. If they guess, they get to open their big present immediately and the rest of the family watches. If they guess wrong, the next person gets a turn and they have to keep guessing till they get it right.

The children play the game too, but on a more modest level. For the "Kringle Jingle," there are no joke gifts and the price limit is fifty dollars. The kids do have to guess who their secret Santa is before opening the gift. (Parents decide when their kids are ready to graduate to the big Kris Kringle.)

Homemade gifts are a tradition in many families, but among the most clever is the family trivia game given to Sam and Sally Pennington by their five children. The game is called "Inlaws, Outlaws and Rugrats," "rugrats" being a slang term for young children, and "outlaws" meaning Nellie Pennington and Nate Hine, who are raising their two children together but have never married. "We got the idea from a book, but we ignored most of their advice," says Nellie. "Basically, our game is based on Trivial Pursuit and we use that board when we play, but we made up our own categories and questions."

The questions cover the minutiae of family lore in six categories: People, Activities, Statistics, Sayings, Oddities, and Places & Events. "They aren't necessarily something people could guess, but a way to learn about the family's history, especially for people who marry into it," says Nellie. There are questions such as "On what occasions did Mom say 'Scat' " (Answer: when family members sneezed) and "What did Nellie and Sarah do when Mom and Dad took the trip to Massachusetts?" (Answer: had a party, which their parents didn't know about till they played the game).

The game cards are made by Nellie on her computer, a different color for each category. The question appears on one side, and on the other is a space for the answer, the name of the person who submitted the question (family members can't answer their own), and the date. To prepare the game, two of the sisters interviewed their extended family and combed through the family archives. Now, the siblings add new questions every year.

There are millions of other traditions involving categories of gifts, but two related to children are worth mentioning because they are so popular and lend themselves to endless variation: the giving of new pajamas on Christmas Eve, and the annual gift of a Christmas ornament.

The pajama tradition, which I have adopted since my son was born, is fun because it adds to the excitement and anticipation of Christmas Eve. Some families actually start it as a problem-solving ritual, worried that their kids' ratty pjs will give the relatives the wrong idea when the Christmas photos are mailed out. Here's a way to guarantee the whole crew will be wearing something clean and new, perhaps even in coordinated colors that will make Christmas morning more photogenic, adding to the sense of the family in its own "tribal" dress. Most families soon find that, like many rituals, kids start getting into it because they know what to expect, but not exactly.

Galen Laughton of Reno, Nev., grew up getting new pajamas every year on Christmas Eve, so now she repeats the ritual for her two sets of twins. "They open one gift on Christmas Eve, and it always turns out to be pajamas, but even the older twins, who are four, haven't quite figured out yet that it's always pajamas." They will.

Monica Hall, on the other hand, always gives her children new pajamas plus a new pair of slippers on Christmas Eve, while another mother gives her kids each a pair of pajamas and a Christmas book. Mindy Robinson's mother always made the pajamas by hand for her kids, even after they were grown-up and married. Mindy says that, by then, her mother would give her a package even before Christmas Eve: on Christmas morning, Mindy would drive over to her mother's house wearing the pajamas over her regular clothes. "My brother and his wife did the same thing," she says.

Another variation on this theme is practiced by Dawn Hale of Clinton, N.J. Her three girls have come to expect that "Herbie the elf" will leave them each a package on the front porch or by the front door, usually while they're out at church on Christmas Eve. "They are either pajamas or nightgowns, always with holiday themes and colors," says Dawn, who confesses that she buys them after Christmas on sale each year and stashes them away until the next year.

The tradition of giving each child a new ornament every year is widespread, again with many variations. In most cases, the ornaments are later given to the children for use in their own households.

One mother in Brewster, N.Y., takes her two children shopping before Christmas and lets each of them pick an ornament, and then takes them a second time after the holiday to buy another, or even two, on sale. The name of the child and the year an ornament was purchased are written on the side of the box, and each year the boy and girl get to choose a special section of the Christmas tree on which to display their collection.

In another family, the parents choose a theme for each child and buy an ornament reflecting it, whether angels, teddy bears, or Santas. Some families buy an ornament every year with that year's date on it, and others pick an ornament reflecting their child's interests, such as a schoolhouse ornament for a kindergarten student.

OTHER GIFT IDEAS

★ The first Christmas after Barbara Gardiner's girls reach first grade, they get a complete boxed set, nine volumes in paperback, of *Little House on the Prairie*. "These books are just so great for girls, and this is about the time when they're starting to learn to read," says Barbara. "Right after Christmas, we start reading them the first one."

★ Pam Pinegar of Detroit, a divorced mother of two girls, describes herself as "a small woman with big feet," and views this condition with humor. Thus the family's annual "goofy slipper tradition," in which she and her daughters try to rival one another with the gift of outlandish slippers. "We have bear claws, fluffy bunnies, cartoon characters, and so on," says Pam, "and part of the tradition is taking our picture in them every Christmas."

★ The Lynches of Merchantsville, N.J., give each of their kids an audiotaped book on Christmas Eve, when they also receive a regular book present from their grandparents.

Being Good and Doing Good

Many families try to deemphasize the materialism of Christmas by creating rituals of giving and sharing, whether it's having their kids set aside used toys every year to donate to needier children or encouraging good deeds around the house.

An old Catholic tradition that remains popular has children place a small straw (some families use yarn) in the manger of the family nativity scene every time they do a good deed: instead of being good so Santa will bring more booty, the emphasis is on doing good so Jesus' bed will be as soft as possible.

Some families set up a decorated box or jar in a well-trafficked room and encourage family members to toss in loose change whenever they get a chance: as the holiday winds down, the family has a meeting to pick which charity will receive the collected funds. Becky Klingbeil uses a decorated box to encourage good behavior. She wraps a box in plain white paper and attaches a gift tag that says "To Jesus, from Caroline and Connor," her daughter and son. Then, each time during December that her children "do something above mere obedience," the good deed is recorded in ink right on the box, says Becky. "Then we talk about how happy Jesus is when we are loving or kind, when we share, and so on."

Caroline, now four, got written up one day because she was playing dress-up with a friend, who was crying because she wanted to wear the outfit Caroline was wearing. Caroline took off the dress and gave it to her friend. On Christmas Day, the family reads all the good deeds on the box.

Another approach is to view the holiday as a chance to thank other people who have done good deeds in the past year.

Jeanne McIver had a long-standing tradition with her four children (now grown) of delivering Christmas cookies to someone special chosen by each family member. "The rule was we had to leave them on the porch, so it was anonymous and we wouldn't be thanked. Sometimes the kids would choose someone from school, like the librarian, or someone who coached a team they were on, or a church member who had been especially nice to them. We'd drive all over town, the six of us, dropping these cookie packages off. It was never on Christmas Eve because my husband is a pastor and that was a busy night, but as close to it as possible."

A related concept is Sue Thurman's "holiday bread," which she explains "doesn't involve bread at all; it's about feeding the souls of strangers." Sue, the mother of one son in Pittsburgh, adopted the idea from a short story involving mittens left by a stranger for a needy child.

"Our tradition is to anonymously give a gift to someone who may not otherwise get a present, or to thank someone who needs to be thanked. We start thinking about it several weeks before Christmas, and each year we do something a little different. The night before Christmas, we'll go to a nursing home or a hospital emergency room or the police station and drop off a package (wrapped with see-through paper so no one fears a bomb lurks inside). We don't give our names, but just explain that it's from Santa Claus for someone who deserves a present."

One Christmas Eve, the Thurmans delivered a poinsettia and a box of candy to the firemen on duty at the local firehouse. Once they took a gift to the nurses and doctors on duty at the hospital's ER, and another time told the same hospital to pass the gift on to "a patient who had no visitors or presents." Sue says that at first the recipients look suspicious; then their reaction turns into "incredulity, wonderment, and often joy. It gives us back a hundredfold whatever we've given. Sometimes we'll just run back to the car and sit there giggling at their surprise. It leaves such warm memories of Christmas."

The Pecoraro family of Livermore, Calif., has a tradition of "secret angels," doing good deeds for one another throughout December. Every Sunday, the parents and two children draw a name and for the entire next week, they perform small chores and provide little treats for that family member.

"We know each other's handwriting, so I made up little notes on my computer that say 'This treat was brought to you by your secret angel,' or 'This chore was done by your secret angel,' " explains Deborah Pecoraro.

In addition, the family has a tradition on major holidays, including Christmas and Easter, of "adopting" a needy family. "We might fill stockings and buy presents for the kids in a family, or put together an Easter meal and Easter baskets," says Deborah. "We usually do this with the other families in our prayer group, and the fathers deliver the presents. We often get the name of an unwed mother or a family where the father walked out from the local crisis pregnancy center."

Deborah says she was both surprised and delighted when the family attended a workshop one Advent and her kids were asked for their favorite Christmas ritual. "They said it was adopting a family. I really think kids are naturally generous and because they help us pick out what food and other items to give, they feel very involved in the giving."

Another woman works with her children each year to help them perform a major good deed "in the spirit of Christmas," such as packing up their old toys for the needy or working in a soup kitchen. Their annual reward is one figure for their own nativity set, so that by the time the kids are grown, they will each have a complete grouping. "I still have the nativity set my mother gave to me," says this woman, "and I still remember what I did to deserve each piece."

One more ritual that has lasted several generations: throughout December, every time a child performs an unselfish act such as helping another with chores, the "Christmas Angel" leaves a small gift under the child's pillow that night. The gifts are very modest items like a small piece of candy or a tiny ornament, but a message is sent that virtue will be rewarded.

Kwanzaa

This is a relatively young holiday, started in 1966 by Dr. Maulana Ron Karenga to strengthen and unify the black community in this country, in part by getting them to celebrate African culture. The word *kwanzaa* comes from the Swahili word for "first" and many of the suggested rituals for the holiday are based on "first fruit" or harvest celebrations common throughout Africa.

Kwanzaa runs for a week, from the day after Christmas through New Year's Day, and each day is devoted to a different principle, including unity, self-determination, and creativity. Each day's celebration is meant to start with the lighting of a candle, as with Advent or Hanukkah, and the holiday culminates in a big feast. African dress, food, music, and crafts are common elements in the festivities, but like many other holidays, Kwanzaa leaves a great deal of latitude for individual interpretation and inspiration. Some families, for example, give gifts each day, but those who also celebrate Christmas tend to downplay that aspect.

While Kwanzaa is now celebrated in thousands of homes and dozens of official city festivals across the country, it isn't universally accepted even within black communities. Some people deride it as artificial and arbitrary, and add that the countries of contemporary Africa aren't themselves examples of unity, but often home to brutal intertribal rivalries and violence.

But the fundamentals of the holiday are praiseworthy, and the seven principles Kwanzaa endeavors to teach children offer a moral and worthwhile philosophy of living. Unity may exist only as a myth, but it is a valuable goal for people and countries to share. Families that use this occasion to pass on the stories of their own ancestors and the historic struggle of their race are fulfilling several of ritual's most important roles, including providing their kids with a sense of identity and values.

Yvette Aidara, mother of a teenage son, has been celebrating Kwanzaa with a group of college friends in Washington, D.C., for twenty years.

"We light the candles every night of the holiday and have a little ritual that goes with that, but basically we're a very fluid group and we don't do the same things every year," says Yvette. "After we light the candles each night, whichever child is going to describe the principle for that night will start by saying the word both in Swahili and English. Then we go around the room, from youngest to oldest, and each person says how they will act on that principle in the year to come."

For most of the seven days of Kwanzaa, the group of friends takes turns meeting at one another's houses, with the host deciding how formal or informal the evening will be. When it's her turn to host, Yvette says, she often starts an exercise where everybody in the group "reminisces about friends or family that died during the year. It isn't morbid at all, but very positive."

Yvette stresses that this is a cultural rather than a religious holiday and her group of friends includes "Muslims, Christians, and people who practice various African religions." On a given night during Kwanzaa, she says, "people who love to cook put out a big spread and those who don't might serve fruit and salads. Usually the host has small presents for the children who come and sometimes for the adults too, but it's not supposed to be anything fancy or expensive. It might be Kwanzaa bookmarks. One year, I gave everybody calendars."

Although many Kwanzaa observers have their big feast on the last night of the holiday, that isn't always so for Yvette's crowd. "It depends on all our schedules and what works for everybody," she says. She adds that in cities like Washington, D.C., with a large black population, the entire month of December is getting to be "Kwanzaa month," with many organizations holding Kwanzaa events before Christmas "because they know most people are doing family things" in that week between Christmas and New Year's. Yvette's son, for example, attended an independent black school in D.C., and every year his school would put on Kwanzaa programs for the students and their families.

Angela Dodson and her husband, Michael Days, didn't start celebrating Kwanzaa at home until after they adopted four boys in the early '90s. The four boys were brothers who had been in foster care together virtually all of their lives.

"As a couple, we had been to a few Kwanzaa dinners at other people's houses," says Angela, "but after we adopted our sons, we decided to start our own celebration. We felt it was something they should know about, and it would help us instill some values in them."

Over the years, the holiday has continued to grow in importance in the family's Trenton, N.J., household. "We put up a Kwanzaa altar on a cabinet top at the same time we get out our Christmas decorations," says

Angela. "We drape it with an African fabric and set up the candles and harvest-related things. Every year we buy a new decoration related to Kwanzaa."

Each evening, starting on the day after Christmas, the family holds a candle-lighting ceremony, led by Angela and Michael or whichever is home that night. Friends or relatives who are visiting join in. "We do a very simple ceremony that includes a reading and the lighting of the candles," explains Angela. "We use a standard book on Kwanzaa and read something from it or from *A Kwanzaa Keepsake*, a cookbook that has more than just recipes, by Jessica B. Harris. Each child will read something, or one child will be picked to read."

Some gifts are given, but not every child gets a gift every evening, and the type of gift is intentionally different from what they receive at Christmas. "We emphasize the giving of less commercial and more academic gifts," says Angela. "It's great because these are often presents that would get lost in the rush on Christmas Day, like a fine book about another culture or a globe or art supplies."

Most years, Angela and Michael hold a major party during Kwanzaa, usually toward the end of the week. "Most people plan a party around one of the principles of Kwanzaa, and the one we usually choose is creativity," says Angela. "We started by doing that one year, and it was a huge hit. Everybody had to demonstrate a talent or tell a story about an ancestor and we had wonderful folktales, original poetry, and so on. One person read from a book he had written." In addition, each guest has to bring a dish "from their part of the African diaspora," says Angela, and this makes for a varied and delicious buffet that evokes even more storytelling.

Angela says she has had plenty of proof that the holiday has had an effect on her kids. The seven principles celebrated during Kwanzaa have worked their way into the family's everyday language and ritual.

For example, one of the principles, self-determination, is called *kujichagulia* in Swahili. It has become customary in the family that when one person has suffered consequences for something they've done, as Angela puts it, the rest of the family will chant "*kujichagulia*" to the person. The word serves as a reminder that all behavior is voluntary, and each individual must control his or her own destiny. In another case, one of the boys gave a family cat the name of another Kwanzaa principle, *ujamaa*.

"Not many people have a cat named cooperative economics," notes Angela with a laugh.

After seven years of Kwanzaa, Angela says her family would never think of dropping the holiday celebration. "These are messages we really wanted our sons to get: that they should be educated people, spiritual people, and people who use their talents and gifts. The messages are strengthened because there is a specific time devoted to them each year, and it is all the better that it comes right after Christmas, when they are focused on 'me-me-me,' and 'what did I get?' "

In Eugene, Ore., Do Mi Stauber and her partner Trisha Whitney observe Kwanzaa with their adopted African-American daughter, Alex.

"The day after Christmas, we take down the Christmas tree and put up a Kwanzaa table," says Do Mi. This carries various symbols of the holiday, such as the candleholder with seven candles (three green, three red, and a black one in the middle), a flag of the same colors, and harvest vegetables. Every day of Kwanzaa, the family lights the appropriate candles while playing African or African-American music, and Alex is given a modest gift, often a book.

"We try to do something every day related to the principle of that day," explains Do Mi. "On collective work and responsibility day, we do a family project like bringing in all the wood for the winter, or shelving the new books. "My favorite day is the second to last one, which is devoted to creativity. We make presents for each other. I always vow to make something in October and end up making it on the day itself, but we all try to be thoughtful. One year I learned a song and sang it to Trish as my present."

In an effort to add a magical element to their Kwanzaa celebration that would "make it important and competitive with Christmas," the two women came up with a wonderful idea for the last night of the holiday.

"On the last night of Kwanzaa (also New Year's Eve), Alex takes an African doll named Osa, puts on her African clothes, and leaves her on the Kwanzaa table," says Do Mi. "In her lap is a traditional trading bead and a note written by Alex about something that makes her proud to be African-American. One year she wrote, 'I'm glad to be African-American because Harriet Tubman was and I like her.' The idea is that during the night, Osa goes to Africa and trades the bead for a present."

In the morning, the bead is gone and Alex finds a present from Africa on the table. One year, it was a drum, another year a push toy made for children in Zimbabwe.

It's hard to find a family that takes Kwanzaa more seriously than the Ruffs of Dublin, Ohio. The family's Kwanzaa decorations remain on the dining-room buffet year round, along with a bowl that is always filled with fruit, even though the candles are lit only during the holiday week.

"To me, Kwanzaa runs a close second to my religious beliefs," says Bonnie Cloyd-Ruff, an engineer with Lucent Technologies. "As African-Americans, we understand the importance of banding together as a family and as a community. We live these beliefs all year, but that week is a time to celebrate our ancestral history."

The family of four has celebrated the holiday for more than a decade, and is famous for its annual Kwanzaa party on New Year's Eve. On that night, as many as thirty families come to the Ruffs' house, each bringing food to share and an inexpensive gift to toss in the children's grab bag.

"We start the evening by respecting our elders with a libation," says Bonnie. "We use a wooden goblet from Africa and pour water on African violets. Everyone then takes a drink of water from a paper cup. Then each adult shares a story about how they got through a difficult time that year, or what they did to reinforce the Kwanzaa principles with their family. Some read poems they've written, others pray."

Then it's time for some history games. In one, the names of famous Africans are pinned on various guests' backs, and they ask questions of others until they guess what their own identity is. Later, after an enormous feast, the children are divided into groups by age and given half an hour to prepare a skit or other presentation about some aspect of Kwanzaa.

To reinforce the ideals of Kwanzaa, Bonnie and her husband, William, direct their children, Jessica and Matthew, now twelve and eight, to prepare a bundle of gifts for a child who isn't familiar with the holiday. Each child is given twenty-five dollars and has to come up with a thoughtful gift to illustrate each of the seven principles. The family usually find the children from names provided at church: they are often from inner-city families, and the Ruffs deliver their Kwanzaa presents in person.

But the Ruffs' Kwanzaa observance doesn't end there. Every year, in June or July, all the families who came to the Kwanzaa party are invited for a barbecue in the park to reaffirm the holiday's principles. There are games for the children, who have to scramble up trees searching for papers listing the principles. And each adult is given a chance to assess how well they have observed the precepts so far.

Five

★ ★ ★ ★

FAMILY FESTIVITIES AND CEREMONIES

A man becomes the song he sings.
—Irish proverb

Most people in this country celebrate a handful of major holidays, but what really sets one family apart from another is how they commemorate more personal occasions. What does it take at your house to set the table with the family silver? To light a candle? To load the whole family into the car for a dinner out?

Family festivities offer vivid proof of what matters to its members. Sports-minded families tend to have detailed rituals for cheering on their favorite professional teams or celebrating a child's Little League home run. Some families make a huge deal out of birthdays, while others invest the first day of school with pomp and ceremony.

Mary Routh celebrates the anniversaries of her four kids' baptism days: the child gets a gift, usually a book, a special candle is lit, and the family dances and sings together. "We sing a song called 'The Father Will

Dance.' It's about how happy God is with us. Like many of our traditions, this one is about bringing our faith into our home."

The festivities detailed below may give you some new ideas about what should be celebrated at your house, and how.

Birthdays

Tradition plays a big role in circus life, so it isn't surprising that circus clowns have their own special ritual for celebrating birthdays: trying to pick a moment when it's least expected, the clowns throw a pie in the birthday person's face. Veteran clowns are exempt, but younger clowns, and even other new performers, will get "pied." Many families have their own singular rituals for birthdays, whether they're designed to be silly or solemnly hail someone's achievements. The purpose is always the same: to celebrate not just a birth but a life, to let someone know that the simple fact of their existence brings joy.

To a child, this is roughly a synonym for bliss. What could possibly be better than a day when everybody else in the family has to be nice to you and give you presents? And all the talk is about how big and impressive a specimen you are. In childhood, almost every year feels like a major milestone, bringing guarantees that you can play with cooler toys, swim in the big pool, go to kindergarten, ride a bike, become a Girl Scout instead of a Brownie.

In my family, birthdays weren't a huge deal. I can hardly blame my mother, considering that all three of her girls had birthdays within one week in March. Basically, we each got to dictate the dinner menu and Mother painted us a birthday card. Instead of presents, we got a modest amount of cash, usually ten dollars, which was never adjusted for inflation. Many families do much the same thing: they let the child pick his or her dinner, however disastrous nutritionally, and they throw in some modest presents.

Those rituals are lovely, but the possibilities for feting a birthday child are endless. Birthdays are measures of growth and change, and some of the most meaningful rituals are quite simple. Like the practice in some families of greeting the child as a changed being: "Hello, four-year-old!" they'll say first thing in the morning. The Cohn family of Davie, Fla., takes this a step further, and will say at bedtime the night before, "Good-bye, three-year-old!" Then, when the child wakes up the next day, they greet him or her as a brand-new creature of four. They'll pretend they don't recognize this big child, so great is the change, as though the trans-formation were of fairy-tale proportions.

One creative way to recognize change is the practice of Gertrud Mueller Nelson, mother of three and a writer whose books include *To Dance with God: Family Ritual and Community Celebration*. Gertrud says that when her kids were growing up, each one received two envelopes on his or her birthday: one was marked "New Privilege" and the other, "New Responsibility." She explains that a child turning six might have her bed-time pushed later by half an hour, but she had to start feeding the dog every evening. Rather than groaning at their new duties, she says her kids (at least until adolescence) were as honored to get the responsibilities as they were to receive new privileges. "It gave them a sense of importance, and made them feel grown up."

If you're ready for a truly radical idea in birthdays, you might follow the lead of the Hassells of Winterport, Maine. In this family of five, the birthday person, whether adult or child, *gives* a present to every other member of the family.

Now, there is one advantage to this system any kid would figure out in a heartbeat. Each Hassell can look forward to getting birthday presents four times a year.

But that isn't why Mary Bliss Hassell thought up this idea when her first child was too young to care. "I grew up as the oldest of seven kids, and I remember being irrationally resentful of the attention my mother was giving to whatever sibling had a birthday," Mary explains. "I noticed that almost everybody was grumpy on birthdays, and I wanted to find a way to make everybody happy instead. I wanted birthdays in my family to be celebrations of the whole family and not just one person."

The Hassells' system runs contrary to the whole American obsession with celebrity and singling out individuals. Most of the time, it seems, people are either made to feel like stars or nobodies in this culture, and that can happen in families just as it does in corporations and on the sets of Hollywood movies. This unusual ritual succeeds in making each birthday special for every member of the family, making anticipation something that is shared, not monopolized. It doesn't so much focus attention *away* from the birthday person as make what he or she gives to other people more important than what that person gets. "I wanted my children to feel that more attention would be paid to them as givers than receivers," says Mary.

At the same time, there is a valuable one-on-one component to this birthday ritual: the pre-birthday planning usually requires a lot of private consultation between one of the parents and the birthday child. "We talk a lot about what to get each person, then we shop for the gifts or make them, and wrap them together," says Mary. Before the kids got money from allowances and jobs, money was provided by their parents to buy gifts, which have never been lavish.

You might wonder whether the Hassell children ever object to this arrangement. "Like most traditions," says Mary, "if you start when your kids are small, they don't know the difference. It was straightforward and easy. We started when the youngest was barely old enough to know what a birthday was."

And lest you think these kids are deprived, Mary notes that they do get some birthday gifts from their grandparents, and from time to time they have hosted traditional parties, to which their friends bring gifts. But the children seem actually to look forward to handing out gifts on their birthdays, a ritual that happens each year after a celebratory dinner (the birthday person does choose the food) and cake, and the obligatory chorus of "Happy Birthday."

The Reichman family of New Rochelle, N.Y., observes birthdays in the traditional way, giving gifts only to the birthday child. But their parties are unusually creative and lavish, and they include a practice that makes the nonbirthday sibling feel central to the celebration.

Whenever Alex or Kayleigh has a birthday, the other sibling is the designated "host" for the party, given such responsibilities as greeting guests, taking coats, helping to set things up. "They seem to enjoy doing this for each other," says their mother, Francine.

Birthday parties are planned around a theme, which is carried out in invitations, food, decorations, activities, and party favors. For example, the "Round-the-World Party" featured invitations that looked like passports, and the cake for the "Medieval Party" was an ice-cream castle with plastic knights, a dragon, and a Hershey-bar drawbridge.

Francine makes a big "photo board" related to the theme, picturing the sour couple from Grant Wood's famous painting for a party with a farm motif. Holes are cut where the faces are, so that kids attending the party can stick their own faces in and have a Polaroid taken. Francine started this activity as an "icebreaker" to relax her young guests, but it quickly became an anticipated highlight of Reichman birthday parties. For a "Space Party," the two characters on the photo board were an astronaut and an alien, while the medieval party featured a knight and a dragon.

Both children are home-schooled, and they research their party themes as part of their regular coursework, sometimes for weeks. Lest you dismiss the notion as frivolous, consider this: when Alex turned eight recently, the theme of the party was "Ancient Lands," which called for a thorough study of ancient Egypt, Greece, and Rome. Alex wrote the name of each guest in hieroglyphs on the back of the invitations. He also helped create such games as "Guess That God": drawings of various ancient gods and goddesses were mounted on the wall, with a brief description, and the guests were given time to study them. Then they had to pull a god's name from a bowl and perform a version of charades, getting the other guests to guess which god they represented.

"We had a ball, and my kids learned so much about this era that we are planning a special trip to the Metropolitan Museum of Art in New York to look at their ancient arts exhibits," says Francine.

The Meisenheimer boys of Suisun City, Calif., are also home-schooled, and the kids get to pick a special subject to study for their birthdays, says their mother, Kim.

"During their birthday week, they don't have to study any of their usual subjects and we arrange our schedules so that this is when they advance to a new grade. The birthday person picks an area to study that week and designs projects related to the topic. One time it was sharks. My son read a lot about sharks, and we took him to the beach and to an aquarium." Also, one of the days is reserved for doing something special with both sets of grandparents, who live nearby. There is only one gift, which is linked to the study topic.

Kim and her husband also observe their birthdays, which are a few days apart, by each studying a subject that interests them. Their sons cook them dinner for the whole week.

There are lots of ways to decorate for birthdays. Sue Straw of Plano, Tex., ties a helium balloon to the chair of the birthday boy or girl before supper, while the Franco girls in Florida wake up with a bunch of balloons tied to the foot of their beds.

The daughters of Ron Greenberg wake up on their birthdays to find a "balloon tunnel" that leads all the way down the stairs: at the bottom is their first gift of the day. Ron uses about fifty helium balloons, tying them with ribbons several feet long to the banisters on either side of the stairs. Then the balloons are intertwined in the middle, leaving just enough room for the children—and even adults—to slide down the stairs on their backsides. The ribbons have crepe-paper streamers woven through them, to close the gap between the walls and the balloons. Ron's girls love these tunnels, and their friends always beg to come over on their birthdays and play in them.

Debbie Midcalf, a mother of three in Palm Desert, Calif., uses balloons for counting down as well as for decoration. It started when her oldest, now seven, was just a toddler and couldn't grasp the concept of how many days until her birthday. "We string them over the dining-room table, up to a week's worth of balloons," says Debbie. "All the balloons are the same color except the last one, the actual birthday balloon. Every day, we pop one balloon and count off a day."

At the home of Julie Stockler, a divorced mother of two living in Upper Makefield, Pa., it's the "birthday fairy" who decorates. "In the middle of the night, I go in and totally decorate their rooms," says Julie, whose daughters are seven and eleven. "There are balloons, sparkles, crepe paper, and all that stuff. Not only that, but the birthday fairy leaves a trail of glitter out the door of their rooms, all through the house, and down the driveway."

If it turns out that the birthday girl is spending that night at her father's house, another night is chosen. "What has always perplexed me is

that the kids never seemed to wonder why the birthday fairy doesn't go to anyone else's house," marvels Julie.

Kathleen Metcalf says her birthday ritual was inspired by a Navajo Indian tradition called a Blessingway. It refers to a ceremony of songs and prayers performed to ensure a long and healthy life, and particular forms of the ritual are used to bless everything from a house to a newborn child.

On Metcalf birthdays, guests are asked to bring small symbolic gifts, meant to celebrate what the child has become in the year just past. "Each family member makes or buys something that celebrates a character trait they admire in the birthday child, or a special event or accomplishment of that year," explains Kathleen, a graphic artist in Park City, Utah. "When my son learned to read, I made him a tiny book with a picture of his favorite book character on it. My mother made a tiny hat with flowers for my teenage daughter, complimenting her on her unique style."

Each of these small tokens is wrapped, and when the birthday child opens it, the giver explains the gift's meaning. A little diary is kept for each child, listing the items and explaining their significance each year. For example, Kathleen reads an entry from her youngest child's birthday diary, her older sister's explanation of a little teddy bear on skis: "Rachel, I gave you the bear because you are doing so well skiing in your first year. And also for bear hugs."

The children attach these gifts to special birthday wreaths hanging in their rooms. Each of the wreaths, which are bought at craft stores, is different, either circular or heart-shaped, and rather plain before the ornaments are added. Kathleen's oldest girl, now seventeen, has a wreath so densely packed with colorful figures and tokens that she can look at it and virtually tell the story of her life.

When the kids were all young, the wreath tokens were the only gifts they received. "When they had parties at an early age, it was simple to ask their friends' parents to only give gifts for the wreaths, but that ended when they were old enough to invite their own guests," says Kathleen. "The wreaths are still the centerpiece of our family birthday celebrations, though. The kids usually get one regular gift, something nice they can really use, like a sleeping bag.

"I wanted birthdays to feel like a celebration of the child's life for that year and not be completely focused on getting presents," says Kathleen. "I think this ritual has accomplished that end."

Two concepts that are immensely popular with some families are "star birthdays" and "half-birthdays." Patrice Kyger, a divorced mother of three in Free Union, Va., celebrates both.

A star birthday is the once-in-a-lifetime occasion when a person's age matches the day of his or her birth: I was born on March 15, so my star birthday would have been when I turned fifteen (Had I known . . .). Some families plan extra-special birthday events on star birthdays, like the Kygers, who heard about the concept from a former baby-sitter.

"We take one of those sparkly tinsel garlands you see on Christmas trees and we wind it around pictures on the wall, furniture, lamps, whatever. We also get candles in the shape of stars and we sprinkle stars all over the cake. We talk about how we are all stars, but this is your star birthday and this is how you fit within the constellation of our family."

The oldest Kyger daughter had her star birthday at six, the middle child at five, and the youngest at four.

Patrice is also a big believer in half-birthdays, which she celebrates with all her kids. "There aren't any presents or games and we don't make a huge fuss, but I think young children change so enormously over the course of six months and it's important to recognize that change and development. What I do is bake a whole cake, but cut it in half (the rest is frozen for later), and put one candle on top. I let them pick the dinner and we all sing 'Happy Half-Birthday to You.' "

The response of her children has far exceeded Patrice's expectations. "I started it about six years ago, and I've seen this little thing produce so much joy," she says. "They feel like, 'Wow, Mom has really noticed how much I've changed,' and that is such a powerful message. Their friends are all envious."

There is power indeed in birthdays, and sometimes it is the power to hurt. Like other days of ritual significance, birthdays create high expectations, and sometimes those expectations aren't met. Also, birthdays prompt a certain amount of soul-searching and sometimes remind people of things that are missing in their lives.

Lucy Steinitz, former director of Jewish Family Services of Maryland, and her husband adopted an infant girl and boy from Guatemala. The children know nothing about their natal families, nor do their adoptive parents.

"From about the age of seven and very clearly when she turned eight, my daughter began getting increasingly sad as her birthday approached," explains Lucy. "It was clear that the timing made her wonder about her biological mother." So Lucy and her husband, Bernd Kiekebusch, dreamed up a birthday ritual to comfort Elsita.

"We told her we didn't know her mother but that we were sure that on that day, she was also thinking of Elsita. I said, 'I'm sure that your mother is looking up at the stars and thinking about you, so on the night of your birthday, why don't you go outside or look out the window and pick a star? She is probably talking to you through a star, so you talk to her through a star, too, and if you do it passionately, you are sure to communicate.' "

Elsita chose her star and said what she had to say to her mother, and she has followed this ritual on every birthday since. "It has made a big difference," says Lucy.

OTHER IDEAS

★ In the Muir household in La Mesa, Calif., anybody over three has to figure out a series of clues in a treasure hunt to find their birthday present. Before Betsy Muir's oldest could read, she would use picture clues: a picture of a refrigerator led the toddler to the fridge, which she opened (with help) to find another clue on the bottom of her juice cup. This was a picture of her toy box, the hiding place for her birthday gift. Betsy makes it much harder on her husband, who has to work his way through a dozen clues, some of which require him to perform embarrassing stunts in public. "I once made him sing 'I'm a little teapot' in a music store to get the next clue," says Betsy. "He did it, hand movements and all!"

★ Another family designates the birthday child as "boss of the family." This means some of the usual stuff, like dictating the dinner menu and the day's activities. But the kids can even do things like send Mom and Dad to bed early, a prerogative they exercise annually and gleefully.

★ The Denson family of Winnetka, Ill., has a special "jumping hug" used only on birthdays. "It's kind of a collision," says Stephanie Denson, mother of two. "You start a few feet back and then you jump up just before you give the person a hug. It adds exuberance."

★ The Pompis of Pittsfield, Mass., believe in starting the birthday celebration at breakfast, borrowing a ritual started by Kelly Pompi's mother. No matter what the birthday person is eating, whether pancakes, eggs, or even cold cereal, the meal must be dressed up a bit, usually with whipped cream, sprinkles, and a candle. Everybody sings "Happy Birthday" and the honored one can open a single gift, with the rest saved for dinner.

★ Sherry Chaney has always given her two stepdaughters a big "birthday box," and her own little girl will start getting one soon. All year long, she gathers small items she knows will be appreciated, including nail polish, socks, stationery, and T-shirts, and puts them in a large decorated box. Because Sherry shops at post-Christmas sales and dimestore clearances, she's able to amass a very impressive array of loot for twenty-five dollars or less. The girls also get one big gift, such as Rollerblades or a bicycle, but "sometimes the small gifts are the most appreciated and loved," marvels Sherry.

★ A family that calls it a "golden birthday" instead of a star birthday—when the age of the person matches the birth date—celebrates by giving the child an equivalent number of gifts. So, turning ten on the tenth day of a given month would bring ten presents (but modest ones).

★ Barbara Franco of Florida, who ties balloons to her daughters' beds, performs another birthday ritual, one that takes place a month before the actual natal date. "The birthday girl and I clean out her room," says Barbara. "We pick out toys and clothes to pass down to her sisters (unless she is the youngest) and pack things up in boxes for poor children. All this helps make room for the new things she'll receive." Not to mention adding to the anticipation and helping each child think of others' needs.

Adoption Days

I know from my own childhood that adopted children don't all react the same way to the fact of their adoption. My adopted brother had only a passing curiosity about his biological parents, while my adopted sister was obsessed for years with finding out about hers. My parents told her they could provide her with almost no information, but I don't think she believed them.

I think it's often hard for adopted kids to grow up amid nonadopted ones, especially if the biological children do better in school, or have more in common with their parents. It's probably pure fantasy on my part, but I sometimes think that if my parents had been able to celebrate Debbie's adoption in some way, held a yearly ritual that told what little they knew of her roots, and singled her out for special praise, perhaps it wouldn't have been quite such a tough issue in our family. Perhaps then she would have felt truly chosen, which is indeed how my parents felt about her.

In any case, more and more families with adopted children are creating such rituals, mostly celebrated on the day the child arrived, often referred to as "Arrival Day," though one family I know calls it "Gotcha Day."

At the Hoddinott household in Columbia, Conn., two of the three children are adopted, both from Korea. The family doesn't want to overemphasize adoption festivities and make their biological daughter feel slighted, but they celebrate what they call "Homecoming Day" on the day each child arrived in this country.

"To us, it's a way to keep the door open, to allow them to ask questions and hear their stories over and over," says Julie Hoddinott. "It's obvious they're adopted because they don't look like us, and it's important to acknowledge their histories."

When the day arrives, Julie doesn't make a big fuss in advance, but quietly announces, "Let's have some cake tonight, because it's Danny's (or Jimmy's) Homecoming Day." No presents are exchanged and no special guests come beyond the immediate family. The only special part of the meal is the dessert, "which is enjoyed by everybody," says Julie.

What she has found is what many adoptive parents discover: her children's interest in the subject waxes and wanes, and the discussion of their background can be easily lengthened or shortened to suit their needs. Ideally, such rituals will let them know that the topic isn't taboo at any time of the year: they can feel free to ask questions as they arise.

"My oldest son, now ten, has started to get much more interested lately, while the younger, at four, doesn't care so much. The older one wants to see an adoption book we filled in with details like the name of the town where he was born," says Julie. "Lately, he's been wanting to watch his homecoming video, which is all about the day he arrived, aged five-and-a-half months."

★   ★   ★

A Minnesota couple adopted two Romanian orphans in 1991, and has taken pains to expose them to the culture of their native land. Among other things, the two children attend a local Romanian cultural festival every year.

The family also observes a minor celebration it calls "Family Day" to honor the adoptions and celebrate the family as a whole. The adoption stories are retold, but this occasion also means acknowledging a family member this boy and girl will never know: the couple's biological daughter, who committed suicide when she was seventeen years old.

After dinner on this day, the family sings "Happy Family Day to Us" and lights five candles on a pie (which the kids prefer to cake), saying each person's name as the candles are lit, including that of the deceased daughter. The date for the celebration is the last full day the girl was alive: the twenty-third of February. The two adopted children were born on the twenty-third of May and December, and were adopted in February.

Some people may feel uncomfortable with this ritual, or worry it sends the children a message that they are meant to replace the dead girl, make up for her tragedy. But I believe it to be a healthy and thoughtful practice that will help bond this family together and show the kids that the children in it are treasured forever.

"The children haven't asked much about her so far," says the mother. But eventually they will. And this ritual will give them permission to ask questions, letting them know that the subject isn't forbidden. It will then serve as a forum in which to comfortably share her history. "I can see the ritual changing in other ways as the kids get older. I'd like to add a part where everybody will say their thoughts about what it means to be in this family."

Clare Bonfanti Braham has four children, three of them grown up and a fourth who was adopted from Korea at the age of six. Clare decided to celebrate her adopted daughter's "Arrival Day," but didn't immediately get the reaction she expected.

"Initially, my daughter wanted no part of this, and when we tried to do things like play the video of her getting off the plane, she said in her then-limited English, 'I not go back.' It took her time to realize we could celebrate this. Now, she gets a kick out of it."

The festivities usually include dinner at a Korean or Japanese restaurant, a viewing of the video, and a reading of the journal Clare kept about the preparations for her arrival. "We saved everything she wore or had with her, including what she was clutching in her hands. We look at all of that."

The lucky adopted children of Leslie Bligh get to celebrate not just their birthdays, but also their "Placement Days," the day they arrived at the Blighs' home, and their "Adoption Days," when the adoptions were legal and final.

"Both days are a lot like their birthdays, but they don't get any presents," explains Leslie. "We retell the story of how we got them and how glad we were to get them and what they were like as babies, and why they were put up for adoption." As with birthdays, each child gets to pick their dinner and dessert, and the honored child eats his food from a red plate that is reserved for big occasions. Upon it are inscribed the words: "You Are Special." There is a blackboard in the dining room, and the appropriate message is written on it, either "Happy Adoption Anniversary" or "Happy Placement Day." For either one, the family sings "Happy Anniversary to Us."

These celebrations became even more cherished when Leslie and her husband got divorced. The two share custody equally, but Leslie worries that the split may have been harder on the kids because they are adopted.

"The kids were just so torn up and the last thing I wanted was for them to think this was their fault, so the celebration of their adoption was even more important. I was determined to show them that they are still very, very much wanted and loved."

The Tarpleys of Nashville, Tenn., have six children between nine and twenty-two, and one of them, Matthew, is adopted. He was brought to this country from Guatemala as an infant by Sara, her husband, and their youngest daughter, then just over a year old. Every year on the anniversary of Matthew's arrival, Sara hangs a paper airplane mobile—his mode of transportation on that day—from the chandelier in the dining room.

"Since most children adopted from abroad come by airplane, a lot of adoptive families refer to it as 'Airplane Day,' " explains Sara. "Our mobile was just a simple one that was part of a craft activity in a children's magazine." To celebrate, she serves a special treat, often cupcakes with candles on them.

In addition, the family celebrates Guatemalan Independence Day almost every year, serving Guatemalan rice with black beans, guacamole, and other ethnic specialties. "We feel it's important because his parentage is unknown," says Sara. "The only thing we can share with him is his national heritage, so we really stress that."

School Days

The first day of school was something I actually looked forward to most years. Buying new clothes and filling a backpack with pristine notebooks were happy rituals for me.

Naturally, there are many children who feel otherwise. But school is a big part of any kid's life, and there are all sorts of ways parents can build rituals into its rhythms. Here are rituals for the first and last days of school, for celebrating good grades and other triumphs, and even for playing hooky.

Celebrating First and Last Days

A few years ago, Nancy and Alan Giehl's firstborn child was about to head off to kindergarten, and they wanted to mark the moment in a memorable way.

"We wanted to make it a big deal, partly to transmit our values about education and learning," explains Nancy, the mother of three in Boulder, Colo. "We decided to start a tradition of a back-to-school dinner the night before, with favorite foods and a simple gift." Just eating in the dining room is a big deal for the Giehls, so "whenever we do, we call it a feast," says Nancy.

Nancy and Alan start by discussing the summer and asking what the kids had liked best. Then they talk about "going to school and how important school is and how we expect the kids to act," says Nancy. "We also try to talk about how much fun learning is and what a good time they'll have." After dessert, which is also a rarity, everyone adjourns to the family room, where gifts are given.

When Julie, the oldest, was starting kindergarten, her parents gave her a child's dictionary. "I was amazed by how much she used it," says Nancy Giehl. "She loved it so much, she took it in for show-and-tell." So Julie's younger brother and sister, the twins, wouldn't feel left out, they were each given a bulletin board. The following year, when the twins started kindergarten, they were each given a special box to keep their markers in, and Julie, headed for first grade, got a map of the United States.

"It may sound silly," says Nancy, "but this is one of my favorite family traditions. It's relaxing, the kids look forward to it, and it isn't wrapped up in a lot of holiday hype."

After a few years of celebrating the start of the school year, Nancy decided the family should also hold one of its feasts on the last day.

The first time this event was celebrated, Nancy made a poster with each kid's name on it and a list of the year's chief accomplishments. After second grade, Julie was described as a "reader, writer, pianist," among other things. During dinner, the Giehls discussed the results of a "family survey" the previous week about what activities various family members wanted to pursue in the summer. "We ranked things and scheduled the top ones right away, like a visit to a local water park," says Nancy.

After the meal, each child was given a letter Nancy had written about the year's highlights and her pride in their hard work. "We don't want to reward them with money every time, but since we had just held a garage sale we also put ten dollars in each envelope," says Nancy. Each child was photographed standing in front of his or her poster, holding the envelope.

In many families, particular care is taken in picking out what to wear on the first day of school each year, and some families have a ritual of taking pictures as the kids head out on that day.

"Every year I get a picture of them wearing their new outfits and standing in front of the door to the house," says Dawn Hale, mother of three in Clinton, N.J. "We always cut flowers from the garden for them

to take to their new teachers. And every year, I videotape them getting on the bus and getting off later in
the day."

The parents of Lucy Steinitz were German, and
she grew up with their tradition of observing the first
time a child goes off to school.

"They give you a huge paper cone stuffed with candy and school supplies," says Lucy. Again, the motive is clear: to add some hoopla, create a
sense of excitement about this major rite of passage, and hint that the
work of school will be accompanied by something sweet.

Lucy and her husband, who is also German, passed on this ritual to
both their children, adopted as infants from Guatemala. "We made the
cones of oak tag, decorated with old wrapping paper," says Lucy. "They
were filled with school supplies like chalk and crayons, a reading book,
and little treats."

The German custom is to give children such cones only once, and
both Lucy and her husband remember getting one on the first day of first
grade. But the Steinitz children received the cones twice, for kindergarten
and first grade. Because mornings are so rushed, they were presented the
night before school started.

Francine Reichman of New Rochelle, N.Y., who puts on the elabo-
rately themed birthday parties, doesn't want her kids, who are educated at
home, to feel deprived when their friends and neighbors head back to
school. So when the regular school year starts, they go to a special "Let's
Not Go Back to School Party."

The Reichmans are part of a local home-schooling group that meets
socially a few times a month, and the whole crew heads to the beach for
this annual event. "We put on a big picnic at the time most kids are going
back to school and we all celebrate how great it is we can be at the beach
while the other kids are locked up in school," says Francine. "The kids
love it."

Both the first and last day of school are celebrated in the Herold
household in Champaign, Ill.

"It goes back to when my oldest son started going to kindergarten in the mornings," explains Minta, a mother of three. "I was working full-time and I couldn't make a fuss about this important step or take him to school, so I decided to take a long lunch hour and take him out to lunch. I wanted to find out what he thought of kindergarten."

So Minta took her son to a diner, where he was allowed to order any-thing he wanted. He discussed his impressions of school so far, and sug-gested that the two of them repeat the exercise on the last day of school. When that big event came around, the discussion focused on "how much he learned that year," says his mother.

Now that her first son is in the sixth grade, the ritual has expanded to include Minta's second son, who is eight. Soon her daughter will start attending kindergarten and these diner lunches will include her. Perhaps she'll order big milk shakes like her brothers always do.

"At the beginning of the year, we talk about their expectations. And at the end, the boys say what they thought of their teachers, what was the best part of school, and what was the worst. It makes them stop and think about the past year," says Minta. "Also," she adds, "we talk about what our dreams are for the future, mine included."

The Fitches of Columbus, Ohio, always make a big deal of the last day of school. Their oldest child, Corey, now seventeen, is allowed to decide every year not only what he wants to eat, but where he wants to eat it.

The ritual began when he was nine and finishing fourth grade. Corey and his parents, Robb and Sally, took a long walk and wound up eating carryout Chinese food on the steps of his elementary school—at mid-night. Why? "It just felt wild and crazy, and he loves noodles," says his mother. "We all sat there and talked about the school year. It was so much fun, he wanted to do it every year."

Over the years, Corey's tastes have changed. One year, he wanted to eat on the floor in a Japanese steakhouse. Then there were several years when the family lived among a community of Yupik Indians in Alaska, and there were no restaurants at which to celebrate. During one of those years, the Fitches took a canoe trip with their son on the last day of school, and then enjoyed a picnic dinner together. Lately, Corey has helped pay for the dinner: an elegant local restaurant gives every honor-roll student a coupon for 50 percent off on a family dinner, so the Fitches always celebrate the last day there.

Corey's younger brothers, twins, are about to start kindergarten, and the ritual will extend to them.

In a number of other families, traditions for the last day of school revolve around a particular kind of food. One mother always makes a giant chocolate-chip cookie for her kids and writes something on it in frosting, such as "We love our school but we love our summer too."

Then there is the watermelon ritual of Jamey Hecht of Freeport, N.Y. Now in his late twenties, Jamey used to end his school year with a huge watermelon fight in the backyard involving seven or eight close friends.

"This was a big, messy, hilarious fight that lasted all afternoon," says Jamey's mother, Marilyn Hecht. "I have no idea what inspired it, but one year my son just asked to do it. I have strong feelings that food should never be used in frivolous ways, but when the boys came and asked my permission, we discussed the ethics of wasting food. Their argument was that watermelon didn't have a lot of nutritional value, and I couldn't dispute that."

The fights didn't cause any permanent harm to anyone or anything, and they may have something to do with the fact that all ten boys have remained friends into their early thirties.

Patrice Kyger always takes her children out for dinner on the last day of school and tells them how proud she is of them. But she also believes in creating rituals of thankfulness, so when her kids graduate from elementary school, which runs through fifth grade, they are given money to buy books for the school's library.

"My kids are big library users, so this made sense to me," she says. Only her oldest child has so far completed this particular rite of passage. "I gave my daughter twenty dollars for this purpose and she chose books that were real favorites of hers, including *Little Women*," says Patrice. "The librarian was absolutely flabbergasted. It was great."

Rewarding Good Work

Plenty of families reward good grades and punish bad ones, hoping to elicit their children's best efforts even if it takes outright bribery or threats. One family I know pays a dollar for each A, while the kids have to pay their parents a dollar for every C. Of course, many parents will tell you that such a system makes little difference: how kids perform in school is the result of many complicated influences and factors generally impervious to such attempts.

Nonetheless, reinforcing good behavior is one of the primary tenets of modern child-rearing, and many families have devised thoughtful rituals to honor their children's school performance.

The Suttons of Casper, Wyo., take their kids out for a "Good Grades Dinner" four times a year when report cards are issued.

"They are generally straight A students, but we would celebrate even if they didn't get all As as long as they continue working hard," explains Mary Sutton, the mother of three between five and fifteen. "We believe in celebrating the effort."

What Mary likes best about the meals is that she and her husband get truly caught up on what is happening to their children at school. "There are no distractions like there are at home, and you're sitting there waiting for the food, so they really end up sharing information about how the year is going," says Mary. "A sit-down dinner in a nice restaurant is an event for us, and it does feel like a celebration."

Barbara Franco, the mother of three girls in Fort Lauderdale, Fla., also celebrates report-card day. She takes the children to Dairy Queen.

"I don't present it as a reward for good grades. I just liked the idea of Report Card Day Ice Cream as a way to be sure we do something special and out of the ordinary at least every few months."

Barbara leaves rewarding high grades to Blockbuster Video, which gives a free rental to any child with a B average or better. She just makes sure the family takes advantage of the bargain.

★   ★   ★

In Chicago, Karen Priebe created a system of stickers that reward good behavior of all kinds, including school performance.

"My son Alex is really smart, but sometimes he doesn't check his work. Even before he started school, I made a sticker chart for him on a bulletin board in the kitchen. He earns stickers for all sorts of things, like doing projects with his dad. But when he needed to be reminded about getting on top of schoolwork, we decided that he could also earn a sticker for every A-plus he brings home on tests."

Alex and his father decide together what the stickers will be good for and how many stickers each reward requires, something like the way frequent flyer miles work. For example, says his mother, "if he gets a certain number, they'll go to a movie together, or he'll get a toy he really wants."

Playing Hooky

Nerd though I was, I really would have loved it if my parents would have "kidnapped" me from school one day a year to do something I loved. I know of a woman who does exactly this with each of her kids: she quizzes one of them in advance to make sure there aren't any special events or tests on a particular day. The kids go off to school just like on any regular day, and about an hour later, after she's had coffee and a shower, this mom plucks one of them up and off they go. The child decides what to do with the rest of the day.

Barbara Franco, the Florida woman who takes her daughters to Dairy Queen on report-card days, looks at it this way: "Adults get to take an occasional personal day when they need it for mental health. Why shouldn't kids in school?"

Actually, only one of Barbara's daughters is in school so far, but she has found this ritual a very practical one. "I let her take one day off school each semester, and this way she doesn't have to 'play sick' if she's having a problem and is afraid to go to school," says Barbara. "She can stay home and talk about it and come up with ways to handle the situation." Or, if everything is going great at school, the girl might just decide to take off for the park or the beach and avoid the crowds, says her mother.

The bottom line: "My daughter loves school," says Barbara, "and I think it has a lot to do with feeling as if she's there by choice."

When Julie Stockler was growing up, she was allowed to play hooky one day a year and she loved it, so naturally, she has carried on the tradition with her own children.

"My mother and I did the same thing every year," says Julie. "We would get all dressed up and go to downtown Detroit to a department store. I'd pick out a new outfit and then we'd have lunch in the ladies' tearoom."

Of course that was the early '60s, and Julie's two kids, now seven and ten, have very different ideas of what makes a day special. "They don't want to get dressed up," she notes. "They each get to pick what to do on their day and it's usually going to the movies or skiing for the day."

UNCOMMON HOLIDAYS

There are a few meat-and-potatoes holidays that are pretty much unavoidable, but there are also dozens, perhaps hundreds, that are more like optional side dishes. Celebrating these minor holidays in distinctive ways adds spice to many a family's annual calendar, and tells a lot about what matters to them. "You are what you eat," as the saying goes. Similarly, let us add, you are what you celebrate.

Take Arbor Day, for example. How many people even know when it falls, let alone celebrate it annually?

Tarrant Figlio wouldn't miss it. Arbor Day and the planting of trees have become a motif in her life, an activity she turns to whenever she wants to commemorate anything of deep significance to herself or her family.

While in high school, Tarrant got some chance mail from the National Arbor Day Foundation, which offered to send her ten tiny trees in exchange for a modest donation (a program that continues today; see Resources, page 347). "I took them up on the offer and just started planting trees. My husband and I met during high school, and we started planting a tree every year on Arbor Day." When the couple got married, it made sense to celebrate by planting a special tree for that occasion, "in our wedding colors." The tree was a purple-leaf plum.

Later, Tarrant worked as a nanny and celebrated Arbor Day by planting a tiny tree with her young charges. She was pleased by how excited the kids were about "their" tree, helping to water it and monitor its growth: she still gets letters from one little boy detailing the tree's progress. When she began having children of her own, she continued celebrating Arbor Day,  as well as commemorating each of her two kids' births by planting a maple tree (a variety she chose "because they are sturdy and live a long time").

"On Arbor Day, we always plant a tree as a family. We don't have a real ceremony, but I tell the kids how special trees are and we talk about how birds nest and how paper is made from trees. They are sort of like mini-science lessons."

The children check frequently on the Arbor Day trees and their birthday trees, measuring them and counting branches in the fall when the growing season stops. Indeed, the Figlios have a special scrapbook for these trees, which the kids call a "baby book." In it are records of the trees' growth, as well as photographs of the children with "their" trees. Pictures of each Arbor Day tree, also called the "family tree," are taken several times over that first summer, and subsequently once a year.

For those still stumped on the date of Arbor Day: it varies from state to state, but about half of them observe it on the last Friday in April.

Nancy Dodge, the mother of five in Princeton, N.J., is a big believer in spontaneous ritual, which helps explain how the family came to celebrate Groundhog Day.

"I'm all for rituals that don't take a lot of advance preparation and revolve around child-fun meals," she says. The Dodges celebrate Groundhog Day because the family needs a holiday about then (February 2). "When the winter is looking endless and bleak, small, impromptu holidays like this give children something to look forward to," says Nancy. "It doesn't have to be wildly exciting for them to have fun."

So the family celebration this past year consisted of watching two rental movies in a row, *The Sandlot* ("to work up our baseball fervor after a long winter," says Nancy) and, not surprisingly, *Groundhog Day,* the Bill Murray comedy. Festive foods served included "chips and onion dip and homemade pizza," washed down with soft drinks. "And we talked about whether it can possibly make a difference whether the groundhog sees his shadow or not," says Nancy.

April Fools' Day is Monica Hall's favorite holiday of all. "I like to do something different every year, so my family never knows what to expect."

Monica, a mother of four living in Maryland, has one very important April Fools' rule: her fooling never involves lying, something she doesn't want her children to think is ever permissible. Beyond that, pretty much anything goes.

"One year, I got up in the middle of the night and set every clock at a different time," recalls Monica. "My husband hated it!" Another year, Monica and the kids all put their clothes on backward to see how long it would take their father to notice once he got home from work. ("It took him a while," she says.)

Her children's favorite April Fools' Day was the year of the backward dinner, when Monica made a meatloaf that looked like a cake, and followed it with a cake that looked like a meatloaf. The meatloaf, for example, was made in a round cake pan and "frosted" with mashed potatoes. The potatoes were colored blue and squirted out of a pastry bag, and the final touch was a candle on top.

Then, for dessert, Monica made a chocolate cake in the meatloaf pan and frosted it with white frosting that included coconut and marshmallows. She colored some vanilla pudding with red-orange food coloring, and put it into an empty ketchup bottle. "The kids thought it was a riot," says Monica. "I wish I had the camcorder filming when we cut into the 'cake.' They sure were fooled."

The Smith family of East Windsor, N.J., has no Asian roots whatsoever, but looks forward to Chinese New Year celebrations that get more elaborate every year.

Clare Smith, the mother of three, is interested in ethnic festivals of all sorts and has experimented with rituals of various countries as a learning experience for her kids. She helps them research particular customs and then try several of them at home. Somehow, Chinese New Year has really taken hold.

"One year we ordered Chinese food and taught the kids to use chopsticks and we kept adding on every year. We always have music and games and work at a related craft, and now we invite another family to celebrate. The kids look forward to it."

The holiday begins on the first full moon after January 21 and lasts for fifteen days: the Smiths usually keep up with it through newspaper stories, and pick a day during the period to celebrate that is convenient for them. Some of Clare's craft projects, including dragon streamers made of crepe paper, come from a book called *Hands Around the World: 365 Ways to Build Cultural Awareness and Global Respect* by Susan Milord. One year, Clare designed simple cone-shaped paper hats, which the family and its guests made and decorated with markers.

"It's a riot to see the kids eat with chopsticks and the novelty of it makes them try food they normally wouldn't try," says Clare. "By now, we have a whole box up in the attic of things we only bring out for Chinese New Year, like little Chinese teacups and lanterns and fans. I found a catalog that sells imported Oriental things, including twenty fans for four dollars. And I found a Chinese food store, where I bought fortune cookies and Chinese tea. I also picked up an audiotape there so we could have authentic music. I think it was actually Chinese rock-'n'-roll, but it sounds very exotic to us."

These holidays are celebrated by multitudes of people every year. But many inventive families make up their own holidays, choosing to celebrate events that might seem eccentric to others but matter very much to them. Or else they just dream up something fun, like the father who occasionally declares "Cabin Night" at his house: for the entire evening, all the lights (and the television) are turned off and the family reads, talks, and snacks by candlelight. Or the mother who helps her kids look up birthdays of famous people: one is selected each month and his or her accomplishments are celebrated with a modest bash on that day.

Made-up Holidays

At various times of the year when her three kids seem to really need a break, Karen Butman of Maryland will declare either a "Pajama Day" or "Movie Day."

Pajama days tend to fall on a day during vacation or on a weekend "when the weather is really awful. We never get dressed all day, unless my husband puts on jeans to run out for a pizza. We might do some cooking and we might not. We will probably watch lots of videos and eat plenty of popcorn."

Movie days are similar, and usually get declared on a hot summer day "when the kids are antsy." Karen will take her kids and their friends to the video store and then to the supermarket to load up on junk food. "We'll make the house all dark and put a blanket on the floor," says Karen. "The kids just love this, and many summers we've done it every couple of weeks."

Not surprisingly, many idiosyncratic family traditions center around food, and the eating of vast quantities of things not part of the USDA's pyramid.

For example, whenever the harvest season for a particular type of fruit starts in Virginia, Patrice Kyger and her three children celebrate by holding a dessert-only dinner. When the strawberries on local farms are ripe in May, the whole family goes on an outing to pick them and Patrice makes strawberry shortcake. On that glorious day, the kids get to eat as much shortcake as they can hold for dinner, and that is *all* they eat.

Over the summer, when the blueberries are ready, dinner is blueberry pie, and when the raspberries are ripe, it's time for a tart. In the fall comes apple-pie night.

The Taylors of Stratford, Conn., have a ritual called "Crazy Food Day." Debbie Gilbert Taylor, the mother of two sons, started this one year when the family had extra time together during Christmas vacation.

"I just got this idea to call it Crazy Food Day and mix up the meals," says Debbie. "We ate lunch for breakfast and breakfast for lunch. The kids just went wild for it and want to do it again and again. I think I'll wait for a snow day or another vacation day where we have nothing planned. That's the kind of day I call a 'gift day.' It's free and you can just follow your whims. We usually stay in our pajamas all day when that happens."

Many kids lobby their parents for a children's equivalent of Mother's Day and Father's Day. And in some families, they succeed.

The Hains of Maryland, for example, celebrate Kids' Day annually, on the third Saturday in July. "My older daughter, then five and a half, heard my husband and me plan a celebration for Father's Day and we had just celebrated Mother's Day," says Sherri Hain. "She wondered why there wasn't something similar for kids, so we decided to invent something for the very next month."

The two girls are given several options for special activities, and they also pick food for the day and each gets a modest gift. "The first time, we spent a family day at the pool and it was a rare event because my husband can't usually do that on Saturdays," says Sherri. "We just used it as an opportunity to talk about how important the kids are to us."

Patrice Kyger was hearing similar questions from her daughter at about the same age. "When I was growing up, the classic answer to that question was, 'Every day is Kids' Day, dear.' But I always considered that mean and untrue. What we decided to do was start celebrating Son's Day for my son, on the second Sunday in July, and Daughters' Day for my girls, on the second Sunday in August."

The Kyger kids get to choose a special activity on their days, as long as it is "local, inexpensive, and something the whole family can enjoy," says Patrice. Past selections have included a picnic and a miniature golf outing. There is also a time to discuss the specifics of these good relationships, helping the siblings to appreciate each other and not just be honored by their parents. "I talk to them about why they are special as daughters or why the boy is special as my son, but I also want them to think about what is neat about having a sister or brother."

Another common genesis for offbeat family holidays is that a mother, especially of small children, will suddenly notice that there are weeks and weeks of empty calendar space coming up before the next major holiday. She improvises a special holiday to fill the gap.

When Nancy Giehl finds a blank patch in her calendar, she declares a doll birthday. Her two daughters each have one of those elaborate American Girl dolls from the Pleasant Company dressed in clothes from a period in American history. When it comes time for a doll birthday, Nancy and the daughter whose doll is being feted bake a cake together, and then the doll gets a gift. (Think tiny tea sets.)

When the girls' brother, then five, got jealous of these occasions, Nancy came up with a birthday for his favorite stuffed animal, an aardvark named Arthur. The aardvark gets a cake and a present too, perhaps a toy car.

"What I like about this is that it creates a special one-on-one time with each child," says Nancy.

The Pompis of Pittsfield, Mass., chose another tactic for making life more festive: they celebrate all their pets' birthdays.

The family has seven cats and one dog. Every cat gets a can of tuna decorated with a candle, and the dog gets a meaty bone from the butcher with a candle. Singing is involved, and the birthday pet gets a modest gift. Five of the cats celebrate on their actual birthdays, but the other two are adopted, so the festivities are scheduled on the anniversary of the dates they were rescued—one from drowning in a lake, the other after being hit by a car.

"The dog gets the biggest party because he is the oldest," says Kelly Pompi. "When he turns fifteen later this year, my son and stepson want to invite the whole family over for a party. It sounds good to me. We'll use anything as an excuse to have everybody over."

And Kris Brakoniecki, a home-economics teacher in Rochester, N.Y., recently started a tradition with her two sons of a special "Oscar Dinner," on the night of the Academy Awards. She attempts to base the menu on the five movies up for best picture. The year *Apollo 13* was a contender, she managed to find some little novelty packets of freeze-dried food. In honor of *Il Postino*, an Italian movie, there was Italian bread, and in honor of *Babe*, the movie starring a pig, the main course was vegetarian lasagna.

SPORTS RITUALS

My husband wouldn't let me write this book without including sports rituals, because he thinks they are such an important part of the "us-versus-them" bond that helps keep families close. That certainly wasn't true in my family. The closest thing to a sports ritual in my childhood was that I usually got free tickets to the Cleveland Indians from a local newspaper for getting straight As. I would grudgingly agree to attend one game every summer with my father, if he would take me shopping for clothes downtown on that morning.

Nonetheless, I recognize that sports are deeply important to millions of American families, and I know firsthand how vital sports rituals are to the wonderful relationship my husband shares with his grown daughter. He was raised in upstate New York as a Cleveland Browns fan, and he passed his passion on to his daughter, Kate, starting at an early age.

They got to attend maybe one live game a year, but they had rituals for watching every televised game. They wore their Browns sweatshirts and hats, hung up a Browns windsock in the hall, and threw a football back and forth during pivotal plays. After major losses, they usually ate a big bowl of ice cream: during games, they were often too tense to consume anything heavier than popcorn.

Win or lose, the important thing was that they celebrated and suffered together, sharing highs and lows of tremendous emotional intensity, and adding to the already close bond between them. They still talk about major victories and key plays, sounding like old soldiers who have been in the trenches together and share the special knowledge of survivors. My husband's Italian heritage is several generations away and doesn't affect his emotions or habits anywhere near as much as being a Browns fan has.

When the owner cashed in and moved the Browns to Baltimore in the mid-1990s, Dick and his daughter mourned together. Like all the legions of betrayed Browns' fans, their anger was partly over the forced rupture in beloved rituals. The fact that my husband was dying to start indoctrinating our son into the Browns cult and now couldn't created a further loss. The pain is so great, as any sports fan knows, because such allegiances are as involuntary as love: one can't simply choose a team out of a hat and feel such devotion. My husband and stepdaughter are fans without a team, and they feel like citizens of a country that's been wiped off the map. Even when Cleveland gets a new team, they fear it won't feel the same.

Yes, the rituals of sports fans are rituals of love, but there is more to it than that. Superstition plays a huge role in being a sports fan, and many of the rituals related to watching and playing sports have to do with trying to propitiate the whimsical gods of sporting chance. In Cleveland, DeeAnn Pochedly's son insists on eating strawberries for breakfast every time he plays in a Bantam Little League game, because that's what he ate for breakfast the first time he hit a two-run triple. If there are no fresh berries in the house, he'll make do with strawberry jam, but he worries about its potency.

Within the actual playing of sports, of course, lie countless rituals: dancing in the end zone, the seventh-inning stretch, and on and on. One woman who coaches a baseball team of five-year-olds drags a helium tank to every game: beforehand, balloons in team colors are inflated and tied to the dugout roof. If the team wins, they all release the balloons into the sky. Should the team lose, the coach pops the balloons. Are these not brilliant metaphors for winning and losing?

Sports traditions also meet the definition for rite-of-passage rituals: people desperately need something to hang on to in a time of transition, that unsettling limbo where one is neither a winner nor a loser, but soon to emerge from a physical trial as one or the other. Having the rituals, acting out the superstitions, can make such pressures easier to bear, and leave families with vivid memories even if, God forbid, their team loses.

Rituals for Players

When Charlene Fischer's sons went to Myrtle Beach over spring break to compete in a baseball tournament, she had to wear her "lucky" gear for every game. This included a sweatshirt with the team's name on it, sold by the team back in Pennsylvania to raise money for the trip. Charlene also had to wear her little teddy bear pins in the team colors, one for each son. And there was a little angel pin she added at the last minute.

"I know we have a very talented team this year, but I feel I have to wear my sweatshirt and all my pins to bring us luck. It must be working: we're now seventeen to two."

What Charlene wears to the games is only part of the Fischer family's sports rituals: before her sons or her twin daughters leave the house for a baseball game, she goes through a checklist with them to make sure they're prepared. "I always ask if they have everything they need, and then I start with the most important thing, the glove, and work all the way down to the boys' jocks," says Charlene. To every question, the obligatory answer is, "Yes, *Mom*."

Finally, no matter whether her kids win or lose, Charlene remembers to tell them after every game, "You did a super job."

Minta Herald's baseball ritual will be all too familiar to any parent who ever embarrassed a child in public.

"My twelve-year-old says he hits better if I'm not around, that I make him nervous. So my primary baseball ritual is that when he is up to bat, I hide behind the bleachers until he's done hitting. I guess it works, because he has had two grand slam home runs in the last two games!"

The Heralds also have a ritual to celebrate those homers. "We always take the family to Dairy Queen for milk shakes," says Minta, who adds that her son also has a good-luck ritual before games. "He always ties the left shoe first."

It's not surprising that Kathleen Chesto, who has written often about religious rituals in family life, created a spiritual sports ritual for her own son.

"My son started running in the seventh grade, and I remembered reading a great passage in Isaiah (40:31) about running. You could recite this for inspiration before almost any kind of sporting event, but it fits perfectly with track meets."

> Those who wait for the Lord shall renew their
>   strength,
> They shall mount up with wings like eagles,
> They shall run and not be weary,
> They shall walk and not be faint.

The Chestos didn't have a formal ritual of huddling during which they'd say these lines before a race, but after reading it to her son at home on several occasions, Kathy would sometimes recite it to him before competitions. And then she found a T-shirt featuring the two middle lines from the passage alongside a picture of a runner in full stride.

"I bought it and tucked it into his Christmas stocking that year. It became his lucky shirt, something he had to wear in every race." And so the ritual continued, unspoken but deeply felt.

Rituals for Fans

When Jay Kriegel was a boy, the Dodgers were in Brooklyn, and every year his father would take him out of school for the first game of the season. At his fiftieth birthday party, his wife surprised him with a cake in the shape of Dodgers Stadium. Though the Dodgers are, sadly, long gone, Jay continues a version of the tradition. Every year, he takes his son out of school for the first Mets game at Shea Stadium. And Jay usually brings his dad.

Not that sports are neglected the rest of the year. Jay prides himself on getting good seats to see the New York Knicks, often taking his stepson or one of his nephews. "Hey, this is at the core of ritual for males," says Jay. "Watching a game together is what we do."

The Brown family of Auburn, Wash., are serious fans of the Seattle Mariners, and during baseball season the family of four can usually be found at the stadium at least once a month.

"We tend to schedule our games by the giveaways," explains Kathy Brown. "By now we've collected backpacks, T-shirts, bats, mitts, posters, pins, and baseball caps."

Kathy, her husband, and their two kids usually stop at a Subway sandwich shop on the way to the game and pick up sandwiches. They always bring peanuts, Cracker Jacks, and licorice, and fill up plastic water bottles with their favorite juices and soft drinks.

They always wear plenty of Mariners gear, and in addition to participating in the wave and other fan activities in the stands, they are partial to a cheer made up by their teenage daughter and a friend. "There's a player named Dan Wilson and they love to shout 'Hey, Mr. Wilson!' like Dennis the Menace does," explains Kathy.

Jeff Butler of Spokane is another fervent fan of the Seattle team. On the first day of the season, his family knows what to expect: sugar cereal, normally forbidden, is eaten to celebrate, and the baseball place mats that his wife, Cindy Phillips, bought are taken out of the cupboard and used until the World Series ends in the fall.

★   ★   ★

Even for the most casual football fan, Super Bowl Sunday is a big deal and many Super Bowl family rituals center on food.

That is certainly the case in the Nabrit household in Westerville, Ohio, where it is also traditionally a day the three Nabrit boys spend with their beloved godfather, who lives in Florida.

"Weeks before the Super Bowl, they're faxing and phoning menu ideas back and forth with their godfather," says Paula Penn-Nabrit, whose three sons are now teenagers. "They want to graze all day long, so the rule is that food must be all over the house, within arm's length, and it must include lots of things they don't usually get to eat."

The boys' godfather hasn't missed a Super Bowl party in more than a decade; during a recent year, when he had business in Chicago, the boys met him there to watch the game.

"Normally, they aren't allowed to drink soda pop, so they always have lots of that," says Paula. "They know they can eat junk food from morning till night and never get scolded, so they do. They usually have big bowls of M&Ms and other snack foods to go with it."

The menu changes yearly, but a burger called a "Big Chuck Deluxe" is standard fare, and even linguistically symbolic of the relaxed Super Bowl atmosphere in the house. Paula's husband, Charles, is a rather formidable man and never addressed by any other name. Except when he makes these "Big Chuck" burgers, which are huge and slathered with peppered bacon and cheese and served on onion buns.

One more sign that Super Bowl Sunday is the Nabrits' time to really relax and let down their hair: it's the only Sunday all year they skip church.

VACATIONS AND FAMILY REUNIONS

There are pioneering families who never vacation in the same place twice, but I suspect that they are rare. Most people find great joy in returning time and again to resorts, national parks, and foreign countries that they love. Not only are there wonderful memories built into every view and feast, but the vacationers depart far more confident that they'll have a great time, which triggers the relaxation impulse early.

In addition, there are vacation rituals people perform no matter where they go: certain games they always play in the car, the method by which a campsite is prepared, a certain posed photograph the family always takes on the first day or the last.

The Cohen family of Wynneword, Pa., vacations at the same beach in Ocean City, Md., every year. They always take fluorescent light sticks, the kind that light up when you break and shake them, and walk the beach one night during their stay, waving the glowing sticks and playing catch with them.

Vacation rituals for the Taylors of Stratford, Conn., start with the annual trip to visit their family's cabin in Maine. "It's about a ten-hour trip in the car, which can be murder with two kids," says Debbie Gilbert Taylor. "So we started leaving in the middle of the night. The boys go to bed in their clothes. We get up, load the van, and carry the kids into the car. They stay awake a few hours, then conk out." Every year, the family has breakfast at the exact same place along the way.

Once they arrive at the well-equipped cabin, the Taylors get busy with a round of activities, including some that have taken on the comfortable patina of ritual. "There's a boat there, and we always bring the dog. There are gorgeous rock formations in this one place, and we always go there and run around. We take a couple of loaves of bread and feed the seagulls," says Debbie. "The kids talk about this trip all year round, and when it gets close, they start counting the days."

The Willners of Brooklyn visit a national park every year, doing research beforehand and reading pertinent history, whether it's the great battles of the Civil War or the settlement of the West.

Every spring vacation, the Lee family leaves Manhattan for a ten-day ski trip, and every summer they go trout fishing. Their teenage son, Derek, says the thing he most looks forward to every year used to be Christmas, but now it's that one day of the year when a guide takes him and his father "to the same spot on the river where we hooked this big fish but lost him."

★ ★ ★

Years ago, the Routh family of Ankeny, Iowa, visited the Rocky Mountains. All six of the Rouths saw a porcupine and pronounced it the strangest creature they'd ever set eyes on outside a zoo. Thus was born the "Porcupine Award," bestowed on the family member who sees the strangest animal on any given vacation (or sometimes just on a hike). "They don't get a tangible reward, but we all consider it a real honor," says Mary Routh. "My youngest is always the last to reach a goal, it seems, but even she has been known to win the Porcupine Award."

Every August, the Majewski family of Wilmington, Del., spends a week vacationing at a secluded mountain cottage in Pennsylvania. Built near a creek by Andrea Majewski's grandfather and uncle in the '40s, the family cottage now has indoor plumbing but lacks such modern conveniences as telephone and television. Even the radio reception is iffy.

Andrea plans the annual trip with her husband and two children to coincide with her parents' vacation, and the extended family enjoys a variety of annual rituals that could only happen at this place. The journey itself includes such rituals as turning off the radio and opening the car windows when the car turns off the main road, because everybody wants to hear the "singing bridge," an old metal bridge that hums when the car travels over it.

"Our trip usually coincides with the annual Perseid meteor shower, and since the cottage is so far away from civilization, there are few lights to compete with the stars," says Andrea. "We usually spend the evenings lying flat on our backs on the grass, watching the shooting stars and chatting into the wee hours." Even the kids, now eight and ten, get to stay up late to watch.

Many beloved daytime rituals take place in the creek, such as "water hikes," during which the kids search for tadpoles and a one-clawed crayfish the Majewskis swear turns up every year, and whom they've named "Crayfish A-Too-Fooey."

At about 4:00 PM on most afternoons, it's time for "drinks in the creek." Andrea's father whips up blender drinks using orange sherbet, juice, and whatever else looks interesting (the kids get a nonalcoholic version), and the family drinks them while floating on rafts in the creek. A

recent addition to the ritual is music: Andrea's parents bring out a cassette player and play their favorite Harry Belafonte tunes, so the whole family sings along to "Cocoanut Woman" and "Mama, Look A Boo Boo," among others.

"There are few things more refreshing than sipping mixed drinks while lounging in a cool, clear mountain creek in the middle of nowhere," attests Andrea, and the kids look forward to the trip for months.

The Siegals of Alexandria, Va., always read to their children by flashlight on vacation, which renders an everyday activity magical. "We'll read at night on the beach by flashlight, or sitting on a dock," says Ann Cameron Siegal. "When my oldest daughter was seven we went to the Bahamas and other than the frog that got into her bed, the only thing she remembers is reading by flashlight on the dock."

Every year, the Webb family of Cleveland heads out to Montana, to stay in a cabin owned by Janet Webb's parents, and on the first night they always stay at the same place in South Dakota.

They refer to their vacations as "adventures" and Janet's two little girls look forward to their surprise vacation boxes. Janet prepares these boxes in advance to give the girls lots of things to do in the car. The boxes are shaped like desks, with a clip on top to hold drawing paper in place. Inside, Janet puts a pair of scissors, small books, a roll of tape, colored pencils, and little games, among other treats. (On the rare occasion when the family flies, the rule is the boxes stay closed until the plane takes off.)

If the girls begin to lose interest in the boxes, Janet pulls out the family's special "craft box," a hard briefcase that holds glitter, glue, doilies, paper plates, sparkly pipe cleaners, and other paraphernalia.

Reunions

Family reunions can be small and simple, like an afternoon barbecue in the park. But families with hectic lives who rarely get to see their siblings, let alone second cousins, increasingly organize big reunions that double as vacations. These can run as long as a week, sometimes in exotic locales or on rented cruise ships, and with special events like talent shows. Edith Wagner, publisher of *Reunions* magazine, says there are now more than 200,000 family reunions a year in this country, each with an average of fifty people attending.

Of course, some families would consider such get-togethers a form of torture. But the need to reunite with one's tribe, and absorb wisdom from the "elders" of the clan, is pretty primal even in our throwaway culture. Even orphans have reunions, such as one held every Easter weekend in Raleigh, N.C.: the old Methodist Orphanage was torn down years ago, but hundreds of men and women congregate at a local hotel every year to catch up with the only family they know.

The Seidemann family settled in Newburg, Wis., back in 1853, and descendants have held a family reunion there every year for more than sixty years. The family patriarch, Ray Seideman (he chose to drop the last *n*), now ninety-five, still presides over the summer gathering of up to 625 people on his dairy farm.

Seidemanns come from twenty-four states and several foreign countries to gather on the third Sunday of July. The event kicks off at

11:00 AM with the feel and bustle of a county fair. Most families bring a picnic, but there is also food to buy on the farm, including bratwursts, beer, and ice cream. The family engages in lots of games and general frolicking. Activities for the kids include sack races, baseball and volleyball, tug-of-war, face-painting, and a watermelon seed-spitting contest. For older Seidemanns, bingo is a favorite, and the prizes include contributed items like jugs of maple syrup.

For those interested in antiques and family history, the barn is divided into "rooms," displaying old furniture from eight generations and many family photos.

These descendants of German immigrants always have a kuchen (coffee cake) contest, and all entries are auctioned off to help defray the reunion's costs. After an afternoon of games and eating, the talent show starts at around 5:00 PM, when the patriarch stands on a truckbed stage and recounts the immigrant journey of Friedrich Seidemann and his wife. The old man usually finishes his performance with a song, and the show continues with other family members dancing, singing, doing magic tricks or comedy routines.

Phyllis Naumann, the youngest of Ray Seideman's ten children, says, "Our bonds are so strong because of this reunion. The longer it carries on, the more it means. My dad has had polio, several types of cancer, and cataract operations, but you would never know it: seeing him going ahead after all these years, you think, what have I got to complain about? To me, family is the backbone of life: we want to keep this reunion going forever."

Less elaborate and more exclusive is the annual "Sisters Convention" conducted for the past decade by Amy Cordell of Oak Park, Ill., and her far-flung siblings.

There are many siblings-only reunions, but in this case even spouses and children are excluded. The six Cordell girls decided to include their only brother, John, after he pouted about it, but refused to change the reunion's name.

The Sisters Convention happens one weekend a year, either at a hotel, at one of the siblings' homes, or at a mother-in-law's beach house. To keep up with the "siblings-only" rule, if the reunion does take place at a sibling's house, that person's spouse retreats to a nearby hotel (children go too). Given that travel costs are wildly uneven, requiring some to travel cross-country while others only go across town, the expenses are pooled and shared equally.

This isn't one of those reunions packed with frantic exertion. "Our main purpose is to *talk*," says Amy, which she admits leads to lots of laughing and inevitably to a little amateur psychoanalysis of their parents. "We talk about our present lives, our future hopes, and our childhoods," she adds. "Because the gap between youngest and oldest is twelve years, this has finally made it possible for all of us to know each other as grown-ups."

Food isn't fancy either. "The first year we went out and bought all sorts of things to make meals, only to find out we were too lazy to cook. We chip and dip our way through the weekends."

The Cordell kids have been known to make T-shirts for everyone present, but it is more usual—an unspoken ritual—to pass out copies of a favorite book or product. It might be as simple as handing out samples of a preferred hair mousse, or a little paperback book on ecology tips. One year, John Cordell found an old manuscript of his mother's called *Dear Peabody*, which consisted of letters sent between the family dog, Peabody, and two older sisters who had grown up and moved out. John retyped the whole thing, had it copied and bound as a hardcover book, and gave one to each of his sisters.

Although having fun remains a high priority of these reunions, the siblings have seen the occasion serve another, deeper purpose. "We skipped a year when one of our sisters died of ovarian cancer," says Amy. "But we now enjoy having the time together to talk about her, remember her, and cry together about our loss."

Some reunions are so relaxed and low-key they don't even think of themselves as reunions, like the annual vacation Steve Borne takes with his five siblings, their spouses and kids.

"We've never thought of it as a reunion because we all live in Louisiana and this isn't the only time we see each other," says Steve's wife, Colleen. "But the Florida vacation was started more than ten years ago because the six siblings wanted to see more of each other than they could at occasional barbecues and baptisms. You see, this was an Air Force family that moved every year, so these siblings are closer to each other than they are to any friends."

Every summer, the Borne siblings head to Perdido Beach, Fla., where they share three or four condominiums for between five and seven days. In August 1998 there will be eleven grown-ups and seventeen children under the age of fourteen.

"We always go to the Pensacola Naval Air Museum, we search for sand crabs on the beach at night using flashlights, and we always play charades," says Colleen. "During most days, we go to the beach or the pool at the condo, and we eat just about every meal together. We'll either cook, or order pizza. To make things real easy, we use a lot of paper plates and we have cups with our names on them."

For thirty years, Anne Cohn Donnelly's family has held a three-generation reunion between Christmas and New Year's.

"As a Jewish family, we always observed Hanukkah, but we got a few presents on Christmas, which we called gift-giving day," says Anne, mother of an adopted five-year-old and stepmother to three. But as Anne and her four siblings started families of their own, buying gifts for everybody in the family got too expensive and time-consuming. Thus was born a family gift exchange, called a Pollyanna, that became the highlight of the Cohn family's annual reunion.

"We've been going to this dude ranch in Arizona for about fourteen years," says Anne, who until recently was director of the National Committee to Prevent Child Abuse in Chicago. "There are about thirty of us, including all my siblings and their kids and my parents. The meals are all organized and we sit together, but our days aren't highly structured. People go swimming, ride horses, or whatever they want, though some of the adults go on long hikes every day."

An entire afternoon and evening are dedicated to the gift exchange, because it involves far more than handing over a package. "Names are usually drawn a full year ahead, and each family member is expected to present a skit, sing a song, or do something special or outrageous," says Anne. One brother-in-law, a rabbi, is an opera fanatic, and tends to sing famous arias with humorously redrafted lyrics. Kids under eighteen exchange gifts in the afternoon, and the adult Pollyanna is set for that evening.

"Some presentations are scavenger hunts, or you have to follow a long string all over the ranch to find your gift," says Anne. The gifts themselves are often wild. For example, Anne has a brother who loves Snickers candy bars, but wishes they came in dark chocolate. So one of his relatives opened all the wrappers on a bunch of Snickers bars, redipped them in dark chocolate, and resealed the wrappers. They were packed in a backpack with a sign that said, "David Cohn, your dream comes true."

Although the Cohns don't consider this a Christmas celebration, and pointedly hold the gift exchange on a day other than Christmas, they do borrow from a much-loved Yuletide tradition. "Rather than put up stockings, we put out our boots overnight in this big room at the dude ranch," says Anne. "The tradition is that each family puts something in every person's boot. There are often prank gifts, like when my mother gave everybody a tube that looked like Chapstick but was indelible purple."

At week's end, the Cohns celebrate New Year's, mostly by laughing and relaxing and going to bed soon after midnight. The next day, they all head home.

African-Americans have held reunions in this country pretty much since there were any families to have them. But after the publication of Alex Haley's *Roots* in 1976, there was a virtual explosion in black family reunions that continues today. They tend to be elaborate and sophisticated, often stressing racial pride as well as the veneration of family.

Ione Vargus, head of the Family Reunion Institute at Temple University in Philadelphia, has been leading an annual conference on black family reunions since 1990. Dr. Vargus says her research shows that most African-American reunions include a worship service, a formal banquet, and a memorial service. Also quite common are scholarship programs for family members. "Black families have really used reunions to reemphasize the whole extended-family notion," she says, "and we're seeing white families beginning to pick up on some of the specific rituals."

Sheila Linton's family reunion is one that was inspired in part by *Roots* and fits many of the patterns of large, successful African-American reunions.

"We are the Bullock family and we started this in 1977 with a picnic at my cousin's house in Virginia," says Sheila, a junior high teacher from Philadelphia. "Now our reunions are three-day events at major hotels, including a semiformal banquet on Saturday nights. We've tracked down 700 family members so far, and there are up to 200 of them at any given reunion."

The Bullock clan gathers each year on a Friday night, usually in July, starting the reunion with a casual dinner and fun activity, often a fashion or talent show. Saturday is devoted to sightseeing and other amusements, and ends with a banquet and dance. The banquet isn't considered complete without the recitation of a special family poem, and recently the Bullocks have started giving out a "Family Member of the Year" award. The reunion concludes on Sunday with a business meeting to discuss such issues as new ways to make money and recent sales of the souvenir T-shirts, mugs, and hats sold at every reunion. Most are adorned with a family crest designed by a teenage family member a decade ago.

All of this requires an immense amount of work, done by five committees organized geographically. One includes all the family members still living in North Carolina, another is based in the Washington, D.C., area, and Sheila's committee covers Pennsylvania, New Jersey, and Delaware. Each committee has to run the reunion every five years, but they are plenty busy in between, holding all kinds of fund-raisers like ski trips to defray the cost of chartering buses.

Sheila, for one, says all the work is worth it. "I can't tell you how moving it is to walk into that glittering banquet with 200 people and to know that every single person is related to you," she says.

Many family reunions include some sort of memorial service to honor departed family members, but the Bullocks' version, held during the Saturday banquet, is particularly dramatic. "You have to picture the lights low, gospel music playing in the background, and we have this candle-lighting ritual," says Sheila.

The first candle to be lit is a thick white one, about six inches in diameter, that represents the patriarch, George Bullock, Sr., and his first wife, Sara. They had twelve children and adopted a nephew, and then George had another child with his second wife. About half of those fourteen children were still alive when the Bullock reunions began, and each of them, oldest to youngest, would walk up and light a small red candle.

White candles represented each of their deceased siblings, and those would be lit in turn by each person's oldest living child.

That entire generation of fourteen is now gone and only white candles are lit each year by the next generation. A fifteenth white candle represents departed Bullocks of subsequent generations. In recent years, a new twist was added: one family member found an enormous candelabra at a yard sale that could hold all the candles. On Sundays, at the business meeting, the candelabra is passed on to whoever is going to lead the next reunion.

The Chambliss family reunion, which brings up to 300 people to the tiny town of Fayette, Miss., includes within it a rite-of-passage ritual for teenagers.

Valeria Primous-Smith of Corpus Christi, Tex., has been attending these reunions on her mother's side of the family since girlhood, and remembers well the "test of womanhood" she had to endure at the age of fifteen. Under the watchful eyes of no less than seven aunts, she had to prove she could bake a cake from scratch.

"The aunts called me into the kitchen and they had all the ingredients on the table. The cake had to pass their inspection," says Valeria. "It was a pound cake, with vanilla icing," she remembers, and she passed with flying colors. (Not so an older cousin, who slammed the oven door and produced a lopsided cake. "Boy, did they give her a hard time!" says Valeria.)

The Chambliss reunion is always held on Easter weekend. After church on Sunday, tables are set up outside for a huge feast, with every family group contributing dishes. "It's all the usual things like chicken and stuffing, macaroni and cheese, but it better be homemade," says Valeria. "If you show up with some bought stuff, you really get talked about."

Between 250 and 300 people come every other year to the reunion of the McNair-Brazil-Scott family. Traced back to two brothers named McNair who left Mississippi in the 1800s for free land in Arkansas, the family is particularly entreprenurial and starts its reunions with a business meeting.

"This year, we'll start on Friday night in Hot Springs, Ark., by discussing such ideas as whether to start an investment club within the family," says Tyrone P. Dumas, chairman of the reunion and director of public works for Milwaukee County. "Some family members think we should raise money by compiling family recipes into a cookbook, and we'll also discuss whether we should incorporate as nonprofit, as some reunions have, so donations to the scholarship fund will be deductible."

On Saturday, the clan will tour an Arkansas cemetery with many family plots, and then head to a local park for a big picnic. Chess will be one of the featured activities, along with dancing. Sunday morning brings a combined church service and memorial service at the hotel. As part of the Sunday program, each graduating high school senior is given a $100 scholarship and reads an essay about his or her goals and plans.

Over the years, the McNair-Brazil-Scott family has learned just how much economic leverage a reunion can have. Lisa McNair, for example, works for the Convention and Visitors Bureau in Birmingham, Ala., and knows well that such organizations often have freebies for reunions that meet in their towns. She also knows that many hotels will throw in a free room when an organization reserves a large block of rooms. "We always insist the free room is next to the suite we've reserved for a hospitality suite," says Lisa, "and the free room is given to that year's host."

Tyrone is famous for actually getting corporate support for the reunions. Before the 1993 get-together, held in Milwaukee, Tyrone wrote to the chairman of Coca-Cola and suggested that giving money to the event would be a small but effective public relations move. In the end, he says, Coke paid for the reunion banquet and donated T-shirts, a banner, and free soft drinks for the picnic. "I can tell you that 250 people left here loving Coke," he says. Indeed, many corporations have turned down such proposals (including Coca-Cola in later years), but recently Tyrone managed to secure two free airline tickets. These will be auctioned off within the family to help pump up its scholarship fund.

OTHER IDEAS

★ Sydney Gines's family has a reunion every year and one traditional activity is the making of a reunion quilt. Fabric, already cut into six-inch squares, is handed out by the family whose turn it is to host. Each family unit attending has to decorate one square in some fashion; those who can't sew or embroider often use fabric paint. The accomplished seamstresses in the extended family take all the finished squares and sew them into a quilt when the reunion is over. Then the quilt is given to the family that hosted that year.

★ Another great idea is to organize a reunion around a theme. "Shipwreck" was the theme at the Bode family reunion one year, but the most successful had an Olympics theme. It kicked off with a parade in which each family represented a different country. The winners of the countless games and contests, including a chug-a-lug contest with Dixie cups of root beer, were hung with "medals" at day's end. And dinner was an international buffet featuring Swedish meatballs, Polish cabbage rolls, German potato salad, and so on.

★ The Walker family hadn't held a reunion for twenty-five years until Alexandra Walker Clark got together with one of her third cousins to organize one in 1995. Her great-grandfather's former farm in Tennessee is now a wildlife sanctuary called Aubudon Acres, and the family was able to get permission to hold its reunion there. The highlight was a performance of the *Walker Follies*, including opportunities for elderly family members to stand up and recount family tales. A cousin played "Amazing Grace" on the saw and a skit Alexandra wrote was performed, depicting her great-grandfather's arrival in Tennessee in 1872. Her son starred as this distant relative and his younger sisters, using two hula hoops and a bedsheet, portrayed a talking covered wagon.

Six

★ ★ ★ ★

Daily, Weekly, and Monthly Rituals

"You have to somehow mark the days. Otherwise, today is Tuesday and tomorrow is just Wednesday. So what?"

—Susan Lynch, Merchantville, N.J.

estive galas and ceremonies to celebrate milestones are important, but daily, weekly, and monthly rituals are crucial. These are the rituals of the hearth that truly keep the home fires burning. Modest activities, gestures, and words that are repeated over and over bring children a unique comfort, proving that their parents' love transcends everything, good days and bad.

There's no telling what will wind up having the most impact on kids. For me, the daily ritual that had the most profound effect was the very pedestrian one of coming home from school and giving my mother an exhaustive rundown of my entire day. She seemed to relish every detail, and there's no doubt her loving interest contributed to my academic successes. Even more than that was the powerful message I got of how much my life mattered to her. And I believe that the practice and pleasure of putting my activities into a daily digest may have figured into my eventual career as a journalist: I've spent my life eagerly learning how other people spend theirs.

And I have seen with my own son how unpredictably these ritual patterns emerge and evolve. It was sheer maternal impulse that caused me to kiss the warm, fleshy soles of his tiny feet when I dressed him, but I still partake of that ritual every morning and every night. Who knows why I started singing "She'll Be Comin' Round the Mountain" every time I dried him after a bath? I added fanciful new verses about his favorite trucks for months, until he decided he didn't want the song anymore. I know one mother who had to read "'Twas the Night Before Christmas" as a bedtime story every night for an entire year: it took her kids that long to get their fill of it.

No one family can or should ritualize every part of daily life. That would cross the line from comfort to suffocation in a hurry. Families who cultivate an atmosphere of easy self-awareness, playfulness, and mutual respect soon find that many rituals pop up spontaneously. At other times, rituals will be needed to smooth over rough transitions like bedtime, and a little experimentation may be required to find something workable.

Don't forget the powerful influence these quotidian rituals have in conveying family identity: they should reflect a family's values and nurture the emotions that matter most to its members. These examples from around the country will provide suggestions and show what it takes to make family time fertile for ritual.

DAILY

The average family doesn't eat together as often as in previous generations; studies show families share dinner, the day's most substantial meal, less than half the time. All the more reason to make every meal count.

First of all, chaos is to families what gravity is to any object heavier than air, and that may be even more true of mealtimes. Everybody comes to the table hungry and self-absorbed. But remember that chewing food simultaneously, while a ritual of sorts, isn't the same as interacting as a family. To impose order on this chaos, real effort must be made, what psychologist William Doherty calls "intentionality."

It's important to eliminate as many distractions as possible: a number of families not only ban television-watching during meals, but decline to take phone calls. Some get really organized and choose a topic of discussion for the meal, or ask each person at the table to share something good and something bad about their day. But there are lots of ways to grab the attention of every family member.

For example, Ann Hodgman, a food writer for *Family Fun* magazine, declares every other night a "reading dinner" at her house. She and her husband and their two kids can either read or draw during the meal, and books and art supplies are kept right by the table in a wicker basket. The alternate nights are designated "talking dinners," and the object is for each person to be as amusing as possible. Because these dinners have talking as their purpose, and because that isn't the case every night, the conversation is likely to take on a livelier tone. To add additional spice, if the family has adopted a new pet—and the household menagerie includes everything from a cat to a hedgehog—it can also join the family at dinner (generally in a cage).

Reading at the table isn't as eccentric a ritual as you might think. When I was growing up, my favorite mealtime ritual was during elementary school, when I lived close enough to walk home for lunch. My mom would read us *Treasure Island* or one of the Oz books while we ate our Velveeta sandwiches on white bread. Sally Pennington likes to joke that what attracted her to her husband Sam was a shared belief that reading while eating should be encouraged rather than forbidden. "We both grew up in households where it wasn't allowed," says Sally. "Needless to say, we raised our five kids to believe that it's just fine, except when company comes."

Julie Young, the mother of six in Arizona (with a seventh on the way), is a big believer in reading aloud to her children at meals, and even when they're just having snacks. "This started because I knew I should be reading to the kids, but I'm just too tired at bedtime to have the patience," she says. "It's an easy matter to read while they eat because I tend to eat beforehand, or after they're done. But I've discovered all sorts of side benefits from this ritual."

Among them: "Because the kids are eating, they don't interrupt me, and because I'm busy reading, I don't spend the whole meal criticizing their table manners." She has also found that the kids tend to stay longer at the table and eat more when they're immersed in a good story, and, because the whole family shares the stories, "we have a lot of common experiences and characters we've come to love." One unexpected bonus: "Sometimes they can't bear for me to put the book down. So they ask me to keep reading while they clear the table and clean up."

Another family's dinnertime goal was to teach children how to research an issue and discuss it. Gloria Uhler and her husband decreed that each member of the California family must come to the table with one topic of conversation, generally related to current events. (Television shows or their characters were taboo.) When it came to their turn, each child or adult introduced his or her subject, and everybody else had to ask at least one related question.

"This was my second husband's idea and at first, my two kids saw it as a bit of a chore, having to research things in advance," explains Gloria, whose children are now grown. "My kids were average students without a lot of motivation, the kind of kids who only did what was absolutely necessary. But once we got to the table, it always became fun. After a little initial resistance, the kids began enjoying the routine."

Gloria remembers in particular a night when the topic was astronauts. She says that the family discussed details about the spacecraft and the distance of other planets, when her daughter piped up and asked, "Hey, how do they pee in those suits?" Gloria recalls that "the discussion got pretty graphic and funny, but this kind of question was indicative of why the ritual was so important. It forced the kids to think about people and situations outside themselves, and of their relationship to the world."

Her kids still didn't turn into Einsteins, but Gloria says the ritual developed in them a desire to learn. She adds, "Think about a kid grudgingly flipping through the pages of *Newsweek* or a section of the newspaper other than the comics, and then finding something that catches his eye. It's a wonderful process to watch."

Other families favor occasional rituals just for fun, like a tradition common to some families of Italian background: whenever pasta is served, the person who finds the bay leaf in his or her portion has to do the dishes that night. "You would be amazed how many trips around the table that bay leaf can make during one little meal," says one mother.

Many families consider saying grace the most important dinner ritual. This often consists of a simple prayer learned as part of childhood religious studies, but a pithy, memorable grace can come from almost anywhere, or be made up on the spot. Some families hold hands around the table while saying grace, while others just sit quietly with closed eyes. In my family, we always took turns saying a simple grace, but many other families say theirs in unison.

The virtues of grace are many. Even for families who aren't religious in a formal sense, saying grace can provide a brief flash of spirituality and a healthy dose of perspective. Most graces remind people that while they eat, others starve. While this family lives surrounded by love, others are abused and frightened. Not to mention that grace is also one of those rituals of transition: it inserts a tiny period of quiet after everyone's day of separate activity and reunites them as a family.

The Michaels of Minneapolis don't belong to any of the local churches, but consider themselves spiritually minded and the family says grace at every meal. "I think it's important that children learn how to say thanks out loud in front of others," says Martha Michael, who has three children. "We say a simple grace and when it's done, we all squeeze hands before we eat. We knew someone else who did that, and we liked it so we adopted it ourselves."

In Columbus, Ohio, Elizabeth Fergus-Jean started by having each of her three children and her husband take a turn saying something he or she was thankful for. But now the family's grace at dinner has evolved into an even simpler ritual: a moment of total quiet.

"I've told my kids that this should be a moment of thanks, but also a moment of connectedness," says Elizabeth. "I think it's important to become quiet before you eat. Sometimes, I'll ask one of them afterward, 'What were you thinking about tonight?' "

Jeanne Mollinger-Lewis was raised Catholic, but doesn't routinely say grace at dinner. She is much more apt to say some sort of prayer when she is sharing an informal meal with her two kids. "Even for a picnic, my daughter likes to say this thing from one of the *Madeline* books. We'll hold hands and she'll say, 'We love our bread, we love our butter, but most of all we love each other.' "

The Hodges of Saratoga Springs, N.Y., love to sing grace, usually holding hands at the table. "Sometimes we'll do something simple, like the Johnny Appleseed song," says Anne Hodge. "The song goes: 'Oh the Lord is good to me, and so I thank the Lord / For giving me the things I need / The sun and the rain and the appleseed / The Lord is good to me.' " But, she adds, "if the extended family is there, we'll sing rounds and do a whole repertoire of songs. During the week, it's hard for my husband to get home in time for dinner, but even then I'll sing with my three kids, sometimes while I'm carrying food to the table."

In Janesville, Calif., the Mowbray family take turns saying grace. "People improvise generally, but whenever someone's imagination gets stuck, he or she will recite the traditional Catholic blessing," says Georgann Mowbray. That prayer is: "Bless us, O Lord, and these Thy gifts, which we are about to receive from your bounty. Through Christ, our Lord. Amen."

But even then, comments are always added to the prayer. "If there is something special the next day, like an athletic event or a test, we ask the Lord to keep that person in his heart. If something good happened, like a great report card, we thank our maker for that. My kids do this too, and they might ask the Lord to watch over Dad or Mom when one of us has a big interview coming or something like that."

One sure way to keep kids interested as they get a little older is to spice up rituals with contemporary cultural references. In the Ezzell family in Westerville, Ohio, the favorite grace is something the kids learned from the youth director at the local Lutheran church. It is sung to the tune of the theme song from *The Addams Family* movie and TV show and it goes like this:

> We thank you for our food, Lord,
> For Mom and Dad & you, Lord,
> We thank you for our food, Lord,

And our family!
Duh-duh-duh-dum [snap fingers], duh-duh-duh-dum
[snap fingers].

Bedtime

Better than a warm bottle, more comforting than the softest blankie, is a good bedtime ritual. This is a monumental moment to a baby or toddler, a time of transition in which parents hold nearly shamanistic power to tame the forces of darkness. Even for older children, bedtime remains immensely important. Although it is a time for separation, it can also be a time of profound connection between parent and child, a time when many astute mothers and fathers find out what is really going on in their children's lives.

A parent's chief job at bedtime is to help a child let go of the day by creating an atmosphere of soothing calm. On summer nights at my house, the first thing my son and I do after "lights out" is to listen together for the rhythmic clicking of the crickets: to do so requires a moment of intense concentration that effectively detaches our minds from the day's thoughts. That pause seems literally to slow time, and as we start a sequence that includes prayers and a "good night" to each of "the people Max loves," sleep seeps in.

The other important task, especially for a young child, is to prepare his or her mind for fear-free dreaming. Reciting prayers, reading books, inventing stories, and talking about the day are all important rituals that further this end. Nightmares are inevitable once a child's imagination starts really cooking, but parents can make a difference by choosing carefully what to read and talk about. Verbally invoking a pack of angels to watch over the bed is still a good idea, but there are plenty of clever rituals that can attack the nightmares head on.

When Matthew Pompi's son started cringing at bedroom monsters, his dad was ready for action. Matthew filled a plastic, plant-spritzing bottle with water and pasted a colorful label to the front. It featured a monster's face with a thick, black "X" written through it.

Whenever Nathan got worried about monsters, the "Monster Spray" was prepared. At bedtime, father and son sprayed in the closet, under the

bed, inside the toybox, and anywhere else monsters might lurk. According to Nathan's stepmother, Kelly Pompi, "it worked wonderfully."

Nathan, now eleven, doesn't need the spray anymore. But he still talks about how he kept it on his bedside table. If he had to go to the bathroom in the middle of the night, he could go armed. He even used to take it along for sleepovers with his grandparents. He's been reminding his dad and Kelly about the monster spray lately, because his toddler half-brother is just getting to the age where monsters can be a problem.

On Bainbridge Island, in Washington, Vicky Adkins draws a circle with her finger on her six-year-old son's forehead at bedtime "to put the good dreams in." Vicky, who also has two older daughters, says her son swears he has bad dreams if she forgets.

Outside Philadelphia, Sue McCandless goes an extra step, actually inventing enchanting dreams for her kids at bedtime.

"I did this with my son, Ryan, who is now fourteen, but it was an on-again, off-again thing that came up maybe every six months, if he had a nightmare," she recalls. "But when my daughter starting having nightmares at two, she really took to the ritual in a big way. We've done it every single night for over two years, and now she gives dreams back to my husband and me."

The invented dreams make the girl the star of a story and focus on activities she loves. "One dream I gave Taylor was, 'Dream you are riding a two-wheeler without training wheels, and you enter a bike race. Your number is ten, your bike is blue, and your helmet is pink. You ride up and down lots of hills through beautiful wooded areas.' Sometimes she will quibble about the details, saying, 'Can't I be number twenty-three in the race, and can I have a green bike?' She asked if she won the race, and I told her to wait and dream how the story ends."

Sue says that the dreams her husband suggests tend to be a bit less elaborate. "He'll say, 'Dream you're flying with Daddy and we fly over Sesame Street.'" Sometimes the girl presses him for details.

In return, Taylor provides some vivid scenarios for her parents to dream. "She even describes what we're wearing," says Sue. "She'll say,

'Mom, you are jumping off a ramp on a jet ski and you're wearing a purple bathing suit.' Once she told my husband he was a prince and he had to find this beautiful princess and marry her, and it was me."

Sue fervently believes that the exercise has helped reduce nightmares for her daughter. "I can't even recall the last time Taylor woke up and said she had a nightmare. She occasionally says she had a bad dream, but they never wake her and she seems to feel in control of them." And yes, Taylor does sometimes wake up vowing that she had the precise dream suggested the previous night.

A final benefit to the ritual is what happens the morning after, when talk of dreams leads to "very stimulating breakfast conversation." From her daughter's recounting of her dreams, her mother says she has gotten countless clues to Taylor's feelings and concerns. And the little girl loves it when her parents share their dreams as well.

Mary Sutton's nightmare-prevention ritual borrows from both Catholicism and Madison Avenue.

Mary says that some years ago, when her oldest child began having bad dreams, she and her husband started tracing the sign of the cross on her forehead at bedtime. "We also wanted to sing a blessing, and I borrowed something I had heard at a prayer group that goes to the tune of the Oscar Mayer weiner song," says Mary. "It goes: May the blessing of the Lord be upon you, I bless you in the name of the Lord."

This simple ritual seemed to help the Suttons' daughter, and was used again when the two younger children needed it. "They go through stages at bedtime where they just want a little extra time and attention," says Mary. "I think this helped relax their minds."

Bedtime can also be an occasion for quiet confidences. There's a biblical admonition to "let the day's own trouble be sufficient for the day" (Matthew 6:34) and one good way for a child to let go of a day is to let go of the emotions it provoked, good and bad, by sharing them.

Lucinda Herring, the writer and ritual maker, created a bedtime ritual for her daughter, Eliza, called "Grateful and Grumbles." The grumbles always came first.

"The idea was to tell the grumbles first so we could shed them before going to sleep. We would end with what we were thankful for in our day, so we could take the grateful with us to sleep. If the grumble was something too big to really let go of, then we asked to receive guidance and help with the problem while we slept."

In Long Prairie, Minn., Barbara DeGrote has found that her three kids will confide in her more readily at bedtime if they are physically relaxed. The children are now between seven and twelve, and don't have as formal a bedtime routine as when they were younger, but several times a week, Barbara will ask, "Do you want your feet rubbed?" She'll slowly rub one child's feet with lotion and he or she will get very relaxed. "It's a nice quiet time, and it's very easy to talk then," says Barbara.

Tim Mullin wanted to end his daughters' days on a positive note, and started a ritual that the family calls "Proud-Prouds." Just before they jump into bed, the two girls are asked if they're proud of anything they did that day. Then their parents tell the girls what made *them* proud.

Cameron, the younger of the two girls, has a sofa in her bedroom, and the family of four gathers there each night to read stories. Once the stories are over, Tim or his wife, Tricia O'Neill, will say, "Now it's time for Proud-Prouds," the signal for Cameron and her sister Kylie to crawl into a parent's lap. The girls take turns so everybody can listen and contribute.

Tricia, who works part-time as director of student affairs at the University of Maryland's law school, says this five-minute ritual is not only something soothing that bonds the family together, but it serves as a window into her children's daytime lives. She finds out what makes her daughters happy and sad, and she and her husband can convey their own values and feelings through their responses.

"Some nights they don't have much to say, but often it's something we didn't know happened at school, like 'I'm proud that I helped someone tie her shoe,' " says Tricia. "Or it might be, 'I'm proud of cleaning my room without being asked.' " In their responses, Tricia and Tim are careful not to imply that only perfection will make them proud. "I say a lot of things like 'I'm proud that you tried your very best to ride your two-wheeler today, even though you fell off a lot,' " says Tricia.

Given that parents necessarily offer generous portions of corrections and criticism, Tricia sees the "Proud-Prouds" as a way to even things out, making sure no day goes by without praise as well. The last thing her daughters hear each day is that their parents are proud of who they are.

Telling stories is a family tradition in countless cultures and another great way to end the day. Kyna Tabor's stories are all about the family's "ever-growing cat nation," a population of felines numbering in the dozens (though only a few live in the house).

Kyna, a freelance artist and writer, says she got tired of reading all the Seuss and Sendak books that she had gotten to know by heart when her son, Mikey, was little, so she decided to make up some stories of her own. The family's cats seemed like a logical place to start.

"I began with a female cat we've had a long time," Kyna explains. "I said she was a princess in another land, and then the other cats like Blackie, Kismet, Patches, Pinky, and so on became courtiers and court jesters. The setting is sort of medieval." The stories often reflect reality, changing when their cats get into scrapes or die, or when a stray kitten is adopted.

The ritual has evolved for Mikey, now ten, and his sister, Kersti, three. "I won't tell the story until they are both in their pjs with their teeth brushed, so they often hurry to get that done," says Kyna. "We start out in Kersti's room, and when she goes to sleep we move to Mikey's room. I have to be careful not to make the story too exciting, otherwise Kersti won't go to sleep. But she loves dragons, so from time to time the kitties have to fight dragons."

The ritual includes pauses when Mikey can jump in and tell part of the story. "I often start by saying, 'I don't remember where we were. How does it go?' " says Kyna. "Or I'll pretend I've forgotten something in the middle, and Mikey will pipe up." In truth, Kyna remembers them all, having written the stories down from the beginning: she is now vowing to learn bookbinding, so she can make these tales into a permanent memento for her children.

Songs are as integral a part of most bedtime rituals as stories are. Infants soon recognize and love the sound of their parents' voices and the standard lullabies have lasted so long because they are genuinely soothing. My own singing voice is atrocious, and though I tried out a rather wide repertoire of lullabies on my son as a baby, he soon said he preferred me to read and tell stories instead, so I gave up long ago. More usual, at least when children continue to express pleasure, is for the same song or songs to be used night after night for years.

Kent Greenawalt, a professor at Columbia University law school, laughs at the fact that the oldest of his three sons, Robert, was still hearing the same two lullabies into his preteen years. The songs were only part of the Greenwalts' bedtime ritual, which was called "Sing and Scratch," because Kent and his late wife Sanja would scratch the backs of their three sons while they sang.

Kent and Sanja both sang a song to the tune of "Twinkle, Twinkle, Little Star" that went "Nee Nee Na Na, Goo Get Soo, Nee Nee Na Na, I Love You." Kent insists that the song isn't total nonsense, but loosely based in part on words that mean "go to sleep" in Serbo-Croatian (Sanja's native tongue). In addition, Kent was also fond of the lullaby, "Sleep, My Child, and Peace Attend Thee."

"We would do the boys one at a time, and it was easiest when they all shared a room. The boys would usually lie on their stomachs in bed, and either my wife or I, and sometimes both of us, would sing and scratch. I'd sing a couple of verses, and then leave the room, but my wife would keep it up with each one until he fell asleep, especially when they were young."

Robert, now twenty-six, remembers the ritual well. "They did 'Sing and Scratch' every night when I was maybe six or seven, and then even when I was older, they would scratch my back and sing if I had had a bad day. We were a physically affectionate family, and to me, this was one indication of our closeness. I know I always went to sleep feeling safe and comforted."

Many bedtimes end with a simple declaration of parental love, often accompanied by one of those age-old admonitions of safekeeping ("Don't let the bedbugs bite!" was my parents' favorite, and like most middle-class kids, I assumed these were mythical creatures).

Nancy Rey of Lakeside, Calif., always says, "I love you a bushel and a peck," to her son as she walks out of his room at night. And he always replies, "I love you a backpack," something he started almost ten years ago, when he was four.

"Even now, the ritual isn't allowed to vary," says Nancy. "I have to start it and if I forget to say, 'I love you a bushel and a peck,' he keeps saying, 'I love you, Mom,' over and over until I realize what I'm supposed to do. And my husband isn't allowed to say it if I'm not there."

Terry Melka has passed on a ritual to her son that she and her father had: she says seven things to him in parting, and kisses him after each one. The seven are: "Good night. Love you. Go to sleep. Be a good boy. Sleep late. Good night. Love you." Even as a preteen, "these kisses have an amazingly calming effect on him," says Terry, who lives in Lyons, Ill. "Even if we have been having a bit of a rough time before bed, he knows these kisses are coming, and so did I as a child."

OTHER IDEAS

★ Keith Schroeder shares a bedtime ritual with his son, Ethan, that started for fun but is also educational. Ethan, who is now nine, has an enormous map of the world on one wall of his bedroom, and every night Keith names a place somewhere in the world. The next night, Ethan has to show his dad where that place is, and the two talk about its culture and history. Ethan's mother, Polly, says the ritual has sparked an interest in all kinds of maps on her son's part, and she's even heard him quiz his friends about geography.

★ In Phoenix, Ariz., Cora Berry got frustrated about her children getting out of bed on five or six pretexts every night. So she created a checklist, and once everything on it is completed, that's it for the night. "Every night we read stories from a bedtime storybook and talk about the moral of the story," says Cora. "Then we say prayers, go potty, have one more sip of water, find our teddy bears and stuffed dogs, and it's lights out." The list is on the bedroom door, and as Cora calls out each item, her children say "check."

★ Each of the three Cohen children gets to have a "midnight snack," although it never happens at midnight. The ritual got started years ago when the kids saw a movie in which an animal friend of Winnie-the-Pooh always had his midnight snack. "They can have whatever they want; cereal, ice cream, cookies, whatever," says Adele Cohen. "I sit with them, and my husband does too if he's here. And we talk. We do it with each child separately because they all have different bedtimes: with the two younger kids, after the snack we go upstairs for teeth-brushing and read a book. But my fifteen-year-old does it at maybe 10:45 PM: he may bring the food upstairs to my room to talk, saying, 'Mom, it's time for midnight snack.'"

★ Suzy Kellett, who had to work full-time while raising quadruplets alone, started a prebedtime ritual when her kids were in junior high that was critical in keeping the family close. "We always loved tea, so at 9:00 PM every night, everybody would stop what they were doing for twenty or thirty minutes, and we would just catch up," says Suzy. "It was usually apple-cinnamon tea, in mugs, and we'd sit in the field behind our townhouse or turn out the lights in the living room. Everybody talked about how the day went, what was going on." Later, after the kids had gone to bed, Suzy would stop by each in turn, and gently probe for unresolved worries. "I could never get them to open up to me if we went out to eat, for example," says Suzy. "My kids talk best when they're alone in bed, in darkness."

Farewells

There's a lot of coming and going in contemporary American households. Moms and dads go to work, travel on business, or dine with friends, while children attend day care and school and sports and music lessons. Many families have found that simple rituals acknowledging their partings and reunions smooth these transitions and remind family members that love follows them wherever they go. It's great to stick a few love notes in your kids' shorts as you pack for camp, but routine good-byes can be just as heartfelt.

Like a number of mothers, Diana Berreman has taught her children how to say "I love you" in sign language.

Diana, a mother of two in Reno, Nev., says her son started learning about sign language in preschool. It was during the Gulf War and she remembers watching television footage of the troops shipping out: one female soldier was shown giving the sign for "I love you" to her deaf child, a moment that commentators milked to the max. "You know how the media plays that stuff up," says Diana, "but I still liked the closeness it expressed and that the last message this child saw at that moment was an expression of his mother's love. So we adopted the 'I love you' sign."

For anybody who isn't sure how to do it, here is Diana's description: "The 'I love you' sign combines the three letters I, L, and Y. To make the sign, you hold your pinky, pointer, and thumb up, while keeping your middle and ring fingers down. The pinky is the I, the pointer and thumb make an L, and the pinky and thumb are the Y. The palm faces out toward the person you're 'talking' to."

Diana uses the sign with both her kids and also with her husband. "It's been a special bond we share. My daughter, now five, will flash me the sign as she walks down the street to school or is riding away in a friend's car. Now that he's ten, my son doesn't use it as often, mostly in response to us. But for us, it's what we do instead of waving."

Some parents have adopted specific rituals for saying good-bye when they drop their kids off at school.

Without fail, the last thing Georgann Mowbray says to her children in the schoolyard is, "Be kind to your friends, listen to teacher, and always remember, Mama loves you." They always chime in and say, "Mama loves you," along with her.

"This started when my oldest, now sixteen, was only four," says Georgann, who lives with her family in Janesville, Calif. "To be honest, I stole it. I overheard another mother saying it and I liked it. I feel that the parting words you say to your kids can often set the tone for the whole day, so why not make it positive and single out what's important?"

Laura Hench has a ritual for seeing her daughter off to kindergarten on the bus. "It's real simple," says Laura, the mother of three in Maine. "Depending on the weather, we walk to the bus stop or drive her. When I spot the bus coming, I say, 'Here's your bus,' and she says, 'Bye-bye, Mommy, I love you.' Then the twins and I say, 'Good-bye, don't forget to wave to us!' She always walks to the exact same spot, a window in the dead center of the bus, and she waves to each of us while we wave and blow kisses."

The children of Jeanne Mollinger-Lewis each have a different ritual with their father on workday mornings. Her four-year-old daughter gives her dad "a kiss and a hug and says, 'I love you,' before he leaves for work," says Jeanne. "If he does it in the wrong order, she won't let him leave."

If he's awake when his father is having breakfast, the couple's son, aged seven, will sit at the kitchen table and have "coffee" (really cocoa) with Dad.

When Galen Laughton's five-year-old twins say good-bye or good night, they each use their own special set of hand signals. "It just evolved by chance," she explains. "I used to do a thumbs-up sign with my son when I said good night, and he'd do it back, and then someone taught him the peace sign. I started it at first because he had a little trouble with dexterity. Well, now he has seven things in a row that he does, including holding his index finger out like a gun and blowing on it."

Naturally, when Carter's twin sister saw this, she had to have a good-bye routine of her own. "To say 'I love you,' she points to her eye, then her heart, and then makes the letter U with two fingers," says Galen. "I do it and then she does it back, and sometimes she mouths 'I love you' while she does it."

The hand signals aren't used for every good-bye, but Galen has noticed that they often appear when the kids are slightly uneasy about an experience. "Maybe it's a pony ride at the fair and they're a little nervous," she says. "They'll look back at me and do their signs."

Galen actually has two sets of twins, and the younger ones are just starting to get interested. "I do a fish-lips kiss with one of them, and she tries to do it back," says Galen. "I can just see what's coming. . . ."

The members of the Dodge family have developed a good-bye ritual that reflects the peculiar circumstances of living in Princeton, N.J., where hunting is illegal and deer are constantly wandering onto busy roads.

"When we first moved here, our car was hit by a huge buck who smashed through the windshield and came very close to seriously hurting my husband," says Nancy. "I became terrified of hitting another deer, and I had read an article in *New Age Journal* about a woman who performs an affirmation ritual she thinks will protect her when she gets into a car. So I decided to make up a sort of blessing about deer. It goes, 'Deva of the field and forest, please keep your creatures safe in the woods and keep us safe from harm.' " (In Hindu mythology, a deva is a good spirit.)

The ritual is now part of a blessing universally applied. Whenever any of the seven family members heads for the car, the others inevitably call out, "Good-bye, and do the deer thing." Nancy laughs about it, but insists it works. "My husband actually saw a deer heading for his car at top speed, but the animal fell down about twelve feet in front of his bumper, as though tripped by a wire," she says. "We haven't hit so much as a squirrel since we started doing this."

Farewell rituals can also serve practical purposes when family members leave home together.

Mary Sutton had very serious reasons for creating a seat-belt ritual. "We were in a car accident and none of us was buckled in. We were just lucky that nobody got hurt."

After that, Mary created a ritual that the family adheres to very strictly. "I start by saying 'Buckle up!' and then one of the three kids says, 'Why do we buckle up?' " That's the cue for someone else to answer, "Because we love each other."

In Arizona, the Young family's farewell ritual is used to make sure none of the six kids gets left behind. "I'm so paranoid about becoming one of those parents you read about who left their child in a rest area or a store," says Julie Young. "So whenever we go somewhere, we count off. My husband is number one, but I'm usually the chauffeur, so I'll start by calling out, 'Two!' The kids echo back in their birth order: 'Three,' 'Four,' 'Five,' 'Six,' and 'Seven.' The youngest can't talk yet, so someone will say, 'And number eight is in his car seat.' "

Then Julie yells out, "And we're off!..." and the kids chorus back, "Like a herd of turtles!" Julie says the turtle phrase came from a friend of hers, and she loves it because "it's an accurate description and it diffuses any grumpiness we've had in getting out the door."

WEEKLY

There is a particular magic, I think, to a ritual that happens once a week, because it is both ordinary and special. It can be depended upon, but you have to wait for it; there is time for anticipation. For parents, that can also mean the difference between a commitment and a burden. I know a number of families who always eat sundaes on Sunday, and a Florida family in which the three girls take turns going to the driving range with their dad on Saturdays.

Remember those investment charts showing how interest compounds, graphically illustrating how a relatively small amount of money can grow into an impressive pile over the years? Weekly rituals work the same way. A relatively modest investment of time can produce staggering changes in family relationships, and it doesn't take years for the benefits to accrue.

The McCandless family is a case in point. Jim and Sue McCandless live outside Philadelphia with their two children, and Jim's workweek runs between sixty and seventy hours. Sue stays home with her four-and-a-half-year-old daughter, and sees quite a bit of her son, Ryan, now fourteen. But when Ryan started junior high, Jim McCandless found himself losing touch with his son.

"Ryan was having a hard time at school and he just wasn't talking to us as much about his life," says Sue. "The junior high principal told us he had gone through a similar experience with his own daughter at that age, where he realized he was losing her and had to do something about it. He suggested Jim institute a practice of weekly 'Dates with Dad.' "

So a weekly ritual was begun that is totally dictated by Ryan. Jim juggles his schedule, sometimes with difficulty, and shows up on that night to do whatever Ryan feels like. "Some days they just go to the park and throw a ball and once they went to a hobby store together. Later, they joined a bowling league," says Sue. "Even when the whole family is off on vacation, Jim and Ryan have their night together."

The results, say Sue, have been astonishing. "It just changed everything. To start with, Ryan used to come down for breakfast and not say a word. Now, he asks his dad what kind of day he's going to have. They're more like friends, and Ryan just wants to spend more time with the whole family. Before, if we gave him the option of going along with us to the store on an errand or staying home, he would always stay home. Now, he usually chooses to go with us."

Weekends

Most families have more time together on the weekends, but for many, time just falls away if they don't pin it down with specific excursions and activities. Turning those plans into a weekly ritual protects that togetherness as nothing else can—it's like a family-time insurance policy.

In religious families, worship provides a built-in weekly ritual, and many have their own ways of observing the Sabbath at home.

For Jews, the Sabbath or Shabbat begins at sundown on Friday. In countless Jewish homes, Friday-night dinner includes prayers, the lighting of candles, and the eating of special ritual foods. But families fill in the details in their own way.

Carolyn Hecht of Freeport, N.Y., didn't want to deny her children candy altogether, and she wanted them to look forward to Friday-night Shabbat. So she cleverly started a ritual called "Friday Candy Day," using most of the candy her kids collected each year at Halloween.

"I didn't want them to have candy for all the standard nutritional reasons, but I didn't want to be mean," says Carolyn. "So after they went trick-or-treating, we'd put the bulk of their candy in a big Tupperware container, supplemented by whatever candy bars we were handing out that year. And every Friday, and only on Friday, they could each pick one thing out to eat."

Her kids are all in their thirties now, but they still remember the ritual, and even remember the Tupperware container. "There are two commandments related to the Sabbath, that you shall keep the Sabbath and you shall *remember* the Sabbath," says Carolyn. "Friday Candy Day helped with the second commandment; it literally made Shabbat sweet."

When Gregg Adkins sits in a church pew with his children on Sunday morning, there's a history lesson going on while the family sings hymns.

"My husband is a history buff, and he has a unique way of getting our daughters involved," explains his wife, Vicky. "Every hymn that we sing in church gives the author and year it was written. What Gregg does is test the girls on the presidents by asking who was president the year the hymn was written."

This is an example of just how flexible rituals can be: they can pop up almost anywhere and don't have to be long to be satisfying. The hymn/history ritual takes place in the short space of time it takes all the members of the congregation to turn to the right page of the hymnal.

Gregg doesn't usually have to say much, he just points to the date, and the girls compete to be the first with the correct answer.

GREGG: 1864.

THE GIRLS: Lincoln.

GREGG: 1841.

GREGG OFFERS A QUICK HINT: Got a cold at his inauguration and never really took office.

THE GIRLS: Harrison.

GREGG: Who came after?

THE GIRLS: Tyler.

Gregg started the game with their middle daughter, Bianca, when she was about nine years old. Her older sister, Aissa, felt left out of the ritual, so she boned up on the presidents and now plays along too. Their younger brother, Casey, is just six and currently attends Sunday school during services, but will join the game eventually.

Indeed, weekend rituals serve all kinds of purposes: getting a family organized, accomplishing chores, and even rewarding good behavior.

In Medway, Mass., Teresa Schultz-Jones lets her three kids "camp out" in the family room during one weekend night, but only "if they have a good week in terms of behavior and getting all their chores done."

They sleep in sleeping bags, watch videos, stay up late, and sometimes get pizza. If all three are camping at home, there is apt to be a fight over who gets to sleep on the sofa. But the privilege of weekend campouts is far from automatic.

"They have lost out plenty of times because of not getting chores done or because they misbehaved," says Teresa.

Nancy Evans is a high-profile executive as well as a mother, and her Saturday ritual organizes the family each weekend. Nancy, who used to be the editor-in-chief of Doubleday, the book-publishing company, and cofounded a cyberspace service called *Parent Soup,* calls it the "Saturday Morning Agenda."

"We start our Saturdays at the breakfast table and we write down an 'agenda.' We call it that because it seems less like work than 'things to do.' We go around the table, taking turns adding to the list. There are things like 'fix bathroom door' and 'pick up dry cleaning,' but we also add in fun things we want to do like 'go ice skating' or 'see movie.' The result is we get a mix of household chores and outings that makes the weekend feel full and great."

College student Wendy Wright grew up in Idaho, the oldest of nine children in a devout Mormon family, and one of her family's weekend rituals was designed to give her mother a break. Both parents worked, but as with most two-income families, the burden of child care and housework fell more heavily on the mother.

So every Sunday afternoon was Peggy Wright's private time. "Mom could either take a nap or do whatever she wanted," explains Wendy. "The rest of us were in the kitchen, baking pies with my dad. We always baked four or five."

In the Berry household in Phoenix, Ariz., all three children are under six and Saturday is family day all day long, ending with church.

"We get up and take baths or showers, pack a snack, and then head out of the house," says Cora Berry. "Breakfast is at McDonald's or we grab a muffin and juice at a doughnut shop. The idea is to do something outdoors all morning, weather permitting."

The Berries may go to the local botanical garden, but a favorite destination is a nearby park with a lake. "We rent a pedal boat and feed the ducks," says Cora. "And the park also has rides. For eight dollars each, my two sons can get unlimited rides on the carousel, bumper cars, and boats, a Ferris wheel, or the train that goes all through the park."

At around noon, they all head off to the playground, where they eat their snacks and then play some more. If the day is beastly hot or otherwise unpleasant, the family will head to the mall or a science museum for children.

By midafternoon, these excursions have pretty much worn everyone out, and it's time to head home for a nap. A late lunch, generally sandwiches and chips, is served after everybody cleans up for the Saturday-night church service, at 6:00 PM.

"It's a nondenominational Christian church with about five thousand members," says Cora, and her kids love the classes there.

The family had been attending church on Sunday, but Cora and her husband liked the idea of consolidating everything into one family-intense day. Cora also likes the fact that Saturday-night services are very informal at her church, so she and the kids don't have to dress up. "I can wear nice shorts and a T-shirt to the service. It ends at 7:30 PM and we head straight to Taco Bell. Then it's home, for bed."

"Now Saturday is family day, and Sunday is for chores," she says. "It's a day to do things around the house and get ready for the coming week."

In Texas, the Brunson family considers Sunday their family day, starting with church.

"After lunch, we always do something together, like skating in the park," says Karrie Brunson. "In the evening, after the kids have their baths, my husband and I read to them, including scripture." But she also wanted family day to include some talking time, and wanted to create a ritual within which her kids would feel free to say what bothers them. So after Karrie and her husband read to the kids, the whole family take turns sharing "a like, a dislike, and a hope."

"I just know that my parents didn't talk to me about much when I was little and I held a lot of stuff in," she explains. "My dad tried to establish a ritual like this, with one night a week when we could tell my parents if we were mad about something. But it didn't last because it always turned into a big fight. My parents divorced when I was five."

Karrie's husband, Joey, came up with the idea that Sunday should be a day "where no one comes over and only the family does something," Karrie remembers. She added "the talking ritual," which takes less than half an hour.

"I definitely feel closer to my kids now," she says. "A lot of family issues and school issues come up. A lot of it is standard kid stuff, like they're mad at a teacher or another kid got to play with a toy longer, or they think their chores are harder than their sister's chores. But one of the things I found out from their likes is how much they all love to play games." So after the talking part of the evening ends, the games begin, usually Uno or Sorry.

Family Nights for Faith

A lot of women's magazines recommend that parents set aside one night a week for husband and wife alone, arguing that relationships must be constantly renewed with frank talk and fun times. The same goes for families.

An excellent way for families to keep connected is by declaring one night a week Family Night, and sticking with that plan through thick and thin. If the hockey tournament falls on that night one week, then bump Family Night to the next evening, but by all means write it into the family calendar, in ink.

Practices vary widely. Some family nights are rather informal and loosely planned, while others are tightly structured, like that of the Vogts of Covington, Ky. Jim and Susan Vogt view their family nights as a chance to pass on their religious values and create a sense of empathy in their kids. Each week, they spend ten minutes to an hour focusing on a single topic. They always begin with the lighting of a candle and end with a special dessert. (If rebellious children don't want to participate, they don't get dessert, which usually changes their minds.)

"We start by singing a little refrain that goes, 'Jesus Christ is the light of the world,' " says Susan. "It's actually an old monastic chant."

Initially, Susan or Jim always led the evening, but now that they're older, the kids take turns. The leader selects a theme in advance and chooses an applicable Bible verse and an activity in which the whole family can share. Sometimes the evening is focused on an international issue; sometimes it is related to an upcoming holiday. When the theme was conflict resolution, the family went through a role-playing exercise in which they took sides, dividing into warring factions and trying to resolve their differences. One night was devoted to the sense of sight, and they each took turns being blindfolded and trying to find their way around the house.

Several of the Vogt kids, now out on their own, say their attitude toward Family Night has improved in retrospect. "We grumbled tons about it as kids and were worried our friends would think it was weird," recalls Heidi Vogt, a student at Yale. "But now I think I became aware of a lot of issues at an earlier stage because of Family Night; I remember some teachers I had were impressed with that. I think it did help shape my values."

It also seems clear that Family Night had an effect on relationships within the family. Heidi remembers a night when "we all drew a paper out of a hat with the name of another family member on it, and we had to write down something we liked about that person. A few years later, I saw that my little brother Aaron still had what I wrote stuck to his bulletin board. I can't even remember now what it was that I wrote, but that was so cool to me."

The Suk family of Evanston, Ill., has Family Night every Thursday. "We didn't start out strictly for religious reasons, but just because my husband and I are so busy, and we wanted to have one night a week when we'd all be at home and not accessible to other people. In fact, we started it even before the kids were born," says L'Tishia Suk, who now has four kids.

The family cooks a special meal ("something that will get no complaints, like tacos") and if the phone rings, it is ignored. "We start the meal by singing a hymn we only sing on Thursday nights," says L'Tishia, who teaches classes on marriage and family issues at her church. Special plates are used for family night; not fancy china, but dishes reserved for this weekly event.

Thursday is also the only night the family prays together, taking turns around the table, offering up prayers for everybody from the president to a favorite grandmother. "We always pray for a girl in Haiti whom we sponsor," adds L'Tishia, "and if we get a letter from her, we save it to read that night." After prayers, the Suks have a treat of ice cream, and this is the only day of the week when ice cream is served.

During the school year, the three oldest children are excused to do homework after dessert, while the youngest plays games with her parents. In the summer, the whole family plans an activity together after dinner. "We'll do things that at least some of the kids like, then switch to other kids' interests next time," says L'Tishia. Activities have included minia-ture golf, visits to the park, and going to a drive-in movie.

Once a month or so, the Suks eat out on Family Night, trying differ-ent ethnic restaurants in the Chicago area. Prayers around the table are postponed until the family gets home and sits down for ice cream.

Keeping families observant together is one of the central tenets of Mormonism, because the faithful believe that if they live "righteous" lives the whole family will remain together after death. The goal for parents is to raise an "eternal family," and to help achieve this aim, the Church of Jesus Christ of Latter-day Saints began in 1915 to advocate a practice called Family Home Evenings. Families are exhorted to devote one evening a week to prayer and spiritual lessons, and most Mormons reserve Monday for this ritual.

"Church members just know not to call one another on Monday nights," says Nanette Hilton, the mother of three in Las Vegas. "Church leaders say that no success can compensate for failure in the home."

The Hiltons always say a prayer together on their Family Home Evenings, and rotate responsibilities for different aspects of the ritual. "We always do it after dinner, and nothing can conflict. One person will pick a song and another will say a prayer and a third person will be in charge of treats for the night. My husband or I will pick the theme, based on what is going on in the family. The topic might be death and eternal life if a grandparent has died, or it might be a lesson about honesty."

Because the Hiltons' children are young, the ritual doesn't last long, perhaps twenty minutes, before the treat is served.

"When I was growing up, my parents rotated, giving us a spiritual les-son every other week. In between, we'd do something fun like go bowl-ing," says Nanette. "But the leaders of our church have since said that the world has gotten so challenging for families that we need to have a solid spiritual lesson every single week." Nanette belongs to a group of women who work together to develop lesson plans for Family Home Evenings.

Luanne Stong of Clearfield, Utah, is also Mormon, but she holds her weekly family nights on Sunday out of personal preference. "I just like the idea of my kids staying reverent all day Sunday," says Luanne, whose four sons are between three and ten.

"We hold ours in the living room after dinner," she explains. "We'll sing songs, with each of the kids choosing a song from the ones they've learned at church. There is often a little lesson, again related to what they are learning in church."

Once the religious aspect of the evening has concluded, the Stongs bring out board games, and have "refreshments." Blender drinks are a favorite, often strawberries or peaches with milk, served with cookies.

"I grew up Mormon, but I wasn't used to this custom," says Luanne. "But my kids must really like it because if we get lazy and are wandering around the house on Sunday, one or the other will start asking, 'When are we going to have Family Home Evening?' I believe that if you start real young, rituals like this become such an ingrained habit to kids, they feel weird if you don't do it."

Deborah Pecoraro is Catholic and started weekly family nights as a form of family self-defense when they lived in a predominantly Mormon area.

"We lived in a part of Arizona that was 95 percent Mormon, and felt a certain amount of prejudice because we weren't. There were some kids, for example, who would tell our kids, 'We can't play with you because you're not Mormon.' "

Deborah chose a Catholic prayer titled "God Made Us a Family" as the theme of the family nights and even made a banner out of blue felt with those words on it. The banner, which hangs in the living room on family nights, has felt figures representing the four family members. "We each made our own figure, down to details like my husband's tie," says Deborah, "and then we put our family logo in the middle. There's a shamrock for my Irish background and a sheep, because my husband's name means *sheep* in Italian."

Dinner was served early on family nights, and then the kids got into their pajamas. They sang a special song and said the "God Made Us a Family" prayer.

"The very first time we did this, we got out a bunch of family pictures and explained how a family tree works," says Deborah. "Sometimes we'd play a board game, and we always ended with a special dessert." At other meetings, the family would get out the colored felt, glue, and scissors and make banners for upcoming holidays, which they still hang when those holidays roll around.

Family Nights for Fun

Of course, not every Family Night has a religious purpose. Many families reserve one night a week just to be together and have fun, and when they say this is "sacred" time, they mean only that it is reverently dedicated to their families above all else.

One family I know, the Van Horns, has a weekly movie night, at which they only watch films that have won the Academy Award for best picture. For the adults, it's a chance to see a classic they love, while their kids get a wonderful education in cinema history.

Quite a few weekly family nights involve watching movies, often rented videos, together. For the Hall family in Maryland, Friday night is movie night, when Monica makes individual pizzas so her husband and four children can each add the toppings of their choice.

"Several years ago, we decided to cancel our cable service and devote the money we saved to building a video collection," says Monica. "Now, we rent a movie once a month and twice a month we watch something from our own library. On that fourth Friday movie night, we buy a new movie."

Anne Hodge's kids are still too young to have killer schedules, so she has three nights a week dedicated to a themed activity.

It started with "Make Your Own Pizza Night." The Hodge family moved from Connecticut to Saratoga Springs, N.Y., about a year ago, and Anne wanted to figure out a good way to meet the neighbors and really feel part of the community. So she decided to have an informal pizza dinner every Friday, and invite a different neighborhood family each week.

"This has been so great," says Anne. "We've met all our neighbors, and it's been one of the best ways we've found to build friendships for the whole family. Also, by now, my three kids love homemade pizza so much, they'd rather have ours than get it delivered or at a pizza parlor."

This was going so well that Anne decided to make Thursday "Game Night," and reserve it just for immediate family.

"It has to be something the whole family can play, like charades or board games. Sometimes, there will be separate chess games, or a couple of kids doing puzzles. We might invite some neighborhood kids eventually, but for now it's just us."

Started recently is "Sunday Kids' Choice," which lets the three kids pick a theme for Sunday dinner, the sillier the better. On "Lego Night," Anne's kids decorated the table with Legos, and then there was "Joke Night," "Song Night," and "Change Seats Night." At one meal, the family could eat only with spoons. The most popular theme so far, says Anne, is "Reading at the Table Night."

But there is much more to "Sunday Kids' Choice." Anne's clever scheme is to start by making the "choice" part of the evening a fun activity, but soon choosing will also include whether the kids would rather plan the menu, cook, or clean up. "We're about to have the first night with a child chef," says Anne. "My daughter Emily has decided to fix deviled eggs and brownies, two things she makes well. I'll supplement that with some parental greens and rice." The two other kids will set the table and clean up.

For Debbie Menichino and her son, every Thursday night is "Dippity Night." On that night, they join Debbie's sister and her daughter, and Debbie's parents and grandmother.

The ritual is very simple. The extended family has dinner every week at a mall diner, where Debbie's son, Anthony, and his cousin love to dip their french fries in ketchup. Thus the preschoolers decided that Thursdays should be known as "Dippity Night." After dinner, the three generations walk around the mall and check out the shops. Right before they leave, it's time to stop at the game room, where Anthony and his cousin each get a turn on one kiddie ride (the kind that jiggles when you put a quarter in). Everybody heads back to Debbie's parents' house for coffee, and more play time for the kids.

★ ★ ★

Finally, let's be honest about the importance and prevalence of television in the average American home. If it isn't overdone, it doesn't have to be a corrosive influence on family ritual, and indeed, many families gather, shall we say religiously, to watch their favorite weekly shows.

If families never engaged in any other shared activity, this would be horrendous. But if television is only a small part of a ritual life and if families watch programs together and use them to generate discussion, it can be a useful exercise. Children can be taught to view television critically, and will learn much about how the world looks and works by watching. Also, having favorite shows and movies in common gives families a shared cultural bond just as loving the same sports team does, or cherishing the same books and songs. I know I'm not the only child of the '50s who fondly remembers the family gathering around the set to watch *Wide World of Disney* on Sunday evenings. And the annual presentation of *The Wizard of Oz* was a wildly anticipated ritual, bringing a rare chance to eat dinner on TV trays in the living room.

For some families, weekly television rituals involve something other than watching the show. One example: in Simpsonville, S.C., Kelly Pfeiffer and her two young children like to turn on the television show called *3rd Rock from the Sun* promptly at 8:00 PM on Sundays. "I don't know why, but we just love the theme song for the show, so we turn it on, dance up a storm, then turn it off and get ready for bed," says Kelly. "Sometimes my husband and I will tape the show and watch it later."

Family Meetings

Like a lot of rituals, family meetings can be arranged many different ways. I know one family that schedules a family meeting only when a major change is coming, such as a new nanny, a big trip, or the start of school. Either parents or kids are allowed to call a meeting when they feel one is needed.

The Vogts, whose family nights were discussed earlier, will sometimes depart from their issue-oriented discussions and activities and have a family meeting instead. A family-meeting list is kept on the refrigerator door, and any member of the family can write down items for an agenda, such as whether the parents want to reassign chores, or the kids want to argue a case for later bedtimes. When family members agree there are enough items to warrant a meeting, one is called. The Vogt children say they learn as much about their parents' values at these meetings as they do during regular family nights.

"There were four kids and only two parents, but we could never convince them to give us an equal vote," says Heidi Vogt. "Still, by arguing with them over things, we learned a lot about what mattered to them. Like we always wanted cable TV, and our parents would explain why they didn't want to spend their money on it. One item always on the list is that we were only allowed an hour a day of television and we always wanted to expand that: they would explain why they had set the limit. I didn't always agree with them, but at least I understood their reasoning."

Some families have had great results with weekly family meetings. But there are caveats. A real key to success is for parents to include fun activities or load on the accolades, so kids don't dread the sessions. One family I know concludes meetings by handing out the children's allowances. But if family meetings turn into parental gripe sessions designed to correct bad behavior, kids will feel more as if they've entered family boot camp than a place where they can comfortably accomplish family business.

For example, the Hassell family includes something called a "spotlight" at every family meeting.

"We rotate this through the five members of the family," explains Mary Bliss Hassell. "It's the time when everybody has to say one nice thing about the chosen person that week."

At these Monday meetings, the family reviews all the events of the coming week and coordinates schedules. There is always a prayer, and each person says something for which they have been thankful that week.

Duties are shared, with one person in charge of refreshments and someone else responsible for coming up with a discussion topic, such as "Where should we go on vacation this year?" or "How do we use this new software for the family computer?" Mary says that when she and her husband are in charge of discussion topics, they might lean more to things like "ethics and morals." If one of the children shows up at the meeting unusually grumpy, there may be a brief discussion of "how to treat someone who is grumpy."

Including dessert, the meetings last less than an hour, and then the Hassells usually play a game. One Monday winter night, they all went sledding. In the summer, the meeting is apt to spill out into the backyard for a family croquet game.

Ellen Brosbe of Santa Rosa, Calif., started weekly family meetings after reading a parenting book extolling their virtues. The family's style of meeting has changed over time, but they have been going on for nearly a decade.

The Brosbes have four kids between eleven and seventeen, and the meetings are held on Sundays now, because that is usually the rare evening without scheduling conflicts. The family is Jewish, but these meetings are primarily devoted to family issues rather than spiritual ones.

Meetings occur in the kitchen, where they've put one of those shiny wipe-off boards on the refrigerator to record the agenda. Any member of the family can add items to the agenda, but "they have to put their initials after them," explains Ellen.

Now that they're older, the four kids take turns leading the meeting. To start, each member of the family has to think of something nice to say about someone else. "It's real mundane stuff, but it's important for people in the family to acknowledge the help they get and thank each other," says Ellen. "One kid might say to a sibling, 'Thanks for doing my chores that day when I was so busy,' and another might say, 'Thanks for letting me use your new video game.' " Then, the items on the agenda are discussed.

"It might be as petty as reminding people to refill the orange-juice pitcher, but it might also be, 'Should we keep going to synagogue as a family when some members are losing interest?' " says Ellen. Since there are three bedrooms for the four kids, they take turns sharing, and a constant item is whether it's time to rotate rooms again.

After the agenda is covered, it's calendar time. The leader reviews every day of the coming week on the family calendar, which is also kept on the fridge. And anybody who has an event scheduled better pipe up and add it to the calendar, says Ellen, because "we have a rule that they can't surprise us at the last minute and say, 'I need a ride now.' "

Ellen gives the meetings mixed reviews. Her teenagers are starting to get a little surly about them because they'd rather do other things, such as hang out with friends, but she believes they have helped the family work through a lot of issues and have been worth the occasional complaint.

Monthly

As a unit of ritual, a month makes a lot of sense. We think of a new month as the herald of a season or the cue that holidays and anniversaries are coming soon. But also, the cycle of the moon is monthly and effects everything on the earth, from the tides to people's moods.

Celebrating the moon's cycle is an ancient impulse, and you don't have to be a pagan to revel in its glow. At certain ages, kids are automatically awed by such natural displays of cosmic change and that curiosity can be channeled into anything, from a study of astronomy to an excuse for a special treat.

The James family of Spokane, Wash., has "full-moon bonfires." Every month on the night of the full moon, the family of four makes a small fire right in their gravel driveway and roasts hot dogs and marshmallows on skewers. "We did it once when my son was six, and it was so beautiful, he said, 'Can we always do this?' " says Judy James, whose son is now eight. "In the summer, the moon isn't out when we eat, sitting on our folding camp chairs, but it's still lots of fun."

In Monroe, Wis., Craig Patchin has a special ritual for full moons the year each of his kids turn ten. Starting with the first full moon after that birthday, Craig takes a walk with that child after dark every month for the whole year. Usually, the walk lasts at least half an hour and the two go to the top of a hill in a nearby meadow where they can see for miles.

The ritual was inspired by a book called *Walk When the Moon Is Full* by ornithologist Frances Hamerstrom. It tells the true story about her family's monthly full-moon walks, including what wildlife they saw in different seasons. Tammy Patchin had just bought the book for her oldest child's upcoming tenth birthday, and her husband seized on the idea. "He felt that he didn't get as much time with the kids as he would like," says Tammy. "So when he got the idea to make this a tradition for our family, he asked if he could be the one to do it. And since our daughter Bethany was about to turn ten, we made it special for that year."

So Craig wrote in the front of the book before giving it to his daughter: "Happy Birthday. I make a pledge to you that we will go exploring every full moon this year and maybe we can write about what we see and hear. I love you, Daddy."

The ritual was so popular that Craig has continued it with his other children. Last year, he did it with his third daughter, Kelsey, and this summer, he will walk with his only son, Micah. Along the way, he has been surprised at how much his kids open up, sharing their lives and asking questions about his childhood. They anticipate the ritual as much as he does.

Kelsey, soon to be twelve, remembers her full-moon walks very fondly, and can even recall what the conversation was about at different times. "On really cold nights, my dad and I sometimes stayed inside, drinking hot cocoa together and looking at the moon out the window. On one cold night, when there was snow on the ground, we took a bunch of blankets and curled up in the hammock outside. My dad had to move a branch of the pine tree so we could see the moon, and we talked about memories and stories. Sometimes, we went to the meadow and we talked about dreams."

In the course of the year, Kelsey says she learned a lot about both life and wildlife. "We saw a flock of bats one time, and you could see the eyes of the raccoons in the moonlight," she says. "It was real neat."

Craig hates to think of the full-moon walks coming to an end after the series with his son, and so do his kids. So they're talking about repeating the ritual before the kids leave home, perhaps the year they turn eighteen.

The most cherished nonfamily ritual of my life is the book group I cofounded more than a decade ago, but book groups or clubs can be a terrific ritual for families as well. I'm a bookaholic, and the conversations are wonderfully stimulating, but the longer the group meets, the more we enjoy a shared history and the more deeply this ritual engages me intellectually as well as emotionally.

Most of the family book groups I know about concentrate on either mothers and daughters or fathers and sons, though there's no reason why a whole family couldn't start one, perhaps joining with another family. At a time when special attention is being paid to the sad loss of confidence among girls starting puberty, book groups for girls are becoming especially popular.

A very successful group was formed several years ago in Washington, D.C., by Shireen Dodson and her daughter, Morgan Fykes, then nine. The two meet monthly with nine other mother-daughter pairs, always on the first Sunday of the month starting at 3:00 PM. To get the gossip and girl talk out of the way, the mothers and daughters meet separately for half an hour, and then it's time for serious business. Each discussion is led by one of the daughters when the meeting is scheduled at her house, and she is expected to come prepared with a list of questions to stimulate conversation (one of the club's unwritten rules is that daughters never show the questions to their moms in advance). The evening ends with supper, often tied in some way to the book.

"The girls were insistent that this wouldn't be like school, so we don't ever read classics," says Shireen, who is assistant director of the Smithsonian Institution's Center for African-American History. "We've concentrated on contemporary books," she says, but the material is far from breezy beach reading. One of the most popular titles so far was a book called *The House of Dies Drear* by Virginia Hamilton, about the Underground Railroad. The mother and daughter who hosted that month set up part of their basement to resemble a stop on the Underground Railroad, so the book group could get a visceral sense of that historic period.

Shireen started the book group because she feared her bond with Morgan would weaken as she approached adolescence. Shireen had just suggested the book-club idea to a friend of hers who was having trouble with a daughter, and since Morgan loved books, she decided to approach her own daughter about starting one. Not only has the club strengthened the ties between mother and daughter, but articles about the group attracted the attention of a publisher, and Shireen has since written a book called *The Mother-Daughter Book Club*, which is inspiring hundreds of others to follow her example.

"The book group has turned out to be two rituals for us. About four nights a week, my daughter and I crawl into my bed and she reads a chapter to me and then I read a chapter to her. And no matter how bad the day has been, it calms us down and brings us together. We'll talk about things that come up in the book, or I might explain any words or concepts she isn't sure of."

Then there's the ritual of the meetings themselves, where "the girls can see that their opinions are valued by their peers and also by grown-ups other than their own parents." Shireen has noticed that the discussions have helped the girls to begin to see their mothers "not just as moms, but as women with histories. It humanizes us," she says.

It has changed the way Shireen and Morgan relate to each other generally. "She is an eleven-year-old girl and there are times we argue. But we'll be in the middle of our old way of arguing past one another and we'll just start to laugh. Then we can really talk and really listen to each other." Shireen reports that virtually all the mothers in the club say they've forged a deeper personal connection to their daughters.

One of the reasons this ritual is so effective and transforming is that it comes at a critical time, when old patterns of childhood like bedtime rituals start falling away. At this tricky age, kids want to be independent, but they still need family traditions. Strong family bonds will help them cope with all the seductions of teenage culture and rebellion, but not if those traditions are stifling or keep children trapped in infantile roles. A book group is perfect, because it treats kids as thinking equals with their own valid opinions.

There are other monthly rituals with an educational motive, but they are most successful when they include elements of fun and when the kids have a say in what happens.

Linda Schissler's husband traveled widely when he got out of the army years ago, and her two sons love his stories of exotic locales. So Linda decided to start a monthly "Trip Around the World" ritual. Each month, the family chooses a country and studies it, learning a few phrases in the language and cooking some authentic dishes.

"I actually got the idea from a neighbor who was a single mom with a little girl," says Linda, an elementary school music teacher in Asheville, N.C. "They used to pick countries and sew costumes for themselves. They'd have a traditional meal from that country while wearing their outfits. I wasn't going to sew with my sons, so I needed to think of other activities."

To start, the Schisslers wrote down names of countries that interested them on pieces of paper. Every month, a paper is picked out of a hat.

"This is partly to get my sons used to looking things up, which my oldest, who is nine, does in school now," says Linda. "So we start with the encyclopedia, looking up things like the country's flag. Then we find the country on our globe. When we can, we look up stuff on the Internet. For example, when we studied Russia and Japan, you could download sound clips that gave the pronounciation of little phrases. We would sit around the computer practicing those phrases. And there was one website where you could download the Japanese alphabet."

In addition, the family would comb through cookbooks looking for recipes they could handle. "For China, we cooked egg rolls from scratch, and they really weren't that hard," says Linda. "I was amazed how good they tasted." If they could find appropriate national music in their dad's international music collection, the Schisslers would play music while eating their ethnic meal.

Unfortunately, the ritual has lately fallen victim to an increasingly complex schedule. "My husband has to work several nights a week and then soccer is very time-consuming," says Linda. "I'm embarrassed to say we've been stuck on Greece now for several months."

But Linda has plans to revitalize the ritual by stretching it out a bit. "It's such a great idea and the kids enjoy it so much that I don't want to give up," she says. "I think we were just trying to cram in too much activity for the time we've got. As it is, it goes by so fast the kids don't retain a lot of what they learned. I'm thinking we should stick with one country for a couple of months, maybe even a year, and really pace ourselves. Then we can do more on language, maybe even try to rent movies from that country with subtitles, which will give us a sense of the language and also a real visual sense of a foreign culture."

Singling out each child for a special activity or recognition every month is a great way to generate anticipation and celebrate individuality.

In Winston-Salem, N.C., the Whalings have a ritual of letting each of their four kids be "king" or "queen" for one day a month. On the first day of the month, Cindy Whaling takes down the large family calendar, and each child takes turns closing his or her eyes and pointing to a date. Whether it's a weekday or weekend, Cindy draws a tiny crown on that day and writes in the child's name.

"On their day, that child gets to select dinner and we usually rent a movie that they pick," says Cindy. "If it's a weekend or in the summer, they can invite a friend to stay overnight, and my oldest, now eleven, has gotten pretty good at pointing his finger at the weekend. My five-year-old always wants to get a Happy Meal and we resist going to McDonald's usually, so he often chooses that when he's king."

The bottom line, says Cindy, is that the ritual doesn't cost the family much and includes pretty normal activities, but because the kids feel in charge, the days seem very special. The kids "even anticipate when someone else is king or queen, because they'll be in on the treat or the movie or whatever happens."

When and If Rituals:
Family Sayings and Doings

There are many family rituals that don't occur at regular times of the day or days of the month, but are linked to certain experiences, situations, or emotions. Some of them are so ingrained in a family's experience that they may not even be recognized as rituals, just seen as the sometimes eccentric habits that lie deep within the culture of a family. Even if you knew about these rituals as a close friend, you might not feel comfortable entering into them. They have an exclusive, tribal quality, like a fraternity handshake, and only family members can belong.

I do a silly thing with my son that we call "beaking." I usually do it when I take him out of his high chair after a meal, and as I scoop him up I start threatening, "Oh, I think I might have to beak you," as I rush to the family room with him in my arms. Then, I throw him on his back on a sofa, pin his arms down, and rub my nose against his nose. He laughs and wriggles away, and I say, triumphantly, "Beak to beak." Now, anytime Max sees a picture of people or animals touching noses, or my husband and I do it, he says, "They're beaking!"

I wouldn't try to argue that this is an educational experience. I'm not giving heavy ethical messages to my son, or imparting ethnic folkways. But I believe that such spontaneous moments of quirky familiar ritual help create real intimacy in families: we are speaking a language spoken only by the two of us (and sometimes his dad).

Every close family, I'm convinced, has some form of this kind of ritual: family words, family hugs, family songs. Cornball though it may sound, these are the pep songs of the family team.

Indeed, some families even borrow directly from team cheers, like the Abbe family. The two kids play soccer and used a cheer while in a huddle, when team members piled their hands in the center, one on top of the other. At the end of the cheer, everyone threw their hands up and out. Now, whenever the family has a car ride full of bickering siblings and is about to make a collective entrance, say at a social event, their mother will call for "family huddle time." The family stacks hands, says the family cheer ("Let's go, Abbes!"), and the reconnected foursome goes on its way.

Another ritual for ending family squabbles was posted anonymously on an on-line bulletin board. This mother calls it the "Indian Hug Cure for Sibling Fights," and says that when the need arises, her three kids are commanded to sit cross-legged on the floor and hug. No talking allowed. Then, after a time, the kids are told to stand up, and hug some more. Their mother swears it works every time.

And then there is the stress-reducing ritual of Kelly Pfeiffer's family. "When we're starting to get grumpy, one of us will shout out 'Crazy Dance Party,' " she explains. "Then we all do a countdown from ten to one, turn on some music, and dance like maniacs until everybody is laughing."

The Brunsons do a "pinkie lock" whenever they want to stress the seriousness of a promise. Two family members lock their pinkies together and say, "I promise on our love." The oldest girl, now five, initiated this practice. One day, for example, she was afraid to go into a swimming pool. Karen, her mother, assured her that she wouldn't let go of her, but the little girl needed more. "Promise on our love?" she asked, and once the pinkie lock was done, she was ready to jump in.

I've even found a family that has a ritual for breaking bad news, based on that well-worn joke about the man who goes on vacation and leaves his neighbor to watch the cats, then calls his neighbor to check on things. His neighbor bluntly informs him that one of his cats died. The grieving vacationer chastises his neighbor for not breaking the news more gently, and suggests it would have been better to start by saying, "The cat's on the roof, and we can't get it down. . . ." and then slowly building up to the sad truth. The man calls back a few days later, and his neighbor says, "Your mother's on the roof, and we can't get her down."

Thus, in the Thurman family, in Pittsburgh, a family member with bad tidings sends a warning by saying, "The cat's on the roof, and I can't get her down." On one occasion when the Thurmans' son James said this to his mother, she replied, "What happened?" and he responded, "Do you want to see the front fender of your car?"

Naturally Sue wasn't happy to hear her son had been in an accident or that her car was damaged, but hearing the punch line first both prepared her for the bad news and activated her sense of humor at a time she really needed it.

Finally, a ritual outlet for many musically inclined families is singing. I've already mentioned how atrociously I sing, but singing doesn't have to be good to be fun, as long as it's done in the proper mood, under the right circumstances. Pamela Pinegar, a divorced mother of two teenage girls, often sings with them. They attempt to harmonize, and call themselves "the Von Krapp Family Singers."

And then there are rare families like the Halls, who sing to and with each other on just about every occasion. "We sing to wake the kids up in the morning, to go to sleep at night, and even to get them to stay on the potty during potty training," explains Monica Hall, a mother of four in Maryland. "We sing after every meal and sometimes before, and once we made the kids 'sing for their supper.' "

That happened on a night when the kids were whining about what Monica was cooking for dinner. "I told them that if they wanted something else, they'd have to sing for it," she says. When they did, loudly and enthusiastically, they were all allowed to make the peanut-butter-and-jelly sandwiches they wanted instead.

Monica says that everyone in the family has a good natural voice, and that she had voice training as a child instead of piano lessons because her mother figured her voice was "already paid for." Monica starts the day by singing a song to her kids that her mother sang to her. It goes: "When you come to think of it, waking up is fun. Open your eyes; what a surprise. Morning has begun." She says the kids groan, but they know they're expected to get moving.

After breakfast, the family performs daily devotions, and each kid gets to pick a song, "and an action to go with it, like marching. We might sing 'This Is the Day that the Lord Has Made,' while hopping around the room. We also try to find out what hymns or psalms we'll be singing for the next Sunday service, and learn the first verse at least."

When they need to combat boredom, the Halls pick from a selection of beloved songs, the sillier the better. "We might sing 'Do Your Ears Hang Low?' or 'Down by the Bay.' For the first one, I'll do something silly like put pants on my head to make ears, and they'll go get their pajama bottoms and do the same. It cheers us all up."

Like everybody else, the Halls have bad days, but at least they can sing the blues together.

Seven

★ ★ ★ ★

RITES OF PASSAGE

While they are very young, the little girls among the Rahūna (in Morocco) go about with their heads shaved except for the front hair and a tuft on the crown; when they reach puberty, they let their hair grow, leaving loose that which is on the forehead and rolling the rest on their heads; when they are married, the hair is divided into two braids which are allowed to hang in back; but when they become mothers they bring those two braids forward over their shoulders on to their breasts.

—Arnold van Gennep, *The Rites of Passage*

I n countless cultures through the ages, the rules and rituals for each stage of life were as clearly prescribed and widely followed as those of the Rahūna. Details such as hair, clothing, scars, and jewelry made it easier for others to know the status and experience of a given person.

Many of life's transitions are just as important today, and not only to the individual and his or her family, but to the community as a whole. Rituals both simple and elaborate evolved to mark and celebrate those changes. In primitive societies, the most important are the initiation rituals that make one a full member of one's tribe. Such rituals are often lengthy, strenuous, and sometimes terrifying, with preparations that may last as long as a year or two. But these rites and the elders who administer them help young people pass through the threshold from childhood into adulthood with a clear notion of what is expected of them, and give them the knowledge and confidence to play their new roles.

Even today, there are transition rituals in other cultures that apply to a whole society, such as Japan's national holiday (January 15) Seijin no Hi, which means "Day of Adulthood." On this day, Japanese citizens who will turn twenty that year are recognized as adults. Young men and women put on their best clothes and pray at Shinto shrines, while local government officials offer lectures (attendance is voluntary) about the rights and responsibilities that come with adulthood in Japan. (As it happens, girls are much more likely to celebrate this holiday than boys, partly because it is one of the few occasions when they get to dress up in elaborate kimonos. After visiting a shrine, many young women adjourn to a fancy hotel for a big party with friends.)

In the ethnic stew that is contemporary America, with extended families a thing of the past and even nuclear families endangered, remnants of such rituals still remain. In Jewish families, the bar mitzvah and bat mitzvah are treated as major rites of passage, as is the vision-quest ritual still followed by many Native American tribes. Latin American communities have the Quinceañera, a religious ritual and family party that lavishly celebrates a girl's fifteenth birthday as her passage into womanhood. Other religions and ethnic groups have ceremonies for important milestones like baptism and confirmation.

But these are scattered examples, exceptions to the rule in a country where major life passages seem more dreaded than celebrated ("midlife crisis"). All too often, even when coming-of-age rituals are enacted they proceed by rote and leave young people unmoved and unchanged. It may sound like crackpot hyperbole, but I really believe that without appropriate coming-of-age rituals, teens and preteens experience a void in their lives. This void can be dangerous because it wants desperately to be filled, and young people are naturally drawn to the chaotic ad hoc initiation rituals of their peers.

Forbidden vices like drugs and alcohol, along with body-piercing and wild hair colors, are among the experiences that tempt teens and preteens as a way of proving their newly independent status. Experts report a near epidemic of teenage girls who cut and scar themselves, members of a secret cult of self-loathing, acting out ceremonies of initiation without a community. Studies show that the average age girls begin mutilating themselves is fourteen, and the cutting or burning is sometimes accompanied by such accoutrements of ritual as candles or incense. In cities and even some suburbs, other kids are seduced by the highly ritualized culture of street gangs, where shooting an "enemy" may be viewed as a rite of passage.

And these impulses are not confined just to kids who see themselves as rebels or outcasts of society. Remember the gruesome videotape of young Marine paratroopers pounding a pin called the "golden wings" into one another's chests until their T-shirts were bloody? "Blood pinning" it was called, and however barbaric it may seem, it shows that the need for initiation rites is a primal one that will remain no matter how "civilized" our society becomes.

In an introduction to a book of essays called *Betwixt and Between: Patterns of Masculine and Feminine Initiation,* Jungian analyst and editor Louise Carus Mahdi says, "The need for some kind of initiation is so important that if it does not happen consciously, it will happen unconsciously, often in a dangerous form." She refers to prisons as "houses of failed initiation."

The question facing parents today is how to address their children's initiation needs in a healthy way. Just what role can and should parents play in this? If parents, as the elders of their family "tribe," don't help guide their children into adulthood, they shouldn't be surprised if their kids never arrive at that destination. It's very easy to get lost on such an arduous journey, and if you don't have a compass and a clear idea of the topography, you'll be more easily seduced by the sideshow barkers along the way.

Because change is one of the few constants in life, it would seem that handling transitions in brave and creative ways would be one of the best lessons a parent could possibly teach. And the earlier the lessons begin, the better.

If children learn at a young age how to face transition head-on with the help of thoughtful rituals, then perhaps the enormous and long-running changes of adolescence won't be quite as frightening. And, by the time the children are grown, they'll possess some of the tools and instincts required to fashion meaningful rituals of their own for such major transitions as marriage, the birth of children, career upheavals, middle age, and death.

While coming-of-age rituals will be the major focus of this chapter, let's start with some of the early childhood transitions. Parents have the authority and ability to make these early changes more triumphant than terrifying, and doing so sends a powerful message that will remain long after the child forgets what it was like to give up bottles.

CHILDHOOD RITES OF PASSAGE

Anybody who has ever raised a child knows how frightening change is to an infant, even a very young one. If Mommy isn't there for bedtime, a child's lamentations might rival something out of Greek tragedy. For the average toddler, the seemingly simple transition from playing to any other activity—even eating, even when the child is hungry—can cause a major breakdown. Simple repetitive rituals guide toddlers through such transitions, and most mothers invent such rituals without even thinking about it. I don't know how long it took me to learn this, but once I helped Max "say good-bye" to all the toys in the community sandbox or a friend's playroom, and promised that we could come back soon, leaving became almost blissfully easy.

But "saying good-bye" becomes more complicated and considerably more frightening when the change is final and when the object to which the child bids farewell is something like his mother's breast, his pacifier, or his crib. At such times, the best rituals accomplish two things: they help a child leap into the nonpacifier future by stressing what a big boy he is, but also demonstrate vividly that the big boy will be loved just as profoundly and deeply as the small baby he used to be.

One effective way of doing this is to entice a child across the threshold to a new status with concrete and tantalizing rewards. While a little girl can't imagine what she'll feel or act like, or how she'll survive without her pacifier, once she has been lured to a pacifierless existence by treats of some sort, she will discover that she can handle her new role after all. And the real pride she feels at her accomplishment makes it easier for her to resist the temptation to regress.

Some might consider this approach simple bribery, but a better way to understand it is that the ritual treat works as a distraction. Indeed, therapist Aaron Hoorwitz, whose work with the "magical thinking" of children was discussed earlier, says that much ritual for both adults and children works as a kind of hypnotic distraction. "What you're doing with hypnosis or ritual is suggesting that someone do something that they are already ready to do, but can't somehow. The ritual distracts the logical part of their brain long enough so that they can accomplish this thing."

One good example of such rite-of-passage rituals is Linda Schissler's potty cake. Linda, an elementary school music teacher in Asheville, N.C., was having a lot of trouble getting her second son, then three, to use the potty at home.

It wasn't a question of whether Gordon was physically ready, because he used the potty regularly at day care. "We tried everything. We bought him a potty seat when he turned two, we got him Aladdin underwear because we thought he'd like wearing it, and we'd say, 'Let's go sit on the potty together.' "

When her oldest son, Carl, was that age, he had simply announced that he was going to start using the potty and wearing underwear, and he did, recalls Linda. But here was Gordon, nearly three and a half, and not the least interested. Linda got the idea of surprising Gordon after dinner one night with a "potty cake." She decorated it with a drawing of a toilet and the words "Happy Potty to You."

Gordon got to blow out the candles after the family sang to him, and then everybody had a small piece of cake. Linda told him that "every time he sat on the potty and something came out, he would get another piece of cake." The result: "He started going to the potty and staying on the potty all the time. In just one day he was going regularly."

The cake ran out in a few days and Linda feared backsliding, so she switched the reward to sugarless cinnamon gum, which Gordon thought of as a distinctly grown-up treat. ("He called it 'hot gum,'" she recalls.) By the time the whole pack of gum was consumed, Gordon was potty-trained for good. "There was part of me that felt I was bribing him, but at that point, I just wanted something to work," says Linda. "I don't know how much was the ceremony and him wanting to be the center of attention and being told he was a big boy, or if he just wanted to feed his face. But it worked, and it clearly didn't leave him warped."

(A caveat: it is important that parents understand that no ritual, however clever or thoughtful, will teach a child to use the potty if he or she isn't physicially able and ready to do so. To try and force a ritual to work against nature could leave a child traumatized. The signs of readiness for potty-training can be found in countless books on parenting, or by calling your pediatrician.)

For many parents, weaning a child from the breast, bottle, or pacifier is a horrendous struggle. Appropriate rituals can be tremendously effective in easing such transitions, as with Eliane Proctor's weaning party detailed on page 24. Incorporating such momentous changes into existing holiday rituals is another strategy.

Andrea Majewski, a mother of two in Wilmington, Del., had a lot of trouble getting her kids to give up their pacifiers, or "sissies" as they called them. Both were still sucking away at four years old. So, one Easter, she and her husband told their older child, Kate, that if she gave all her "sissies" to the Easter bunny, he'd probably leave an extra-special treat in her basket. On Easter eve, the pacifiers were placed lovingly in a special box and Kate said good-bye to each and every one. The next morning, the box was filled with special candies and a note from the Easter bunny about "how grown-up Kate was becoming." Andrea adds, "It sounds dopey, but it sure worked."

Thus, a few years later, when Kate's brother Steven was four, the Easter bunny received another batch of pacifiers. "It was even easier with him, because Katie had very enthusiastically described the wonders that awaited him." says Andrea. "He could hardly wait to see if it lived up to his expectations." It did.

Rachel Klein, who lives on Long Island, N.Y., used a different approach to get her older son, Max, off pacifiers.

"He was so attached to pacifiers it was like an addiction, like he was enjoying a cigarette," she jokes. "Finally, when he was three, we started reading this little book about Miss Piggy giving up her pacifiers by throwing them out in the garbage. But I didn't think he could handle anything so abrupt."

So Rachel came up with the idea that Max would take his pacifier to bed as usual, but stick it under the pillow. It would be safely within reach but symbolically distant. Indeed, he wound up fishing it out from under the pillow during the first few nights, says Rachel. But by the end of the week, he realized he could sleep without the pacifier and the transition was accomplished. He and his mother sang a little made-up farewell song as they ceremoniously threw out his pacifiers.

MILESTONE BIRTHDAYS

All birthdays are important to children, but some are truly pivotal, signaling the arrival of new powers and privileges. Creating rituals that recognize and define the meaning of those milestones helps kids come to grips with what is changing and what remains the same.

My son just turned three, and to us that felt like a milestone, partly because most of the interesting toys come with warnings that say: "Not for children under three." Even more important, he started nursery school just before his birthday, so it feels as if this year will truly mark the end of infancy and toddlerhood. His life as an independent creature really begins, because, for the first time, he'll be having daily experiences over which I'll have no control and, often, I worry, no knowledge.

When I thought about what rituals to devise, other than eating a cake with trucks on it and giving gifts with small parts, I kept coming back to this notion of releasing him into the larger culture. I wanted a ritual that would celebrate the excitement of his emergence into a new world of possibilities, one that would feel like an adventure.

I loved the idea of creating a physical threshold he would have to cross, which conjures up images of heroes venturing bravely into the unknown. I bought an inexpensive full-size sheet at Wal-Mart, and used his brightest paints to write "Happy Birthday Max" in huge letters, then painted balloons floating to the top. I decorated it with symbols of his "big-boy" triumphs and privileges, including wearing underwear, eating popcorn, and using scissors. At the bottom I cut a slit just taller than he is, and painted giant threes on either side.

After dinner on his birthday, Max was detained in the dining room while the sheet was taped over the wide entrance to the family room. Once it was in place, he was carried over to it, and I pointed out the symbols. I told him how proud we were of him and how many exciting adventures he had ahead. I explained that his presents were on the other side of the curtain, but first I reached underneath and pulled out a small metal Volkswagen Beetle, a model car my father had given me and that Max had coveted practically since birth.

"Now that you're a big boy," I said, "this belongs to you." Never have I seen his eyes so wide! Clutching the yellow car, Max bolted gleefully through the opening in the curtain, exclaiming at the pile of presents on the other side. The biggest testament to his appreciation of this ritual is that Max wasn't immediately interested in opening his gifts. He first had to dash back and forth through the curtain repeatedly, till he'd gotten enough of this new thrill. When the curtain was taken down a day later, he asked to have it reinstalled and then it was used as a playroom tent for months.

Here are some other milestone birthdays and the rituals parents have devised to celebrate them.

Reaching ten is unquestionably a big deal: by then, school is old hat and friends are becoming more and more important. Kids have lost baby teeth, learned to ride a bike, probably kept a secret from their parents. They know by now that they're really good in karate, or the best singer in the class, and they've got a set of passionate likes and dislikes: in other words, they've begun to form a real sense of identity.

But what lies ahead is pretty scary. This first year in the double digits means that the chaos of puberty is coming, with all its horrors and uncertainties. So this is a good year for rituals and gifts that recognize enhanced maturity, but in a reassuring way: things that dwell more on the excitement of being at the peak of childhood rather than hinting at the confusion and changes ahead. Kathy Chesto gave each of her kids their own radio alarm clock when they turned ten. "They were thrilled because it meant they were finally grown-up enough to wake themselves up in the morning," she says, "like Mom and Dad and the older kids."

Another example is the Swiss Army knives that Jeff Butler gave to his sons when they turned ten.

"This all came up because we were camping once when our sons were maybe four and five," explains Jeff's wife, Cindy Phillips. "The boys saw Jeff using a Swiss Army knife and they really, really wanted one. Clearly they were too young, and my husband just picked a number out of the air. He said, 'When you turn ten, you can get your own Swiss Army knife.'"

From that point, this special knife was much anticipated by both boys (Kyle, who is adopted, is only eight months older than his brother, Tristan, who is not). So it was decided that when each of the boys turned ten, he would be taken by his father to a fancy knife shop.

"The first time, I went out to dinner with my son, Kyle, just the two of us," says Jeff, who teaches high school physics and calculus. "Then, we went knife-shopping. I wouldn't let him get the $5,000 model, but he sort of already knew which attachments he wanted, like the little scissors and the cool toothpick. He also wanted a fish scaler on his, because we go fishing a lot. But I really believe in throwing them back in, so he hasn't used that feature yet."

When his turn came, Tristan too was excited about getting his Swiss Army knife. But he also got the chance to do something special for his tenth birthday that pretty much eclipsed everything else.

"Because I'm a teacher and I'm friends with the high school football coach, the coach said that for Tristan's birthday, he could be the ball boy for the team at an away game," explains Jeff. "So Tristan and I went to the game and we stayed in a hotel that night, just the two of us. He loved being 'in' the game and being around those big football players. We went shopping for his knife the next morning, but I'm afraid it paled next to the experience of being ball boy at the game."

Jeff and Cindy's daughter is now seven, so she will have a crack at the ritual in a few years. "I imagine my daughter will want a Swiss Army knife just like her brothers," says Jeff. "She goes camping and hiking with us too. We'll have to see when the time comes."

Getting a knife of one's own does carry a powerful, age-old symbolism, suggesting that a child is entering a phase when he must learn to care for, and perhaps protect, himself. There are other powerful symbols for such a stage that Jeff and Cindy might want to consider for their daughter. For example, when Sara Tarpley's daughter turned ten, she was allowed to do something she'd been begging for for years: get her ears pierced. This ritual of body piercing also feels very primal, an ancient step enacted in many coming-of-age ceremonies.

The objects and activities that represent maturity vary from family to family, but when Susan Lewis was a child, the grown-up experience that tantalized her was drinking coffee.

"When I was a young girl in Council Bluffs, Iowa, I remember the smell of freshly brewed coffee in the morning, and the obvious pleasure my mother took from sipping her cup," remembers Susan, who is now an actress in theater and television. She often asked her mother if she could have some coffee, and her mother always replied, "Not yet." Until, on the morning of her twelfth birthday, Susan ran downstairs to discover a piping hot cup of coffee ("two parts milk and one part coffee"), at her place in the kitchen. Her mother said, "Go ahead now. You're old enough, young lady," and Susan savored both the drink and the sense of initiation. She was one of seven children and had observed her big brother's first cup of coffee.

"It really meant I was special, that I was seen as grown-up now," says Susan. "The fact that when we got our coffee it was in front of all the other kids was important. Boy, our egos flourished on that morning!" She laughs now at how she really lorded the privilege over her younger siblings. "I didn't really want coffee that often after I turned twelve, but if I was having a quarrel with one of my sisters, I might say to my mom at breakfast, 'She's having milk. I'll have coffee.'"

Susan, who now has a four-year-old son, says she prefers herbal tea as an adult. But her son has become fascinated with Grandma's coffee on visits to her home in Omaha, Neb., and he has started to anticipate that forbidden treat on his twelfth birthday.

Another archetypal male milestone that remains even in the late twentieth century is the first time a boy or young man is considered old enough to go hunting.

For Kim Meisenheimer's two sons, that moment comes when they reach their twelfth birthday.

"About a month before, they get to take a weekend-long course with their father so they can learn how to shoot and do target practice," says Kim. "The men in this family like to hunt deer and duck, so they consider this a very big deal. At this age, the boys are so impressed with all the grown-up things dads can do, so this birthday seems to be a big transition for them."

The ritual gift for this big year: hunting gear. As Kim puts it, "This is one of the few times the boys are actually happy to get clothes for a present." The following October, the boys are guaranteed a chance to go deer-hunting with their firefighter father and his friends from the station.

"They wait for so long to do this. They ride motorbikes out there and hike through the mountains and camp in tents, so it's a whole outdoor week." She adds that her older, quieter son, Chad, was both excited and wary before his hunting trip, concerned that maybe he wasn't up to it and wouldn't have a good time. "It was a lot different from what he expected," says his mother. "I think it built a lot of confidence that the trip went well. But the best part for him was being with the guys, not being the little boy who stayed home while Dad went away hunting."

Her younger son, Brent, practices archery already, and can't wait until it's his turn. He plans to take the rifle lesson, but is eager to try shooting a deer with his bow and arrow.

For most kids, sixteen is a magical year. They can drive at last and driving means freedom. All rites of passage begin with a separation from family and tribe, and in our culture, kids separate on wheels. Behind the wheel of a car, a teenager finally finds himself equal in stature to adults, a peer with equal powers and responsibilities.

Baxter Murphy of Seattle was as car-crazy as any teenager and his father is a man who still loves cars. Baxter's big sister had received a car for her sixteenth birthday, and Baxter could hardly wait to get his.

Under the circumstances, his parents, then divorced, decided to make cars the theme for all the events of that day.

"In the morning, he got the keys to a new Toyota sports car from his dad," says Lynn, who works as a movie scout. "I gave him a wallet into which we had already put his driver's license. Then we went to a nice auto shop and he picked out a key chain and we got him a car-cleaning kit. His father had already ordered floor pads for the car with his name on them, so we picked those up too."

For dinner, Baxter was taken to his favorite drive-in, one where they still attach the metal tray to your car door. He was joined by some of his closest friends. Then, it was time to go play "Whirlyball," a game his mother describes as "basketball in bumper cars." The game requires at least six people on a team, and Baxter and his friends numbered more than a dozen, so the game was on. "Basically, you have these plastic scoops, sort of like for jai alai, and you zip along and crash and try to get the ball and race to the net," says Lynn. "We all had a blast."

I suppose the age most associated with *really* reaching adulthood in this country continues to be twenty-one, the legal age for booze, although young people have already been legally drinking beer, driving, and even voting for some time.

Cindy Phillips remembers vividly that, in her childhood, her father was "a very old school" disciplinarian about children minding their manners around grown-ups. He was famous for telling all the kids in the neighborhood, "You can call me by my first name, the day you turn twenty-one." What ended up happening is that as each of the kids reached that magical milestone, they would show up on Cindy's doorstep and ask to see her father. "He would pour them a drink, and they would call him by his first name. It was a real big deal."

Today, when teenagers show even less respect for their elders, it's hard to imagine such a ceremony. But some parents have found profound and personal ways to mark twenty-first birthdays.

Lynn Murphy did include some drinking on her daughter's twenty-first birthday, but the full day of festivities celebrated Amy's past and future as well. "I set up special activities all through the day, but one of the themes was that everywhere we went, she would run into, or get a phone call from, someone who was important in her past."

After breakfast, Lynn and her daughter went to Seattle's Pike Place Market, where they "bumped into" one of her best friends from high school who had also recently turned twenty-one. Lynn took the two young women to a spa, where they each had a professional massage.

Amy was given little cards telling her what came next, and one announced "gift stop," which turned out to be a clock store. "I thought of a clock as something permanent, and told her to pick one she liked," says Lynn. "She chose a whimsical one that she still has, at twenty-seven."

Lynn had also decided that picking out a womanly perfume was an important milestone, so another "gift stop" card guided her and Amy to a perfumery in a hotel. "The woman who served us really turned it into an event," says Lynn. "She was very exotic and went into all this detail about body auras and all. The whole thing took an hour."

Then it was time for a champagne toast, at a picturesque spot in the hotel called the Bookstore Bar. "The symbolic first drink with Mom," says Lynn.

Before dinner, Amy and her mother went out for hors d'oeuvres, where Amy was surprised and delighted to find her high school swimming coach and his wife and a girlfriend from the team. The coach had been a special mentor and Amy was a champion swimmer.

Later, it was time for a family dinner at Seattle's dramatic Space Needle restaurant. There were more champagne, presents, and more phone calls. "It got to the point where she'd say, 'Oh God, here comes another waiter paging me,'" says Lynn.

Of course, many parents who want to celebrate their children's twenty-first birthday have to plan around the fact that the kids are away at college. That didn't stop Alma Fisher from creating a memorable ritual for her oldest son, Scott.

Alma, who lives in Lake Bluff, Ill., got the idea from a friend. For at least a year before the big birthday, Alma had been collecting special birthday cards, knowing she was going to send her son one card for each year of life, and wanting each card to represent something notable about a particular year. For example, on Scott's fifth birthday, a friend of his had slammed the door of the treehouse on his fingers, and Scott felt his parents went overboard reassuring his friend that the accident was a trifle: the photo for that year showed a little boy with a suitcase walking out the front door of a house.

The cards started arriving at his college fraternity twenty-one days before his birthday. Enclosed with the first one was a photograph of Scott during his first year, and a letter from his mother recounting the details of his birth. There was also a dollar bill.

The next day, Scott got another card with another letter, a photograph from his second year, and two dollars. And so it went, day after day. By the time his birthday arrived, Scott had collected $231 in cash, the story of his life in words and pictures, and a demonstration of motherly love he will never forget.

Alma says his response made the effort worthwhile. "He said, 'Mom, I can't begin to tell you how much this meant; even the guys in my fraternity were completely undone by it.' He also told me he saved all the stuff I sent. And someday he wants to do it for his own children."

She is getting ready to repeat the ritual with her younger son, Trent.

COMING OF AGE

When exactly do children "come of age" in this society? Is it when they can or do have babies? When they graduate from high school? Move out of the house? When they can drive? Or vote? Or drink?

To make things even harder, we live in a permissive society that puts individual fulfillment far ahead of community well-being, and our tribal drums, which we call media, relentlessly celebrate adolescent behavior. Where are the enticing images of wise but cool adults to emulate? The cultural "heroes" are mostly athletes, moguls, and movie characters who break the rules as gleefully as any toddler. Thus, even if we could figure out *when* one becomes a grown-up in late-twentieth-century America, how do we help our kids grope their way toward that lofty state?

Well, necessity is the mother of invention, and that includes the invention of good ritual. And necessity is where this all starts. We may not have the models and mythology that fed the primal rites-of-passage rituals in ancient tribes, but even our current culture includes images of profound coming-of-age experiences, and their very popularity tells us how deep-seated this need lies.

Take a look at the *Star Wars* trilogy and Disney's *The Lion King.* George Lucas has said he based the story for his trilogy on coming-of-age mythology in the work of Joseph Campbell, and that material clearly touched a deep chord in audiences hungry for stories that reach beyond special effects. Luke Skywalker goes through many trials and battles, learning from such wise and heroic elders as Obi Won Kenobe and Yoda how to face his father and death, and prove his manhood.

The Lion King, a fable that Disney invented, is a classic coming-of-age story. The cub must survive the death of his father and a period of solitude in the wilderness before reaching maturity, passing such difficult tests as defeating a shrewd enemy and accepting his responsibilities. Until he has faced down all his demons, he isn't able to love another or rise up to his destiny as king.

But what are the trials today's young men and women must face to come of age? And where are the Jedi knights who will lead them into adulthood?

Increasingly, as the pain of uninitiated teenagers becomes more intense and destructive, a community of teachers and leaders has begun to emerge. Margaret Mead, the famous anthropologist, organized a seminar in the '70s to explore how rites of passage could be adapted to contemporary Western society; little came of it at the time, but now many are working toward that goal. Rites-of-passage programs are springing up all across the country, within churches, schools, inner cities, and even within the juvenile justice system. Therapists and wilderness guides are building new camps and programs formed specifically to help adolescents complete this crucial transition.

The rituals themselves differ considerably, whether they are wilderness journeys, school projects, or religious ceremonies. But the basic principles are the same ancient patterns distilled decades ago by anthropologists. What they realized is that the coming-of-age rituals for all these primitive tribes and societies shared a three-step process of separation, initiation, and return to society. The more psychologists studied this phenomenon, the more convinced they became that these steps are psychologically indispensable; each of us must complete a mental journey away from our parents, must confront and understand our emerging personality (or soul), and must be recognized as an adult by our parents in order to grow up ourselves.

One of the more established rites-of-passage programs is the School of Lost Borders in Big Pine, Calif., run by Steven Foster and his wife, Meredith Little. The two, who also train adults to lead such programs, have spent several decades guiding teenagers into the mountains for what they call a "vision fast," based on Native American vision-quest traditions.

It takes ten days, including four of intense instruction and preparation, before the young people spend three days and nights camping alone in the mountains with water but no food. Before their time of solitude, each kid finds a special "fasting place" and stashes water there. The kids are paired with buddies, and told to make a rock pile each day where they will leave a note telling their buddy they are all right. Instructors discuss the effects of fasting and tell the kids how to prepare themselves to receive a "vision," including making a circle of rocks on the last night of the fast and sleeping inside that "purpose circle." They are given tarps, but not tents. Despite all the preparation, some kids get scared or frustrated and return early to the base camp.

After the time alone, the questers reunite for several days, during which they celebrate and share their adventures with "elders," including their parents. These mentors help them clarify in their own minds the meaning of their "ordeal," and what it taught them about themselves.

"Usually we take about ten kids at a time, often graduating seniors," says Steven. "When it's all over, and the kids are reunited in that ceremony with their parents, we ask the parents to give them some kind of right or privilege to mark the attainment of a new maturity. Parents often tell them that from this time on they won't bother them about their hours, their friends, or their homework. Often parents bring a symbolic gift. One mother gave her son her dead father's wedding ring. A father gave his daughter a journal he had kept between the time she was conceived and the time she was born.

"The big three elements in rites of passage have been hunger, seclusion, and exposure to the elements, and that's what this experience provides," says Steven. "Kids come to terms with their childhoods and their parents and begin to see who they will be as adults. It's a very powerful thing, and we hear from these kids years later that it was one of the most important experiences of their lives."

Like Steven Foster, Joe Benton came to see the need for such rituals, but with a very different group of "clients." Joe is director of community programs for the Department of Juvenile Justice in Columbia, S.C., and after growing frustration at how ineffective traditional therapies were in turning around troubled African-American teens, he started a "manhood training program" in 1990.

The rites-of-passage program is attended by young men chosen by their probation officers, and it runs three days a week all summer long. "We teach values and history, and the development of identity, purpose, and direction in their lives," says Joe. "There's a ritualistic structure to it, including a pledge they say every day. They pledge to respect elders, teachers, and parents, they pledge to assist the community, and they pledge to try to stop people they know from doing negative things."

Myth and ritual are important in any rite-of-passage program, and Joe's come from African and African-American sources rather than the Native American ones that inspired Steven and Meredith. For example, the class reads Alex Haley's *Roots*, and discusses the lessons Kunte Kinte's father tries to teach him in Africa before he is captured and enslaved. The father tells his son "never to run toward danger," and Joe tries to impress on his charges that the advice would also serve them well: there may not be lions or slave-traders waiting to pounce on them, but these kids need to question their own instinct to do things like "run toward the sound of shots, or a fight in school."

Also based on African principles is the ceremony that ends the summer program. It begins by "pouring a libation (water) on the earth," and this is done by a prominent African-American from the local community. A drum corps of young boys performs African drumming routines, and the "graduates" take turns telling the audience, which includes their parents, what they have learned, and repeating the pledge they have taken. In the end, the boys must kneel before their mothers and explain what they have learned; then the mothers say, "We consider you a man now."

There is no question that the manhood program is successful: roughly half the young men drop out of the program, but of those who complete it, about 70 percent haven't appeared in court since. Some are now in college.

But what about ordinary parents of ordinary teenagers, who have no models in their families or communities to inspire them? What can they do to help their children ritually move toward adulthood?

Many experts say that because the process is fundamentally about separating from one's parents, mothers and fathers can't do this entirely alone. "When it comes time for a young man to prove himself, he must do that without his father," says Stephen Foster of the School of Lost

Borders. He says groups of parents can work together and serve as mentors for one another's sons and daughters, but he firmly believes that "even the best-intentioned parents can't initiate their own children," and he acted on that belief with his own five kids.

Many parents disagree with that position, and I have found some who have fashioned incredibly thoughtful and worthwhile initiation programs. But even those who say parents can't manage the entire process with their children agree that their role is vital, and that there are many ways parents can spur and guide the transformation.

For example, even when a child has the advantage of a comprehensive spiritual coming-of-age ritual, such as a confirmation or bar mitzvah, there is plenty of room for families to supplement and enhance the experience: a girl from Scarsdale, N.Y., wanted her bas mitzvah celebration to include not just good food but good works, so she invited several dozen friends to help her perform restoration work for a day on a nineteenth-century synagogue in Manhattan.

Here are some examples of family-made coming-of-age rituals, some simple and others complex, that parents and their children have found worthwhile. I believe these families are pioneers in a long-neglected territory, and that they will be joined by others with different approaches. Obviously, the survival skills kids need to become functioning adults in our culture are very different from those of primitive tribes. They need to know how to make choices and how to handle constant change, but I don't think we've come to grips yet with how to enhance such abilities through rites-of-passage programs. Nonetheless, pioneers such as the ones below have much to teach us by their examples.

Robbie Fergus-Jean of Columbus, Ohio, calls it "my manhood trip." Like his brother before him, Robbie set off in the family van with his father, John, for a three-week trip out west the summer after he turned thirteen.

The idea of some sort of rite-of-passage journey originated with the boys' mother, Elizabeth Fergus-Jean, but she and her husband agreed that he should be the one to lead these expeditions. Both times, father and son hiked and fished and explored and talked, and listened a lot. They listened to each other, and to a series of audiotapes that John brought along, especially *Black Elk Speaks,* from a book published in 1932 about the life and beliefs of a Sioux holy man.

"We talked about how the passage from girlhood to womanhood is marked by a definite physiological change, but that this isn't true for boys, and there really isn't a ceremony for a male child to show he has reached maturity," says John, a college professor and former museum curator. "We shared ideas about what it means to grow up and the responsibilities involved. It wasn't like: here's the cookbook on how to be a man, do these eighteen things and you'll get these seven rewards. It wasn't so much: this is a lesson, and this is how you'll apply it to a job, but a way of understanding things that gives you a different outlook."

The ultimate destination on both trips was Yellowstone Park, but each time, father and son drifted along at a leisurely pace. "We went to Custer's battlefield, the Black Hills in South Dakota, and anything else where the topography intrigued us," says John.

Both boys went to the Fire Hole River in Yellowstone, which is warmed by thermal springs. It is bracketed on both sides by steep stone cliffs, and many visitors jump from there into the deep river below despite Park Service warnings. "It takes a lot of courage because you're jumping basically into rapids and these cliffs are high," says John. Nevertheless, both of his sons decided this was a challenge they must face. "Jamie did it on his trip and then Robbie, having heard about it, had to do it too. And it was important to Robbie that he jump from a higher place. Believe me, people looked up at where he was and were just stunned.

"Each boy found his own 'secret spot' while at Yellowstone," says John. "Jamie's was a spot where the hot water and cold water meet. It was almost like a hot tub." Then Robbie "found a spot in a more remote part of the park, in the mountains by a stream. He arranged rocks there in the shape of his initials to mark it."

Another milestone for both boys was smoking their first cigar. "We learned about how the Indians viewed tobacco, how it played an important role as a magical way to connect with spirits, and we partook of tobacco after understanding it in that way," says John. "The message was that with something as powerful as tobacco, it must be done in moderation: you don't treat it as a child would, but as a reflective person would."

Neither boy brought back the usual touristy souvenirs, but reminders of the natural world and their experiences in the West: porcupine quills, fur from mountain goats, the beard of a buffalo. They also saved the paper rings from their cigars. Jamie's collection of treasures is stored in a special deerskin bag, along with a twist of tobacco, and hangs from the fireplace mantel. Robbie's keepsakes are arranged on a special table his mother made.

Elizabeth says both boys were deeply affected by their trips: Jamie, the oldest, began referring to his siblings as "the kids" from the time he returned.

John says the trips definitely changed his relationship with his sons: "We shared so much at an age where it isn't always easy to share with your kids. We slept together, ate together, hiked together, and shared the bonds of common experiences and common fears. My sense is that they came back knowing more about themselves and their place in the world, and they don't feel they're powerless. It was important to them that they jumped off that cliff, not so much because of the actual jump, but because they overcame fears."

The Fergus-Jeans will focus next on creating a coming-of-age ritual for their daughter, Christin. After hearing about her brothers' awesome journeys west, she is clamoring for one of her own—but with her mother as a guide.

Coming-of-age ceremonies don't have to last for weeks to acknowledge that a milestone has been reached.

Kate Downing's family wanted to do something special to recognize the significance of her thirteenth birthday. A big dinner was planned and a special room reserved at the Athletic Club in St. Paul, Minn. "We're not a backyard-barbecue type family," says Kate's aunt, Deborah Gelbach.

Kate's parents and grandparents and aunts and uncles stood in a circle and offered toasts to her. Aunt Debbie said, "We have always called you Katie, but you have stopped referring to yourself in that way, and we vow to call you Kate from now on." It was a formal recognition that she had outgrown her childhood name and that her family would respect her maturity and her choices.

The evening's most important gift was a poster made by Kate's father's mother, which she referred to as "a lineage of teenagers." Featured in rows are photographs of four generations of family members, all taken at the age of thirteen (or as close as they could come). In the top row are photographs of Kate's great-grandparents, then a row of her grandparents, and then pictures of her parents and their siblings, and finally a recent photo of Kate.

"It is just the neatest thing, going from faded browns to crisp black and white to color," says Marcia Downing, Kate's mother. "It provoked a great discussion about what we remembered about that age, and how this is a new beginning. We all laughed about how fashions and hairstyles had changed. Kate just loved it, and she keeps the poster on her closet door."

When her first son was a year away from turning thirteen, Diane Sanson of Malibu, Calif., started searching for a coming-of-age ritual she could use for both her boys. She and her husband, Mike, didn't belong to a church or know any families who had created their own initiation rituals.

Diane was working on her doctorate in human behavior and training to be a marriage and family therapist. She decided to seek help from Jack

Zimmerman, a counselor and teacher who is a fervent advocate of "councils," sessions in which people sit in a circle and pass around a "talking stick." Only the person holding the stick can speak, and the others must listen with respect. Native Americans have ancient traditions for such ritual meetings and usually use decorated sticks, but other objects such as shells or stones can also be passed to designated speakers. Zimmerman trains private clients, including families, in how to use this communication tool and has also introduced councils into a special curriculum in some California public schools. He outlines his methods in *The Way of Council*, a book published by Bramble Books of Las Vegas.

Having studied with Zimmerman and belonged to a women's group that met as a council, Diane wanted the council method to be part of her coming-of-age ritual. She believed it would help teach her sons "how to listen, and how to express their feelings. I want them to be emotionally articulate."

The Sansons believed that the experience would be more valuable if the boys were part of a small group of boys and fathers. "Among other things, I thought it was important for them to observe more than one model of manhood," says Diane. Kai, her older son, was told to invite his friends and boys he thought he wanted to get to know; in all, five sons and their fathers signed on for that first multifamily rites-of-passage program.

With Jack Zimmerman's help, the Sansons designed a nine-month-long program that borrowed some elements from traditional tribal coming-of-age practices, including physical trials and times for solitude and reflection. Once a month, the men and boys would meet together in a council, discussing everything from what it means to be a man in our culture to what activity or challenge they should take up next.

Each father-and-son team was to complete some physical trial on its own, while the group undertook a series of outdoor challenges that included two camping trips. Each of the Sanson boys committed to hiking all 240 miles of the John Muir Trail with their father, though that feat took several summers to accomplish.

Each boy in the group was also required to perform some sort of community service; as a group, they served lunch to homeless people at a shelter. Individually, they took on different tasks—one boy worked with Habitat for Humanity to help build a house for a needy family.

Each boy was instructed to keep a journal about the process, and to describe his dreams and goals, though some weren't very conscientious about it. The boys were taken several times to a cliff above the ocean at dawn for solitude and reflection: they were to sit alone for forty-five minutes, "contemplating and writing down their thoughts," says Diane. Afterward, the boys would surf and have a big pancake breakfast. Forty days in the wilderness it wasn't. As Diane says, "We had to have some fun elements like the surfing and pancake breakfast, or the kids just wouldn't go for the serious, quiet parts."

The whole process started in September, when Jack Zimmerman met with the boys and their parents on the beach, where they gathered driftwood to make a talking stick. Jack explained how councils work and answered questions. He calmed some of the more skeptical parents, including a religious woman who worried that her son would be doing "weird and unsafe things," says Diane. The woman decided to keep her son in the group.

To kick off the process, they enacted an aspect of ancient tribal coming-of-age rituals, in which boys are literally kidnapped from their huts and carried away, while their mothers rant and weep about the separation. The fathers came to each house in turn and took the boys away, and in most cases, the mothers emoted on cue as their sons departed. The boys were then taken to a camping area for their first physical ordeal.

After camping overnight, the boys were wakened at dawn, given paddleboards, and instructed to paddle six miles in the ocean, along the coast, to a pier. One of the dads paddled along in a kayak, to make sure the boys were all right.

"They had to all make it and help each other if necessary," says Diane. "A couple of the boys got way behind, but in the end they all reached their goal. The mothers were waiting for them at the pier, and we had a big lunch for them."

This trial, which was called "Paddle to the Pier," turned out to be a great way to start off, says Diane, but it wasn't easy getting all the parents to agree to it. "Creating rites of passage is such a hard thing to do in this culture. We agreed it had to be a real challenge for the boys in order to have meaning, but it also had to be safe. None of us was willing to risk our sons dying in the ritual," a tragedy that sometimes happens in primitive tribal initiations.

Later, the boys and men decided that they wanted to explore the issues of aggression and war. So they went to one of those places where people have mock battles with paint-filled guns, and staged their own war. One father had lost a son to gang violence and refused to participate because it was too painful. His reaction was discussed in a council meeting afterward. "I was opposed to the whole thing," says Diane, but she says she has decided over time that "exploring war and fear and aggression is important to men," and that perhaps it was helpful for the boys to talk about their reactions to fighting and the appetite for violence they feel in themselves.

In June, the rite-of-passage program ended with a ritual of solitude and separation and the traditional Native American trial of a sweat lodge. "The boys went to the mountains with their fathers, and sat talking with them after dark," says Diane. "Then the boys were to go up higher on the mountain and spend the night alone, apart from their fathers."

The next morning, the sweat-lodge ceremony was performed. With Jack Zimmerman's help, the Sansons found a Native American guide who could lead the boys in the ritual, which was held in a typical lodge made of willow branches covered with canvas and blankets. A sweat lodge is small, the air is close, and enormous heat and steam are generated by pouring water over scalding hot rocks in the center of the room. The lodge is meant to be symbolic of the womb, and such ceremonies a kind of rebirth. Participants are sometimes naked, but in this case the boys wore bathing suits.

"They would go in there for fifteen minutes at a time, and the leader would say blessings and prayers," says Diane. "My sons said the boys were asked to talk about their grandfathers and other family elders and also to talk about their vision of being men. They went in there four times and I understand it was quite an ordeal, very uncomfortable."

When the Sansons' second son, Brett, participated, all the boys in his group decided after leaving the sweat lodge that they wanted to jump off the nearby cliffs into a river below, much like the Fergus-Jean boys did in Yellowstone. Diane laughs at how naturally the boys were drawn to this leaping: "Here we had done all this work creating this ritual, and here they were just spontaneously creating a challenge of their own," she says. "I think it shows that the impulse to do this sort of thing is already there in kids. But you have to provide a context in which it can come out."

Both groups ended with a big family gathering to celebrate the "graduates." "Each boy had to stand and speak for ten minutes," says Diane, "about what he had learned and what kind of man he wanted to be."

The coming-of-age ritual had a big impact on the Sansons' older son, Kai, who chose it as the subject of his college application essay to the University of California at Santa Cruz. Five years later, his younger brother Brett is still in close contact with all but one of the boys who shared the experience. "It's a bond that will last forever," he predicts. Of the toughest challenges, including the Paddle to the Pier and the sweatlodge ritual, Brett says, "I learned that nothing is easy, but the feeling of accomplishment overcame the pain."

Diane, who is now divorced from Mike, went on to write her Ph.D. thesis on rites of passage for adolescents. She felt it was important to be versed in the experiences of girls as well, so she designed rite-of-passage programs for several groups of young girls, and what she has learned may help others.

Her sons had taught her that nine months of ritual and ceremony is nearly impossible to schedule with half a dozen hyperbusy preteens, so she created programs lasting six months or less, working with groups of four to six girls and mothers.

Diane led a weekend rafting trip with one group, and brought along a college student as a fellow guide. She felt that girls should conquer their fears of physical effort and the natural world as well as boys, though she discovered that some girls had trouble getting through a whole weekend without a telephone.

Particularly successful was a ritual Diane created to cap the rite-of-passage program. All the girls in the group had gotten their period by then, so each of them and their mothers came to the backyard ceremony dressed in red. The mothers were given flowers to weave into their daughters' hair.

Then there was what Diane calls a "water ceremony." The women stood in a circle and a pitcher of water was passed around: while holding the pitcher, each woman spoke about some positive memory or feeling about being a woman. When all the women had spoken, the pitcher was passed again and each mother poured some of the water on her daughter's hands. Finally, each mother whispered a special private blessing to her daughter.

Another wonderful model of a parent-driven program was designed by Paula Penn-Nabrit and her husband, Charles, for their three teenage sons in Westerville, Ohio.

Paula and her husband didn't want to emphasize the physical aspects of manhood, believing their sons got enough of that sort of testing by playing football and practicing martial arts. The Nabrits focused on intellectual and spiritual growth, and stressed two fields of study: scripture and African-American history. The boys were given extensive reading assignments in both areas, and extensive writing assignments as well. Although the Nabrits' program is highly original, it was influenced in part by a pamphlet called "Bringing the Black Boy to Manhood: The Passage," written by educators Nathan and Julia Hare. (The Hares' plan focuses more heavily on community involvement, suggesting such exercises as adopting a senior citizen and having boys communicate with local elected officials.)

The Nabrits made deliberate choices about the specific values they wanted to transmit, then designed the ritual around them. Their goal was for the boys to appreciate and celebrate not just their approaching manhood, but the context of community and culture within which they would stand as men. "We want them to be spiritually healthy and intellectually challenged for their entire lives," says Paula.

There is no question that the three boys found their rite-of-passage assignments challenging; there was much grumbling about what a lot of work their parents required, and how none of their friends were suffering a similar ordeal. But several factors contributed to the boys' cooperation, including their parents' promise that the program would end with a big party complete with a local DJ. It helped that, the first time out, the twins Charles and Damon had each other for mutual support and commiseration. Two years later, their younger brother, Evan, just accepted that his turn had come.

The Nabrit boys had been schooled at home for several years, so they were accustomed to accepting scholarly assignments from their parents. Nonetheless, I believe that some version of the Nabrit program could work in virtually any family where the kids are disciplined; the number and type of assignment could be modified to fit the time kids have available, and different rewards could help keep them interested.

The reading period for the Nabrit boys lasted between six and nine months, with each being expected to read a total of sixteen books by such authors as Langston Hughes; Steven Biko, the murdered South African antiapartheid leader; Malcolm X; Nelson Mandela; W. E. B. Du Bois; and Martin Luther King, Jr.

The boys were generally given ten days to complete each book, and five days to write an essay on it several pages long. They would turn in an outline for each essay, and when that was approved by their parents they would produce a first draft, and so on. As revisions were made, there would be discussions between the parents and the boys about the content of the books and also about the finer points of writing.

Paula says she and her husband were not just looking for a "logical flow" and organization in these essays, but also for a solid analysis that showed critical thinking. For example, writing about Dr. King's *Letter from a Birmingham Jail*, says Paula, the couple wanted their sons to notice its similarity to epistles in the Bible. But they also wanted them to "explain the concept of justice as a value, and say why they thought it was good."

The boys were also assigned a number of chapters in the Bible related to the religious doctrine of their Pentecostal church, and had to write an essay about each of those chapters.

The rewards for all the Nabrits were plentiful. Though Paula and Charles expected the moaning and groaning, they were thrilled with the progress they observed as their sons wrote essay after essay. "We saw a lot of outstanding analysis, and you could see this development right before your eyes," says Paula. And they were pleased to watch the twins work closely with their younger brother when his turn came. "We sort of expected them to say, 'This is stupid! It was stupid when they made us do it and we can't believe you have to do it too,'" says Paula, but that didn't happen. Instead, "they helped critique Evan's work, and I was surprised by how much they had retained. I would overhear them asking, 'Now what does Steven Biko mean in this essay on black consciousness?' "

When all the reading and writing and discussing was done, the boys were prepared for a ceremony several hours long that was held in their church on a Saturday, attended by members of the congregation and the Nabrits' extended family. The boys had to memorize a greeting to the congregation in Ashanti, an African language spoken in Ghana and elsewhere. The choir sang, the pastor spoke, and each of the boys had to read a series of three essays he had written about the past, present, and future of the African-American male.

Finally, each boy gave a brief speech, summarizing what he had learned and thanking those who had helped him. Charles said, "I used to think my mother was just exaggerating when she said I would feel good when I saw the results of writing and rewriting the same essay. Now I realize she was telling me the truth. . . . Because of this experience, I have begun to think seriously and critically about my life and what I believe."

At the close of the ceremony, the pastor, Eugene Lundy, said to each boy, "We welcome you to the honored realm, challenges, and responsibilities of black manhood." Then various relatives stood up and spoke, from great-grandparents on down. And then it was time to party.

The boys still grumble today about the work they had to do, and how they're still waiting for all the rewards of manhood. But two years after his rite of passage, when I asked Damon what it means to be a Nabrit, he replied, "It means having a lot of responsibility."

Not every parent has the time and energy to devote to such extensive rites of passage, and there are doubtless some kids who would participate with reluctance. But there are alternatives, like the dinner the Downings held for their daughter, which allow parents to celebrate and recognize their children's maturity.

One important thing to remember is that this is a time not only to grant more freedom to children, but also to demand more from them, just as young men and women who complete bar and bat mitzvahs are expected to play a bigger role in religious ceremonies, such as fasting on Yom Kippur. In the secular world, this change can be registered quite powerfully in fairly simple ceremonies.

★   ★   ★

One option for families is to write a family contract like the McCandlesses did. When her son Ryan was in junior high school, Sue McCandless found herself engaged in constant battles over issues like his messy room and how he organized his time. Ryan felt he was too old for such constant nagging and that he didn't have enough say in scheduling his after-school time.

Finally, the parents sat down with him and negotiated a contract, which they all signed. Ryan's parents agreed to stop bugging him about whether his room was clean or his teeth brushed, and Ryan agreed to reserve the time from 6:00 to 7:00 PM for homework, and the next hour for reading "some kind of book." From 8:00 PM until bedtime, Ryan is free to do as he pleases. As a result, says Sue, "The fights ended and we have no more power struggles. I had a hard time letting go of my demands to keep his room clean, but now if we have company I just shut the door."

In agreeing to step back and give Ryan more freedom over his hours and his room, Sue and her husband were creating a milestone. They were formally giving up some of their authority, which served to both applaud and encourage the maturation of their son's self-reliance and judgment.

Rituals that mark such transitions don't have to be solemn to be memorable. One mother used to cut off a pair of apron strings and present them to each of her children as they got ready to leave home. Then there's Richard Boardman, a Wisconsin guidance counselor who lets his children give him "the haircut of their choice" when they complete eighth grade. "You could say I'm courageous or just stupid," he says, "but I wanted a rite of passage that would give my children a total sense of power over me, and in this case, I literally put my head in their hands. I know it's something they'll never forget."

Richard has so far endured two haircuts. His oldest boy, Dathan, gave him a military-style buzz cut, and his daughter, Tria, who threatened a pink Mohawk for at least a year, also cut it very close to his head. The kids might have done something more outrageous, but they wielded this awesome power carefully, says Richard, knowing that they'd have to be seen in his company afterward. "The rule is I have to wear it that way for a whole week and though I can cover it with a hat when I leave the house, the kids can order me to remove it," says their dad. Only after that week can he retreat to the barbershop for revisions.

The Boardman children found the experience thrilling and reveled at every strange look their father endured at church or in a restaurant. Their friends were bowled over by the audacity of it all, and the other boys on Dathan's baseball team took to rubbing his dad's head for luck until the hair all grew out. Indeed, the exercise has been such a hit that Richard decided recently to grant the kids a second chance to cut his hair, as a reward for graduating from high school.

There is no magic age or stage that determines when a rite-of-passage ritual should be conducted, and there is no rule about having only one such ceremony. Parents should be alert to developmental and social milestones, and seize upon those that carry real significance for their children. Using that logic, two pivotal events that deserve to be marked and celebrated are a girl's first period and the bestowing of a driver's license.

First Periods

Countless baby-boom women who came of age with the dawn of the feminist movement vowed that their daughters would have a more positive introduction to menstruation than they did. We all swapped horror stories about how our mothers could hardly broach the topic, and then, when they did, only emphasized the discomforts of "the curse." We set about banishing the age-old attitude that produced the Jewish folk ritual of slapping a young girl's face on the day of her first blood, as if to say, "Wake up, girl, and get ready to feel a woman's pain."

Many thoughtful mothers now try to celebrate this transition in a way that will help their girls enter womanhood with more anticipation than dread. They want to give their daughters what they wish they'd had themselves. And in a time when girls get their periods and are sexually active at an earlier age, there are critically important values and health lessons to be shared. But eager mothers must be careful not to put their own wishes and needs ahead of their daughters'. Most young women are still self-conscious and embarrassed by this change in their bodies and dread family recognition, let alone celebration.

Pat McCarthy of Casper, Wyo., learned this the hard way. The mother of four served her oldest daughter dinner on a red plate with white hearts "that we save for special occasions" on the day the girl had her first period. There was little ceremony beyond that, but her daughter was mortified. Her discomfort was so obvious that her younger sister didn't tell her mother about her period until she'd been menstruating for months and figured it was too late to celebrate.

But more public ceremonies are being performed in workshops offered for mothers and daughters across the country. Karri Hays-Walzer teaches a workshop for parents and daughters in Park City, Utah, based on material developed by Tamara Slayton, the founder of a program for adolescents and families called The Coming of Age Project, and based in Sebastopol, Calif. Slayton has created group rituals for teenage girls that celebrate their bodies at this important time, but also, she says, "their souls and spirits."

So, in Karri's workshops in Utah, the girls not only hear about the biological changes ahead, but each shares her life goals and makes a uterus of felt and a paper crown. At the end of the day, the mothers give the girls flowers and a gift, and their fathers come to place the crowns on their heads. The fathers read such lines as "Remember you are a river, your banks are red honey where the moon wanders," taken from Ntozake Shange's novel *Sassafrass, Cypress and Indigo*. Karri says that some young girls are moved to tears by this ceremony, but others "just want to get out of there." Though I admire the intention, I hope that families only do this when their daughters are eager to, and with full knowledge of the program.

Indeed, Rabbi Debra Orenstein of New York, author of *Lifecycles*, a book about the life passages of Jewish woman, advises parents to resist the impulse to celebrate this event even as a family. She suggests that mothers offer such simple one-to-one rituals as "practical advice, tales of their own experiences . . . a hug (rather than a slap), a special mother-daughter outing or gift," or a jointly recited prayer. The rabbi then presents a prayer that a woman can say when she gets her first and each subsequent period, requesting from God "a month of goodness and blessing, healing and vitality, fruitfulness and abundance. . . ."

I agree that mothers must remain sensitive to their daughters' potential for embarrassment. There are many families that have delighted girls with thoughtful but private tributes.

For example, Marilyn Clark and her husband of West Virginia have taken each of their daughters to the jewelry store to pick out a ring as soon as they start their periods. The girls can admire that new ring every day and feel pride at what it signifies without telling a soul, if that's what they wish.

A much more ambitious course is that taken by Barbara and Kevin Gardiner of Stanchfield, Minn., who created a lengthy coming-of-age program culminating with the first period of each of their three girls.

"When our oldest started to develop and go through all that preadolescent stuff, we decided we wanted to do something so she would grow up knowing more than we did at that age, and in a wholesome way," explains Barbara. When she came across a book called *What's Happening to My Body? Book for Girls* by Lynda Madaras, Barbara planned to read it with her oldest girl, Diana, then ten, but Diana wanted to read it with her father instead.

The reading evolved into a kind of ritual, with father and daughter sitting together, often on Sunday afternoons. Kevin, a computer programmer, has "a jovial sense of humor," says his wife, and she could often hear Diana and Kevin laughing together as they read the material in the book. "It was a kind of bonding experience for them," says Barbara.

To stress that becoming an adult involved more than just physical changes, the Gardiners talked about how this was a time of mental and emotional change, too, and they encouraged the girls to seek out new challenges. Diana started swimming lessons at the local high school. This was a big step because she was schooled at home by her mother and didn't know anybody there. But Diana loved the sport and soon excelled at it. She was an experienced baby-sitter, and decided to get training in CPR; she also took a special course so she could coach handicapped people in a horseback-riding program.

In addition, the Gardiners told Diana she could choose a new middle name for herself, which they would legally add to the existing one. This new name would reflect her thinking about her emerging adult identity. "I got this idea from a friend who has a daughter about the same age," says Barbara. "That woman wanted her daughter to align herself with some god or goddess, and that just isn't us at all. But I liked the idea of the girls choosing a name for themselves." Indeed, this is an element of many ancient rite-of-passage experiences, including that of Native Americans; in many tribes, young people choose a new name after a period of fasting and solitude produces a vision of their identity and purpose.

Diana began keeping a list of possible names on the refrigerator, with the "meanings" next to them, crossing off those she rejected and adding new candidates as the months went by. In the end, she chose Carmen, "because it means *song* and she loves to sing."

The Gardiners discussed their celebration plans before the big event: Kevin would bring home flowers, a special family dinner would be served, and Diana would be given a unique gift, "something she would cherish all her life," says Barbara. "If she had seemed embarrassed about the whole family celebrating, then I guess Kevin and I would have taken her out to dinner alone. What we do with the other two girls will depend on their preference."

Several days after Diana started menstruating, she was feted and applauded over dinner. Her father presented a special gift to her, a gold coin called a double eagle, with an eagle on one side and Lady Liberty on the other. With it came a long, thoughtful letter, warning Diana that the time ahead would be a confusing one and gently suggesting that she "still enjoy being a kid" whenever possible.

The letter also talked about the symbolism of the gift. "The beauty of gold cannot compare with the gift of potential motherhood. It is something of great value that must be protected. Many would try to steal it from you. The coin, like your body, is a special and private thing that should not be freely given but should be carefully shared with only the most trusted friend, one in whom you can place the trust of a lifetime."

A young girl whose passage to womanhood is celebrated with such love and seriousness isn't likely to view her virginity as a frivolous embarrassment, an outdated encumbrance to shed at the first opportunity. She may actually treasure it, uncool though such an attitude might be, and understand why losing it isn't what makes her a woman.

Others who want to celebrate privately might get some ideas from DeeAnn Pochedly of Cleveland. When her daughter started menstruating at age twelve, DeeAnn let her stay home from school for the day and took her out to lunch. On the way home, DeeAnn stopped by a drugstore to get her daughter "some of the little necessities," and that night, she tucked her preteen into bed with extra words of love and pride. Even the girl's siblings weren't given the scoop about why she played hooky: their mother just said, "Big Sis needed a day off," says DeeAnn. The next night when DeeAnn's daughter came home from school, she found a surprise present, says her mother, "three pairs of new undies in a different color for her to wear on those 'special' days."

DeeAnn says her daughter called her "Mommy" that day for the first time in a very long while. She figures she must have done something right, because her oldest daughter has already told a younger sister that "getting your period isn't so bad. You get a day off school, and Mom will buy you stuff."

★   ★   ★

In one Kentucky family, an all-female dinner is scheduled for around the time when a girl is expected to start menstruating. The girl's mother hosts, and all the women of the family bring a special gift, such as a ruby ring or jewelry handed down from a grandmother. All the women tell stories of their first periods and what being a woman has meant to them. Whenever the girl actually gets her period, she is expected to phone all her female relatives, no matter the hour of day or night.

Nancy Goddard, who leads wilderness journeys for women and teenagers, was once asked to create a ceremony for a woman's two daughters; one had just started to menstruate and the other soon would. Nancy gathered the girls together with some of their friends and their friends' mothers. Each girl lit a candle set on a simple altar decorated with flowers and other symbols of femininity.

The group sat in a circle, girls and mothers alternating. They were each given a slip of paper and asked to write, anonymously, between one and three "fears they had about becoming a woman or being sexually active," says Nancy. The mothers had to fill out the slips too, and mostly wrote questions they thought the girls might be too embarrassed to ask, such as "What's an orgasm?"

All the papers were stuffed into a hat. The hat was then passed around the circle, with each person pulling one out. As a question was read, Nancy asked each person to try to answer it. "I wanted the girls to be able to communicate what they knew, and at times to act as teachers to the women as well as each other," explains Nancy. "It was sort of amazing to me to realize how little these rather sophisticated girls actually knew." But this ritual was a way for them to learn important information without passively enduring (and ignoring) a one-sided lecture from Mom.

Afterward, Nancy had the women and girls hold hands and led them in several chants, including one that goes, "We are women on a journey, shining in the sun. . . . We are women on a journey, standing as one." The afternoon ended with a celebratory potluck feast, with each mother bringing her daughter's favorite dish. "Part of the notion was to welcome them to the sisterhood of women and create a community of people they could go to in the future with questions," says Nancy, who has repeated the ceremony, with some variations, many times.

CELEBRATING A NEW DRIVER

In a culture built around mobility, individualism, and speed, becoming a licensed driver is one of the few universal recognitions of maturity. It's even constructed like a ritual: initiates into the realm of drivers must complete a "trial" by passing a written test and proving to an objective expert that they can drive and park.

The jubilation of teenagers who pass the test and earn the right to drive is very real, and the impact of this change on their families is equally profound. If there was ever a clear-cut example of a rite of passage in contemporary America, this is it. Coveted new privileges are bestowed on a person, but awesome new responsibilities are imposed.

In a primitive tribe, a young man would learn how to kill with weapons, but he would also be taught the proper circumstances for doing so. In our culture, we put teenagers behind the wheel of a complicated, powerful machine that has the potential to kill or maim in a single moment of carelessness. Don't we owe them an initiation into the duties of the newly powerful? And shouldn't it be felt as a change in relationship within the family, and not just the official pronouncement of a state agency?

Families can at least celebrate and discuss this event, and some may want to add "trials" of their own, such as testing the child on how to care for the car, what to do in an accident, and how to handle specific quirks of the family's car, such as its alarm system. Although it is far from a common phenomenon, some families have created rituals to mark this passage as the coming-of-age event it truly is.

The Vogts of Covington, Ky., felt strongly about creating a specific ceremony when each of their four kids started driving. "When they pass the driver's test, we have this ceremony, which includes giving them a special key case with a house key and a car key of their own," says Susan

Vogt. "We usually do this at dinnertime, because that's the easiest time to get everybody together." Including the house key adds to the symbolism and seriousness, granting the new driver a greater freedom within the family.

Most of the Vogts' rituals have a religious element to them, and this one is no different. "We say a simple prayer, to the effect, 'God bless our child as he gains independence and a new stage in life, and bless this car, and keep our son safe in his travels,' " says Susan.

Kathleen Chesto also advocates performing a special driver's license ceremony, and wishes she had thought of the idea for her own three kids. She decided that the new driver should have to recite a sort of pledge promising to obey not only the driving laws, but the family's rules of the road. For her book *Family Prayer for Family Times: Traditions, Celebrations, and Rituals*, Kathleen asked her youngest daughter, then eighteen, to write such a credo for a just-licensed driver.

As part of the ceremony, Kathy suggests, one of the parents might begin with a prayer such as, "God of protection, we place [child's name] in your care. We rejoice with her in this accomplishment, and challenge her to live up to this new responsibility."

Then comes the part written by Kathy's daughter, Liz, which Kathy suggests could easily be modified to suit the circumstances of the young driver in question:

> I believe that driving a car is a serious responsibility, to myself, to passengers in the car, to those in other vehicles, to pedestrians, and to the environment.
>
> I believe that traffic laws have been made for our protection and I will obey them.
>
> I believe that others have as much right to the road as I do and I will attempt to always be courteous.
>
> I believe that a car is a means of transportation, not a symbol of power, and I will use it wisely and share in the responsibility of being a driver in this family.
>
> I believe that a car is an expense that should be shared justly by all who use it.

I believe that the less parents know, the more they worry, and I will try my best to call when I am late and to keep them informed.

For their own kids, the Chestos drafted a written agreement about how and when the family car was to be used, and the children had to sign the pact. It covered such issues as how many passengers the new driver could carry and how far they could travel. There was also a rule that each kid was allowed one accident and one speeding ticket each. After that, such offenses would result in a loss of driving privileges for a certain period of time.

"I think such rituals of maturity are as important to grown-ups as to children, because they remind us that these children do not belong to us," says Kathleen. "I know from my own experience that when your kids start driving you really face the reality that you have to let go. And it's hard."

Part 3

How

Eight

★ · ★ · ★ · ★

MAKING RITUALS FROM SCRATCH

The making of ritual is a creative act fundamental in human life. It is also a divine gesture. Genesis tells us the first purpose of such creative action is to give form to what is formless: "In the beginning, God created..." Through ritual and ceremonies we people in turn make order out of chaos. In endless space, we create a fixed point to orient ourselves: a sacred space. To timelessness we impose rhythmic repetitions: the recurrent feast. And to untamed or unbound matter, we give a shape, a name, a meaning.

—Gertrud Mueller Nelson, *To Dance with God*

itual is intimidating. Ceremonies often make us squirm or giggle. Most of us have attended a wedding, funeral, or other religious ceremony in a faith different from our own. We know firsthand that feeling of tense confusion: How will I know when to sit or stand? What is expected of me? What does the ritual mean? Can I ruin it accidentally?

It might seem, then, that the only thing scarier than being asked to participate in an unfamiliar ritual is to have to make one up ourselves. But the truth is, we've been doing it all our lives.

As children, we made up playground ceremonies and believed in their magic. When we got married, we made choices about how and where we'd gather, what music we wanted, and what flowers we'd hold, and many of us wrote all or part of our vows. As parents, we create rituals constantly and often spontaneously, whether to calm our children's fears or to celebrate a big occasion. Much of what makes our daily lives rich and binds us together as families is ritual, but we often don't call it that or think about how it got that way.

Mostly, we cling to what we know. We embrace holiday traditions handed down from previous generations. Sometimes it's because we love them, but sometimes it's because it seems like too much bother to make up new ones. On the way to adulthood, we've learned how to feed ourselves, how to drive a car, and how to earn a living, but few of us have learned how and when and why to make rituals. To do so seems impractical or awkward, something exotic and impenetrable, something done by priests and shamans, not ordinary people.

And then, perhaps, an unusual and important event will appear on the horizon, and we'll feel as if we ought to do something special to mark it. But if we lack models and encouragement and don't know where to start, the occasion will pass without flair, perhaps acknowledged with an awkward toast or two. And we'll be left feeling mysteriously deflated, wondering why this triumphant moment in our lives didn't *feel* triumphant.

Working on this book made me more conscious of ritual than I've ever been before and forced me to examine the areas of my life that call out for it. I've learned how hard it is to create a ritual from scratch, but also why it's worth doing.

After I'd been researching the book for about a year, I legally changed my name because I wanted to have the same last name as my son. At the same time, I decided to change my first name from the name I'd been given at birth (Margaret) to the name everybody actually calls me (Meg). In the past, I'm sure this change would have happened entirely on court documents and other pieces of paper, and I wouldn't have given much thought to why it was taking so long to *feel* as if this new name belonged to me.

But then I started thinking about what a perfect occasion this was for a ritual. I remembered how the marriage ceremony that I spent months writing and preparing had functioned as a rite of passage. This helped me to actually *become* married and *feel* married by publicly speaking and behaving in a certain ritualistic way. I thought about how much more it would mean to me if my name change were celebrated in a similar spirit, a public declaration of transformation, acknowledged by my friends and family.

There are plenty of models for marriage ceremonies, but I didn't know a single person who had ever created or attended a name-changing ritual. Then it occurred to me that there was an element of baptism in it, which suggested the idea of immersion. I wanted it to feel total and extreme, and to carry me out of my usual experience, and I concluded that having someone daub water on my forehead simply wouldn't cut it.

My brilliant flash of inspiration was this: why not dive into my friend Carol's swimming pool with all my clothes on? That could be the central action of the ritual, which would be supplemented by vows of a sort. And the ritual would end with a champagne toast with my husband.

Then came the hard part: asking my friend to allow me to stage this bizarre ceremony in her backyard, and asking my intensely private husband to participate. Carol, a free spirit at heart, was immediately enthusiastic. My husband wasn't at all convinced I was in my right mind. "Can't we just pour some water on your head while you stand in the kiddie pool on the deck?" he wondered. Eventually he agreed to participate if I didn't demand that he engage in any histrionic gestures, but he made it clear he was only humoring me.

I sent out invitations to a small circle of friends, ordered a cake, painted a special T-shirt for myself to wear when I emerged from the pool, and wrote some remarks. It was a warm Saturday afternoon in early September, and everybody gathered in summer dresses and straw hats, some clutching babies. When everyone had arrived, I began.

I stood before the small group and explained why my new name suited me so much better. I said I was throwing away my "Social Security name" and replacing it with a combination of my journalism byline and my married name: I now had a name for my work and a name for my life, and one nested inside the other. Wearing a casual cotton dress, I then mounted the diving board, faced my friends, and before plunging in head-first, said, "With pride and happiness, I become Meg Cox Leone." Underwater, I could hear nothing and felt the water surround me, but when I popped up for air and swam to the shallow end, I heard clapping and cheering. I got out and my smiling husband handed me a glass of champagne. Then I cut the cake and put on my T-shirt: "At Long Last, Leone," it said.

One more thing: although I had sensed my husband's resistance to the ritual, on the morning of the big day he surprised me with a gift. It was a black leather Filofax with my new initials embossed on the cover, a wonderful symbol of the change and proof that it mattered to him too.

The ritual "worked." Although it would take months before all my credit cards, financial statements, and passport were changed, I started getting comfortable with my new name in a few weeks. It wasn't just acting out and pronouncing the change publicly that did it, but also the assistance of my friends. If I would phone one of them and refer to myself in the old way, he or she would teasingly correct me. Change is always hard, but I believe that if acknowledged externally, it can be internalized more naturally and easily.

Knowledge is power, they say, and understanding what has made rituals work over hundreds of years can help all of us fashion new rituals with more confidence. Whether they're derived from Native American customs, religious traditions, or the habits of aboriginal tribes, the basic building blocks of ritual are essentially the same.

THE ELEMENTS OF RITUAL

It is true that some rituals happen casually and spontaneously in families: you take a long walk on the night of a full moon or get carryout Chinese food after your son's basketball game. Everybody has such a great time, it becomes a ritual. Whenever there's a full moon, you walk, and when your son's game is over, you all automatically head for the Chinese place. The same is true of many satisfying rituals, from bedtime routines to major holidays.

But sometimes rituals grow up like weeds and must be pruned or replaced to fulfill the real needs of a family. More elaborate rituals are often called for, ones that take considerable thought and planning. Parents who want their traditions to create a lifelong bond between family members and pass on their values in a vivid way have to craft special rituals that reflect their true intentions. To do so, they must understand the enormous power of ritual and learn to use it wisely.

Ritual requires structure, and the three stages observed in rites of passage make sense and hold true for almost any ritual. First comes the stage of preparation, then the stage of action (and often transformation), and finally the stage of integration and celebration. If this seems like a strange concept, then think of ritual as having a beginning, a middle, and an end. Even the simplest grace at dinner has these three parts: a nod or verbal cue that grace is to be said, the grace itself, and an "amen" at the end.

In this way, rituals are like stories: the stage is set, the hero or heroine has an adventure or solves a problem, and then that change is assimilated (Cinderella marries the prince, the Lion King takes over his kingdom). In the case of a holiday celebration, the change might just be greater awareness within participants: in a Christmas ritual, the family will be more conscious of what the holiday means to them when the celebration is performed. At a birthday party, the transformation of the honored person to a new age and stage is recognized and feted by all attending.

But what is it that makes a ritual powerful and memorable? This is the question that obsesses me, and after a lot of thought and analyzing hundreds of effective family rituals, I think I know the answer. What is required is an intense focus that screens out all the distractions of everyday life, and the evocation of an emotional or psychological truth using symbols or actions that speak deeply to the people involved.

The rest is smoke and mirrors, sometimes literally. Many of the "props" of ritual, like music, candles, and special clothing, are designed to help people enter into the focused state they need to experience a ritual, a state that can be trancelike at times. But at the heart of it, the action of the ritual must portray a deep-seated belief held by those performing the ceremony.

Let me illustrate what I mean. On pages 341–342 is one of the most powerful rituals I found, the adoption ritual created by Gail Simpson. It was held in Gail's church during a regular Sunday service and included the baby's mother. To me, what made the ritual so poignant was the combination of action (the literal handing over of the three-week-old infant from the mother to Gail), the simple power of Gail's words, and the fact that there was a role for every party involved.

Those actions and words were powerful because they didn't shrink from expressing potent and even painful emotional truths that are often glossed over: this young woman was giving up this baby, and her loss was another family's gain. Gail and her husband made vows to raise the girl with "faith, hope, courage, dignity, wisdom, and humor," and added,

"We humbly receive this child, awestruck by the mysterious forces which delivered this particular child to our care."

The ceremony closed with a perfect hymn, set to a poem by William Blake, about how tightly joy and sorrow are intertwined. And that is another secret of ritual's power: it allows us to experience and comprehend the opposites inherent in reality. To do so is pretty much impossible in the ordinary flux of life, in an everyday state of mind. Most any ritual of transformation contains such paradoxes, just as a wedding is both sad and happy, the end of a single way of life and the beginning of couplehood. The act of embracing those contradictions by means of a ceremony puts people in touch with the deepest mysteries of life, an experience that can only be called spiritual.

This core element of emotional truth can make any ritual more meaningful, even the simplest bedtime routine. The emotional truth being acknowledged may be the child's fear of the darkness or of being alone. Elinor Craig's good-bye ritual as she leaves her son at day care profoundly addresses a basic emotional truth, too. She recognizes her son's fear by putting him in a position of taking action.

Think of a ritual as a party; people need to be put in the proper mood, one of intense focus, and this is true whether the ritual is essentially silly or solemn. Anthropologists write about "ritual space" and "ritual time" as separate from ordinary space and time, and a spell of sorts must be cast so that people have a sense of crossing into a new territory.

There are many ways of doing this, including physical markers or barriers: people walking through a doorway covered with balloons know they are entering into ritual party space. In primitive tribes, just marking a big circle in the dirt and sitting within that circle signaled the entrance into sacred space, and a circle is still a powerful symbol. Placing chairs in a circle serves a similar purpose today. Having people hold hands, whether at the dinner table or in a circle of chairs, also serves the purpose.

But there are other ways as well. To be in the grasp of a ritual is to have a kind of heightened awareness, and stimulation of one or more of the five senses is one way to get there. Think of how the smell of incense awakens associations of sacred places. Or how the familiar clink of silverware against a glass hushes a roomful of people, who anticipate the ritual of a toast or speech. What separates ordinary time from ritual time can be as simple as a moment of silence, or the lighting of a candle in a darkened room. A change in music, like a trumpet fanfare or the peremptory boom of a gong, has a similar effect.

The next step is the ritual itself. Ritual implies performance, usually a combination of action and words, and the action performed must correspond closely to the purpose and emotional truth of the ritual to be effective. For example, a ritual of letting go might suggest such actions as burning or burying something, say an object from childhood in a coming-of-age ritual. Or a young person could write down childish qualities that he hopes to outgrow on slips of paper, tie them to helium-filled balloons, and release those balloons into the wind.

Ask yourself: what am I trying to accomplish or change with this ritual? Then try to think of a way to act out, or dramatize, that change at its most basic level. If it's a ritual about maturity and growth, one action that suggests itself is the literal crossing of a threshold.

Lucinda Herring, a writer and educator who teaches a course called "Living a Spiritual Year," works a lot with what she calls "gateways," and talks about how prevalent they are in our lives. "Every season is a gateway to the next, and even every day is a new gateway. When I work with children and we're celebrating the coming of fall, I'll often erect a threshold out of fallen tree branches nailed together. The children will help fill one side with summer flowers and the other with autumn leaves, and then we'll walk through it."

Similarly, Lucinda created a gateway for a woman to walk through to celebrate her fortieth birthday. The woman was a herbalist who made her living crafting beautiful wreaths, so the archway was made of tree branches and decorated with special herbs and flowers. Forty candles were lit and her female friends made a circle around the threshold as the woman walked through it, making a symbolic passage into the second half of her life. Those friends who were over forty also went through the gateway: before passing under it, they described their lives before reaching that age, and on the other side, they talked about their life since.

Many such ritual actions are ancient and primal. In his pivotal study of cultural celebrations, *The Rites of Passage*, Arnold van Gennep collected examples of different types of historic rituals and analyzed the activities commonly employed. For example, rites of union such as weddings include binding two people together with ribbons or cords; an exchange between the two of food, blood, or personal objects; washing or anointing each other, and so on. Though no one in our society is ever likely to conduct an initiation ritual that involves bathing in the sea with a live pig, as some ancient Greeks purportedly did, bathing or cleansing oneself remains a primal act symbolic of purification. For example, California-based psychologist and author Kathleen Wall advises many clients for whom she designs personal or relationship rituals to begin by taking a bath, to cleanse themselves symbolically as they do so literally.

When searching for a suitable framework for ritual, you really can't go wrong by starting with the four elements: earth, air, fire, and water, and devising a ritual around the one most closely associated with your intentions:

> ★ **Earth.** Earth is used for burying things, but it is also symbolic of growth and new beginnings. A wonderful ritual to mark the beginning of anything, from a new baby to a new venture, is to plant something; a tree, wildflowers, whatever

seems right. Roni Carr of Reno, Nev., plants sunflower seeds with her three kids every year to celebrate the advent of spring.

Long custom has associated various plants, flowers, and trees with specific human qualities and aspirations. Our grandmothers probably knew these by heart, but you can still find them in old books or by questioning experienced florists: gladioli are said to represent strength of character, red tulips a declaration of love, and ivy means fidelity or friendship. The appropriate plants or flowers can be placed in a special garden or given to someone with an explanatory card.

In her book *Lights of Passage: Rituals and Rites of Passage for the Problems and Pleasures of Modern Life,* Kathleen Wall tells of a mother who planted a young apple tree with her daughter. The girl was six and the nursery estimated that the tree would start bearing fruit in six or seven years. As it happened, the first apples appeared just as the girl started menstruating. The mother told Dr. Wall that she and her daughter had carried on many conversations under that tree over the years, and the emergence of the tree's fertility gave the girl "more comfort" in her own budding fertility than any lecture could have done.

★ **Air.** Air suggests wind and balloons, which are pretty foolproof in ritual. Releasing helium balloons into the wind can be useful in any ceremony about letting go of the old to make way for the new, but there is also the implication of buoyancy and breeziness. And the bubbly euphoria of celebration: remember the woman who has her Little League team tie balloons to the dugout roof, and release them after a victory? Having balloons, whether tied to trees or furniture or flying away, just makes a person feel as if there's air in her step.

Then there are kites. I remember when my sister and I were trying to think of a symbolic action to celebrate my father's seventy-fifth birthday. We decided to fly down to North Carolina and surprise him with a visit, but that didn't leave much money for a present. We wanted a gift that would celebrate how we saw him, which was young in spirit. So we bought him a kite, and I'll never forget taking him down to the beach that September and flying it with him. It soared above us, frisky and brightly colored, and we passed the string from hand to hand, running and giggling like children.

Wind can also propel pinwheels, streamers, or anything else that gets carried aloft (if you have the money, hot air balloons, gliders, airplanes, or even blimps would be great ritual props). And there are soap bubbles, which children love and which help adults regress to childlike joy: *The New York Times* once featured a wedding where all the guests blew bubbles as soon as the bride and groom were declared husband and wife.

★ **Fire.** When I think of fire I think of bonfires, so terrifically witchy on Halloween, and of rituals around the hearth. That includes Christmas, of course, and hanging up stockings. But I also have fond memories from childhood of the electricity going out in our house and my parents letting us roast hot dogs and marshmallows for dinner in the basement fireplace.

Fire can both warm and destroy, thus becoming an apt symbol for rituals of paradox: out of death grows new life. One great New Year's ritual is to write down on slips of paper bad habits family members want to drop, or unhappy incidents of the year, then toss them into the fire and watch them burn. The year ahead can now begin on a clean slate.

Perhaps the greatest of ritual staples is the simple candle. A candle is portable fire, but the symbolism it carries is less about burning and purging than about illumination, the forces of light and good, and also faith and intimacy. If ever there was a tool made for shutting out the tyrannical appliances of modern life and providing the pure focus ritual demands, it is the candle. Staring at a flickering candle flame is wonderfully hypnotic, and empties the mind of accumulated trivia.

Many religious rituals practiced at home involve candles, including lighting Advent wreaths and lighting candles for Friday night Shabbat services. This book also includes many family-designed rituals that revolve around candles. For example, Joyce Taylor's Christmas Eve ritual, in which family members each light a candle as they tell of a prayer God has answered that year. Or the Kellett quadruplets' Christmas Eve tradition of lighting candles and carrying them up to bed.

In rituals for the winter solstice, candles symbolize the warmth and illumination of the sun, as family members vividly mark and celebrate the fact that the days will now start getting longer.

And Diane Sanson, who created a lengthy rite-of-passage program for her teenage sons, used candles in a leaving-home ceremony. "It was the end of the summer, before each one went off to college," she says. "When it was their turn, each son was allowed to invite a number of good friends and their families over for dinner, and after dinner we stood in a circle outside in the backyard. There was one candle, which was passed around. Each parent said something about their wishes for their child, and each boy said something about what he was thinking."

★ **Water.** Water, which purifies, renews, and makes life possible, is perfectly suited to rituals of baptism, both religious and secular. It is also very powerful in rituals of cleansing.

One example of a public ritual using water was the reaction several years ago to the police corruption scandal at a Harlem police precinct. Soon afterward, Reverend Jesse Jackson and local black leaders scrubbed the sidewalk in front of the station, using buckets and sponges and cleanser. This ceremony sent a visceral message that the community demanded to be part of the cleanup.

Of course, water rituals don't all have to be solemn. Remember the Elkin family's ritual of soaking their father in the bathtub every year on Thanksgiving? Water can also evoke the mischievous playfulness of childhood: how about getting in a supply of squirt guns for a "welcome to summer" celebration, or pack them for a family beach or pool vacation?

Beyond these four elements, the action of ritual is often suggested by the event and its associations. Researching a particular event or holiday at the library, or digging into family or religious history, often leads to new ideas about how to celebrate a holiday. Reading about the historical past of the real St. Nick, for example, might inspire a family to create gift-giving rituals around St. Nicholas Day, December 6, and reserve actual Christmas for mostly religious observances.

The admonition to "know thyself" is especially critical to good ritual. No matter how perfectly an action or gesture might seem to suit a particular ritual, if it doesn't fit the personality and temperament of the participants, the ritual will seem forced or awkward. So families should build ritual actions around their passions: if they love sports, family rituals can be organized around sports and contests. If many family members like to sew, then organizing a family quilting bee might be a great idea. Musical families can include singing or playing instruments in many rituals, while a family that loves sailing may choose to celebrate on the water whenever possible.

One example: Jim Sanford, the Vermont architect who practices the Scottish ritual of First Footing on New Year's Day, loves to hike and organizes "birthday hikes" for his sons and their friends. Cakes are completely optional, and the boys don't miss them. Jim says he prefers the hikes over regular parties because they seem less aimless; "the boys get from here to there," he says. They accomplish a goal, together.

If you're having trouble pinning down your passions and feel as if work and family leave you too busy to have any, follow Lucinda Herring's advice: ask yourself " 'What do I still take the time to do, no matter what?' That's a key to what matters to you" as a person, and to your family.

Often, after the actual ritual is performed, it's time to celebrate, and that usually means eating and drinking, ritual actions themselves. In her book *The Rituals of Dinner*, classics professor Margaret Visser talks about how deeply the act of eating together connects people, and always has.

"We eat whenever life becomes dramatic," she says. She describes a ritual among a tribe in Tanzania: to heal a bitter feud, a goat is slaughtered and its liver removed. The two parties to the quarrel each hold half of the goat's liver in their mouths, inches apart, as a priest cuts the organ in two.

Then the two people eat their halves, and peace is declared officially restored.

In Margaret Visser's words: "Only food—all-necessary, visible, divisible, an external object which becomes internal, and which then turns into the very substance of the eater—could give rise to such a clear yet mysterious and effective ritual." Her vivid analysis helps explain why breaking bread together is a sacred bond between people: by eating the same dish at the same time, we become one, at least for a time.

WORDS

Most rituals require words, and that scares a lot of us. People persist in believing that ritual requires flowery or portentous rhetoric, but many of history's greatest speechwriters, Abraham Lincoln among them, knew better: simple words expressing simple truths are much more powerful.

The words of a ritual, particularly in a rite of passage, are often vows or promises, pledging to be guided by explicit values. Making such a pledge out loud, before witnesses, can be a transforming act, as in a wedding.

The basic guideline is to use words that convey the central emotional truth of the event. When all else fails, stop trying to sound like a greeting card, and try saying what's in your heart. That doesn't necessarily mean winging it, unless you're one of those lucky people who are spontaneously profound. For me, it's much harder to speak simply and powerfully if I haven't thought in advance about what I feel and mean. I do better when I can condense my message, be choosy about my words, and say my piece clearly. Then the words appear almost like a chant or a prayer I know by heart, and I feel what I'm saying as I speak the words.

However, one of my favorite rituals was created by my friend Anne Kalik, and the words were made up on the spot. Anne needed a ceremony to transform her into the fairy godmother of a dear friend's daughter. This eleven-year-old girl, let's call her Jenny, decided she'd rather have Anne as a godmother than the one she had. Anne explained to Jenny that godmothers are for life, but confided that an older woman had recently become *her* fairy godmother and had helped guide her through some rough times.

Jenny and her mother loved the idea, so Anne determined to make the arrangement official. The three had planned a vacation in Sun Valley, Idaho, so Anne brought some things she thought might be useful for a ritual: face paint, feather headdresses (like kids wear at birthday parties to play Indians), and a "smudge stick" used in many Native American rituals, a simple wrapped bundle of herbs, mostly sage, that Anne had purchased at a New Age bookstore in Sun Valley. Traditionally, a smudge stick is set ablaze, and the aromatic smoke is waved through the air in a gesture called smudging.

While camping along the Salmon River, Anne and her friend decided it was time for the fairy-godmother ritual. Another mother and daughter were along on the trip, so they would be included, but the fathers of the two girls were sent off down the beach. Anne said she borrowed some aspects of the ritual from what she has studied about Native American traditions, but it was basically a spontaneous ritual, made up as she went along.

"After dinner, I took the two girls into my tent and painted their faces with stars and moons, and I tied the feathers on their heads," says Anne. "We all went to the bank of the river, and I drew a circle in the sand with a stick. The five of us walked inside the circle and sat down just as the stars came out."

Anne says she lit the smudge bundle and "asked for the Great Spirit's blessing, summoning wind and presence from the four directions. Jenny's mother wanted to give her an Indian name, and she decided to call her Big Heart, hoping she would be a loving soul. I put my hands on Jenny's head and said, 'You have a beautiful spirit. I promise I will keep my eye on you, and love you always.'" Anne says the smudge stick was passed around, and each of them said "something from our hearts." Then the girls and women all hugged. To end the ceremony, Anne threw the smudge bundle into the river, where it hissed and disappeared in the current.

Not only was the brief ceremony fun for everyone involved, Anne says it had a big effect on her relationship with Jenny. "I've loved this child since she was born," she says, "but the ritual made me feel I had formally made a promise to be responsible. It added something special; I pay more attention. If I see she's interested in soccer or art or whatever it may be, I take pains to encourage her."

The words Anne used in her ritual were simple and direct, expressing the emotional truth of the special bond she was trying to create. The circle, the smoke, even the stars overhead made it easier for her to say these things as intensely as she felt them.

Thankfully, many family rituals have been occurring for generations and there are often countless precedents to help supply the words we need. There are many other resources, both for familiar and unusual occasions. The Bible is a great source of expressive wisdom and has something to say about every major human crisis and milestone. Poetry is also wonderful, even the words to popular songs. Cole Porter, the Beatles, and Broadway musicals are eminently worth quoting when the proper ritual comes along. Children's books are a great resource too: on fitting occasions, our family likes to chant the slogan of a valiant troop of bugs in William Joyce's *The Leaf Men and the Brave Good Bugs.* The "doodle bugs" proclaim: "Tiny of body but brave of heart, we always finish what we start."

Even if it's a ritual without known precedents, there are places to look: Marilyn Labendz of Montville, N.J., who creates Jewish rituals for all occasions, once invented a ceremony for a woman who wanted to celebrate the renovation of her seventy-five-year-old Steinway grand piano. "It really wasn't so hard," she says. "Music plays a big part in Jewish tradition and I was able to find a text about a prophet who couldn't prophesy until his minstrel was brought to him."

A common mistake is making ritual words too serious, forgetting to exercise a sense of humor. After all, even a memorial service has room for levity: haven't we all been to services where an anecdote about the deceased left us laughing through our tears? How good that felt, the reminder of the joy and happiness that person spread in life, which in turn is a measure of our loss. Our sense of humor is part of what is distinctive about each of us, and if our rituals are going to work, they must reflect our true personalities. One family I know sometimes ends grace by saying, "Amen, and we really mean it."

Finally, although most rituals require a leader, it's not a good idea for that person to be the sole speaker. Otherwise, the activity is less a ritual than a speech. Ritual is shared by people and requires give-and-take, an altering of relationships. In family rituals, it's vital that children have a voice, even if that means a teenage child interjects a mocking remark when a moment threatens to get solemn. Except for religious rites and highly scripted ceremonies, rituals should encourage kids to speak in a natural, comfortable way. Indeed, the playfulness of children makes them very much at home in ritual and spectacle, where pretending and play-acting are the highest art forms.

For example, the Brock family of Cheney, Wash., decided to try to make family dinners special one night a week. Barb Brock, a professor of recreation management at Eastern Washington University, uses nice plates on Thursdays even if the food itself isn't anything special. What makes Thursday special is the words. Well, actually the toasts.

"I have no idea how it got started, but we just make a lot of toasts, and from the time Adam was two years old that just made him feel so important and so included. For the longest time, his favorite toast was 'To the future!' and he said it over and over. Now he's gotten more creative, and his little sister usually says, 'To the future!' "

Nuance

In ritual, with its heightened sense of anticipation and sensation, the little things mean everything.

My brother-in-law in Indianapolis, Rob Smith, is one of the people who taught me this important lesson, on the first anniversary of his marriage to my sister. Tracy had been moaning for a while about how she never got flowers, so Rob decided to do something about it. But he didn't do the expected thing and send a bouquet to her office.

One Sunday when Tracy got to the church door, the official greeter for the week handed her one red rose and wished her a very happy anniversary. As she walked into the church, friends from the choir and other members of the congregation walked up to her, one by one, and gave her more roses and more good wishes. The final rose came from the pastor himself. In the end, Tracy got her dozen roses, but she got so much more than that. Rob declared his love and respect for her far more loudly than if he had spent ten times the money and filled her office with flowers. Instead he allowed an entire community to express affection for Tracy on their anniversary, and at the place where the wedding had occurred. Naturally, she would have been grateful to receive a dozen roses in the usual way. But it wasn't the roses that left Tracy teary-eyed, it was the ceremonial way in which Rob gave them to her.

"God is in the details," goes the familiar saying, and those details are also one of the secrets of powerful family ritual. Nuance is what keeps an old tradition still personal and relevant, and what makes the simplest of everyday routines profoundly affecting.

Nuance means all the little things: flowers, music, food, and decorations, but also where you stage a ritual, the order in which you do things, the names you call things.

To zero in on the details that will make a difference, start by asking yourself these two questions: who is this ritual for, and what can I do that will give him (or her, or them) the sensation of being the star of the moment, of being cherished? Being singled out and honored for exactly who one is is one of the ultimate joys of life, and for children, it surpasses any bakery confection known to man.

Doing this requires empathy and genuine intimacy, because you have to *really* know the people involved and understand how they feel in different situations. Also, it requires you to think in advance about how the ritual will play out and such thoughtfulness requires time, which is another rare gift to those we love.

Remember, ritual is a performance, and so the stage must be set, the lighting selected, the music or sound effects arranged, the "costumes" considered. If you think of ritual in that way, as a sort of play that requires stage directions (and a director), it will help you to anticipate and make choices about the flow of the action.

Take something as simple as toasting. Drinks are poured, perhaps champagne, and everybody raises their glasses as someone says appreciative words about the hero of the evening. That's all fine, but because the routine is so, well, routine, tiny variations in it really make a splash.

William Doherty, a therapist who wrote the book *The Intentional Family: How to Build Family Ties in Our Modern World*, talks about a special party for his wife. A simple and profound decision was made: every time a person made a toast, they got up from their own place and sat next to her, turning to look into her eyes as they made their remarks. When a person's toast was finished, he or she would say, "Who else would like the chair?"

"It was so much more powerful than if they had just stood up and talked. I guess it was the added intimacy of sitting next to her. I get teary-eyed just thinking about it."

For similar reasons, I was moved by the description of a party given by designer Giorgio Armani for his top employees. The party was reported to be part of an orchestrated publicity campaign to make Armani seem more personable and less remote. The staff lunch was the only event without celebrities, but it included a ritual gesture by the host that seemed to come from the heart.

Now when most bosses, or bosses of families, stand up and talk about how much they love and value everyone in the room, they usually stand or sit in one place and declaim. As Armani spoke about each person, he simply stood behind his or her chair, a gesture that conveyed respect and a sense that he needed to be physically close to them while describing their special contributions. Giorgio became a man rather than a figurehead of Armani Inc. in a distant chair. "Many left the lunch in tears," *The New York Times* reported, and it's easy to see why.

Because we are all such creatures of routine, it doesn't take much variation in the usual order of things to make rituals seem very special. One way to create a sense of celebration is simply to do ordinary things in unexpected places or at unusual times. Like families who eat Christmas Eve supper on the floor under the Christmas tree. Take the novelty of the situation, the permission to do something ordinarily forbidden, and add dramatic lighting, using only candles and the lights on the tree, and you have a ritual that children will look forward to all year.

That ritual "recipe" of tweaking the expected can be adapted for all sorts of occasions. Like the boy who was allowed to celebrate the last day of school by eating carryout Chinese food on the steps of his school at midnight. Or the families that turn everyday dietary rules upside down by declaring an all-dessert dinner. Or the families that are normally very strict about bedtimes, but plan after-dark walks when the moon is full.

Gift-giving is another staple of family ritual and it, too, can benefit from attention to small details, like the roses given one by one.

To be honest, we've all opened gifts in a frantic frenzy, like children, and found ourselves left feeling, as they do, "Is that all?" The antidote to this is the ritual focus we've been talking about, getting people to slow down and really experience what is happening to them. In order to do this, the presenting and opening of the gifts needs to become more structured, more of a conscious ritual.

Again, there are many ways to achieve this, such as requiring kids to solve clues or follow footprints to find hidden gifts, like the children who have to follow ribbons downstairs from their beds to find their Easter baskets. Anything that delays gratification and builds anticipation is going to be more fun and memorable than just having everything handed to you in a pile.

Another approach is suggested by the wonderful birthday ritual Kathleen Metcalf created for her three children (see pages 168–169). Each has a wreath on his or her bedroom wall, and on birthdays, every family member hangs on it a small object representing a quality they admire in the child or an important event of the past year.

There are countless variations on this idea, which, like many rituals we've discussed, has ancient antecedents in diverse cultures. Kathleen Chesto created a special ritual bestowing of gifts for her children as they left for college. She planned a special dinner for each one about a month

before their departure, and gave them a basket of gifts, each with an explanation. They were far from lavish presents, but the basic essentials any kid needs, like shampoo and a dustpan. She also threw in fun items like a jar of bubble-blowing liquid.

The ceremony for bestowing the gifts included a reading from Genesis about leaving home, and then Kathy voiced a parental wish for each item, in a way that also conveyed the family's values. For example: "I give you soap. Never be afraid to get your hands dirty in the service of others." And "I give you this dustpan and brush. May it remind you never to sweep unpleasantness under the carpet, but to pick it up and deal with it." Finally, "I give you this bubble stuff and wand in the hope that you will never leave your childhood totally behind."

Fundamentally, this gift-giving ritual provides a basic structure with which to convey a lot of diverse wishes to a loved one, including sentiments we often have a hard time expressing. Sharing our hopes and dreams for our children *with* our children is something we do far too seldom, and an effort they will genuinely appreciate.

I discovered this myself when I orchestrated something similar for my stepdaughter's law school graduation. My husband, her mother, and I carried on various conversations about what good things we wished for her in her future, then thought up half-a-dozen gifts that would represent those wishes. For example, we hoped that she would get to travel a lot, which she loves, and gave her luggage. But we also hoped she would be a compassionate person, and so gave her a small gold heart necklace. To add some levity but also focus on the importance of remaining optimistic in life, we made some pretend "future Super Bowl" tickets for the Cleveland Browns. (She and her father are deeply upset about the team being moved to Baltimore and eagerly await the formation of a new team in Cleveland under the old name.)

The exercise was fun for all the parents, and Kate was truly touched by both our effort and our wishes for her.

Finally, though we've discussed the importance of words in ritual, let's not neglect names: sometimes just having a special family name for the tiniest of rituals makes a huge difference.

For example, Barb Brock was trying to think up ways to keep her daughter amused during a period of patched-together day care. On Tuesdays, when Sydney is watched by a friend of her mother's, Barb picks her up after work and takes her to a little coffee stand in Spokane. Sydney is too young to drink coffee, but the owner makes her a special cup of frothy warm milk with almond flavoring, which she and her mother call a "White Cloud." Just knowing she is going to go to the stand and get her White Cloud on Tuesdays makes Sydney look forward to those times.

The Sauvey family of DePere, Wis., has a good-bye ritual that I suspect many other families follow: when Marie or her husband leaves for work, they blink the car headlights on and off several times. The Sauveys call this ritual "headlight kisses." The special name elevates the ritual into something very tender, just as Paul Sauvey hoped it would. "He's a charter pilot and is gone for days at a time," says Marie, so he wants his good-byes to be memorable and loving.

Like members of a secret society, or practitioners of a profession that has its own slang, families who have special names for the things they do feel the bond of the initiated, protected against outsiders by their knowledge and love.

Nine

★ ★ ★ ★

WHEN RITUALS NEED CHANGING

Ritual is sufficiently powerful that the yearning for it ought to be accompanied by a relentless criticism of it. Ritual fails as often as it succeeds, but even in its failure it can exercise power like some dying, fiddling emperor.

—Ronald L. Grimes, *Marrying and Burying:*
Rites of Passage in a Man's Life

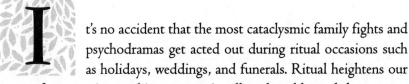

I t's no accident that the most cataclysmic family fights and psychodramas get acted out during ritual occasions such as holidays, weddings, and funerals. Ritual heightens our sense of expectation, making us emotionally vulnerable, and these events become symbolic repositories of all our previous family ceremonies. Family members use these events, albeit subconsciously, to act out their primal relationships to one another, and it isn't always a pretty sight.

We enter into family rituals anticipating peak experiences, nursing personal fantasies of the perfect family Christmas or the blissful wedding, and then are sometimes depressed when the reality doesn't meet our hopes. If the ritual is to honor us, we visualize a ceremony that drenches us in the perfect love and admiration we feel we deserve, but we are almost certainly doomed to disappointment.

The fact of the matter is that rituals can fail and that the pain when they do isn't trivial. There's a way in which rituals, especially major ones, resemble big exams. Such rituals require a great deal of advance preparation before the deadline, and then there is immense pressure on the big day to perform one's role perfectly, to do one's best. The possibility of failure is genuine, and if the worst happens, the terror and feeling of defeat will be every bit as powerful as the euphoria and sense of accomplishment that come from successful rituals.

We have all watched rituals fail, and the feeling of pain, even humiliation, can be so acute that it haunts us for years.

I will never forget the funeral of my grandfather, my mother's father, a jeweler, musician, amateur filmmaker, and craftsman. We wanted to be reminded of his accomplishments and to be shown that he wouldn't be forgotten. Instead, the dim-witted funeral director read a pro forma speech and every time he mentioned my grandfather, mispronounced his last name. It felt like a desecration. I was a teenager then, but I felt the mistake viscerally each time he made it. I watched in horror as my mother's face turned white, her anguish palpably mutating into even greater grief.

Some years later, I witnessed another ritual failure that made a big impression. It was a milestone birthday party for a member of my family. Much care had been taken, with invitees coming long distances and spectacular foods being prepared. But when it was time for a series of champagne toasts, things got off on the wrong foot. The first person launched into a high school anecdote that was amusing, but showed how sharp-tongued the birthday person could be. Suddenly, that tone took over the event, and the toast became a roast. Guests meant to be teasing, but when it was all over, not a single nice thing had been said of the honoree, who ended the evening in tears.

Even though these ceremonies were intended to honor people and were attended by their nearest and dearest, they backfired in ways that nobody expected. They demonstrate why ritual must be approached with attentiveness and knowledge. Ritual is not the enemy, but like a powerful drug that has the potential to heal or harm, it must be respected and used wisely.

How to Prevent Ritual Failure

The failed funeral left me mad and the failed birthday left me sad, but both taught me a great deal about preparation for ritual. There is no such thing as ritual insurance, but let's start by looking at how these two disasters could have been prevented or mitigated.

Planning a one-time-only ceremony, such as a wedding, funeral, or milestone birthday, is a bit like producing a major play, except that it only runs for one performance. Thinking ahead and practicing whatever can be practiced is absolutely essential. That's why weddings have rehearsal dinners.

Lots of family rituals don't give you that option. But before my grandfather's funeral, someone should have sat down with that funeral director and explicitly detailed the family's wishes, and asked for a copy of his remarks. Even a casual conversation about Grandpa would have revealed that the funeral director didn't know how to pronounce the man's name (though it was clearly his job to make sure that he could).

That funeral taught me the importance of playing a ritual out, at least in one's head, and imagining what every step will look like from the "audience." Even when one is grief-stricken, the details must be attended to.

Similar lessons were learned from the birthday fiasco about how chaotic and wrongheaded rituals can be if left too entirely to their own devices. Friends and family had been told in advance that they'd be encouraged to make remarks, but no parameters were set. If the toasters had been steered in a particular direction or given a theme, everything would have worked better. It might have been "the funniest thing I ever saw her do," or "something she taught me." Or people might have toasted "what I most admire in her," or something they wished for her future.

If the event had been declared to be a roast from the start, everybody's expectations would have been different, and the cumulative effect of all that carping would have been comedic. Even so, I believe, someone should have served as a sort of master of ceremonies, and wrapped up the proceedings on a positive note.

Which brings me to another important lesson from this failed ritual: never, ever should a ritual be purely negative. People can't tolerate that, and, more important, it doesn't reflect life.

There are many examples in this book of family rituals that *include* negatives, such as bedtime rituals where children list a good thing and a bad thing that happened that day—Lucinda Herring's "grateful and grumbles," for example. But all of these rituals are balanced with something positive, so that children can reflect on the duality of life and develop the discipline of acknowledging a compensating bright side.

Karrie Brunson, a mother of three, learned as a girl what happens when rituals embrace only the negative. Her father tried to institute a weekly ritual in which family members could air their gripes, but the sessions always escalated into family fights. The practice was soon abandoned; Karrie's parents were later divorced. Thus, when Karrie was trying to create weekly family days for her family, she hit on the notion of having each person state "a like, a dislike, and a hope."

If Karrie had taken the opposite extreme from her father and only allowed family members to share their "likes," the ritual might have become artificially sweet, and, eventually, dreaded. This way, her kids can share their real complaints within a larger context that forces them to pause and reflect on the good things in life too. Adding a third piece to the ritual was a brilliant stroke, and the one Karrie chose was excellent. Sharing a hope is a deeply personal gesture reserved only for those one trusts; it implies that one expects to be understood.

Extended family rituals are a whole other kettle of fish, with additional difficulties to overcome, such as mind-boggling travel logistics. Not to mention the dynamics of clashing ritual styles and personalities, and the necessity of inviting the aunt nobody likes because you're asking the aunt everybody loves.

There's a brilliant scene in Barry Levinson's movie *Avalon*, about an extended family of immigrants in Baltimore. By tradition, the brother who always hosts Thanksgiving doesn't carve the turkey until everybody arrives. But one year his brother's family arrives even later than usual, and the brother hosting the feast finally gives up and starts slicing. "You cut the turkey!" shouts the latecomer, and sweeps right back out the door with his family. This break in tradition is viewed as such a betrayal, it opens up a rift in the family. "You might as well have stabbed me in the heart," the offended brother says later.

Family ritual conflicts also get exacerbated when the matriarch or patriarch of a family dies, or gets too infirm to host big gatherings.

"It seems that, every holiday, something goes wrong," says Tammy Cardwell, a mother of two in Texas. Ever since her husband's grandmother, a great cook and the official family hostess, died, "We never know from holiday to holiday whose house we'll be going to or what we'll do. Family members change their plans constantly, with Christmas jumping around from this house to that, and we didn't have any family Thanksgiving for two years. Somebody is always mad at somebody else."

Tammy finally adopted a strategy of not taking any Christmas plans seriously unless they are communicated to her "within two days of the holiday and even then, I call to confirm." As for Thanksgiving, she and her husband have started new traditions to replace the lapsed family ones, generally going to a friend's house with their kids.

The sad thing is that her childhood holidays were "magical" and she misses them. She realizes now that the magic was the result of her parents having "worked out the kinks that I'm now forced to work through, leaving me free to be a child."

It seems to me that Tammy's fond memories of childhood ritual point to a remedy: what she should be concentrating on now is creating that magic for her own children, even if it makes holidays less fun for her. And that may mean taking a tighter grip on the festivities, creating new traditions that matter a lot to her immediate family and fitting any extended family gatherings around those.

Indeed, some families I know have reluctantly bowed out of huge and cantankerous holiday get-togethers and announced they'll wait for less stressful occasions to see those family members. One woman I know simply announced that Christmas would be celebrated with immediate family only, because that was her favorite holiday and the stress of including everybody else was making her dread it. After consulting with various family members, she turned the Fourth of July into the "big family holiday," and everybody now seems satisfied.

Like most people, I have botched rituals myself. For my fortieth birthday party, my husband arranged a dinner with friends in the cozy wine cellar of an Italian restaurant in New York. He orchestrated many of the details, including a fanciful and witty cake decorated with forty winks, forty carats (carrots, actually), forty thieves, and so on. Gathered around me were many of my dearest friends, in a beautiful space eating delicious food. It should have been wonderful, but I blew it.

It came time for remarks, and I was more than ready. I had spent a great deal of time looking up pithy quotes about aging and lists of the brilliant and famous who hadn't produced masterpieces until they were over forty. I had thought hard about what it meant to me to be this age, and I wanted my friends to listen raptly while I told them, and then shower me with tokens of their affection (verbal and otherwise). Instead, shortly after I started pontificating, two of my more boisterous friends began to make light of my remarks, in the manner of siblings ribbing a too-pompous relative.

I'm embarrassed to admit that I didn't take it well. I crumbled and couldn't go on, feeling angry and hurt like a small child. I said I had nothing else to say, when clearly I did, and just clammed up. I let an awkward silence sit there, eroding all the good cheer in the room. And though various rituals rushed in to fill the vacuum, such as the blowing out of candles and the bestowing of gifts, the fizz was gone, the party had fallen flat.

I've thought about that party a lot since then and what I could have done to turn things around. The power was in my hands, but I abused that power and I still feel awful about it. Yes, it was okay for me to be annoyed, but it wasn't all right for me to sabotage my own party, to puncture a beautiful evening for my friends, whom I love. It wasn't just that I didn't act like a grown-up and banter back, letting my friends know, in a tone that matched theirs, that I wanted to continue. I had tried to create a ritual that was all about *me*. A ritual that is designed to make just one person happy is doomed to failure.

From the beginning, I had wanted to have a fortieth birthday party that was as memorable and sustaining as the one I hosted when I turned thirty-five. But I ignored the essential element that made the earlier event so special: on that occasion, every step I took was aimed at creating a magical event for my friends. *That* was my gift to myself, and I believe that is why the evening went so well.

I love dressing up and I wanted to declare the dinner a black-tie affair, but I didn't want it to feel the least bit stuffy. So instead of hiring a staid string quartet, I searched for music that was sassy, even rowdy. I hired a trio of women singers and explained the effect I was after. They showed up wearing '50s prom dresses and cowboy boots, and they sang both "Happy Birthday" and "Happy Trails," with guitar accompaniment. Before they sang, they made me close my eyes while they gave all my guests silly paper hats to wear, and put a cardboard tiara on my head. The contrast of tuxes and gowns mixed with paper hats and country and rock music was perfect: everybody stomped their feet and howled and hooted.

Then the singers left and we ate a fabulous dinner. I made few, if any, remarks, and there was just one simple birthday toast. But the evening made me feel like the sophisticated New Yorker I always wanted to be, and the joy in my friends' faces made me feel I deserved them.

So, think ahead, don't be selfish, and don't take yourself too seriously. Also, don't ever assume that people will come to a ritual with the same goals and purposes you have.

No matter how prepared and how loving we are, some of our rituals will inevitably fail because we are human. But even when that happens, our efforts won't be wasted or our good intentions ignored. Family rituals born of love may crash and crumble, but the love will outlast the disappointment. Pat McCarthy's daughter Katie, who recently finished a stint as a missionary nurse in Belize, has long since forgiven her mother for the unwanted first-period ritual: she sees it as the proof of motherly love it was, however misguided.

"Even though I wished she had ignored it, even then part of me knew what she was trying to do," says Katie. "Yes, it's a huge deal to know that your body is now able to make a baby, but here I was eating off this blood-red plate for my period, thank you very much." At the time, Katie found it impossible to express her feelings with anything but a blush. But now, she says, "We laugh about it."

If we are going to teach our children that succeeding doesn't matter as much as trying, then this is a good place to set an example: we can't be seen weeping too much over the spilt milk of failed ritual.

A further caveat: don't confuse ritual reluctance with ritual failure. Kids, spouses, and all manner of relatives may balk when presented with the idea for a new ritual and kids often whine and complain about such recurring rituals as family nights, especially if they aren't strictly devoted to fun. That doesn't mean the ritual is a failure or should be abandoned. You might consider, as a family, whether some tinkering is in order, but don't give up too easily if you think a ritual is generally helpful.

When and How to Change Ritual

Families aren't static, and rituals can't be, either. Growing children may still need and want a bedtime routine, but they won't need the part of the ritual about scaring away monsters. Janet Drey of Des Moines, Iowa, only realized after the fact one Christmas that nobody remembered to put out cookies for Santa: her kids expressed no regrets, so it was dropped from the family's annual holiday preparations. Indeed, some ritual changes almost serve as an index to maturity: children anticipate the time when they're old enough to light candles themselves, or help cut down the Christmas tree.

Parents need to be sensitive to children's reactions over time to even the most ingrained ritual exercises. For example, the McCarthys of Casper, Wyo., have been making the sign of the cross on their children's foreheads at bedtime since the kids were infants. "We cross them with our fingers," explains Pat McCarthy. But when her oldest, Kate (the one who hated her first-period ritual), became a teenager, she was obsessed with the idea "that crossing on the forehead causes pimples."

Rather than enter into a battle about religion or hygiene, the girl's parents worked out a compromise: Kate would lean down and her parents crossed her on the top of her head instead. "I believe you have to respect where they are," says Pat, and she and her husband automatically made the change when their three younger children became teenagers.

Sometimes the signs that a ritual needs changing are crystal clear, especially when a child is outgrowing a once-cherished routine. I remember how proud I was of the rather elaborate bedtime ritual I created for my infant son: all his stuffed animals would kiss him good night in different ways, then I would help Max turn out the light and get used to the dark in my arms, singing a lullaby about him.

But even before his first birthday, he began interrupting the ritual. I would start reaching for animals, and he would impatiently implore "bed, bed," while trying to dive headfirst into his crib. My feelings were hurt, but dropping the ritual sure made for an efficient bedtime.

Often the need for ritual to change isn't so clear. For example, by the time Kathleen Chesto was diagnosed with multiple sclerosis in 1986, she had been dragging herself around in a weakened state for several years. Doctors kept telling her there was nothing physically wrong, and it never occurred to her to try and scale back the extensive work she did for major holiday rituals. But it was all more than she could handle, and the festivities lost much of their joy for her.

"At the time, the kids were old enough to have taken on some of the work, but they just didn't want to," says Kathy. "Finally, we talked it out and decided to switch to menus that were easier and less formal. Instead of making a big turkey with all the trimmings for Thanksgiving and Christmas, I would make roast beef." The silver lining in the disaster was the exercise of reevaluating the holidays with her husband and three kids: "We were able to ask ourselves, 'What really matters to us about the ritual?' and it wasn't that we ate the exact same thing every year. It was clear that family mattered more than food."

The ritual was modified again when the Chesto children were older. "We added back some of the elaborate dishes, because now the kids love doing the cooking themselves."

When death strikes a family, rituals can become a painful reminder of how things were before. Deciding what and how much to change, however, is bruisingly tough: does one modify existing rituals only slightly and carry them on in tribute to the deceased person? Or is it less painful to look resolutely forward and revamp the rituals entirely?

Those were some of the decisions faced by Sally Weber of Los Angeles, when her husband Jerry was killed. As described on pages 77–80, it took Sally several years of agonizing and study before she was ready to take over leadership of the family's Passover seder.

Sally's decision was made largely as a result of her teenage daughters' insistence, and she saw how keenly they missed the ritual. In the end, she changed the Passover service slightly to reflect her personality and her talents. Her annual seders serve as a loving tribute to her husband's memory, but they have also strengthened her own religious faith immeasurably.

But Sally and her daughters didn't follow the same pattern with all the family's religious rituals. While they had been used to getting very dressed up and holding rather formal Shabbat dinners on Friday nights, after Jerry's death they found it too exhausting. "The girls and I instituted what we call 'pajama Shabbat,' and it gave us this wonderful feeling. We are continuing a tradition, but it was a great feeling to loosen it up."

As other rituals arose for discussion, Sally and her daughters discovered that proposing changes could be unsettling to one another. "We finally agreed that if any of the three of us was uncomfortable with a change, we just wouldn't make it. That was important because it meant we could change things without feeling the whole structure was falling apart."

In cases where a family loses a matriarch or patriarch who presided over major holidays, families find that if they don't consciously reinvent rituals for their extended family, the vacuum remains unfilled. Sometimes, the younger generation finds itself breaking into smaller groups, planning events for immediate family only, which is fine if that is what people prefer.

As painful as death is, changing rituals after divorce can be just as distressing, if not more so. Often, the spouse who gets custody seems to also get custody of the major rituals, and celebrations of all sorts have to be doled out or reconfigured. Competitive ritualizing, stressful for everyone, is likely to ensue. Having a vastly different bedtime ritual with Dad than with Mom can serve to reinforce a child's sense of dislocation, and the big holidays are even worse. Celebrating fragments of ritual in parental shifts may make it nearly impossible for kids to feel the unalloyed euphoria that marks the best of childhood holidays.

Even emotionally mature parents who love their children dearly and want to prove that divorce hasn't diminished their love don't find the going easy.

When Sherry Sturch got divorced from her childhood sweetheart after twenty years of marriage and three children, her first impulse was to try to soften the blow by continuing as many of the usual family celebrations as possible. "At first, we tried to have regular Sunday dinners as a family but it only lasted a couple of months. The kids would say, 'You guys get along so well, why aren't you still married?' It felt false to them, so we dropped it."

They continued to celebrate all the major holidays together as a family for about five years, but that practice also came to feel forced. Sherry says excluding her husband from Thanksgiving that first year was hardest on her daughter. From then on, the children would share the main course with one parent at Thanksgiving, then travel to the other's place for dessert. On their birthdays, Sherry spent the day with the kids and then their father would take the birthday boy or girl out to dinner. "I've finally learned that you can't go back and change what was, but you always have the chance to create something new," says Sherry.

One of the most stressful times for kids of divorce is house-switching, moving between the home of one parent and the home of the other. Like all life transitions, this one can benefit from thoughtful rituals.

For example, Suzy Kellett, the mother of quadruplets, raised them pretty much alone after her husband left her when they were ten months old. The father later became more involved in the children's lives, and the quads began visiting their out-of-town dad for a month every summer. Spontaneously reacting to a need to embrace their mother tightly before the journey, the quadruplets started a ritual of sleeping in Suzy's room the night before they leave. "I have no idea what started it, but they all bring their sleeping bags and sleep in my room."

Most kids move back and forth more often, many on a weekly basis, and they too would benefit from having transition rituals for each house.

In the book *Lights of Passage: Rituals and Rites of Passage for the Problems and Pleasures of Modern Life*, Kathleen Wall talks about a family in which the two children change houses four times a year. After they fly to their dad's house, they always stop at the same pizza place on the way from the airport, and when they get home, they curl up in familiar blankets in front of the television. On the morning they leave their dad's house, they always take a long walk in a nearby park and eat breakfast at their favorite diner. They've worked out a different set of arrival and departure rituals for their mother's house. All family members share an understanding that on these transition days, the tempo will be slow and gentle and issues like scheduling and discipline will be deferred.

There are no general rules, but postdivorce rituals, like every other kind, need to honestly reflect reality, even if that sacrifices some stability. If the reality within a family is that everybody gets along well even though Mom and Dad are better off unmarried, then inclusive rituals of celebration are more possible. If that is simply not the case, finding a fair way to divide the calendar is better for everyone.

Although it's generally not healthy, and usually not possible, for a family's major rituals to remain unchanged after divorce, this isn't a good time for either parent to forget a birthday or ignore a major milestone. Younger children especially, who might go through a stage of believing the divorce is their fault, will become convinced of it if they don't get their usual birthday cake, or no one notices a great report card. Kids need to know that they won't get lost in the shuffle, and keeping kid-focused rituals center stage is one way to do that.

Further complications result, naturally, with remarriage and the introduction of stepparents. This is definitely a time when existing rituals have to become inclusive, and new rituals designed that help give this awkward group a common identity. Often rituals of inclusion start with a wedding.

When Arlene Goodrick of Camp Pendleton, Calif., got married for the second time, she gave her four-year-old daughter a central role in the ritual. The little girl walked her mother down the aisle, and stood by the altar for part of the ceremony, making vows of her own. "The three of us made a circle by all holding hands," says Arlene. "Then the minister asked her if she would love us and honor us as her parents and always keep the lines of communication open with her family. He asked if she would promise to do these things, and she answered, 'I do.' "

During the reception, the little girl got to make her own wedding toast (using apple juice), and helped pass out the cake.

After her mother's remarriage, the daughter continued to spend a lot of time with her father. But her stepfather has wisely carved out his own relationship with the girl, teaching her how to tie her shoes and ride a bike. He has also created some new rituals just for the two of them, including getting up with her on Saturday mornings, making her breakfast, and watching a Disney movie with her.

So, while it is important to have rituals that help bind a new family together, it is also vital that stepparents create more exclusive rituals that can develop an individual bond with their stepchildren. Best of all is to find an activity that reflects a shared interest, so the time together is focused on that interest and having a good time. Otherwise children may expect a lecture or an artificial attempt at chumminess and will dread rather than anticipate the event.

My relationship with my own stepdaughter could have been helped greatly by scheduling activities just for us. We are now comfortably close, but it took years for us to get there. I was so wary of seeming to usurp her intense relationship with her mother in any way that I held myself too distant. Even monthly get-togethers early on would have broken that down, I believe, and helped us appreciate each other sooner.

Flexibility, always vital to ritual, becomes even more important in such patchwork families. For example, one stepmother wondered how she could celebrate Christmas with her stepdaughter on the weekend before

the holiday without ruining things for her own young boys. She came up with a creative solution generous to all concerned: when the stepdaughter arrives for the weekend, the family celebrates "Practice Christmas." Santa fills the stockings for all three kids, bringing multiple gifts for the stepdaughter and a token gift for each of the two little ones.

On Christmas Day, the two boys get the rest of their presents, plus their stockings are refilled by Santa. All the kids loved the ritual from the start, and the proof of its success is that it has lasted more than a decade. Creating a brand-new holiday in honor of the stepchild was a great idea, especially since it didn't exclude the children from the father's second marriage. In the end, a holiday was created that exists only for this particular group of people, the kind of ritual bond that can help people feel more happily related than blood relations sometimes do.

Ten

★ ★ ★ ★

MAKING A RITUAL LIFE

The function of ritual, as I understand it, is to give form to the human life, not in the way of a mere surface arrangement, but in depth.

—Joseph Campbell, *Myths to Live By*

What does it mean to make a ritual life?

Ellen Brosbe has a very clear idea of what it means to her family. The vast majority of the Brosbe family rituals have a single source: the Jewish religion. Even the most prosaic of the family's rituals reflect Jewish principles, including the way the Brosbes play Monopoly. "Jews believe in tithing (giving 10 percent of income to charity)," says Ellen, "so when you pass Go and collect your two hundred dollars, you have to set aside twenty dollars."

This precept is followed in the real world by the Brosbes. Every member of the family puts money into a special container on Fridays before the Sabbath begins, and the family meets several times a year to choose charities to receive the money. But applying that practice even to a game makes the lesson more vivid, demonstrating that this belief runs deep within the family culture. It was one of the Brosbe kids who pointed out that the family's practice of putting the Monopoly money for tithing in "free parking," where it again becomes available as prize money, is not quite kosher as charity. "What can I say?" Ellen responds. "We also haven't figured out how to designate low-cost housing in Monopoly. But at least we discuss it."

Living a ritual life to the Brosbes means living their religion. To them, faith isn't conveyed by stuffy admonitions but by active rituals that are creative, even whimsical.

So Herb Brosbe likes to make a "Parting of the Red Sea Cake" at Passover, swarming with little plastic Lego and Playmobil figures. And when the Brosbes observe the Jewish harvest festival of Sukkot and decorate the temporary harvest hut in which families are supposed to eat and celebrate, lollipops hang from the ceiling along with a string of lights in the shape of chili peppers.

For other families, making a ritual life has little to do with formal religious observance. The faith and passion that tie their rituals together have more to do with putting family first, keeping people close.

Like the Trieschman family of Baltimore, some of whose rituals were discussed in the holiday chapters. The Trieschmans celebrate every major holiday and a lot of minor ones too, bringing together an extended family of more than twenty.

Christmas means caroling together and the family's outrageous Kris Kringle gift exchange. At Easter, there's an elaborate egg hunt and one of the adults always dresses as the Easter bunny. Both Labor Day and Memorial Day are spent at Cindy's mother's Delaware beach house, and every year the family picks a different state fair to attend en masse.

So close is the family, that Cindy's father recently purchased an old blue church bus so he could drive the entire extended family around. It's used not only on major holiday excursions, but even for impromptu outings. "He'll decide it's a good time for a snowball fight, and drive around and pick up all the grandchildren," says Cindy. "My kids get so excited when they see that bus pull into the driveway. Next thing we're going to do is give the bus a special name."

All these rituals have not only kept the extended family close together, but also inspired Cindy and her siblings to create additional rituals of their own. "I'm a sponge: I want more and more family rituals and I love starting them," she says.

Cindy will draw inspiration from just about anywhere. She's about to start a Christmas ritual she saw in a catalog: "You can order this dill pickle–shaped ornament and the idea is to hide it someplace on the tree," she explains. "Whoever finds it first gets to open whatever present they want first. I'm just waiting for my baby to be old enough to participate."

For large families, the drive behind living a ritual life is also fueled by a practical need for organization. Religion is important to L'Tishia Suk of Evanston, Ill., but she cites the need for order in a family of six as the principal impetus behind many of her rituals.

"I do workshops on being organized and I think traditions help you in this," says L'Tishia. "At Christmas, we do certain things, and it's Saturday night, so we eat pizza, and Sunday morning is waffles. I find such rituals simplify life. I've been making pizza every Saturday night for twenty years, so it's something I don't have to spend a lot of time planning."

It's L'Tishia who bundles her family into the car every year for a picnic in the park on the first day of spring. For fifteen years, the family has sat down together for a special breakfast on Thanksgiving morning, taking turns declaring what it is for which they're thankful that year. On Christmas Eve, the Suks act out the nativity story after dinner. "There is a Joseph and Mary, and then one of us is all the shepherds, one plays all the angels, and so on," says L'Tishia. "It only takes ten minutes, and everybody has a great time."

QUALITY AND QUANTITY

The message is inescapable: in order to build a ritual life that is genuine and deeply felt, both quality and quantity are important. Just stringing together a bunch of rituals in which family members woodenly go through the motions wouldn't create much more than exhaustion. In the way that hollow religious rituals lead to diminished church memberships, such empty family rituals might actually drive family members away in search of more rewarding pursuits.

Conversely, having only a few cherished rituals wouldn't be sufficient either, even if they were remarkably thoughtful ones. Time in a child's world moves very slowly, and ritual needs to happen every day, not just on special occasions.

It's the combination that makes a ritual life, the fact that rituals are both personal and persistent, threaded through the days and the years, something you know as well as your name.

Fortunately, committing ourselves to both quality and quantity doesn't demand that we all quit our jobs and become full-time ritual producers. Ritualizing every part of family life would be disastrous, snuffing out the joy of spontaneity and becoming a grind. Even families who are passionate about ritual know when to draw the line, when to let chaos rule, and what events are better left uncelebrated.

Cindy Grubb, for example, admits that she has virtually no bedtime rituals and little enthusiasm for cooking in any form. L'Tishia Suk doesn't do much for birthdays other than decorate the birthday person's chair. "I guess it's because I'm just worn out," she says, laughing.

It took me three years of research and analysis to reach this conclusion, but I believe there is no perfect model for any family. I've come to see that when it comes to family ritual, one size emphatically does *not* fit all. While these ritual paragons have many lessons to teach, and I have borrowed specific rituals from these and other families, a ritual life is something unique, and each family must build its own.

I could never emulate the Brosbes because I'm not Jewish or even overtly religious, and my extended family is much too scattered to celebrate the way the Trieschmans do. As for the Suks, L'Tishia's organizational zeal puts me to shame, and my husband wouldn't put up with half that much regimentation. Besides, though I now wish I had started much earlier and *could* have a large family, rituals that provide structure for a family of six would overwhelm us.

Like many people, I didn't think much about the ritual in my life until a baby was on the way. Once Max was born, it was a whole new world, demanding rituals of all kinds to protect, comfort, and celebrate this new being. How would we do bedtime? Observe his birthday? Make bathtime fun? Explain the meaning of the Fourth of July?

Slowly, certain things became clear. One was that no matter my zeal for ritual generally, I couldn't conjure it out of thin air. It had to be tied to a need of my child's or a real passion of mine and my husband's, or it just didn't happen. People who devoutly follow a particular religion have a built-in ritual schedule that we don't have: creating rituals in the absence of such a framework can be a challenge.

When I try to find the recurring themes in our ritual life, the most obvious one is books and reading. Dick and I are both bookaholics and our house is stuffed with books. Many of our family rituals involving Max also revolve around books.

We not only read to him often during the day and before bed; almost as soon as he was sitting in a high chair for solid food, we started reading to him during meals. Maybe it helps explain why he's such a good and unfussy eater: he would happily sit there for an hour as long as there was a pile of books on the table. He was also encouraged to keep a small stack of books next to his potty seat. Reading there helped foster the patience necessary for "success." And early on, we started a ritual of going to the library every week to borrow books.

Much as I love reading, I would never try to argue that it should be the only passion fueling our family rituals. For us, I think the pivotal driving force will be, like the Trieschmans, our love of family and desire to get and stay as close as possible. I know that the older Max gets the more attractions we'll have to compete with to get his attention, and I want to lay the groundwork now for a whole set of family rituals that will pull him home like a giant magnet.

I feel especially strongly about creating rituals for important transitions in Max's life, but I have already learned that different kinds of transitions require different kinds of ritual, and some require just the merest notice. When he started nursery school, for example, I spent days dreaming up the perfect good-bye ritual, words of wisdom that I would impart day after day when I dropped him off. I had this fantasy that someday he would look back and remember those words he had heard so often, and realize they had made a huge impact on his life, helping to make him hungry to learn.

Hah. From the first day, he was so immediately immersed in rolling Play-Doh and picking up toys he didn't even turn around to wave good-bye. I tried talking to him, but he paid no attention. The fact is, he didn't need a ritual of transition. He had already shifted gears internally from home to school, and my words were extraneous. I didn't want to just slink off in silence, so I whispered in his ear, "I'll be thinking about you." He may not have needed it, but I felt better.

As a family, I want us to fashion a ritual life that both teaches us who we are and helps us to become more than we thought we could be. I want rituals that are as organic and indispensable as breathing, and celebrations so enticing we're jealous of ourselves. I want to demand a lot of ritual, but I expect to give a lot of myself to create it. I know I still have much to learn about ritual and what my family needs from it, and I'm eager to learn.

But enough about me. What should *you* do?

The Basics—A Ritual Inventory

How does a family start making a ritual life? And how much ritual is enough ritual?

No matter how old you or your children are, an excellent place to start is with a ritual inventory. Take out two sheets of paper, and label one "Daily/Weekly/Monthly Rituals" and the other "Special Occasion Rituals." This can also be done on the family computer. Leave plenty of space between rituals because you'll be moving things around later. If possible, do this exercise as a couple and if the kids are old enough, include them. Write down absolutely everything you can think of, using the categories from the "What" section of this book, but also adding any rituals that don't meet these classifications. Most families have far more ritual in their lives than they think they do.

When your lists are complete, study them. Are there general themes or purposes behind your rituals? Have most been handed down from your parents? Are they predominantly religious in nature? Did they arise spontaneously, or did you invent them out of particular needs or desires? Most likely some are celebratory rituals and others solve problems, like getting the kids to bed at a decent hour: what's the ratio between the two?

Does the theme or purpose you came up with fit your family's personality? Does it reflect your values and goals as a family? Since rituals provide one of the most basic definitions of a family, ask yourself what it *means* to be a Smith (or whatever your family name is) based on these rituals? Does that definition seem accurate? Does it make you feel proud?

No matter how you answered, even if you feel your rituals are far from ideal, don't do anything drastic like ditching them all at once. It's important to have continuity, and even if you feel that you need to transform some of your rituals and add a bunch of new ones, changing all of them at once is too traumatic. Even for grown-ups, let alone small children.

Don't worry about every single ritual being educational and wholesome or strictly meeting your goals. I'm a big believer in balance, and just as you need a few fatty foods and sweet treats in your diet, you need to include some rituals that are just about being silly, letting off steam, or eating forbidden foods. I'm sure I'm not the only one whose favorite childhood rituals included eating doughnuts.

Take your two lists and underline all the rituals your family wants to continue. If there are some you want to eliminate completely, perhaps because the family has outgrown them, cross those out with a marker, or delete on your computer screen.

Now it's time to do some cutting and pasting. Cut out those rituals you want to amend and paste them on a new sheet of paper marked "Old Rituals/New Ways." Write down the details of how you would do those rituals differently. Do you want to celebrate a holiday in a way that is more overtly religious, such as celebrating not just Christmas but all of Advent? Can you think of a bigger or different role for the kids to play now that they're older? Has the full Thanksgiving feast gotten to be too much work for Grandma, and might you organize your siblings to turn the holiday into a more casual affair, with everyone contributing a dish? Do you want to open up a family celebration to a wider community and invite close friends or neighbors to participate? Do you need to alter a tradition because the children are growing up and including their dates or spouses? Most questions can be answered best by staging a full-family brainstorming session.

Once you've figured out how to revitalize your existing rituals, the scary but exciting part starts: what should you add? Ask yourselves— what's missing?

Take out another sheet of paper or open a new page on the computer and write "New Rituals" at the top. Grab the family calendar for the coming year and ask yourself whether there are any significant dates you don't currently celebrate, such as anniversaries, holidays, vacations, first days of the seasons, or any milestone events at school. Let your imagination run far afield. In their book *Ideas for Families* Phyllis and Merle Good talk about how they commemorate the recovery of Phyllis and the couple's two daughters from a serious car accident. "As an annual ritual of gratefulness and celebration, we return to the hospital for a meal in their cafeteria."

Use the paper marked New Rituals to map out specific events you'd like to celebrate as a family that you haven't in the past, but don't write anything into your calendar until you've chosen which ones you're going to add. And don't try to add too many new events in a given year.

To zero in on what you should celebrate, ask yourselves: Do you have a rough idea of what your plans will be for all of those dates that really matter to your family? Are there parts of the year that seem empty of celebration? When was the last time you had a really special family vacation or adventure with lots of planning and high expectations? Do you sufficiently celebrate the changes of season; is there a local harvest festival you'd enjoy attending? Are there ethnic holidays you've neglected that would help teach your children about their roots or introduce them to a branch of the family they barely know? Is it time to start a family reunion or revive a reunion tradition that has lapsed? Do your existing rituals adequately reflect the depth of your spirituality?

Ask yourselves what you consider the primary goals of your family rituals, and if you feel that some of them aren't being sufficiently addressed, then concentrate on creating new rituals to meet them. For example, if your extended family is scattered and one of your ritual goals is to keep everyone feeling close, you might try something like what the Gines family does, as discussed on page 116. On the day before Thanksgiving, Betty Gines's six grown children synchronize their watches and bake pies at the same time.

If you've got small children and you're looking for fresh occasions to celebrate, an excellent resource can be found in your local library. It's a fat volume called *Chase's Calendar of Events,* and a new edition is put out by

Contemporary Publishing Co. every year. In it you'll find not only the dates of every religious holiday and full moon, but loads of historical anniversaries, international festivals, and every holiday ever proclaimed by a president. Granted, some of it is silly stuff, like January being Oatmeal Month (so says Quaker Oats). But there are all sorts of occasions that would be fun or educational to celebrate with children, such as National Poetry Month (April) or Freedom Day (February 1), the anniversary of the day when slavery was abolished.

You can find clever ways to celebrate many of these events in a fabulous book, *Happy Birthday, Grandma Moses*, written by two sisters who used *Chase's* as a guidebook themselves. Clare Bonfanti Braham and Maria Bonfanti Esche cover more than a hundred special days, presenting a craft or activity for each one. They show how to make a piñata and maracas for Cinco de Mayo, a celebration of Mexican independence, and teach kids how to spell their names in sign language in honor of Helen Keller's birthday. The book is organized chronologically, so you can consult it at the beginning of a year or even monthly to see if there's something that's right for your family. We used a recipe for honey cookies and had a tea party to celebrate the January birthday of A. A. Milne, author of the Pooh books.

As you evaluate your calendar and ponder what to add, ask yourself these additional questions: Do your existing rituals reflect your values and your passions, or is there an activity or celebration you should start? Do you love cross-country skiing but realize you haven't done it since you bought skis five years ago? Maybe you should plan a short winter vacation this year and take the whole family skiing.

If you feel strongly about helping the needy, do you have family rituals for acting on your good intentions? Maybe you can vote to pick a family charity once a year and then plan a series of fund-raising events, such as a garage sale in the spring and a backyard fashion show or play in the summer, for which the kids sell tickets. Or, you can organize your kids and their friends into a minichoir and practice a small program of songs, then entertain the residents of a local nursing home at Christmas or on the first day of spring.

Once you've looked ahead a whole year and narrowed down which special-occasion rituals on your list you're committed to trying, take a look at the paper for daily, weekly, and monthly rituals. Do these routine rituals also reflect your burning convictions and values? For example, if you want books to be important to your kids, try something mentioned in Jim Trelease's indispensable guide *The Read-Aloud Handbook,* and put a new book under your kid's pillow every weekend.

Do you feel you have enough everyday and weekly traditions to stay in close emotional touch with your children? Can you name your child's closest schoolfriend off the top of your head? What issue most troubled your son this week? How did your daughter perform on the school team in her most recent game? If not, maybe it's time to add a dinnertime or bedtime ritual where family members share something about their day.

Is everybody on top of their chores? Has it been a long while since the whole family just did something for fun? Perhaps you ought to institute weekly or monthly family meetings, or a weekly family fun time.

If you're just getting started and looking for some general advice about what's sufficient, I would suggest that you make sure to have at least one daily family ritual that allows direct communication with each of your children. This could be a dinnertime ritual or a bedtime conversation, but if it works better for you, it could be a special morning good-bye ritual, or something that happens when a child comes home from school.

I'm a big booster of some sort of weekly family night that requires the active interaction of the whole family, not just watching television or a movie together. Videos could certainly be part of a weekly family time, but if you're going to do that, make it clear the movie is part of the "treat" portion of the evening and make sure you also discuss family and personal concerns, preferably beforehand. The "working" segment that covers issues of substance, resolves conflicts, and may include prayers or songs can often be completed in twenty minutes, leaving plenty of time for eating, playing games, or watching shows. There are tons of ideas in Chapter 6 about different ways to conduct family nights and meetings.

RITUAL PRACTICE AND THE NEED FOR SPONTANEITY

We all look forward to the big holidays, with their special decorations, food and music and parties and presents, but there's a sense in which we can't celebrate these occasions fully unless we keep our day-to-day rituals vital. There are several reasons for this. It is the small and constant rubbing together through the familiar actions of ritual that makes and keeps us close as families. Without that closeness, we wouldn't care so much about celebrating the big events and holidays, and we might as well go to a big stadium, or Times Square, and celebrate them with total strangers.

But there's something else everyday rituals do for us, something Ronald Grimes calls "ritual practice" in his book *Marrying and Burying.* Grimes, who went to Methodist seminary but later took up Zen Buddhism before becoming a professor of ritual studies, believes that people simply won't get much out of big-event rituals if they haven't cultivated the focus and readiness that come from more routine ritualizing.

"In my view," he writes, "the staple of ritual is practice, which takes a variety of forms depending on one's tradition. Weekly worship, daily prayer and hourly meditation are among the more traditional forms...." All such practices cultivate a "basic, contemplative attitude characterized by receptivity and reverence.... Contemplation is a way of valuing the givens in life. Without it, all the drum-beating and organ-playing in the world is noise."

The author, who doesn't believe in how-to books for ritual and probably wouldn't approve of mine, might disagree with my analysis, but I think that what he says applies to family ritual. If families are going to build a ritual life together, they must find ways to incorporate into their lives the kind of daily quiet thoughtfulness that he describes. It is indeed a kind of foundation upon which other things can be built, and again, there are millions of ways to do it, including various kinds of grace at dinner or thoughtful bedtime rituals.

Another idea is to adapt the ritual of Nancy Freimuth of Appleton, Wis., the mother of two small children. "I had been really struggling with issues of religion and spirituality. So much of life with kids today is focused on negatives or on what they want at a given moment, and I needed to find a place for the spiritual in our lives."

So when her daughter was three and her son only two, Nancy started a very simple ritual done daily, or every other day, usually in the late afternoon. "We'll clean up the toys first and then sit in a circle," says Nancy. "I have a little Tibetan prayer bell, and I ring it. We simply close our eyes and listen to it resonating, in silence. Then we hold hands and each take

turns saying what we are thankful for." Her daughter might be thankful for Barbie, and her son for his Power Rangers, but Nancy treasures the moment of closeness and quiet. She usually uses her turn to tell her children how thankful she is to have them.

Parents can plan ahead to incorporate small moments of ritual practice into their daily schedules, and the big events can be blocked off on family calendars. But a full ritual life should also be open to spontaneity, for celebrating on the spur of the moment, for a basic readiness to rise to an unexpected occasion. As we all know, many of the best things that happen aren't planned in advance.

It's important to acknowledge the major triumphs of childhood as they arise: good grades, hitting the first home run, getting a lead role in the school play. Some rites of passage also can't be scheduled: who knows what day your daughter will have her first successful ride on her two-wheeler or start her period? Or what day your son will shave for the first time? Whether you decorate the dining room with paper banners, serve the celebrated one dinner on a fancy plate, pick up a special dessert on the way home from work, or take the family to your favorite fast-food joint, don't neglect to honor these milestones with fitting ceremony and some special words of praise.

Other unexpected events of a less pleasant nature will also benefit from ad hoc ritual, such as the death of a pet. Burying a cherished pet in its favorite corner of the yard, marking the spot with painted rocks, and taking turns remembering the animal's most outrageous stunts help children learn the comfort of grieving.

Another change that sometimes happens without a lot of warning is moving, which can be very traumatic to kids. Rituals for saying good-bye to an old house and hello to a new one can be reassuring for the whole family. To say farewell to the old place, perhaps you can get your family to make a special "house photo album" to take with you, or bury a small time capsule in the backyard containing mementos from special family occasions that took place there.

When arriving in a new place, consider a house-blessing ritual, an ancient practice that offers many possibilities. Once at the new house, plant a tree as a family or hang up a "guardian angel" over the fireplace. You can even have a special ceremony and, pouring a libation of water on the front stoop to bless it, bestow a name on your new house, as though it's a country estate of enormous character. In her book *Bless This House,* Ann Wall Frank offers many suggestions, including lighting a candle at the front door and saying, "Bless this house. Keep it safe, sound, and full of love." Carefully carry the candle indoors, and offer a blessing for each room in turn.

Whatever you do, make sure your rituals grow naturally from the reality of your life and the preferences of everyone in the family, not some fantasy you have of how you wish things were. Nanette Hilton, a Nevada mother of three girls, says she introduces new rituals more slowly and sparingly than she would personally prefer because her husband, she says, is "one of those people who think rituals are a burden, that they take the spontaneity out of life."

The context of your family's life will provide much of the information you need about what rituals to start. Observing and respecting such simple existential conditions as where you live and the timing of family events is like pointing your sailboat into the wind. You'll get where you're going much faster, and the ride will be a lot more fun.

Like the family that lives in Oregon but often doesn't get snow for Christmas: every year, a kindly uncle takes a forty-five-minute trip to the nearby mountains and brings back a truckload of snow late on Christmas Eve to his sister's house. Her kids wake up to find their yard is the only one on the block with even a dusting of snow, and are told that Santa and the reindeer shook it off when they landed.

Another example: when my son went trick-or-treating for the first time as a toddler, I was suddenly confronted with the problem of what to do about all that candy. We let him eat only one piece a day, but I didn't relish the idea of the rest sitting around for weeks or months. I mentally ran over our family calendar for the next month and it hit me that his birthday comes only two weeks after Halloween. Bingo. I told him that if he left the plastic pumpkin still half-filled with candy outside his bedroom door, the "Good Witch of Halloween" would come and take the candy for children who had none, and leave a birthday present instead. When he woke up on his birthday, the pumpkin was full of small gifts, including individually wrapped plastic train cars and a menagerie of farm animals. He was thrilled.

Rituals should also reflect reality in other ways: don't neglect their power to heal. Some mothers have special routines to cheer up a child home sick from school, like one who keeps a special activity box with craft items and inexpensive handheld games that can only be opened on such days.

My friend Walter recalls a time when his father had to be away on Christmas Eve to nurse sick relatives and when he telephoned home, his father said he was feeling very sorry for himself, like Charlie Brown. On the day their father returned, his four children and wife met him at the airport carrying colorful balloons. In full view of the surging holiday crowds, they draped him in a sheet on which one of his sons had painted the words, "Poor Sweet Baby." Thus was born a favorite family tradition, the "Poor Sweet Baby Blanket," and whenever any of them suffered a misfortune or setback from then on, he or she was enveloped by the sheet and comforted by the entire family.

Kathleen Chesto actually advocates having a "celebration of failure" when things go wrong, an important proof to children that love and attention aren't doled out only in return for good performance.

"We all learn much more from our failures than we do from our successes, if we are willing to stop and examine them," she says. It's not that children should be rewarded for failing, but that they need to have the failure put in perspective. Her recommendation, as usual, is that this be done in the form of a brief prayer.

In the case of a big disappointment, such as a failing grade or not being picked for a team, she suggests parents lead a prayer asking God to "help us remember that we can't always succeed" and that dark clouds often have silver linings. Within the context of that prayer, asking God to help "others who are hurting tonight" helps remind children that they aren't alone in adversity, says Kathleen, and kids can be prompted to specifically name others they know who are hurting for the same or different reasons. The generosity of praying for these other hurting souls may lessen the sting of the child's own pain.

When it comes to rituals, the hardest thing for many families is just getting started. Parents feel a hunger for activities that will bring their families together, but they worry that their kids will reject their plans. They are terrified of looking silly, of getting it wrong, of not being in control. These are legitimate fears, because, as we've discussed, rituals can fail and they don't work well if they're rigidly imposed. At some point, parents must relinquish control in order for a ritual to be truly shared.

But that fear and difficulty point to one of ritual's greatest virtues and the secret of its success: while we must be the leaders in ritual, our children have much to teach us. By bringing together our moral focus and knowledge of the mechanics of ritual with our children's exuberance and natural joy, we can create rituals that embrace and transport the entire family.

Sometimes all it takes is the simple act of will that propels us off a diving board into shockingly cold water. We must get past the initial awkwardness and make that leap into playfulness ourselves, knowing in advance that it will take us a little time to adjust.

The important thing is simply to start. Kathy Chesto believes the answer is to "take one step and discover it moves you forward. So you take another. Sometimes, you will fall down."

Vicky Kelman, a Jewish religious educator and mother of four, has a similar response. "What I say to people who are overwhelmed by Jewish tradition is that they should start by taking lots of baby steps. In our family, we observe the Sabbath for twenty-five hours, but nobody has to start there. You can begin by spending three minutes lighting the candles on Friday nights. After a while, you add the blessings for the bread and wine, then you add a family discussion or a family walk. As you keep adding on, eventually you start going to synagogue on Saturday, and your Shabbat has grown with you."

Whatever you do, don't wait too long. Rituals are easiest to start when children are young and in awe of their parents' powers, and the longer the rituals go on, the greater their magic. People complain about how kids spend too much time with television and their peers. But if powerful, consistent rituals are started in a child's toddler years, he or she will have been participating in them for fifteen years by the age of eighteen: that's a major force that will form character, not just habits.

Take Barbara Franco's word for it. This mother of three in Florida can distinctly recall her mother and father "deciding we needed family time and inventing some ritual that would last a few months and then fall by the wayside."

What went wrong? Barbara says her parents simply waited until it was too late. "We were in our preteen years and I think my parents suddenly panicked that we never did anything together." As a result, Barbara has worked very hard to establish a wide range of rituals for her girls, who are between one and seven. "Some of our traditions spring up spontaneously. But even then I make a conscious effort to continue them."

Thus, while the family isn't rich financially, its rituals are abundant. They have bedtime rituals, rituals for good grades, and every Saturday the girls accompany their father to the local driving range. When they wake up on birthdays, balloons are tied to the foot of their beds. On Thanksgiving morning, while watching the parades on television, the girls go through the toy ads in the paper and make out their "wish lists" for Santa. The next day, their parents do most of the Christmas shopping from those lists, then take the girls out to buy Christmas ornaments: each child gets to pick out two or three special ones. Every once in a while, on a summer day, Barbara declares "naked time," and the girls run wild and bare in

their fenced-in yard, skinny-dipping in the wading pool and chasing each other through the sprinkler.

So ask yourself regularly: what doesn't work anymore in our ritual life? Did we truly celebrate this past year? Perhaps you can make this part of your New Year's traditions. Or plan an annual family retreat, a weekend away from home that mixes goofing-off time with a serious look at the family's "bottom line." Every family member should get a chance to discuss their personal goals and their goals for the family, covering family rituals as well as other aspects of family life.

Nurture your rituals and they will provide sustenance to your family all your life. Chances are, your best rituals will outlive you, sending your love into generations to come. Bend yourself to the honest hard work of ritual, and the bountiful crop you harvest will be joy.

Appendix

*Gail Simpson's Open-Adoption Ritual

GIVING AND RECEIVING CEREMONY
CELEBRATING THE OPEN ADOPTION OF SOPHIE

Minister: In our community we recognize life's major events through ceremony. John, Susan, Mary [Adopting Father, Mother, Sister], and Karen [Birthmother] invite you all to join with them in marking the Giving and Receiving of this child, Sophie [Baby], in open adoption.

Karen, would you pass Sophie to John, Susan, and Mary as a symbol of your choice to have them adopt her and raise her as their daughter and sister.

John, Susan, Mary, Sophie, and Karen invite those of you who are part of the adoption triangle to join them in the reading below. Any person who has adopted a child is invited to rise now and join John and Susan in the reading by the Adopting Parents.

ADOPTING PARENTS TO BIRTHPARENT

We solemnly receive this child, accepting the unfathomable responsibility of parenting her, committing ourselves to the daily renewal of spirit needed to raise children with faith, hope, courage, dignity, wisdom, and humor.

We humbly receive this child, awestruck by the mysterious forces which delivered this particular child into our care.

We joyfully receive this child, anticipating the tender pleasure of our journey with her.

Minister: All adopted children, young and old, are invited to rise now and join Nancy [an Adult Adoptee] who will read, for Mary and Sophie, the reading by the Adopted Child.

ADOPTED CHILD TO BIRTHPARENTS and ADOPTING PARENTS

I bring you together in this mysterious intersection of nature and nurture which is adoption. I am the music to which you will dance of love and loss for a lifetime. Dance well. My melody is the sweet yearning for life. Teach me the language of love from which to compose my lyrics.

Minister: Any person who has given a child for adoption is invited to rise now and join Karen in the reading by the Birthparent.

BIRTHPARENTS TO ADOPTING PARENTS

I give this child to be raised by you as your child. She is a part of me

> *Whom I have nourished with my blood and spirit;*

---

* Names have been changed.

*Whom I conceived in innocence of the
awesome power her life would command;*

*Whom I have borne in the pain of fear,
childbirth, and separation;*

*And in whom I rejoice, reveling in the
miracle of my own creation and in the gift
beyond measure which I now give to you.*

Minister: Will the rest of you please
join in reading the words of the
Community.

Community to Adopting Parents

*Treasure this child's life as you treasure your
own. Act in Karen's stead to provide the daily
substance of nurture and love. In the fullness of
time, let her know how love brought us together
in this vulnerable moment of giving and
receiving.*

Community to Birthparents

*Go forth to fulfill the promise of your future
knowing that we celebrate your life and the story
you continue to create. We honor you as this
child's proud heritage.*

All Sing: *Every Night and Every Morn* (William Blake, ca. 1803; Ralph Vaughan Williams, 1911)

*Every night and every morn,
Some to misery are born.
Every morn and every night,
Some are born to sweet delight.*

*Joy and woe are woven fine,
Clothing for a soul divine,
And through every grief and pine
Runs a joy with silken twine.*

*It is right, it should be so.
We were made for joy and woe.
And when this we rightly know,
Safely through this world we go.*

SELECTED BIBLIOGRAPHY

Barnett, James H. *The American Christmas: A Study in National Culture.* New York, NY: The Macmillan Co., 1954.

Berg, Elizabeth. *Family Traditions: Celebrations for Holidays and Everyday.* Pleasantville, NY: Reader's Digest Association, 1992.

Bossard, James H., and Eleanor S. Boll. *Ritual in Family Living: A Contemporary Study.* Philadelphia, PA: University of Pennsylvania Press, 1950.

Braham, Clare Bonfanti, and Maria Bonfanti Esche. *Happy Birthday, Grandma Moses: Activities for Special Days Throughout the Year.* Chicago, IL: Chicago Review Press Inc., 1994.

Carey, Diana, and Judy Large. *Festivals, Family and Food.* Stroud, Gloucestershire, England: Hawthorn Press, 1982.

Chesto, Kathleen O'Connell. *Family Prayer for Family Times: Traditions, Celebrations, and Rituals.* Mystic, CT: Twenty-Third Publications, 1995.

Coles, Robert. *The Spiritual Life of Children.* Boston, MA: Houghton Mifflin Co., 1991.

Dodson, Shireen, with Teresa Barker. *The Mother-Daughter Book Club.* San Francisco, CA: HarperCollins Publishers, 1997.

Dombro, Amy, and Leah Wallach. *The Ordinary Is Extraordinary: How Children Under Three Learn.* New York, NY: Simon & Schuster (Fireside), 1989.

Driver, Tom F. *The Magic of Ritual: Our Need for Liberating Rites That Transform Our Lives and Our Communities.* San Francisco, CA: HarperCollins Publishers, 1993.

Eliade, Mircea. *Rites and Symbols of Initiation: The Mysteries of Birth and Rebirth.* Woodstock, CT: Spring Publications, 1995

Eyre, Linda and Richard. *3 Steps to a Strong Family.* New York, NY: Simon & Schuster, 1994.

Frank, Ann Wall. *Bless This House: A Collection of Blessings to Make a House Your Home.* Chicago, IL: Contemporary Books, 1996.

Fulghum, Robert. *From Beginning to End: The Rituals of Our Lives.* New York, NY: Villard Books, 1995.

Gennep, Arnold van. *The Rites of Passage.* Chicago, IL: University of Chicago Press, 1960.

Gillis, John R. *A World of Their Own Making: Myth, Ritual, and the Quest for Family Values.* San Francisco, CA: HarperCollins Publishers (Basic Books), 1996.

Good, Phyllis Pellman and Merle. *Ideas for Families.* Intercourse, PA: Good Books, 1992.

Grimes, Ronald L. *Marrying and Burying: Rites of Passage in a Man's Life.* Boulder, CO: Westview Press, Inc., 1995.

———, ed. *Readings in Ritual Studies.* New York, NY: Simon & Schuster (Prentice Hall), 1996.

Hare, Nathan and Julia. "Bringing the Black Boy to Manhood: The Passage." San Francisco, CA: Black Think Tank, 1985.

Hutton, Ronald. *The Stations of the Sun: A History of the Ritual Year in Britain.* New York, NY: Oxford University Press Inc., 1996.

Ickes, Marguerite. *The Book of Festivals and Holidays the World Over.* New York, NY: Dodd, Mead & Co., 1970.

Imber-Black, Evan, and Janine Roberts. *Rituals for Our Times: Celebrating, Healing, and Changing Our Lives and Our Relationships.* San Francisco, CA: HarperCollins Publishers, 1992.

———, Richard Whiting, et al. *Rituals in Families and Family Therapy.* New York, NY: W. W. Norton & Co. Inc., 1988.

Krythe, Maymie R. *All About American Holidays.* San Francisco, CA: HarperCollins Publishers, 1962.

Lieberman, Susan Abel. *New Traditions: Redefining Celebrations for Today's Family.* New York, NY: Farrar, Straus & Giroux (Noonday Press), 1991.

Mahdi, Louise Carus, et al. *Betwixt and Between: Patterns of Masculine and Feminine Initiation.* Peru, IL: Open Court Publishing Co., 1987.

———. *Crossroads: The Quest for Contemporary Rites of Passage.* Peru, IL: Open Court Publishing Co., 1996.

Mead, Margaret. *Coming of Age in Samoa.* New York, NY: William Morrow & Co., 1928.

Meade, Michael. *Men and the Water of Life: Initiation and the Tempering of Men.* San Francisco, CA: HarperCollins Publishers (Harper San Francisco), 1993.

Nelson, Gertrud Mueller. *To Dance with God: Family Ritual and Community Celebration.* Mahwah, NJ: Paulist Press, 1986.

Ochs, Vanessa L. *Safe & Sound: Protecting Your Child in an Unpredictable World.* New York, NY: Penguin USA, 1995.

Pipher, Mary. *The Shelter of Each Other: Rebuilding Our Families.* New York, NY: G. P. Putnam's Sons, 1996.

Roberto, John, ed. *Family Rituals and Celebrations: A Guide.* New Rochelle, NY: Don Bosco Multimedia (Catholic Families Series), 1992.

Robinson, Jo, and Jean Coppock Staeheli. *Unplug the Christmas Machine.* New York, NY: William Morrow & Co., Inc, 1982.

Ryan, M. J., ed. *A Grateful Heart: Daily Blessings for the Evening Meal from Buddha to the Beatles.* Berkeley, CA: Conari Press, 1994.

Schmidt, Leigh Eric. *Consumer Rites: The Buying and Selling of American Holidays.* Princeton, NJ: Princeton University Press, 1995.

Shenk, Sara Wenger. *Why Not Celebrate?* Intercourse, PA: Good Books, 1987.

Strassfeld, Michael. *The Jewish Holidays: A Guide and Commentary.* San Francisco, CA: HarperCollins Publishers, 1985.

To Celebrate: Reshaping Holidays & Rites of Passage. Elmwood, GA: Alternatives, 1987.

Trelease, Jim. *The Read-Aloud Handbook.* New York, NY: Penguin Books, 1982.

Tuleja, Tad. *Curious Customs: The Stories Behind 296 Popular American Rituals.* New York, NY: Crown Publishers Inc. (Harmony Books), 1987.

Visser, Margaret. *The Rituals of Dinner: The Origins, Evolution, Eccentricities, and Meaning of Table Manners.* New York, NY: Penguin USA, 1991.

Vogt, Susan, ed. *Just Family Nights: 60 Activities to Keep Your Family Together in a World Falling Apart.* Elgin, IL: Brethren Press, 1994.

Wall, Kathleen, and Gary Ferguson. *Lights of Passage: Rituals and Rites of Passage for the Problems and Pleasures of Modern Life.* San Francisco, CA: HarperCollins Publishers, 1994.

Walter, Mildred Pitts. *Kwanzaa: A Family Affair.* New York, NY: William Morrow & Co., Inc. (Lothrop, Lee & Shepard Books), 1995.

Wolfson, Ron, with Joel Grishaver. *The Art of Jewish Living: The Passover Seder.* Woodstock, VT: Jewish Lights Publishing, 1996.

Woodson, Meg. *Making It Through the Toughest Days of Grief: Anniversaries, Holidays and Other Landmark Days.* San Francisco, CA: HarperCollins Publishers (Zondervan Publishing House), 1994.

Zimmerman, Jack, with Virginia Coyle. *The Way of Council.* Las Vegas, NV: Bramble Books Co., 1996.

Resources

Organizations

1. **Alternatives** is a nonprofit, interdenominational group created in 1973 to combat the commercialism of Christmas. It now has a broader role within the simple-living movement and a goal of celebrating responsibly year-round by "emphasizing relationships and traditions over things." **Alternatives** publishes a free quarterly catalog and sells books, pamphlets, and videos, many of which contain ritual ideas for families. It also sponsors workshops and speeches.

     Address: 3617 Old Lakeport Rd., P.O. Box 2857, Sioux City, IA 51106
     Phone: 800-821-6153
     E-mail: AltSimLiv@aol.com
     Website: http//members.aol.com/AltSimLiv/simple.html/

2. **The Family Reunion Institute** at Temple University holds a conference on African-American reunions and extended families, usually conducted one weekend in March. People planning a family reunion are welcome, and workshop topics generally include such areas as how to organize and fund a reunion, and how to trace your family's roots.

     For information, call 215-204-6244 or write:
     Family Reunion Institute
     School of Social Administration
     Temple University
     Philadelphia, PA 19122

3. **National Arbor Day Foundation** encourages the planting of trees on Arbor Day, which occurs the last Friday of April in most states. If you send $10, they'll send you ten trees to plant. The type of seedling trees will depend on what thrives in your part of the country, but often they are Colorado blue spruce. You'll also get membership in the organization and a subscription to a bimonthly magazine with tips on how to plant and care for trees.

     Call the toll-free number, 888-448-7337, or write:
     National Arbor Day Foundation
     100 Arbor Ave.
     Nebraska City, NE 68410

Publications

1. *Reunions* magazine carries stories about reunions of families, schools, and military organizations, and includes how-to information. Published quarterly, subscriptions cost $17 a year. Also publishes a forty-four-page guide on how

to plan a family reunion, including state-by-state listing of reunion-friendly hotels and resorts. The guide costs $10, but comes free with a subscription.
Phone: 800-373-7933
E-mail: reunions@execpc.com
Website: www.reunionsmag.com
Write: P.O. Box 11727, Milwaukee, WI 53211-0727

2. *Family Fun* magazine was mentioned so often by mothers I interviewed for this book that I got my own subscription. Each issue is packed with rituals and activities to do with children, including ideas for seasonal parties, suggestions for great vacations, or craft projects to make on a rainy day. It costs $14.95 for 10 issues.
    Address: *Family Fun*, P.O. Box 37032, Boone, IA 50037-0032
    Phone: 800-289-4849

3. *Chinaberry Book Service.* If you have children, you owe yourself a regular look at this special publication. It's one of those catalogs you actually look forward to getting. The editors list books by age group and only offer books they love. In their blurbs, they explain why your kid will love them too. Books for teens and adults are also included. Call for free quarterly catalog: 800-776-2242.

4. *Making It Through the Toughest Days of Grief.* This book by Meg Woodson should be very helpful to anybody who has lost a loved one. The author is a professional grief counselor with advanced degrees in theology and psychology, and also a mother who has endured the deaths of two children, a son at twelve and a daughter in her twenties. Ritual is a major part of the book, which focuses on how to get through major holidays and anniversaries, including the anniversaries of death. The book is available in paperback, published by Zondervan (see Bibliography).

5. *The Read-Aloud Handbook* by Jim Trelease. Any parent who wants to raise a child to love books should read this. It offers statistics that prove why reading aloud makes a difference, and is packed with real-life success stories, ending with a long list of great books for reading aloud to every age group. Available in paperback, published by Penguin (see Bibliography).

6. *Just Family Nights: 60 Activities to Keep Your Family Together in a World Falling Apart* edited by Susan Vogt. Susan and Jim Vogt have raised four terrific kids and are big believers in a weekly family night. Susan's book is an excellent collection of ideas for family nights, from her family and others, including suggested scripture readings, activities, and discussions. Some are seasonal and many are concerned with topics of social justice. The book is published in

paperback by a small publisher, Brethren Press, and if you have trouble getting it through your local bookstore, send a check for $18.95 to Parenting for Peace & Justice Network, 523 East Southern Ave., Covington, KY 41015.

RITUAL-MAKERS

Nancy Goddard. A mother who lives in an "intentional community" in California that shares common spaces and beliefs, though its members live in separate homes. Nancy's rituals for winter solstice and the first period of a teenage girl are included in this book. She conducts wilderness rite-of-passage trips, primarily for teenagers and groups of women. Some of these trips are domestic, but she has also taken groups to Mexico, Nepal, and India. In addition, Nancy runs a day camp for teen and preteen girls for two weeks every summer in Sebastopol, Calif. For information about the camp or wilderness trips, write to Nancy at 9051 House A, Mill Station Rd., Sebastopol, CA 95472, or call her at 707-829-0171.

Marilyn Labendz. Marilyn, a mother of three, has a budding business creating Jewish-centered rituals for others. She has invented rituals for Jewish baby-naming ceremonies and bar mitzvahs and once created a ceremony to dedicate a refurbished grand piano. Her business is called Ritefully Yours, and she can be reached at 9 Woodland Rd., West Caldwell, NJ 07006, or by e-mail at MSL428@aol.com.

Diane Sanson. Diane gives seminars on rites of passage and can be hired for help in designing programs for other parents. You can write to her c/o Counseling Center for Growth & Healing, 22761 Pacific Coast Highway, Suite 240, Malibu, CA 90265, or call her at 310-456-2909.

Steven Foster & Meredith Little are a married couple who run the School of Lost Borders in Big Pine, Calif. The school teaches others how to conduct wilderness rites of passage, but the two also run at least one program for teens themselves annually. After careful preparation, the participants spend up to three nights alone in the mountains. Their program is described in this book. Call them at 619-938-2943 for information.

PRAYERS

There are some excellent books at your library or local bookstore that suggest prayers for meals and bedtime. Here are the most commonly used mealtime graces favored by three major religions.

1. From the Father of Protestantism, Martin Luther: "Come Lord Jesus, be our guest. Let these gifts to us be blest. In the name of the Father, Son, and Holy Spirit. Amen."

2. A lovely traditional Jewish blessing: "Lift up your hands toward the sanctuary and bless the Lord. Blessed are You, O Lord our God, King of the universe, who brings forth bread from the earth. Amen."

3. A well-known Catholic grace: "Bless us, O Lord, and these Your gifts, which we are about to receive from Your bounty. Through Christ, Our Lord, Amen."

ACKNOWLEDGMENTS

First and foremost, I owe thanks everlasting to my husband, Richard. His editorial suggestions were invaluable and his encouragement vital. He adds the sense to my sensibility, and he was definitely worth the wait. Also to our wonderful son, Max, who taught me why ritual matters and inspired me to write this book. And thanks, too, to brilliant, feisty Kate, who never made me feel like a "stepmonster."

My agent, Geri Thoma, was my friend long before she made any money from me, and I know she always will be. She was exactly the right match for me, and kept my sentimental streak from taking over the book.

During the five years in which I covered publishing for *The Wall Street Journal,* I fantasized about who my perfect editor would be should I ever write a book. I decided it was Ann Godoff. I was right. Her unflappable associate, Enrica Gadler, was an added bonus.

I am also indebted to my illustrator, Janet Payne, who understood what I was after and delivered it more beautifully than I ever could have hoped.

I am grateful to the organizations and individuals who helped me find the families in this book. Among them I owe special thanks to the Chinaberry Book Service, which is much more than just a catalog. It functions as a community of book-loving families, and its founders invited that community to send me examples of their rituals. Dozens of families did so, many of whom will find themselves in these pages. *Parents* magazine was also helpful: they printed an early article of mine on holiday rituals and allowed me to attach a questionnaire that produced hundreds of responses.

A good share of the families in this book were found in cyberspace. I must single out a wonderfully down-to-earth service on AOL, Moms Online, whose far-flung editors were active and resourceful partners. Moms Online published an essay I wrote on rituals that was hyperlinked to a lengthy questionnaire, and the mothers who responded had some of the most ingenious rituals I found anywhere. I also found families at Parent Soup on AOL.

Thanks to Edith Wagner, publisher of *Reunions* magazine, who helped me locate many of the reunion rituals mentioned here.

Family therapist Carol Stacks was good enough to read the manuscript and verify my information about the psychological impact of rituals on children. I'm extremely grateful to religious educators Vicki Kelner and Kathleen O'Connell Chesto, who led me to remarkably thoughtful parents and patiently answered questions about religious rituals in their respective faiths. If I have committed any religious faux pas in this book, it is my fault alone.

I feel a special gratitude to therapist and author Mary Pipher, who believes in the healing power of family rituals, and whose early support convinced me this work was worth doing. Professor of religion Elaine Pagels was another major influence.

As I began my work, she asked whether I thought a homemade, secular ritual could ever rival the power of a religious one with centuries of tradition behind it. I think she'll find the answer here.

My friends provided much comfort and aid. Thanks especially to Kathy Markel for asking every one of her friends to share their rituals, and to Blair MacInnes for suggesting excellent books and finding them when necessary. Joan Kron, my former colleague and surrogate mom, has long inspired me by her passion and energy, and her support never flagged. Sandy Graham, an early reader, shared her wisdom as a mother and an editor. Others who read the manuscript and offered valuable help include Dick Einhorn, Jim Shannon, and Paula Penn-Nabrit. Thanks to Walter Mead for his enduring friendship and for planting the seed of this book by making me jealous of his family's rituals. And to Carol Mason for giving me love and encouragement and for letting me throw myself into her swimming pool as part of a name-change ritual I created.

Much is owed to Teresa Veary, our former nanny, who took such good care of Max that I could work in peace and contentment. She is a natural ritual-maker in her own right, and she taught me a great deal.

Thanks, too, to all the friends and acquaintances who gave me advice, mailed me articles, offered theories, and shared rituals at dinner parties. I can never adequately repay the hundreds of people who generously told me about their rituals, including the more than two hundred families who appear in the final text. To the many people I interviewed but didn't include: your rituals are no less valid or powerful for not being included here, and your children are fortunate.

I will always be grateful to the fine editors of *The Wall Street Journal,* where I spent seventeen years. I have them to thank for teaching me to make every word count and to never tell my readers something I could show them instead.

Author's Note

If you would like to share your family's traditions with me for possible inclusion in a future edition of this book, please write me at: Random House, Inc., 201 East 50th Street, New York, NY 10022, or send an E-mail to: MegMaxC@aol.com.

Index

About the Author

Meg Cox was a staff reporter at *The Wall Street Journal* for seventeen years, where her beats included everything from agriculture to culture. She now lectures about family rituals and writes for a variety of publications. She lives with her husband and son in Princeton, N.J.

About the Type

This book was set in Centaur, a typeface designed by the American typographer Bruce Rogers in 1929. Centaur was a typeface that Rogers adapted from the fifteenth-century type of Nicholas Jenson and modified in 1948 for a cutting by the Monotype Corporation.